The
Paris
Opéra

The
Paris
Opéra

**An Encyclopedia of
Operas, Ballets,
Composers, and Performers**

*Genesis and Glory,
1671–1715*

SPIRE PITOU

GREENWOOD PRESS
Westport, Connecticut • London, England

Library of Congress Cataloging in Publication Data

Pitou, Spire, 1912-
  The Paris Opéra.

  Includes bibliographies and indexes.
  Contents: [1] Genesis and glory, 1671-1715.
  1. Opéra de Paris—History. I. Title.
ML1727.8.P2P5 1983   782.1'0944'361   82-21140
ISBN 0-313-21420-4 (lib. bdg. : v. 1)

Library of Congress Catalog Card Number: 82-21140
ISBN: 0-313-21420-4

First published in 1983

Greenwood Press
A division of Congressional Information Service, Inc.
88 Post Road West, Westport, Connecticut 06881

Printed in the United States of America

10 9 8 7 6 5 4 3 2 1

TO MY WIFE, DORIS

CONTENTS

PREFACE

Histories of opera begin ordinarily and logically with accounts of the early operatic performances in northern Italy during the sixteenth century, and they proceed with their subject by considering the outstanding works staged during subsequent years in countries fortunate enough to have had a Mozart, Wagner, or Verdi in their population. This overly selective approach to the history of opera has allowed many interesting operas and composers of lesser magnitude to slip into oblivion, and the resultant accounts of the lyric stage in the West have tended to become more and more concerned with international repertory.

France is a case in point. None of the recent histories of opera describes in reasonable depth the French lyric theatre between the time of Lully and the period of Gluck, although some surveys do feel obliged to pay fleeting homage to Campra and Rameau. The nineteenth century might seem to fare better at first glance on account of the attention accorded to such figures as Meyerbeer, Gounod, and Massenet, but this celebrated trio was responsible for only a small percentage of the works produced in the rue Le Peletier and at the Garnier palace before 1900. As for the Paris Opéra during the twentieth century, it is not difficult to believe that this theatre might easily close its doors without offending French composers and musicians because in recent years only Italians like Giuseppe Verdi and Giacomo Puccini, Austrians like Arnold Schoenberg and Alban Berg, Germans like Richard Wagner and Richard Strauss, and Russians like Modest Mussorgsky and Alexander Borodin appear to be worthy of billing there.

This encyclopedia, therefore, will try to remedy the present situation by offering a more extensive account of the entire period of French opera and ballet from 1671 onward and by examining every extant work produced at the Opéra since the moment when Louis XIV granted to one of his subjects the first license to mount lyric tragedies and ballets within the confines of his kingdom.

Yet it must be admitted immediately that it became evident to the author and editor of the present work that any serious inquiry into the entire range of operatic and balletic activity at the Opéra would involve a large corpus of material. Thus, it was decided that this study should be divided into four separate sections with the initial volume of this quadripartite report extending from the founding of the Opéra in 1671 to the death of Louis XIV at his Versailles residence on 1 September 1715. The second section begins with the establishment of the regency of Philippe d'Orléans on 2 September 1715 and extends to the end of the Napoleonic era in 1815. The third volume, including the remaining years of the nineteenth century, closes with the outbreak of World War I on 1 August 1914, while the final pages of the work deal with the years of the modern period.

The present volume, devoted to the classical age of 1671-1715, is the first in a series of four volumes, therefore, and it has its particular format by reason of being devoted to the earliest phases of opera and ballet at the Opéra. It opens with an overall introduction to the entire 1671-1982 span of time, and the introduction is designed to furnish an immediate orientation to the entire subject over the past three centuries. Events transpiring at the Opéra-Comique during this same period are reported concurrently in this section because this theatre and the Opéra have produced similar works, have suffered parallel reverses, and have enjoyed comparable triumphs. The development of the ballet since 1671 is also traced in this introduction because the dance has always been an indigenous part of operatic programs in Paris.

The second portion of the present work contains the Opéra encyclopedia itself for 1671-1715, and the material presented herein is arranged alphabetically and includes the titles of balletic and lyric compositions as well as the names of authors, performers, and administrators. Subsequent volumes employ the same format to permit the rapid retrieval of information, but only this initial tome offers rosters of the outstanding singers and dancers for 1671-1982 in its appendixes. Each of the entries in the encyclopedia section pertaining to an opera or ballet identifies its composer, librettist, choreographer, costumer, set designer, and the performers contributing to its creation and important revivals. An analysis of its action, scene by scene as well as act by act, is provided. The select bibliographies concluding each entry when feasible are added to direct the reader to other studies or compilations containing supplementary bibliographies and other salient facts considered pertinent.

The third and last major section of this volume presents a chronologically arranged bibliography of all lyric and choreographic works still extant and performed at the Opéra between 1671 and 1 September 1715. In this portion of the present work, the names of the composers, the librettists, and the choreographers are recorded with the titles and genres of the compositions, and the date of premiere of each work at the Opéra or Versailles is noted. Also, it will be seen that, for the convenience of readers, separate 1671-1715 bibliographies of ballets and operas are offered in this third section.

To recapitulate, then, the present work is divided into three principal parts: an introduction outlining the 1671-1982 history of the Paris Opéra and its cognate theatre, the Opéra-Comique; an encyclopedia of the operas, ballets, composers, and performers associated with the Opéra between 1671 and 1715; and a listing of works given at the Opéra before the death of Louis XIV in 1715.

Abbreviations used in the second section will be explained on the pages prefacing the encyclopedia portion of the book. The asterisks appearing throughout the text of the entries after proper nouns indicate that entries discussing these names and titles have been incorporated in the same volume. Whenever the entries are located in another volume, direct references to the other volume will be furnished in parentheses after the proper noun, for example: (For Berg, see twentieth-century volume).

It is hoped that this manner of presentation for information dealing with the repertory, composers, and artistes attached to the Opéra before 1716 will prove efficient and effective for readers and researchers interested in ballet and opera in France. It is also the author's genuine wish here that his study meets the two requirements prescribed by Horace for all written works when he insisted that they be pleasing as well as useful. And the author prays with fervor that his errors of commission and omission are neither numerous nor enormous.

Many works have been consulted in gathering information for this study, and a special debt is owed to each of the publications mentioned in the list of abbreviations preceding the second section of this book. Yet certain publications must be indicated here as having been especially useful. First and foremost, a strong acknowledgment of precious aid must be extended to the bibliographical compilations by Théodore de Lajarte, Oscar Sonneck, and the late Stéphane Wolff as well as to the indispensable *Enciclopedia dello spettacolo* in 9 volumes, the *Die Musik in Geschichte und Gegenwart* in 17 volumes, and, inevitably, Grove. The critico-historical publications of Chouquet, Guest, and Larousse have also been consulted without hesitancy as have been the books on ballet by Cyril Beaumont, Horst Koegler, and Louis Oster. The dictionaries and encyclopedias by Chujoy, Ewen, Kobbé, Martin, Riemann, Slonimsky, Thompson, and Vinton have been employed on countless occasions and always with profit. It is impractical to mention here all the studies of individual works, composers, and artistes that have helped the author of the present encyclopedia during the past decade.

An undertaking like the present book can scarcely be accomplished by one person alone, and the author wishes to point to at least some of the kindly individuals who have assisted him with his recent labors. Dr. James Sabin has been an incredibly patient and understanding editor at all times, and a full measure of gratitude must be extended to him. It is also a pleasure for the author to voice his appreciation of the support supplied by Dean Helen Gouldner of the University of Delaware; she has had the courage to believe from the start that this project could be completed. Similarly, President Arthur Trabant must be thanked for his generosity during the final stages of the work. Dr. John Dawson, director of libraries at the University of Delaware until 1978, has been extremely helpful in procuring materials, and thanks must go similarly to him and to the staffs of the libraries of Wesleyan University and Yale University in Connecticut; Cornell University, Fifth Avenue Public Library, and Lincoln Center in New York; Princeton University, Monmouth College, and Ocean County Library in New Jersey; University of Pennsylvania in Philadelphia; and the Library of Congress. An earnest expression of gratitude is extended to the American Philosophical Society of Philadelphia for financial help in the early years of the project, and thanks must go in like fashion to the personnel of the Service Photographique and the librarians of the music collection at the Bibliothèque Nationale in Paris. Also, Mme Martine Kahane and Mlle Marie-Josée Kerhoas of the Bibliothèque de l'Opéra have been constantly sympathetic and helpful. Lastly, my most patient wife is to be thanked generously for her willingness to spend so much time and effort in helping to gather materials during our sojourns in Paris between 1970 and 1982.

The
Paris
Opéra

INTRODUCTION

Genesis: 1659–1670

The genesis and early growth of a musical theatre in France was another manifestation of Renaissance creativity that spread from Italy into the rest of Europe during the sixteenth and seventeenth centuries. Like the cognate legitimate theatre, it evolved from misunderstandings about the conventions governing the ancient stage and from the newly acquired conviction that a live performance designed for representation before spectators should offer dancing, singing, and drama in a unified composition recalling Greek tragedy.

The first serious and still extant achievement in this new musico-literary genre was *Euridice* by Peri and Caccini. An essentially Italian work that had its French premiere in Paris during the last decade of Henri IV's reign (1604), this archetypal composition boasted a prologue in recitative form, and its first scene offered a chorus of shepherds singing and conversing with the heroine during the celebration of her wedding. Euridice invites all present to join in a dance before she is poisoned by the viper. The second episode involves the hero's descent into the underworld, an event that will be repeated many times at the Palais-Royal. The conclusion is based upon the happy couple's safe return from Hades. As early as 1604 this seminal work of Italian origin with a libretto by Rinuccini featured ballet dancing, choral singing, and a mythological drama moving toward a happy ending as love triumphed over all obstacles, even death. It was of no importance that the music hardly ever managed to match in pathos the moving situations in which the principals kept finding themselves.

Henri IV and Marie de Medici were similarly responsible for placing strong emphasis upon the carousel that bore a close resemblance to the ballet, but the most impressive of these productions was not held until 1612 to salute the impending marriage of Louis XIII and the Spanish Infanta. Quadrilles were executed, music accompanied lavish spectacles, and horses were employed in figured dances. Subsequently Louis XIII kept the French tradition of theatrical dancing alive, and he prevented the musical theatre from being monopolized by the new art form imported from Italy and causing such a sensation with its novel music and striking use of *castrati*. He made the *ballet de cour* the principal entertainment of his Court and appeared himself in *Le Ballet d'Armide* (1615) based on Tasso's epic with music by Guédron and dances by Belleville. Later, in 1619, he sponsored *Le Ballet du roi* and *Le Ballet de la reine* at the Louvre. Two of the most sumptuous displays on the stage arranged during his reign were *Le Ballet de la marine* (1635), hailing the recently expanded French navy, and *Le Ballet de la félicité sur le sujet de l'heureuse naissance de monseigneur le dauphin* (1639), celebrating the birth of the future Louis XIV. When the latter monarch inherited the crown as a child in 1643, music and theatrical displays on the grand scale had become a means of convincing the world of the power, resources, and leadership of the French nation. This was especially true of *Le Ballet de la prosperité des armes de la France*, in which the confident appearance of La Victoire on the stage and the references to valiant warriors doing the will of their fearless prince were more than mere theatrical devices. It is no surprise that propaganda-minded Richelieu was largely responsible for this work. He brought the famous machinist Torelli from Italy to construct for its representation special machinery capable of creating new and more expressive effects in its production.

When Louis XIII and his minister died within months of each other in the winter of 1642-43, Mazarin took Richelieu's place under the regency of Anne of Austria, and one of his first acts was to restore Italian opera to its previous position of importance at Court. He summoned an entire Italian company of artistes to Paris without delay and made a special and expensive effort to import the singer Leonora Baroni. Other performers like the *castrato* Atto Melani followed her example and came to the French capital for financial or other reasons. Italian opera enjoyed a fresh resurgence in France, and nearly a dozen compositions were staged between 1645 and the moment when Louis XIV reached his majority. These works included Cavalli's *Egisto* (1646), Luigi Rossi's *Orfeo* (1647), and Carlo Caproli's *Le Nozze di Peleo e di Teti* (1654). This last work featured machine effects by Giacomo Torelli and a ballet by Isaac de Benserade that left foreign dignitaries speechless. The king himself danced six parts in it, and, as Apollon, he gave a hint of things to come by declaring, "Earth and Heaven have nothing that resembles me." It was quite obvious that the Italians were trying to improve their position at Court by exploiting the aspects of operatic production that were particularly well liked by the French: machine spectacles, pastoral scenes, and ballet. Francesco Cavalli's *Ercole amante* (1662) was the last Italian work mounted in the capital for many years; the king dismissed the Italian artistes in 1666 because he had tired of them and wished to nationalize music as he had done with the other arts. The stage was being set for French opera, and Isaac de Benserade's ballets and Jean-Baptiste Lully's music for Molière's comedy-ballets were the seeds from which it would grow.

Isaac de Benserade created accomplished *ballets de cour* in the last decade of Mazarin's ministry, and his compositions were usually the highlights of courtly programs drawn up to celebrate royal and noble marriages, out-standing victories won by Louis XIV's generals, or the signing of treaties returning peace to Europe. His characters were from the three categories of personages that would populate the stage of the Palais-Royal until the eighteenth century: allegorical, historical, and mythological. Louis XIV danced in these colorful productions, which grew more dramatic as time went on, while Lully's music for them became more popular than Ben-serade's choreography and librettos. Yet the combined talents of the two men produced an impressive array of theatrical entertainments, and they created such contemporary successes as *Le Ballet de l'Impatience* (1660) and *La Naissance de Vénus* (1665).

In 1664 Lully began to collaborate with Molière, for whom he created entrées to be placed between the acts or scenes of such comedies as *Le Mariage forcé, La Princesse d'Elide, Monsieur de Pourceaugnac,* and *Le Bourgeois Gentilhomme.* These works were quite popular with the public and at Court, where the king performed in them from time to time, but the most spectacular accomplishment of the actor-author Molière and the composer Lully was *Les Plaisirs de l'Ile enchantée,* written to celebrate the opening of the château at Versailles as a royal residence. The festivities lasted for a week; royalty, nobility, and musicians connected with the Court along with Molière's troupe shared in this extravagant pageant featuring music, dancing, song, and drama composed almost exclusively by Lully and his collaborator. Lully had about 150 musicians at his disposal at this time, and the entire experience at Versailles must have suggested to the Florentine that musical spectacles could be a popular and profitable undertaking.

Finally, in 1670, Louis XIV decided that he would no longer dance in ballets, although he would continue to show an active interest in the theatre. He had seen the Italians come and go, and he realized that the dance, the drama, the spectacle, and the song had emerged as the elements of theatrical entertainment performed best and enjoyed most by the French. When it was suggested to him that the government might do well to form an Académie d'Opéra to combine and to promote these aspects of theatrical activity, Louis XIV agreed. The man who voiced the wish to undertake this task was not Benserade, Molière, or Lully. His name was Pierre Perrin.

Pierre Perrin's ambitions became evident as soon as he adopted the title of *abbé* to guarantee himself a certain social standing despite his humble birth in Lyons in 1620. The ruse was effective, and it was not long before he obtained a position presenting ambassadors to Gaston, duke of Orléans and brother of the king; he shared this honor with the famous poet and friend of Mme de Rambouillet, Vincent Voiture. The year of his arrival at Gaston's Court, he embarked upon a musical career by presenting ten performances of *La Pastorale* at Issy in the home of M. de la Haye. This idyllic work in five acts for which Cambert had done the music became known as *La Pastorale d'Issy.* Its score has been lost, but it is known that its authors were bold enough to bill it as "the first French comedy in music" offering the best possible combination of French song and Italian music. It is obvious that Perrin and Cambert were already attempting to displace the Italian artistes because they went on to write *Ariane ou le mariage de Bacchus* and a third composition on the death of Adonis that was never published. These musical efforts brought Perrin more than transitory applause and superficial compliments, and *La Pastorale* was especially effective in enhancing its authors' reputations. Its presentations were crowded with nobility eager to hear the work, and they brought news of its success back to Paris posthaste. The king and Mazarin heard about it inevitably, and it was mounted at Vincennes on 1 May 1659. Loret reviewed it in his *Muse historique*. This publicity alone was enough to call attention to Perrin and his accomplishments, and he was licensed by Louis XIV on 28 June 1669 to establish an "academy of opera." The letters patent issued on this occasion guaranteed him the monopoly of staging musical performances in the French language. The privilege extended to "the entire extent of our kingdom" and was to be valid for a period of 12 years.

Perrin was now armed with royal permission to exploit a waiting market, and he set about immediately to recruit personnel qualified to cope with the tasks ahead.

It goes without saying that he enlisted the services of Robert Cambert as his composer. Born in Paris about 1628, Cambert had studied under Chambonnières, harpsichordist to the French Court, and he had obtained the post of organist at the church of Saint-Honoré before he was 30 years old. He was the author of an impressive series of musical compositions and had evinced a lively interest in developing opera in France on the grand scale. In 1658 he had produced in his own home *La Muette ingrate*, which has been lost. It was in the following year that he joined forces with Perrin to stage *La Pastorale d'Issy* (1659), the success of which induced Mazarin to commission the two authors to write *Ariane ou le mariage de Bacchus*. This composition was supposed to be given during the celebration honoring the marriage of Louis XIV, although it never found a place on the program. Perrin almost had to make Cambert part of his plans: he had shared in his previous efforts and triumphs; his interest in opera and his connections at Court made him eminently qualified.

It was likewise reasonable that Perrin should select Pierre Beauchamps to take charge of the ballets. He was ballet master for Louis XIV and had written most of the music for Molière's *Les Fâcheux*. He was held in such high esteem by the king at this time that he was named chancellor of the Academy of the Dance in 1671.

The fourth member of the newly formed organization was Alexandre de Rieux, marquis de Sourdéac, the extravagant Norman nobleman who had already brought the entire troupe of the Marais theatre to his home to stage Thomas Corneille's *La Toison d'or*. It is difficult to know what to think of the marquis, if only on account of the strange report that Tallement des Réaux gives of him in the section of his *Historiettes* devoted to individuals whom even Tallement considered curious and bizarre. He writes of Sourdéac:

He is a real character. He has himself chased by his peasants just as a stag is hunted; he says that he does this for exercise. He has a mechanical bent and does marvelous work with his hands: there is not a better locksmith in the world. He once had the idea of producing a musical play in his own home, and he had a theatre constructed on his estate at a cost of at least ten thousand *écus*. If he had not worked on the seats and galleries, the amount expended would have been twice as large.

Here, then, was a man with a swollen purse, a theatre, and an obvious liking for bold enterprises, and his mechanical knowledge could not help but be a boon to the production of spectacles relying upon machines. Yet Sourdéac was a dangerous associate if one believes Tallement's allegations that he was a counterfeiter, a usurer, and a pirate. It is easy to understand why he spent so much time practicing the art of eluding pursuers.

Finally, Laurens Bersac, the financier who fancied himself as M. de Bersac de Fondant de Champeron, lent to the venture the power of his purse and the prestige of his name, while La Grille and Pierre Monnier set out for Languedoc to plunder church choirs for singers.

This was the group that joined forces in December 1669 to present the first officially sanctioned French opera in France, and the musical tradition that they founded with their ill-starred organization would endure for more than 300 years despite the many dark and bloody days that were in store for the nation and its capital.

Le Jeu de Paume de la Bouteille, 1671–1672

The new troupe intended to start their schedule of programs with a representation of *Ariane*, a comedy in music that Perrin and Cambert had mounted at the Hôtel de Nevers in 1669, but this work was set aside in favor of *Pomone*, a pastoral that these same two men had just completed. But first there were obstacles to overcome, especially the lack of a theatre and the new singers' inexperience with the stage and the pronunciation of Parisian French. Perrin solved the first problem by signing a lease for the Béquet tennis court. In the meantime rehearsals were held at Sourdéac's country home in Sèvres during May and June 1670 to coach the vocalists in the ways of the stage and the use of the language. A legal dispute then broke out over the Paris theatre that Perrin had hired, and the company was obliged to transfer to the tennis court in the rue Mazarine called La Bouteille. Financial difficulties increased when it came time to build a stage at this second tennis court and when it was found necessary to fit new loges there. A large excavation also had to be dug to make room for the machinery to be installed, and the structure itself had to be extended 25 feet into a neighboring lumberyard. These alterations were completed, but the company had yet to pay for them. The opening of *Pomone* could not be delayed, therefore, and the Academy of Opera opened its doors for its first premiere in March 1671.

Since expenditures had been heavy, management decided to recoup as quickly as possible by charging high prices for admission and by making the servants of nobility purchase tickets. The public did not take kindly to either extraordinary measure, and there were loud protests and bloody brawls at the box office. So violent was the demonstration that the chief of police was allowed complete freedom to deal with the unruly lackeys who rushed the guards and forced the doors. The fracas produced serious injuries on both sides, but *Pomone* was a success in nearly every way despite the turmoil. It ran for at least eight months and is credited with having earned the handsome sum of 120,000 *livres*. Perrin has left a report in which he alleges that the public left as much as 4,000 *livres* at the box office on better days.

Pomone was a profitable undertaking, therefore, and the troupe should have had enough money left after paying the 2,400 *livres* monthly rent to please all members of the company, even if expenses had been high. Yet such was not the case, and the artistes, as well as management, were dissatisfied with their situation and suspicious of each other in certain instances. This lack of harmony in the Academy of Opera was the result of a curious set of circumstances. The license to produce opera was issued in Perrin's name, and he was legally responsible for debts incurred; Sourdéac was business manager and handled the cash from admissions with his henchman, Champeron; Perrin lacked the money to settle the company's accounts because Sourdéac did not feel inclined to give even the most necessary sums of money to him. No contracts existed among the members of the enterprise; no books were kept. The rift between Perrin and Sourdéac widened when their estimates of the profits derived from *Pomone* differed by thousands of *livres*. Finally, Perrin agreed to a salary instead of a share in the income, but he and the performers were still not paid. In a word, Perrin was being swindled, and his swindlers could still present *Pomone* because the lease to the theatre was now in their names and he had given them public consent to stage his work. Outraged and frustrated, Perrin went to the courts to sue his partners, and he gained some temporary financial respite by selling half his license to Sablières, intendant of music for the duke of Orléans. He was awaiting the outcome of events when, on 15 June 1671, he was thrown into jail for indebtedness.

The performances of *Pomone* were not interrupted, however, and Perrin's partners continued to enjoy the fruits of its success. All that Perrin could do was to sell the remainder of his license and rights to Sablières. He then proceeded to offer these same rights to a second party, La Barroire. The latter purchased them in good faith, and this newly acquired money enabled Perrin to pay his debts and to regain his freedom on 17 August 1671. It was not long before La Barroire found out that he had paid good money for rights that had already been sold, and he had Perrin thrown into prison again on 29 August 1671. The affair had now assumed the aspect of a scandal, and one wag observed that the Opéra was now inoperative.

With Perrin removed from the scene by all this knavery and involved litigation, Sourdéac and Champeron had a free hand to go on with business as usual, because Sablières and his librettist Guichard were occupied with the Versailles production of their own opera, *Les Amours de Diane et d'Endymion*. But if Sourdéac and his accomplice had their freedom and a theatre and the effrontery to continue as if nothing were amiss, they lacked a librettist now that Perrin was more hostile than ever and back in prison. This problem was solved when they found a willing collaborator in Gabriel Gilbert, a dramatist who had fallen into disrepute after one of his compositions proved to have too close a similarity to Corneille's *Rodogune*. It may be said that a pirate and a plagiarist produced the second work for the Académie d'Opéra under the license of a man in jail.

The date of the premiere of this second work, *Les Peines et les plaisirs de l'Amour*, is uncertain, but accounts agree generally that it was sometime in February or March 1672. Its success was never in question, and the public was again leaving large sums of money at the box office in the rue Mazarine.

But it was the very success of this new work that was finally responsible for the closing of Sourdéac's theatre on 1 April 1672 because the large crowds seeking admission to the Opéra were attracting the attention of Jean-Baptiste Lully, who had once said in all seriousness that French opera was an impossibility. Now, however, at this very moment that Robert Cambert's second work for the company was proving so popular at La Bouteille tennis court, the dramatist Donneau de Visé's *Les Amours de Bacchus et d'Ariane* was a hit at the Marais, and the spectacular machine play *Psyché* was being revived for another successful run at the Palais-Royal. Sablières and Guichard were casting about for a place to perform for the public the works that they had just produced to entertain the king and his brother. While this rage for opera and machine plays was at new heights and still growing, Lully went to see Perrin in his cell in the Conciergerie. He made this trip across the Seine because he was certain that Perrin's present predicament and lack of funds would induce him to sell his license or what was left of it, if mathematical niceties had to be observed at this point. But whether Perrin owned part or all of the license made little difference, as long as he sold what he had, because Lully was the king's favorite, and His Majesty's government could hardly deny the validity of a license purchased by him or contend that the manner in which it was sold or bought was illegal. Lully had accomplished his first step, therefore, when he left the prison where Perrin was being held. He came away with what Perrin had agreed to sell, and he was willing to sell all the interest that he had or that he pretended to have in the rights to produce opera in France. Lully had purchased not merely another partnership; he had gained sole possession of all rights formerly belonging to the prisoner. Perrin had sold his monopoly for the third time.

Lully had not been duped because he was quite capable of recognizing fraud and detecting deceit. The truth of the matter is that he had accomplished what he had set out to do: to gain the advantage of having a claim to the license, even if this claim were doubtful or spurious. All he had to do now was to let the magic of his influence at Court transform his partial or imagined claim into the total, sole, and exclusive right to stage opera in France. He had the king on his side, and there was nothing that Louis XIV could not do in Paris in 1672.

The Florentine had been able to gain this initial and important victory because Perrin saw in him a potential and powerful enemy of Sourdéac and Champeron. But Lully did not rush into the second phase of his campaign because Molière had to be reckoned with, too; he was similarly a favorite of the king. Lully remained content for a while with his share of the one and only license that had been in force since 28 June 1669. He cast about for ways to turn his back on his former collaborator on comedy ballets, but he could find no solution to his dilemma except to act directly. His maneuvers proved successful, and he accomplished the second stage of his plan by promoting the issuance of the second license that he had been seeking all along. This new document of March 1672 solved all problems by nullifying Perrin's dispersed license and by founding the Royal Academy of Music under the directorship of Lully, who now had the monopoly to stage "plays in music." Molière was still free to mount his *intermèdes*, but he protested formally against Lully's exclusive right to employ "dancing, ballets, concerts of lutes, theorbos, violins and all sorts of music and other things." The expected protests in other quarters were also forthcoming. Sourdéac and Champeron disputed Lully's favored position on the inevitable grounds that they were the rightful licensees, while Sablières and Guichard objected that it was they who held a valid license purchased legally from Perrin. Solomon, with all his wisdom, would have been hard pressed to find a solution to this involved quarrel, but the Crown was not listening to arguments and acted almost immediately. On 30 March 1672, La Reynie, the chief of police in Paris, was given the order to close down La Bouteille tennis court. Molière was still protected at the Palais-Royal, where he could give his comedies without interference; Perrin had had his revenge, even if his cherished license was gone; Lully was in possession of his official document guaranteeing him the right to produce "plays in music."

This was the proverbial lull before the storm, however, because pandemonium broke loose suddenly in every quarter. Not only the teams of Sourdéac-Champeron and Sablières-Guichard but also the actors, creditors, workers, and even Perrin in his cell produced a deluge of complaints, suits, and appeals. Lully answered all claims and charges calmly and briefly and won favorable verdicts from the Parliament of Paris. Yet Sourdéac and Champeron thought privately that they had really won the day because they were allowed to keep the theatre, which they considered to be the one and only facility in Paris available and suitable for the representation of opera. The enemy would have to come to them eventually and with hat in hand. But they were underestimating Lully, who already had a solution to the same problem that had faced Perrin when the latter had had a license to produce opera but no theatre in which to stage it. He had been unable to get the space at the Louvre that he had requested, but he had managed to obtain a short-term lease for the Béquet tennis court, also known as the Bel-Air tennis court. And, as if by magic, a royal decree was issued immediately to prevent Sourdéac from using his well-equipped opera house. He was ordered "to dispose of said tennis court and its furnishings and machines to whomsoever and howsoever" he saw fit. Lully was now in control and free from all encumbrances.

The Bel-Air Tennis Court, 1672

After Lully had hired the Bel-Air tennis court in the rue de Vaugirard near the Luxembourg palace, he entered into an agreement with the set designer and architect Carlo Vigarani whereby the latter was to ready the stage, the machines, and the other installations necessary for the accommodation and entertainment of audiences. He selected the dancer Desbrosses to organize and to rehearse the members of the ballet, and he found places for most of Cambert's idle singers. He agreed to rent the tennis court for eight months and to return it to its owners in good condition.

The Florentine had obviously been quite busy while maneuvering himself into the position of director of the new Royal Academy of Music, and he had not yet found time to compose a special work to celebrate the inauguration of his theatre. But he did hit upon the expedient idea of collecting a series of airs that he had already written for Philippe Quinault, Benserade, and Molière, and he welded them together into a pastoral pastiche to which he gave the title of Les Fêtes de l'Amour et de Bacchus. The work was billed as a royal production and was well received by the public; the king's triumphant return to Paris after his campaign in the north aided its success. It opened on 15 November 1672, the day of the inauguration of Lully's theatre, and it ran until 1 February 1673, the date of the premiere of Lully's second composition for the Royal Academy of Music. Incredibly enough, the composer had been able to stage his first work at his new theatre only eight or nine months after Les Peines et les plaisirs de l'Amour had been mounted at La Bouteille tennis court. The events leading up to the foundation of the Royal Academy of Music and to the premiere of Les Fêtes de l'Amour et de Bacchus are reported in Le Journal de l'Opéra in six terse entries for 1672:

13 March.	Letters patent bringing control of the Royal Academy of Music to Lully.
30 March.	Letter from the king to M. de la Reynie ordering him to stop performances of the Opéra.
14 April.	Decree of the king's Council of State at the request of Lully for the execution of the license granted to him to establish a Royal Academy of Music at Paris. Given at St.-Germain en Laye.
13 August.	Letters patent: License in favor of Lully of the Royal Academy of Music.
20 September.	Royal license in favor of Lully for the printing of operas.
15 November.	Theatre occupied by the Opéra: Bel-Air tennis court, rue de Vaugirard, near the Luxembourg.

If Lully had a theatre, a troupe, and a successful work at this point, he still did not have a librettist, and it was obvious that *Les Fêtes de l'Amour et de Bacchus* would not run forever. His choice fell upon Philippe Quinault, an accomplished and proven dramatist with whom he had already collaborated on *La Grotte de Versailles* for the king in the summer of 1668. The first result of this partnership was *Cadmus et Hermione*, a lyric tragedy in five acts and a prologue that had its premiere in April 1673. Lully's success was almost beyond the bounds of belief. The king approved the work and announced that he would attend its performances, whenever it might be staged, if he did not have to be in Holland fighting the Dutch. The famous lady of letters, Mme de Sévigné, admitted that it had moved her to tears. It was applauded continuously by the crowds that kept coming to the theatre to hear it in the spring and summer of 1673.

But there was a serious problem that had arisen as early as the beginning of the year: the theatre in the rue de Vaugirard was in poor physical condition because Vigarani had not undertaken extensive repairs on account of Lully's short lease on the building. The structure was now deteriorating under the weight and traffic of large crowds, and its weakened condition constituted a real peril to performers and spectators alike. Lully did not wish to curtail his programs and diminish his financial success by closing down production, but he knew that he had to take some measures. Suddenly fate intervened once again on behalf of the Florentine: Molière died after a performance of *Le Malade imaginaire* on 17 February 1673. The comedian's troupe had been giving plays at the Palais-Royal since 1660, but this did not deter Lully. He asked Charles Perrault, architect and author, to intercede with Jean Colbert, Louis XIV's finance minister, on his behalf, and he obtained the Palais-Royal shortly after the king had attended a performance of *Cadmus et Hermione*. *Le Journal de l'Opéra* notes on 28 April 1673, "Permission given to sieur de Lully to present musical works in the theatre of the Palais-Royal"; this same document adds later that Lully moved into his new facility on 16 June 1673. The Royal Academy of Music performed at this new location in the rue Saint-Honoré between the rue de Valois and the rue des Bons-Enfants for 90 years without paying rent. Molière's bereaved company was transferred to the abandoned La Bouteille tennis court.

La Salle du Palais-Royal, 1673–1763

After Lully was given permission to move into the Palais-Royal on 16 June 1673, it was clear that his position was secure beyond all question and that he was now the dominant musical figure in all France. The Royal Academy of Music was amply funded and firmly founded; in addition to paying no rent and being free to charge high prices for admission, this institution could use in Paris all scenery and costumes that the Crown might purchase for productions at Versailles. If there were alterations or repairs to be made in the theatre, Colbert was authorized to pay for them with government money. As if these financial subsidies were not sufficient reassurance of constant stability, Molière's troupe was forbidden to use more than two vocalists and six instrumentalists in their performances.

The Florentine's only responsibility was to produce operas to justify his license, and he discharged this obligation with faithful regularity by billing a new opera almost every year at the Palais-Royal between the beginning of his tenure as director of the Royal Academy of Music in 1673 and his death in early 1687. The subjects of these new compositions were often suggested by the king, and they were always criticized by the Academy of Inscriptions after Quinault or his substitute submitted the first draft of the libretto to the scrutiny of this body. But Lully had the final say on the finished product, and it was he who set the poem to music after learning it by heart in its final form. It was at this stage of the development of the tragedy that Lully used the knowledge that he had gained by going to the legitimate theatre to listen to the rhythm and intonations of French alexandrine verse composed of syllables. His arias and recitatives were thus formed in such a way that the words were distinguishable and the drama unimpaired. Contrary to the Italian fashion, the music was added to the words in French opera. Most of the compositions so created were based upon mythology, and most of these librettos were suggested by Ovid's *Metamorphoses: Cadmus et Hermione* (1673), *Alceste* (1674), *Thésée* (1675), *Atys* (1675), *Isis* (1677), *Bellérophon* (1679), *Proserpine* (1680) *Persée* (1683), *Phaéton* (1683). Lully then renounced mythology after 1683, probably because the king had grown tired of such subjects, and he turned to Herberay des Essarts's romance for material for his own *Amadis de Gaule* (1684). The two great epics of the Italian Renaissance by Ariosto and Tasso inspired his *Roland* (1685) and *Armide* (1686).

In one fell blow, then, Lully and his librettists, usually Quinault, established the basic genre of serious opera in France with the composition of these 12 lyric tragedies. These works were always preceded by a symphony and a prologue glorifying Louis XIV, his generals, or his admirals. Each of the protagonists overcame seemingly insuperable obstacles by virtue of his courage, magnanimity, or willingness to sacrifice himself for his beloved or the commonweal; appropriate gods and goddesses were always present to lend a helping hand. These representations of extraordinary heroism were interspersed with ballets and choruses composed of characters of supernatural origin in most instances, and the dancers and choristers ranged from magicians and devils to shepherds and sprites. The constant theme was love triumphant, providing that the love was not violent or treacherous; the main character was the embodiment of chivalry and constancy, although he might stray momentarily under the charm of a seductive sorceress like Armide or Circé. Striking costumes and breathtaking spectacles achieved by means of machines furnished the visual appeal that was stressed in opera because it was completely lacking in regular tragedy. Violent and bloody acts were likewise offered to the spectators, and the unities of time and place meant nothing despite their inviolability on the legitimate stage. Even comic scenes were licit at first until they provoked objections. But if the Aristotelian rules governing legitimate tragedy did not always apply, the dramatic format of the lyric tragedy was discernible at all times and did not vary except in certain minor features of the intrigue: an exposition revealed the love interests and conflicts of the principal characters; a subsidiary love affair was introduced; the problems of the unfortunate couples were complicated only to be resolved. The great difference between the lyric tragedy and the traditional tragedy was that the former did not aim at a catharsis. Its task was simply to entertain, to move, or to amaze spectators. It was not concerned with eternal values or the verities of human existence despite its constant allusions to love and glory because it did not attempt to interpret life. It hoped to adorn it.

The multiple scenes provided by Lully's librettists furnished him with ample opportunity to use a variety of music between his symphony in a slow and then fast movement and his jubilant *chaconnes* of the grand finales. The battles, triumphs, duels, and demonic dances were accompanied by fanfares and martial passages designed to heighten the excitement of these spectacular moments that called for loud drums and blaring trumpets. A more gentle manner was reserved for the oboes describing the sleep scenes in works like *Armide*. The pastoral interludes were patent invitations for the composer to point to the quiet moods of nature, but his talent for pictorial music also produced descriptions of the chill winds of winter and the loud violence of storms as well as of chirping birds and wafting breezes. The choruses were antiphonal in structure, for example, the exchange between the jailers and their prisoners in *Amadis*, I, 3. The basic and preponderant portion of the score was the recitative because the drama depended upon it for its forward motion. Wedded to the poem, the music of the recitative was regulated in tempo and modulation by the language of the poetry alone, and no Italianate ornamentation was allowed to superimpose itself. Lully followed the pattern of French versification for this aspect of his score, and his music progressed in the recitatives by measured units within the limits of the hemistich or whole verse. Thus, Lully's compositions were exactly as he described them, lyric tragedies, since they were dramas in fact presented by the recitative but interspersed with arias underlining the important moments of decision, success, or pathos and with choruses reflecting the action in the manner of Greek tragedy.

Lully ruled with an iron hand over the Royal Academy of Music because he viewed himself not as the manager of a theatre but as the director of a mobile unit of professional performers that had an unsurpassed knowledge of their specialty and the discipline to maintain their skills at the highest level. The members of his company were expected to rehearse and to perform flawlessly and on time. His musicians were to follow the scores before them and to refrain from indulging in independent displays of virtuosity. Lully attended rehearsals and was quick to correct any fault, vocal or instrumental, that marred the execution of the work being prepared. His performers were supposed to be effective actors as well as competent singers, and they were disciplined for any attempt to call attention to themselves by departing from the established schema of representation. A personnel manager as well as a conductor and director, Lully tolerated no emotional displays and was quick to detect and to suppress the slightest display of jealousy or temperament. His dominance of the situation is evident in his having created the music for every operatic production sponsored by the Royal Academy of Music during his lifetime. As already indicated, Philippe Quinault did most of his librettos, but these texts were given their ultimate and definitive form by the composer. When Quinault was in disgrace and Thomas Corneille was engaged for the composition of *Bellérophon*, it is reported that the latter dramatist had to write the equivalent of three tragedies before he managed to produce five acts acceptable to Lully.

As might be anticipated, then, no one stepped forward to occupy Lully's unique position after his death on 22 March 1687, and the fate of the Royal Academy of Music was shaped more by political and economic events than by the emergence of any great composer or by the impact of some other new musical influence. The Opéra passed through three periods of political change during this lull in its development before the appearance of Jean-Philippe Rameau on the operatic scene in 1733, and its history in the

1687-1733 period parallels the history of most other cultural institutions in France during this interval of nearly 50 years, which saw the end of Louis XIV's reign (1687-1715), the regency of Philippe d'Orléans (1715-23), and the first decade of Louis XV's rule (1723-33).

When Lully died, he left such a deep imprint upon opera and the Royal Academy of Music that no one entertained the idea of renouncing or altering the traditions and practices that he had established so quickly for the composition and official production of musical works at the Palais-Royal. His forms and style as a composer and producer lived on by sheer momentum. His continuing influence was further promoted by the fact that subsequent administrators, composers, and performers were his relatives or had been trained professionally by him and were not of a disposition to dispute his precepts. Yet not all the members of the company were possessed of the character and dedication required to maintain the discipline that Lully had enforced. Certain artistes began to indulge themselves in fits of temperament and pretended to be ill so that they might not be burdened with rehearsals and other mundane tasks. The female members of the troupe found themselves pregnant with increasing frequency, and the Palais-Royal began to acquire the reputation of being a disreputable corner of Paris. The promiscuity of some dancers was so evident or even so spectacular that popular songs and doggerel verse began to circulate on the subject of their sexual habits. The new head of the Opéra was Lully's son-in-law, Jean-Nicolas de Francine, but neither he nor his associate, Hyacinthe Goureault, had the capacity to suppress these disruptive influences.

At this very moment when the Royal Academy of Music was in need of strong direction and support, Louis XIV was becoming less attentive to its affairs. He did issue a decree in 1713 pertaining to the conduct of certain matters at the Palais-Royal, but his concern was too late in manifesting itself and dealt principally with small adjustments in salaries, pensions, and royalties besides ordering the artistes to remain in their dressing rooms. These were really minor details as far as the future of the Opéra was concerned; the royal directive did not reach the heart of budgetary matters and production money, since Louis XIV's lavish building program and costly wars had already increased the national debt far beyond its reasonable limits. If the Sun King had been inclined to support the Royal Academy of Music unreservedly, moreover, it was unlikely that his staid and pious companion, Mme de Maintenon, would have allowed him to do so without opposition, and her influence over him was now total. The clergy was also waging a vigorous campaign against every aspect of theatrical activity, and the aged king was becoming more sympathetic with their convictions and arguments because of his concern over his own fate in the hereafter.

A relative lack of superior musical talent compounded these moral and financial difficulties, and too frequently the new librettos submitted to the company lacked unity and forcefulness. The dramas were insufficient or diffuse. Lully's carefully structured recitatives were too often replaced by ornate passages encouraging individualistic performances. The ballet was becoming more and more important, but its libretto was frequently only an excuse to introduce the increasingly popular danseuses. The lack of talent necessary to create a work of prime quality for the Royal Academy of Music was apparent in the short runs that many new compositions had and in the regular revivals of Lully's works that were always well attended. André Campra made a serious effort to fill the void left by Lully's death, but his *L'Europe galante* (1697), *Tancrède* (1702), and *Les Festes vénitiennes* (1710) could scarcely provide enough material to sustain Paris audiences until 1733.

Yet it must be acknowledged in retrospect that the Royal Academy of Music fulfilled its function during the first 44 years of its history under the aegis of its founder, Louis XIV. The artistes staged no fewer than 88 compositions in their three theatres between 1671 and 1715. They mounted *Pomone*, an entertainment, a *pastiche*, two ballets, and four pastorals in the period before Lully's demise, but it was the Florentine's 14 lyric tragedies that made up the bulk of their offerings to the public in 1671-87. This was the triumphal period of French opera, and it corresponded chronologically to the days of Louis XIV's greatest glory. Curiously enough, then, the beginning of the Sun King's decline and the death of his superintendent of music coincided. The Opéra was the official musical institution of the land, and it could not avoid reflecting some of the changes in taste marking the decline of a brilliant era in France between 1687 and 1715. The lyric tragedy continued to constitute the basis of repertory through sheer momentum, and 42 of these compositions were produced at the Palais-Royal. It will be noted, however, that these works did not run as long as Lully's tragedies; his 14 lyric tragedies had sufficed for a period of 15 years, but an entire array of composers and librettists had to furnish 42 works in this genre to fill the subsequent gap of 28 years. A second feature of the 1687-1715 programs was the number of ballets selected for representation: 18 opera ballets, comedy ballets, and straight ballets were added to repertory. The continuing favoritism shown to the lyric tragedy and the increasing interest accorded to dancing resulted in the pastoral falling from favor, and only two heroic pastorals were accepted by the management.

If one examines the components of operatic repertory in Paris during the last 44 years of Louis XIV's reign, then, one finds that the most popular type of production in this interval was the lyric tragedy: 56 titles were in this genre. The demand for this sort of program ran parallel to the current trend favoring pure tragedy in the legitimate theatre of the time, but, since tragedies were becoming increasingly devoid of decoration and spectacle, the Opéra was gaining in popularity by producing works offering a purely physical appeal to the senses. The artistes did not confine their efforts to creating colorful and extraordinary spectacles in the context of tragedy, moreover, since they varied their programs by mounting pastorals and a gradually increasing number of ballets. More importantly, the growing interest in shorter and lighter works pointed to the shape of things to come during the regency when the ceremonious formality and baroque pomp of Louis XIV's Court disappeared before the growing frivolity and *galanterie* of a new age.

The establishment of the regency of Philippe d'Orléans in 1715 was accompanied by a feeling of release that swept over the kingdom if only because the conclusion of the Sun King's long rule promised the possibilty of lower taxes and continued peace as well as the closing of Versailles and the end of Mme de Maintenon's domination at Court. The government moved to the Palais-Royal, where the regent made his home, and the artistes' theatre acquired sudden prestige merely by its location. The Royal Academy of Music did not alter the substance and style of its programs abruptly because the major contributors to the repertory continued to be André Campra, Pascal Colasse, Henri Desmarets, André Destouches, La Coste, the elder Rebel, and Stuck. Jean-Joseph Mouret joined this group, but he brought his talents rather than a revolution to his art. Campra was the outstanding composer of the time, and he had been present on the operatic scene since the premiere of his *L'Europe galante* in 1697. Yet this stage in the evolution of French opera continued throughout the regency and until 1733, not because this year saw the performance of Campra's last work by the Royal Academy of Music, but because Rameau's first opera, *Hippolyte et Aricie*, had its premiere at the Palais-Royal on 1 October 1733.

It must be realized that many of the 1671-1715 works continued to appear on 1716-33 programs. Nine of the first 15 compositions mounted by the company were revived once or twice during the regency and the first decade of Louis XV's rule: *Alceste* (1716), *Amadis* (1718, 1731), *Bellérophon* (1718, 1728), *Isis* (1717, 1732), *Persée* (1722), *Phaéton* (1721, 1730), *Proserpine* (1727), and *Roland* (1716, 1727). And the illusion of sameness in the theatre was strengthened by the fact that the personnel of the troupe did not change suddenly or to any great degree with the death of Louis XIV on 1 September 1715. When *Polyxène et Pyrrhus* had its premiere on 21 October 1706, for example, the leading vocalists had included Mlle Journet and Thévenard; Mlles Prévost and Guyot had danced in the ballet with Dumoulin and Dangeville. After the death of Louis XIV, Mlle Journet appeared in the title-rôle of *Camille* on 9 November 1717, while Mlle Guyot and Dumoulin performed in its ballet. Thévenard filled the leading male part in *Le Jugement de Paris* on 14 June 1718; Mlle Prévost starred in its ballet. Dangeville danced in *Polydore* at its premiere on 15 February 1720.

Yet there were changes in repertory, and the new works accepted for production in 1716-33 have a pertinent significance because they reflect clearly the efforts of the Royal Academy of Music to cater to the changing taste and disposition of their paying public. These later additions to repertory are usually shorter than their prototypes and do not make such heavy and sustained demands upon the attention of spectators. A more obvious feature of the new titles as a whole is their variety because no fewer than nine different types of compositions are involved, although only 26 works had their premieres in this period of 17 years. And only slightly more than half of them were lyric tragedies derived for the most part from the Homeric tradition and bearing such titles as *Ajax*, *Ariane*, or *Le Jugement de Paris*. Others, like *Pyrame et Thisbé*, issued from a Roman literary source, usually Ovid. But there was one innovation even in this genre, *Jephté*, which drew its inspiration from the Bible but failed to enjoy a long run because the archbishop of Paris did not feel that a religious subject should constitute the basis for an operatic entertainment at the Palais-Royal. The company also placed greater stress on the dance in their productions, an especially congruous development since the regent's residence had become the scene of masked balls. This preference for ballet forms manifested itself in the fact that no fewer than 15 new compositions in this genre were performed between 1716 and 1733, while the opera-ballet established itself as a separate type of theatrical presentation with each of its acts containing a complete plot with its own characters supporting a central theme. These opera-ballets included *Les Ages* (1718), *Les Eléments* (1725), and *Les Sens* (1732). Four other choreographic works were billed as heroic ballets. *Le Parnasse* (1729) was billed as a straight ballet. Compositions of a lighter sort were similarly stressed, and two comic intermezzos, two entertainments, and a "Persian comedy" called *La Reine des Péris* rounded out the 1715-33 additions to the repertory designed to capture the fancy of a less heroic age.

At this moment, when the tide was turning against the lyric tragedy and the theatrical style of the seventeenth century was losing favor, Rameau burst upon the operatic scene on 1 October 1733 at the age of 50 with *Hippolyte et Aricie*, a love story that Racine had dramatized with such success in *Phèdre*. This opera left many spectators more puzzled than enthusiastic at first because they were taken aback by the unfamiliar sounds of Rameau's chords based upon his theory of music and they were reluctant to accept his disciplined treatment of more lively rhythms, his calculated control of melody, and his logical execution of a more complex orchestration involving strings, bassoons, flutes, oboes, trumpets, and horns. All these innovations were too much to assimilate readily and rapidly after more than a half century of music inspired more or less by Lully. The critics of Rameau's manner saw in his music a betrayal of the great French master and pointed to the coloratura passages in the last act of *Hippolyte et Aricie* as a definite sign of the composer's capitulation to Italianism. They overlooked Rameau's choice of a subject treated by Racine and his abiding by the rules that Lully and Quinault had observed in wedding music to words and claimed instead that his contrapuntal style was evidence of pedantry in an age when the natural was to be cherished above all else in art. Yet Rameau's innovative manner was the result of careful deliberation, since the composer considered the lyric tragedy to be the crowning achievement of a musical career. He was to set only three other librettos in this genre: *Castor et Pollux* (1737), *Dardanus* (1739), *Zoroastre* (1749).

Rameau had also lived up to earlier expectations with *Les Indes galantes* (1735), an opera-ballet successful enough financially and esthetically to validate this genre as an undisputed operatic form, and *Castor et Pollux*, which mobilized the defenders and opponents of Rameau under the banners of the Ramoneurs and Lullyistes. The quarrel concentrated upon the supposedly excessive use of semiquavers by the composer. Since *ramoneur* means chimney sweep in French, the ensuing implication was that a page of Rameau's music could look soot-swept. The author of *Castor et Pollux* was more perplexed than hurt, and the publicity boosted receipts on the dates when his work was performed.

Rameau had had to wait a long time before he had his first composition mounted by the Royal Academy of Music, but his growing acceptance by the public now reassured him, and he went on to create according to his own convictions and with confidence. After *Dardanus* (1739) had added new fuel to the Lullyiste-Ramoneur conflagration, he completed three heroic pastorals entitled *Zaïs* (1748), *Naïs* (1749), and *Acanthe et Céphise* (1751) as well as two lyric comedies, *Platée* (1745) and *Les Paladins* (1760). He finished *La Princesse de Navarre* to honor the marriage of the dauphin and Marie-Thérèse. After the success of *Les Indes galantes* (1735), he could scarcely renounce the opera-ballet, but *Les Fêtes d'Hébé* (1736) and *Le Temple de la Gloire* (1745) proved to be somewhat disappointing, and *Les Fêtes de l'Hymen et de l'Amour* (1747) and *Les Surprises de l'Amour* (1757) lacked enough dramatic interest to justify the importance that the dramatist and librettist Louis de Cahusac attached to them. There were also other scores in a single act that Rameau contributed to the repertory, and even a cursory description of his compositions for the stage reveals his constant interest in the Royal Academy of Music for more than 30 years. Rameau was the most prolific composer of his time as far as the French theatre was concerned: his dramatic production includes at least 25 titles amounting to approximately 80 acts. More importantly, Rameau did not reject the manner of Lully and his disciples completely in these works. He remained with the mythological tradition in the choice of his subjects, and he acknowledged the importance of the ballet while retaining the general structure of his predecessors' overtures and drama. In a word, he refined and expanded but did not reject the formula developed by Lully to present a tragedy musically and with dancing and spectacle. It was really the style of his music that made his work seem either strange or Italianate to astonished listeners because he refused to adhere to the pattern of applying one note to one syllable ad infinitum as in the earlier fashion of Lully.

The composer of *Castor et Pollux* was not the only musician to contribute to the repertory between 1733 and 1774, the year of the premiere of Gluck's *Iphigénie en Aulide* in Paris. The distinction of being the second most frequently accepted composer at the Opéra during these 40-odd years belongs to Antoine Dauvergne, who provided the artistes with three lyric tragedies, two heroic ballets, an opera, an opera-ballet, and a comedy-ballet. Originally a violinist in the orchestra and considered to be the creator of the first French comic opera, *Les Troqueurs* (1753), he was especially close to the musical scene and held a number of positions in the government of Louis XV including the directorship of the Opéra. Jean-Joseph Cassanea de Mondonville was the next most frequent provider of scores with three lyric tragedies, a pair of heroic ballets, a comedy-ballet, a tragedy, and a piece designated as a "pastorale languedocienne" done in his native dialect to demonstrate that the French language could be as musical as Italian. Louis-Joseph Francoeur, alone or in collaboration with his uncle, was responsible for a heroic ballet, a heroic pastoral, an entertainment, a lyric tragedy, and two opera-ballets. As can be seen from this simple catalogue of these three musicians' works at the Opéra, the weakening of the position of the lyric tragedy in repertory resulted in the composers casting about in other quarters for success. Bernard de Bury, Jean-Joseph Mouret, and Joseph-Nicolas-Pancrace Royer did three works apiece for the artistes. Curiously enough, however, it was the more than 20 creators of only one or two new works who accounted in large measure for the diversity and quantity of bills posted between 1723 and 1774. It might also be noted in reference to repertory that Rameau died on 12 September 1764 and that only 16 new works were mounted by the artistes after his death and before Christoph Willibald von Gluck's appearance in Paris a decade later with *Iphigénie en Aulide*. These ten years were in fact a lackluster period for the Royal Academy of Music. *Le Journal de l'Opéra* reveals that a profusion of programs consisted of *spectacles coupés*, that is, a set of two or three acts extracted from different works. Every third, fourth, or fifth bill between 2 January and 22 May 1772, for example, was made up of entrées or acts from assorted compositions, and only the revival of *Aline* on 26 May 1772 interrupted this run of patchwork programs. Each of the early 50 performances staged between 13 May and 5 September 1773 was a *spectacle coupé*. But box-office returns continued to remain low and to reflect a growing apathy on the part of the public. Daily receipts fell below 1,000 *livres* more and more frequently, while returns did not even amount to 500 *livres* on many days. Only 222 *livres* were collected on 28 November 1771.

Yet there was an evident variety in the offerings at the Opéra in this period of 40 years preceding Gluck's arrival in Paris, and a tally of the 1733-74 titles billed at the Royal Academy of Music reveals that the artistes accepted 92 new works during this interval if one includes the 11 Italian intermezzos of 1 August 1752 to 12 February 1754. The most popular genre was the heroic ballet with 15 authors producing 19 of these compositions. In contrast to the eras of Lully and Campra, the lyric tragedy was now the second most frequently performed work; a dozen composers had only 15 of them approved for staging. The 14 opera-ballets approved for representation by management furnish additional evidence of the increasing popularity of the dance in the eighteenth century, when the stage was elevated to enhance ballet presentation. The strength of this trend is apparent again in the fact that seven ballets, two comedy-ballets, two *ballets bouffons*, and a heroic ballet had their premieres at this same time. Nor was the pastoral forgotten: five heroic pastorals and four straight *pastorales* were among the new offerings by the Academy. Strangely enough, only a single work was posted as an opera, Rameau's *Naïs*, considered by some critics to be an opera-ballet. Four other types of composition were likewise billed once: the lyric comedy (*Les Amours de Ragonde*, 1742), the entertainment (*Les Augustales*, 1744), the *fête* (*Le Temple de la Gloire*, 1745), and the *opéra burlesque* (*La Scaltra Governatrice*, 1753). Ten of the 11 Italian works were described as intermezzos. Finally, the continuing custom of giving fragments, either heroic or pastoral, reveals the tendency of programs to lean more and more toward the *spectacle coupé* made up of single acts from such compositions as *Les Festes de Thalie* (1714), *Les Amours des dieux* (1727), *Les Sens* (1732), and *Les Indes galantes* (1735), which provided *La Provençale, Apollon et Coronis, La Vue*, and *Les Incas du Pérou* for a number of these bills. *Le Journal de l'Opéra* records many examples of this sort of program, but one sample should suffice: the representation of 1 October 1769 consisted of the second and third acts of *Les Fêtes de Paphos* (1758) and *La Provençale*. Sometimes a new title was coupled with a pair of acts from established works, as on 4 October 1771, when *L'Air* from *Les Eléments* (1725) and *La Sibylle* from *Les Fêtes d'Euterpe* (1758) were mounted with *Le Prix de la valeur* (1771).

This policy of providing such a variety of offerings was part of an effort to raise money at the box office, of course, and a glimpse into the business affairs of the company reveals the reason for this preoccupation with finances despite the favored fiscal position of the Royal Academy of Music. The situation became serious, it appears, when François Berger replaced Eugène de Thuret as director of the Opéra in 1744 because the latter's health had become undermined after 11 years in office. Berger had been director for only three years when he had to be dismissed because the debt of the Academy had risen to 400,000 *livres* during his directorship. His successor, Guénot de Tréfontaine, was faced in his turn with a deficit of 250,000 *livres*. Finally, the city of Paris had to intervene to assume direction of the company on 25 August 1749. But, by 12 March 1757, the debt of the Royal Academy of Music had climbed to the awesome total of 1.2 million *livres*. The municipal government of the capital was obliged to discharge this extraordinary obligation so that the doors of the Palais-Royal would not be closed.

If Louis XV had continued to see the Opéra in particular and music in general as effective and official instruments in promoting the national interest, the Academy would not have fallen into such regrettable circumstances. Louis XIV had made ample provisions for the payment of expenses, and he had written guarantees of financial independence into the letters patent that he had granted to Lully. But Louis XV did not display the same interest that his great-grandfather had taken in the Opéra. He regarded it more as a form of entertainment, as an agency to point to certain family events, or even as another form of amusement for Madame de Pompadour. Thus, *Le Journal de l'Opéra* abounds in notations confirming the presence of royalty at the theatre and indicating scores of trips that the artistes made to Fontainebleau and Versailles. The doors of the Palais-Royal were closed promptly to mourn deaths in the royal family, and special programs were mounted to celebrate the births and weddings of royal personages. The greatest collaboration between royalty and the Royal Academy of Music took place on the occasion of the marriage of the dauphin and Marie-Antoinette in 1770. This incredibly lavish program and the theatre built for it at Versailles were so costly that the more earthbound members of government began to worry about the effect of the celebration upon the national budget. The log of the Opéra lists the days set apart for the artistes to perform in the nuptial festivities as 3, 10, 13, 15, 16, 22, 24, and 25 May and 8 June. The production of *La Tour enchantée* alone required the services of 800 vocalists, dancers, and extras as well as the use of 16 horses. A few years later, in 1773, 350,000 *livres* were spent at Versailles to celebrate the marriage of the count d'Artois, for whom the company mounted *Bellérophon* and *Isménor*. Specifically, Louis XV appears to have expected the artistes to amuse and to honor him without concern for expense, but he never seems to have entertained the possibility that it might further the purposes of the Crown to relieve the company of anxiety over finances and to make them an arm of policy as they had been in the days of Louis XIV.

The argument over the relative merits of Italian and French opera was also renewed toward the middle of the century, when Friedrick Melchior Grimm, philosopher and critic, attacked French music in the *Mercure* (1750), and when the Italian artistes known as the Bouffons arrived in Paris to perform Pergolesi's *La Serva padrona* on 1 August 1752. The pro-French forces realized that only Rameau could serve them as a more effective leader, and even his former enemies, the Lullyistes, closed ranks with the Ramoneurs to defend their national music. The leaders in this group were Jacques Cazotte, Elie Fréron, Jean-Baptiste Jourdan, and other lesser known figures who gathered in "the king's corner" of the Palais-Royal to present a united front to the pro-Italian faction in the "queen's corner." Pamphlets and pronouncements inundated Paris; no café was without its daily quarrel. Inevitably, Jean-Jacques Rousseau joined the fracas with *Le Devin du village* (1752), and Grimm picked up his pen again to belittle

Rameau, Jélyotte, and Mlle Fel in his *Le Petit Prophète de Boehmischbroda* (1753). In the meantime, *La Serva padrona* had returned double the usual receipts to the box office, and the management of the Opéra saw no reason to turn its back on good fortune, national pride notwithstanding. The policy of mounting *opera buffa* or *intermezzi* continued, as gods and heroes of Olympian stature were rejected for characters of more humble dimension. The Academy had offered 41 consecutive Italian programs to the public between 1 August and 7 November 1752, and they had benefited to the happy tune of 75,662 *livres*. But protests were being made in influential quarters against Italianism at the Palais-Royal, and Dauvergne's *Les Amours de Tempé*, with a libretto by Louis de Cahusac, was given its premiere there on 7 November 1752. A deadlock had been reached apparently, and the only solution to the problem was to stage both French and Italian works to satisfy the Bouffons, the Ramoneurs, and whatever Lullyistes were still active. This compromise could not continue forever, of course, and the Academy made an effort in the second half of 1753 to wean themselves and their public away from the Italian type of entertainment. *Bertoldo in Corte* was mounted on nine dates in the first two months of 1754, however, and *I Viaggiatori* was presented for the first time on 12 February 1754 for a brief run of five billings. *Le Devin du village* was performed seven times in this same interval of two months. But this score of representations proved to be the last appearances of the Italian artistes for some time to come. The quarrel subsided for all practical purposes with Charles-Simon Favart enjoying a success at the Théâtre Italien with *Le Caprice amoureux ou Ninette à la cour* (1755), a parody of *Bertoldo in Corte* (1753).

L'Opéra-Comique, I: Before 1762

Self-indulgent performers, strained budgets, and foreign troupes were not the only threats to the prosperity of the Royal Academy of Music after the death of Louis XIV. A rival theatrical group was now emerging in Paris to compete for spectators. This peculiar sort of competition for a theatrical company holding a royal monopoly on a certain type of production was a new problem, but it had taken a long time to develop. In fact, it had grown out of the Saint-Germain and Saint-Laurent fairs of the Middle Ages, which had offered such unsophisticated forms of entertainment as tight-rope acts, performing animals, and marionettes. These shows assimilated an element of music quite easily when the vaudeville or popular song was included in the rudimentary entertainment they afforded. The fairs were municipal institutions and continued into the seventeenth century as a form of amusement patronized principally by the people, but the process of commingling music and words on the stage in a sort of mixed genre was repeated at Court with the arrival there of Mazarin's Italian troupe of singers and actors in 1642. The trend toward the use of words and music on the same theatrical program was reinforced by Lully's composing *intermèdes* for Molière's ballet comedies. No one seemed to sense any conflict in these developments until Lully managed to deprive the legitimate stage of the use of nearly every sort of music after the death of Molière in 1673. Then, in 1697, the Italians were expelled from the capital after angering Mme de Maintenon with possible allusions to her in *La Fausse Prude*. The injunction levied against music at the Comédie-Française and the disappearance of the Italians led the players at the fairs to believe that new theatrical vistas had opened up for them. They began to enrich their repertory with parodies of operas and tragedies, scripts appropriated from the Italians, old texts rejuvenated for the occasion, and even modified modern French works. They hired a limited number of professional actors to assist them in their new theatres, and it was only a matter of time before they provoked the Opéra by using music and the Comédie-Française by exploiting what could pass for drama.

The lines of conflict were now defined, and the police had to warn the actors from the Saint-Laurent and Saint-Germain fairs in 1699 and 1706 not to present plays containing dialogues. Threatened, they managed to purchase the right to employ singers and dancers from the Opéra in 1709. This ploy was successful, but only for a while, and their leader Charles Alard had subsequently to give programs without speaking or singing; his actors displayed their speeches printed on cards for the audiences to read at the proper moment. This system of cue cards was clumsy, and appropriate vaudeville airs soon replaced the written speeches. The orchestra struck up the popular tune, the theatregoers recognized it and sang the pertinent words. A refinement was added when the words to be sung were displayed on a banner visible to all spectators. Thus, the comic opera was born of this device of substituting songs for dialogue to develop lighter rather than tragic plots. The term "opéra comique" was used for the first time in 1715.

This newly formed theatre soon began to specialize in parodies of works offered by the legitimate actors at the Comédie-Française and the artistes of the Royal Academy of Music. But some authors like Alain-René Lesage and Jacques-Philippe d'Orneval saw that a profit could be turned by creating texts for this new theatre for which Catherine Vanderberg had purchased from the Opéra the right to mount plays mingled with songs, dancing, and symphonies. Such well-known authors as Alexis Piron, Charles-Simon Favart, and Louis Fuzelier submitted plays that were acceptable to the new group that established itself definitively in 1752 under the direction of Jean Monnet. Intent on success, Monnet enlisted the services of the famous painter François Boucher, the well-known choreographer Jean-Georges Noverre, the musician Antoine Dauvergne, and the authors Charles-Simon Favart and Jean-Joseph Vadé. The latter writer wrote the first new work for the company, *Les Troqueurs* (1753). After Monnet yielded his license to Julien Corby and Moëtte in 1757, the Opéra-Comique was joined by a quirk of fate to the Théâtre-Italien (1762). This sign of approval was an obvious assurance of success, and such writers as Pierre-Alexandre Monsigny, André Ernest Modeste Grétry, François-Joseph Gossec, and François-André Danican Philidor had no reluctance about submitting their works to this newly formed organization.

The Tuileries, 1763–1770

The Royal Academy of Music suffered a most unexpected blow on the morning of 6 April 1763 when a fire broke out in the Palais-Royal. It was caused by painters working on new scenery. The flames could not be suppressed, and the theatre was destroyed. After the conflagration, the artistes moved into the Tuileries for a series of 28 concerts lasting from 29 April until 16 December, with the concert on 20 June being held in the Tuileries gardens for the inauguration of the king's statue there. These concerts were composed of overtures, *divertissements* excerpted from longer compositions, or separate entrées selected from works already produced by the company. *Le Journal de l'Opéra* for January 1764 records that the Opéra found new quarters in "the new hall of the Tuileries on 24 January. . . between the pavilion of the Clock and Marsan." The troupe would remain here until 1770, although they would have to suspend activities temporarily from 17 December 1765 until 12 January 1766 on account of the dauphin's illness and death on 20 December 1765. They produced seven new works here in this interlude of seven years, but the first of these compositions was not staged until 15 April 1766, more than two years after the fire. The tendency to favor the ballet in all its forms continued: two lyric tragedies and four ballets were introduced into the repertory. The other new work was a pastoral in a single act entitled *La Fête de Flore* (1771). The favored composers of this 1763-70 interval were Pierre-Montan Berton and Jean Claude Trial, who were directors of the Royal Academy of Music at the time. They managed to guide their *Erosine*, *Sylvie*, and *Théonis* safely onto the stage while piling up a deficit of 500,000 *livres* for the Opéra.

Le Palais-Royal, *bis*, 1770–1781

The new Palais-Royal theatre was inaugurated on 20 January 1770 with a performance of Rameau's *Zoroastre*. Excited and curious, a large crowd milled about the doors of the theatre on this occasion, and it was necessary to rely upon the municipal police to maintain order. Once the unruly theatregoers were inside the new structure, they found it quite large because it had been constructed to accommodate 2,500 spectators, and its designer, Louis-Pierre Moreau, had decided to extend it as far as the rue des Bons-Enfants. It was laid out in an oval shape, the first time that this architectural form had been used for staging opera in Paris, and its spectacular and really overdone interior with its lavish ornamentation bespoke the ambitious plans that management had for its new facility. An orchestra of approximately 70 pieces, a ballet company of nearly 100 dancers, and a staff of almost 75 singers were available to entertain the public. Prices of admission were higher now, and a special administrative unit was established to handle the sale of tickets on a daily and annual basis. As protection against another fire, water was kept on hand, and a fireproof curtain was installed.

The Royal Academy of Music was to remain in its new home only until the end of the evening performance on 8 June 1781, but certain noteworthy innovations took place during this relatively brief period of a dozen years besides the novel stage effects attempted in the series of special programs of 1770 at Versailles to celebrate the marriage of Marie-Antoinette and the dauphin.

The first of these departures from tradition involved the ballet, which was undergoing a reform in Europe as it changed from a display of posturing and acrobatics into a pantomimic interpretation of the tragedy unfolding on the stage. Thus, the ballet became ancillary to the principal action, and it was elevated to a position of prime importance instead of being proffered as a supplementary amusement in another form. Jean-Georges Noverre was one of the leading champions of this new attitude towards the ballet, and, when Jean-Benjamin de La Borde's *Ismène et Isménias* was performed in Paris on 11 December 1770, it incorporated into its representation a pantomime-ballet entitled *Médée* by Jean-Georges Noverre. The striking aspect of presenting these two works in combination was not simply the fact that *Médée* was a ballet without words but that it was not part of another piece. As such, it constitutes the prototype of later ballets offered as indigenous yet silent portions of operas, although they were accompanied by their own music and sometimes became as important as the matrix work itself.

While François André Danican Philidor, Pierre-Alexandre Monsigny, and André Ernest Modeste Grétry were providing successful works for the prospering Opéra-Comique in this period prior to the Revolution, the repertory at the Palais-Royal remained rather dull. Etienne-Joseph Floquet was called upon to answer cries of "Author! Author!" on 7 September 1773 after the staging of his ballet *L'Union de l'Amour et des Arts*, the first time that a composer had been honored in this fashon at the Opéra. But this occasion was unique, and mediocrity was really the order of the day. The fresh sets and costumes created after the fire of 1763 helped to enliven the spectacles at first, but this bright note alone could not sustain spectators' enthusiasm forever. Then, on 16 June 1773, Marie-Antoinette and the dauphin came to the theatre, and the future queen found the program of *Théonis* and *Zélindor* so dull that she set into motion a series of events to improve the offerings at the Opéra: she decided to have her former music teacher, Christoph Willibald von Gluck, produce a program at the Palais-Royal without delay. The project was simple enough, because François Louis Lebland Du Roullet, a member of the staff at the French embassy in Vienna, had come to know the composer in Vienna and had already given him a French libretto in three acts based upon Racine's *Iphigénie en Aulide*.

The Royal Academy of Music might be reluctant to bring Gluck's music to the Paris public lest their own offerings suffer by comparison, but they could scarcely contravene the wishes of the future queen. Gluck's first Paris composition was presented to a full house on 19 April 1774. The applause was deafening; no premiere had ever before returned such a handsome sum to the box office in the hundred-year history of the Opéra: 6,212 *livres*, 10 *sols*. Encouraged, Gluck went on to do a French version of his *Orfeo*, wherein he substituted a tenor for a contralto in the title-rôle on account of the Parisians' dislike for *castrati*. His other works for the Palais-Royal included *Cythère assiégée* (1775), *Alceste* (1776), *Armide* (1777), *Iphigénie en Tauride* (1779), and *Echo et Narcisse* (1779). These seven compositions earned one million *livres* for Gluck in Paris.

Gluck's music had a maximum impact upon contemporary audiences because it was based upon the composer's conviction that operatic scores should be purged of certain persistent conventions deriving from Italian *opera seria*. This reform of opera had become almost a fixation with him since the time when he had joined forces with Raniero de' Calzabigi and count Durazzo to banish Pietro Metastasio's ornate style from the operatic stage. Gluck published his ideas in his various prefaces and in a letter he wrote to the *Mercure de France* in October 1772 before coming to France. In the preface to *Alceste*, he announced that his ambition was to keep his music free of the "abuses" that have made music "ridiculous" in Italy. Specifically, his aim was to achieve the true, the simple, and the natural in art, a sentiment that won him the support of Jean-Jacques Rousseau. He believed that music should transcend national frontiers and be unified at all costs with each element of the composition serving the production of the universal drama being presented. The ballet, the score, and the chorus must serve this single purpose instead of trying to stand by themselves. The aria must be a part of the flow of the drama, not a moment of song inserted into the recitative. In a way, therefore, Gluck summed up the generations of previous French composers by virtue of his Lullyian insistence upon the importance of drama in opera and on account of his Rameau-like quest for purity and logic in music. His whole musical attitude was in sympathy with the baroque customs and institutions about to be swept away in the approaching holocaust, and there is poignant significance in the fact that his chorus of "Chantons, célébrons notre reine" started a riot in 1790.

Yet Gluck had enemies, and he got his first taste of the resentment and hostility he inspired in Paris when *Iphigénie en Aulide* went into rehearsal and the recalcitrant musicians objected to his music, his manners, and his threats to report their insolence to Marie-Antoinette. After the success of his first production in the French capital, his enemies suggested to Mme Du Barry that she proclaim herself a patron of the arts by importing the Italian composer Niccolò Piccinni to serve as a rival to Marie-Antoinette's Gluck. Du Barry was favorably disposed toward this proposal, but the death of Louis XV suppressed all activity relating to the Opéra for a while. Finally, negotiations were resumed in Naples, and the Opéra acquired another alien star: Piccinni left Naples for Paris on 16 November 1776. After his arrival in the capital, he and his librettist Jean-François Marmontel labored daily and note by note to produce a new version of Lully's *Roland*. It was at this point that Gluck learned that the Royal Academy of Music had invited Piccinni to compose a *Roland*, although he, Gluck, had already embarked upon a version of this subject. He consigned the pages of his unfinished score to the flames of his fireplace. The bitter struggle between the Gluckists and the Piccinnists reached its climax at the time of the premiere of Piccinni's *Roland* on 17 January 1778, and the question of the relative merits of these composers' works and styles replaced America and progress as the favorite topics of conversation at the café de la Régence. Ultimately, Gluck returned to Vienna after the disappointing reception accorded to his *Echo et Narcisse* (1779), while his rival remained in Paris to do *Atys* (1780), *Iphigénie en Tauride* (1781), *Adèle de Ponthieu* (1781), and his great success, *Didon* (1783). Piccinni would add two more titles to repertory before his return to Naples on 13 July 1787: *Diane et Endymion* (1784) and *Pénélope* (1785).

The 1763-81 repertory of the Royal Academy of Music was dominated by Gluck and Piccinni, but these two composers contributed to the Opéra only 15 of the 65 compositions that had their Paris premieres in this interval of 18 years. Pierre-Montan Berton and Jean-Claude Trial alone or in collaboration had five titles accepted by the company before Gluck made his initial appearance at the Palais-Royal, and Floquet considered himself a serious rival of the author of *Alceste* with his *L'Union de l'Amour et des Arts* (1773), *Azolan* (1774), *Hellé* and *Le Seigneur bienfaisant* (1780). Jean-Georges Noverre and Maximilien-Léopold-Philippe-Joseph Gardel had nine ballets performed. The list of foreigners besides Gluck and Piccinni providing compositions for the Academy is quite long because Anne-Pierre-Jacques Devismes de Valgay tried to compensate for the lack of native talent by inviting other eligible Italians and Germans to enrich his programs; Pasquale Anfossi, Johann Christian Bach, Giovanni Cambini, and Luigi Cherubini were but some of these guest composers. This lack of creativity among French musicians was matched by a parallel dearth of talent among domestic librettists, and the familiar lyric tragedies of Quinault in five acts were revived in a reduced form of three acts to avoid boring eighteenth-century audiences. It might be noted finally that a young man named Mozart had his first work for the Opéra performed on 11 June 1778, but no one paid much attention to him. Spectators were more interested in the choreography that Noverre had done for *Les Petits Riens*.

The Porte-Saint-Martin Theatre, 1781-1794

The program of 8 June 1781 had just concluded when a small fire broke out on stage. The entire proscenium was engulfed in flames before counter-measures could be taken, and the Palais-Royal theatre was reduced to ashes in moments. After the fire of 1763, a tank and pumps had been installed in the theatre by the architect Louis Pierre Moreau to prevent the repetition of such catastrophes, but no one had taken the precaution to keep the reservoir filled with water. This oversight was responsible for the deaths of 14 people in the spectacular blaze fed by the paint, alcohol, and other volatile materials found backstage.

It was less than a fortnight after the conflagration that the company turned to giving a series of 14 concerts between 19 June and 10 August before moving on 14 August into temporary quarters in the theatre of the Menus-Plaisirs du Roy located in the rue Bergère. The building here was small, and the police had to be summoned to direct traffic in the neighborhood during the artistes' brief sojourn in this inadequate facility, where François Lays, Augustin-Athanase Chéron, and J. Rousseau refused to sing and dared to quit the company even under threat of imprisonment. The Opéra opened in the rue Bergère on 14 August 1781 with a bill composed of *Le Devin du village* and *Myrtil et Lycoris*; they remained with this stage, which had been the theatre of the Saint-Laurent fair, until 23 October 1781. They were able to mount 22 programs in the interval between 14 August and 23 October 1781, and they managed to prepare Jean-Baptiste Rochefort's version of Pasquale Anfossi's *L'Inconnue persécutée* for its premiere on 21 September.

The task of providing a new, permanent, and ample theatre for the Royal Academy of Music was undertaken personally and immediately by Marie-Antoinette, who selected a site and charged the architect Samson-Nicolas Lenoir to begin construction immediately. She promised him the order of Saint-Michel and a pension of 6,000 *livres* if he could complete his task by 31 October 1781. Lenoir recruited two work crews and labored around the clock; he finished in time to open his theatre on 27 October 1781, and he ingratiated himself with the queen twice over by incorporating her statue into his facade. No one appeared concerned over the building having cost 400,000 *livres*, not 200,000 *livres* as planned, and the only troublesome feature about the entire project was the rumor that the edifice was weak and unsafe for public programs. It is reported that the building did sag a few inches under the weight of the spectators who crowded into the Porte-Saint-Martin theatre on the day of its opening, but this structural deviation was apparently viewed as a detail of no consequence, and Piccinni's *Adèle de Ponthieu* had its premiere without incident on the free inaugural program given to celebrate the birth of the dauphin. The building was strengthened in 1782, when it was decided to increase its seating capacity. The company remained in the Porte-Saint-Martin theatre until 7 March 1794.

The years immediately preceding and following the fall of the Bastille were a time of many changes for the Royal Academy of Music, and the most obvious of these innovations were in its title, which was converted to the single word, "Opéra," on 24 June 1791. A decision was made on 29 June to rename it the "Académie de Musique," and, on 17 September, its original title of "Académie Royale de Musique" was restored. The royal family came to the theatre on 20 September, apparently to show their approval and to express their gratitude for this third change in four months; 1791 was the last year in which the queen paid her annual rent of 7,000 *livres* for a box at the Opéra, which became the "Académie de Musique" once again on 15 August 1792. The growing wave of republicanism led to the Opéra next being designated simply the "Opéra" for the second time on 12 August 1793 and as the "Opéra National" on 18 October 1793.

And it goes without saying that the administrative reforms taking place within the structure of the Opéra were numerous in these troubled times. The company entered the prerevolutionary period with the supervision of its affairs withdrawn from the city of Paris and with Henri-Montan Berton as its director. He was answerable to the Crown. He died almost immediately on 14 May 1780, however, and Antoine Dauvergne replaced him with François-Joseph Gossec as his aide. The king tried to excise all superfluous expenditures from the budget in the ensuing decade, but the deficit remained large and rose to more than 150,000 *livres* on occasion despite the extra rents, royalties, grants, and other auxiliary sums the Opéra managed to extract from its tenants and the public. Even extraordinary windfalls like the 40,000 *livres* from masked balls in 1784, along with a subsidy of 60,000 *livres* from the government of Paris, did not seem to help. Dauvergne could not stem the tide of excessive expenditures and poor management, and he stepped aside to give Morel an opportunity to bring some order out of the prevailing chaos. The first thing that ingenious Morel did was to set up a private business selling opera librettos obtained for a pittance. He made the mistake of including the count de Provence's works in his venture and was dismissed from office. Dauvergne returned to the directorship at the king's request, but the Revolution broke out, and the municipal government of the capital assumed control of the affairs of the Opéra once again in 1790. The new administration was scarcely an improvement with its deficit of 627,590 *livres*, and they transferred the management of the company's affairs to Louis-Joseph Francoeur and Jacques Cellerier for 30 years. Once again the remedy proved worse than the disease, and these two officers were declared suspect on 8 March 1792. Cellerier fled from the country, and Francoeur was thrown into prison. Inevitably, a committee of citizens beyond reproach was formed, but there was still a deficit of 276,507 *livres* weighing down the Opéra when it came time to leave the Porte-Saint-Martin theatre.

This irresponsibility in fiscal matters had its effect upon the performers, who decided to make life as easy as possible for themselves. Mlle Antoinette-Cécile Saint-Huberty had to be threatened with jail before she consented to live up to her agreement with the Opéra by singing whenever she was required to do so. Other artistes attempted to have their stage appearances reduced by 60 percent. When conduct reports on each performer were compiled, it was found that even the great Auguste Vestris indulged in blatant insolence and impudence, while Mlles Hilisberg and Rose followed his example. Etienne Lainez reported sick whenever he had more pleasant tasks to perform, and it is said that another vocalist neglected his duties to chase women of easy morals in gambling houses.

Three other miscellaneous events must be indicated here, although they had nothing to do with personnel and finances. Louis XVI founded a school known as the *Ecole de Chant et de Déclamation*, which was organized to train vocalists and actors aspiring to a career in theatres supported by the Crown. This institution became the Conservatoire in the course of time. Secondly, the "Liberty of Theatres" was decreed and described in documents dated 13 January and 2 March 1791. This corpus of regulations governing public representations for a profit gave any citizen the right to establish a theatre merely by indicating his intention to the proper authorities. The works of any author dead five or more years were considered to be in the public domain and could be mounted without interference or hindrance from another person or agency, but the writings of living authors were protected by law. Lastly, the new government came to understand very quickly the value of the Opéra as a vehicle for propaganda, and they turned to promoting such works as *Le Triomphe de la République* or *L'Offrande à la Liberté*. This cult of theatrical republicanism was spontaneous at first, but, on 2 August 1794, the government issued an order that the theatres should honor the era of liberty, fraternity, and equality three times a week by mounting works serving this purpose. A spate of politico-patriotic programs resulted from this edict despite the lack of applause prompted by these works, which appear today to be nothing more than idle exercises in absurdity. Yet they seem to have entertained or even to have stirred audiences in their day, when spectators at the Opéra seem to have been mostly "dilettantes sans culottes."

The troupe added 60 titles to the repertory during their stays at the Menus-Plaisirs and Porte-Saint-Martin theatres. Curiously enough, the lyric tragedy in its abbreviated form of three acts enjoyed a revival with 16 of them being mounted for the first time between 1781 and 1794. Only two of them were in five acts, the length preferred by Lully, and *Thésée* (1782) alone was in four acts; four of them had their premieres in 1786, and three of them enjoyed their initial performance in 1788. Many of them were derived as usual from ancient history or legend, but *Pizarre* (1785) and *Adèle de Ponthieu* (1781) were based upon incidents in more recent Spanish and French history. The next most popular genre was the "opéra," which could be described as being the lyric tragedy under another name. The artistes produced 14 of them, which boasted protagonists as diverse in origin and personality as Oedipus, Alexander the Great, and Louis IX; most of their other heroes were figures found in ancient mythology. *Electre*

(1782) by Jean-Baptiste Lemoyne, *Chimène* (1783) by Antonio-Maria-Gasparo Sacchini, and *Dardanus* (1784) also by Sacchini were billed simply as tragedies, but it is difficult to understand why these three works were not offered as lyric tragedies. In fact, if the works designated as operas, tragedies, and lyric tragedies are counted as being compositions of a single sort, no fewer than 33 of them fall into this category and constitute more than half of the new works staged. The other offerings by the company included eight lyric comedies, one comedy opera, one heroic comedy opera, an *opéra-féerie*, a *divertissement*, and the two "fragment" programs of 1782 and 1784, which presented one new act apiece. The choreographic creations consisted of four pantomime ballets, two heroic ballets, an action ballet, and a comic ballet. The sudden surge in patriotic spectacles in 1793-94 resulted in the birth of such anomalous types of productions as the patriotic tableau, the lyric act, and the lyric entertainment.

These 60 works were scored by 23 composers whose contributions to repertory ranged in importance from a single act in a program of fragments to a cluster of lyric tragedies. Mozart's second offering to the Opéra, *Le Mariage de Figaro*, was staged for the first time in 1793, and six other musicians also set but a single libretto for the company in 1781-94. Another half-dozen composers, including Etienne Nicolas Méhul and Jean Christophe Vogel, completed two scores apiece for the artists, while an identical number had three titles posted at the Opéra in this same period. Niccolò Piccinni saw his *Didon* (1783) and three other works given at the Opéra before he left for Naples with his family on 13 July 1787. Antonio-Maria-Gasparo Sacchini, André Ernest Modeste Grétry, and Jean-Baptiste Lemoyne were responsible for five, seven, and eight new compositions, respectively, but none of this trio may be said to have dominated this span of 15 years by virtue of the originality of his style or the scope of his concepts.

The Opéra-Comique, II: 1762–1797

The comic opera established itself beyond all doubt as an important genre of theatrical music when the Opéra-Comique and the Comédie-Italienne joined forces on 3 February 1762 to offset the latter troupe's deficit of 400,000 *livres*. The new company used the most popular and gifted actors and actresses from the two troupes, including Mme Favart, Carlin, and Laruette; they opened at the hôtel de Bourgogne with a welcoming discourse and the representation of their two recent hits, *Blaise le savetier* by François-André Danican Philidor and *On ne s'avise jamais de tout* by Pierre-Alexandre Monsigny.

The company enjoyed considerable financial success in 1762, and their fiscal position was improved the following year by the unexpected fire of 1763 at the Opéra, but after 1764 they found themselves handicapped by being obliged to limit their offerings to whatever compositions were already at the disposal of the two troupes before their consolidation. They had to restrict their programs to the works that had been mounted at the Paris fairs or the Théâtre-Italien, although such compositions as *Le Cadi dupé*, *Cendrillon*, and *Le Maréchal ferrant* did make a better and almost novel impression on the larger stage of the theatre in the rue Mauconseil. Carlo Goldoni helped them to some degree by furnishing new scripts, but the real solution to their problem of a limited repertory was solved when certain librettists and composers understood the potential of the license that the company had acquired from the Crown and threw in their lot with them. Anseaume, Charles-Simon Favart, Jean-François Marmontel, Louis Poinsinet de Sivry, and Michel-Jean Sedaine furnished them with fresh librettos which were set by Egidio Romoaldo Duni, Grétry, Monsigny, and Philidor. It was largely on account of the talents of these nine men that the theatre and its programs grew to become an integral part of the theatrical scene in Paris during the next 25 years.

Since a steady stream of finished works poured into the Théâtre-Italien during the next two decades, it would be impossible to list here all the contributions to the repertory made by this first group of authors alone. But it should be obseved that the first few years that the company passed at the hôtel de Bourgogne saw them produce at least a half-dozen hits popular enough to be revived with regularity and confidence: Monsigny's *Le Roi et le fermier* (1762), Philidor's *Le Sorcier* (1764), Monsigny's *Rose et Colas* (1764) and *Aline, reine de Golconde* (1764), Duni's *La Clochette* (1766), and Monsigny's *Le Déserteur* (1769). If one examines the works that just one of these composers created for the hôtel de Bourgogne in the ensuing decade, for example, Grétry's, one finds that he alone had a series of nearly a dozen titles accepted by the company between 1768 and 1778, including such well-known compositions as *Le Huron* (1768), *Lucile* (1769), *Zémire et Azor* (1771), and *La Fausse Magie* (1775).

These new comic operas were essentially regular comedies with spoken dialogue interspersed with songs written especially for the composition of which they were an indigenous part. Resembling modern musical comedies in format, they relied in part for their appeal upon their settings, which could be laid in the exotic Orient, a simple French village, or an imaginary locale. Since their intrigues unfolded so frequently in rural France, the heroine was often an innocent and trusting peasant courted by a young and manly hero who was her social equal and dedicated to protecting his threatened beloved. The general tone of the score was simple, lyric, and romantic to harmonize with the characters and plot. Love and virtue triumphed without fail, and the finale was based upon a vaudeville tune that left everybody happy and smiling. A most interesting development in the subject matter employed in comic opera took place a few years before the Revolution when the *Bibliothèque universelle des romans* began to appear with its abbreviated versions of medieval romances and the librettists for the Opéra-

Comique seeking fresh material became interested in them. They produced an entire series of compositions bearing such titles as *Aucassin et Nicolette* (1780), *Richard Coeur-de-Lion* (1784), and *Raoul Barbe-bleue* (1789).

The Théâtre-Italien and the Opéra-Comique had combined their resources in 1762, and it was now evident that it was the latter company that had emerged as the dominant partner in their marriage. The letters patent issued to the company on 31 March 1780 had recognized this situation by alluding to the corporation as the Opéra-Comique, although Parisians would refer to "the Italians" for several years out of sheer habit. Yet whether the troupe was designated as the Opéra-Comique or as the Italians, it was obvious that the artistes in the hôtel de Bourgogne now had little or nothing to do with Italian plays but were giving their total attention to French lyric compositions described as "comédies à ariettes." They were earning more and more money, and their current facility was becoming increasingly inadequate on account of their growing popularity. It was accordingly decided that the financial condition of the troupe and constantly larger audiences were sufficient reason to build a new theatre. The municipal authorities agreed because the danger of another fire in the populous section of Paris had become a possibility to be avoided at all costs since the conflagration at the Palais-Royal in 1781. Arrangements were made to construct a new opera house on the site of the gardens of the hôtel de Choiseul. The architect Heurtier was placed in charge of construction, and his position as chief building inspector with the government enabled him to expedite matters to the degree that the artistes moved out of the hôtel de Bourgogne on 4 April 1783 and into their new home in the boulevard des Italiens on 28 April 1783.

The corporation had contracted debts amounting to 600,000 *livres* in the course of their new venture, and the severe freeze of the 1788-89 winter compounded their problems because an economic depression as well as the biting cold immobilized the inhabitants of the capital. Prices soared, and charitable agencies had to provide food and fuel for the unfortunate. The theatre did not even open its doors on some dates because no spectators appeared at the box office, and receipts fell to less than 200 *francs* on other days. The troupe also encountered new competition from the theatre opened by the queen's hairdresser, Léonard Autié, and the violinist Giovanni Viotti. The king's brother, as well as Marie-Antoinette, promised their protection to this group, which came to be known as the théâtre Feydeau because it moved into its new quarters in the rue Feydeau after leaving the Tuileries. Most importantly, their programs consisted of Italian opera, French comic opera, comedy, and vaudeville, and these offerings tended to attract the same sort of audiences that frequented the Opéra-Comique theatre. This latter organization, which also came to be known as the *théâtre Favart* and the *théâtre de l'Opéra-Comique national*, had to compete openly and bitterly with the *théâtre de Monsieur* in the rue Feydeau until September 1801. On this date, the two companies acknowledged the futility of their struggle and joined forces to form a single corporation with the approval of the government. The new unit retained the title of Opéra-Comique and planned to present a regular schedule of programs in the Feydeau theatre while retaining the Favart theatre for less regular representations. The former facility was redecorated and opened its doors on 16 September 1801.

An incredibly large number of lighter compositions in the lyric manner were produced in the French capital between the time of Louis XVI's accession to the throne in 1774 and the end of the Revolutionary era in 1801, but it is possible to discern that the comic operas staged in Paris during this interval of 27 years fall into two chronological periods of 1774-89 and 1789-1801 by reason of the identity and styles of the composers involved as well as on account of the impact of political events. The comic operas billed in prominent Parisian theatres during the earlier 15 years reflected the continuing popularity of both French and Italian music. Violinists and voice teachers from Italy were on the scene, and they were quick to supply Parisian theatres with compositions inspired by Pasquale Anfossi, Niccolò Piccinni, Giuseppe Sarti, and Tommaso Traetta. These pre-Revolution musicians writing Italianate scores for French comic operas were facile, skilled, and alert to provide the music for whatever libretto might come their way, and their French rivals were hard pressed to compete with them. François Bianchi set two French librettos, *La Réduction de Paris* (1775) and *Le Mort marié* (1777), while Antoine-Barthélemy Bruni earned a reputation among French theatregoers with *Coradin* (1786), and Jean-Joseph Cambini did the score for *La Rose d'amour* (1779). Alexandre-Marie-Antoine Frixer DIT Fridzeri tasted success with *Les Souliers mordorés* (1776); Alessio Prati contributed *L'Ecole de la jeunesse* (1779), for which Egidio Romoaldo Duni had already created a score without success. The French composers having no difficulty competing with the immigrant Italian musicians included Nicolas Dezède with *Julie* (1772), *Les Fermiers* (1777), *Blaise et Babet* (1784), *Alexis et Justine* (1785), and a dozen other works produced at this time. Stanislas Champein's *La Mélomanie* (1781) proved to be the author's most popular composition although his *Les Dettes* was well applauded in 1787 for its scenic effects and pleasing music. Henri-Joseph Rigel had hits in *Le Savetier et le financier* (1778) and *Blanche et Vermeille* (1781), but he could scarcely equal Nicolas Dalayrac, whose inexhaustible inspiration and lively imagination did not fail the composer even after he had set *L'Amant statue* (1781), *L'Eclipse totale* (1782), *Le Corsaire* (1783), *Les Deux Tuteurs* (1784), and *La Dot*. The most striking feature of these works collectively is their tendency to fall into the two categories of comic opera that this genre will embrace in the more mature stages of its growth: the suspense-and-rescue type of work and the romantic tale of persecuted love triumphant in the end.

The repertory of the Favart and Feydeau theatres was affected profoundly by the Revolution in the last decade of the eighteenth century because the number of completely propagandistic works billed at these two theatres was exaggerated by a governmental decree ordering that republican and patriotic compositions be included on the programs. As might be suspected, these works, like *La Prise de Toulon par les Français, Le Réveil du peuple*, and *L'Intérieur d'un ménage républicain* of 1794, were of no lasting value and are of interest today only as curious symptoms of the revolutionary fever epidemic in France at the time. The significant contributions to the Opéra-Comique and its rival company were made by composers of the calibre of Etienne Nicolas Méhul, whose initial composition for the musical stage was his famous *Euphrosine et Coradin* (1790). After creating this work, which sufficed to make him known throughout Europe, Méhul went on to set *Stratonice* (1792), *Mélidore et Phrosine* (1794), and *Adrien* (1799), and his career had not yet come to an end. As indicated previously, Nicolas Dalayrac began the second phase of his writing with *Les Deux Petits Savoyards* (1789), a composition that would have a history of 40 years in the theatre, and he did another five titles for the Opéra-Comique before the turn of the century: *Camille* (1791), *Tout pour l'amour ou Roméo et Juliette* (1792), *Léon* (1798), *Adolphe et Clara* (1799), and *Maison à vendre* (1800).

It was on the eve of the Terror that Luigi Cherubini arrived in France to produce his first Paris work, *Lodoïska* (1791), which was followed by *Eliza* (1794), *Médée* (1797), and *L'Hôtellerie portugaise* (1798). Jean-François Lesueur started his career in 1793 with his most applauded work, *La Caverne* inspired by Alain-René Lesage; he did two other works for the Feydeau theatre before the Empire, *Paul et Virginie* (1794) and *Télémaque* (1796). And a word must be said about Henri-Montan Berton, who was prolific to the point of composing nearly 50 operatic works that all bear more or less the stamp of his well-known *Montano et Stéphanie* and *Le Délire* of 1799. Other composers to add to the steadily increasing corpus of comic operas despite the outbreak of a war and a revolution included Blavius, Charles-Simon Catel, François Devienne, Pierre Gaveaux, François-Charlemagne Lefebvre, Jean-Pierre Solié, and the younger Jean-Claude Trial.

As can be seen by the titles of certain works accepted by the artistes, the comic operas of the end of the century exhibited a tendency on occasion to become more comic or more serious than earlier composers and librettists might have allowed. The comic operas of this period never laid claim to being lyric tragedies in the grand style, but they did show themselves capable of displaying a more sober attitude toward subjects as traditionally tragic as those treated in Cherubini's *Médée* and Dalayrac's *Tout pour l'amour ou Roméo et Juliette*. Lesueur's *Télémaque* had in fact been written in operatic form for the stage of the Opéra before its rejection dictated that it be revised for performance at the Opéra-Comique. The more comic of the comic operas were designed to appeal openly and unabashedly to the populace and were based upon the usual highly complicated plot of the farce involving ordinary people in improbable situations as in Devienne's *Les Visitandines* (1792) and Jean-Pierre Soli's *Le Secret* (1796): the former was based upon a valet mistaking a convent for an inn; the latter follows the fortunes of a man believing falsely that he has killed his rival in a duel. These new directions taken by the growing comic opera before Napoleon's emergence upon the national scene promote interesting speculation about the possible future of this musico-literary genre, especially since only one company was to be involved in its future after 1800.

The Montansier Theatre, 1794–1820

La Montansier née Marguerite Brunet began her career as a theatrical impresario by directing the theatre at Nantes and by obtaining royal permission in 1768 to manage the small theatre in the rue Satory in Versailles. She went on to manage the Court theatres after 1774 and became responsible for the fortunes of the Théâtre Beaujolais at the Palais-Royal in October 1789. After the outbreak of the Revolution, she publicized her sympathy for the new government by outfitting, at her own expense, a contingent of soldiers to help repulse the invading Prussians, and her political position seemed secure despite her earlier dealings with the royal family, when she was called before the committee of public safety and charged with plotting to strike and to circulate a medal commemorating the "martyrdom" of Louis XVI on 21 January 1793. Her record as a patriot supported her refutation of this accusation, and she was soon free to found another theatre, the Théâtre National located in the rue de Richelieu, now renamed the rue de la Loi. La Montansier was a skilled promoter by the summer of 1793, and the success of her venture seemed certain, but her enemies were still active, and she was denounced again and accused of financing the construction of her new and sumptuous theatre with money given her by Marie-Antoinette, now called "the Austrian she-wolf" by her alienated subjects; her enemies said that she had mixed the mortar for it "with the blood of the people." She was condemned and taken to la Petite Force; the doors of her theatre were padlocked. The Opéra then left the Porte-Saint-Martin facility to occupy the confiscated salle Montansier now designated as the Théâtre des Arts. The artistes would remain here from 26 July 1794 until 13 February 1820, and their theatre would be known in this period of 27 years as the Théâtre des Arts (1794), the Théâtre de la République et des Arts (1797), the Théâtre des Arts (1803) once more, the Académie Impériale de Musique (1804), the Académie Royale de Musique (1814), the Académie Impériale de Musique again during the Hundred Days of Napoleon, and the Académie Royale de Musique (1815) for the fourth time since 1672.

The Opéra continued to have its affairs managed by the city of Paris after the disgrace of Louis-Joseph Francoeur and Jacques Cellerier in 1793, and the first committee supervising its activities in the rue de la Loi was composed of François Lay DIT Lays and Laïs, Lasuze, Jean-Baptiste Rey, and Jean-Baptiste Rochefort. The Directoire replaced these municipal appointments with Antoine-Joseph Bonnet de Treyches and Anne-Pierre-Jacques Devismes du Valgay on 12 September 1799, but the former administrator had to be removed from office within a year, and his coworker, Antoine-Joseph Bonnet de Treyches, assumed the directorship without assistance on 23 December 1800. Jacques Cellerier then returned to become director in 1801, although he had fled from Paris on 17 September 1793 to escape charges of malfeasance in office. Napoleon introduced a completely changed table of organization on 26 November 1802: he ordered the Opéra placed under his prefects with Etienne Morel de Chefdeville and Bonnet de Treyches as its principal officers. A general superintendency of theatres was created in 1807 to oversee the major theatres of Paris, and this historic decree placed the corporation and its assets under the control of the Imperial Chamberlain with the dramatist Louis-François Picard appointed its director. After the second exile of Napoleon and the dissolution of his empire, Papillon de La Ferté replaced Picard with Alexandre-Etienne Choron and Louis Luc Loiseau de Persuis as his principal aides. Choron had to retire before long after causing too many quarrels among personnel, but Persuis was retained and named musical director of the Académie Royale de Musique in 1816. The violinist Giovanni Viotti was appointed director of the company on 30 October 1819.

These official events involving management were interspersed with the sporadic issuance of decrees pertaining to programs and other matters involving the artistes and the stage. The edict of 2 August 1794 demanding the weekly production of patriotic compositions in the theatres and the financial subsidies awarded to encourage this policy as well as the persistent public enthusiasm for the principles of the Revolution in certain quarters were decisive forces affecting the repertory of the Opéra during the first years of the artistes' sojourn in the rue de la Loi. *Denis le tyran* (1794) depicted a statue of Liberty arising from the ruins of a schoolhouse directed by a cruel schoolteacher; *La Rosière républicaine* (1794) offered the edifying spectacle of the altar of Reason displacing the village church. The year 1794 ended in the apotheosis of Jean-Jacques Rousseau with a hymn sung in his honor on 11 October: "L'Education de l'ancien et du nouveau régime." The walls of la Montansier's theatre rang constantly with the strains of "La Marseillaise" and other anthems; a dozen of these Jacobin spectacles were mounted at the Opéra between 1794 and 1798. These were extravagant days at the Théâtre des Arts, and the degree of this extravagance can be appreciated only when it is remembered that these celebrations in honor of Reason, Liberty, Nature, and the Convention were accompanied as often as not by salvos of artillery on the stage.

But these almost hysterical protests against tyranny and superstition lost their novelty, appeal, and pertinency after a while, and as early as 1795 there were isolated instances of spectators throwing the texts of anti-republican poems on the stage for the actors to declaim. Other spectators dared to destroy the plaster busts of revolutionary heroes placed in the theatres for the edification of audiences. At the turn of the century, Paris witnessed a revival of interest in classical subjects on the stage, moreover, and the production of *Anacréon chez Polycrate* in 1797 was the occasion of an uninhibited announcement by management that the public could now return to the Opéra without fear of being bombarded by propagandistic tirades. Greek mythology provided the inspiration for at least 16 ballets, operas, and lyric tragedies performed for the first time between 1797 and 1807; for example, *Héro et Léandre* of 1799, *Hécube* of 1800, and *Astyanax* of 1801. A concomitant interest in Roman heroes and history was evident in such compositions as *Adrien* of 1799 and *Le Triomphe de Trajan* of 1807. As had been the case during the years of the monarchy, librettos based upon more exotic civilizations were offered by the artistes to provide variety: Assyria was represented with *Sémiramis* of 1802; Islam was exploited in *Mahomet II* and *Le Pavillon du Calife* of 1804. Works hinged to some aspect of Celtic or French culture were likewise favored in this early decade of the romantic era when the French became especially interested in their national past, and *Ossian* of 1804 as well as *Paul et Virginie* of 1806 matched the literary trend of the day by catering to their desire to see the patrimony of France glorified. It must be acknowledged, however, that the opera of this time did not yet develop the romantic manner to the same degree that it evolved in the poetry, plays, and novels of Hugo, Dumas, and Lamartine.

But it will be recalled that Paris was now on the eve of becoming the operatic capital of the world. Soon composers would not feel that they had reached the summit of their career if they did not have a hit or at least an address in the French capital. It is accordingly curious that the 14 years between the arrival of the troupe at the Montansier theatre in 1794 and the world premiere of *La Vestale* by Gaspare Spontini in 1807 is supposed to have been a time when the singers in the troupe were relatively weak and almost totally eclipsed by an especially gifted group of dancers. A glance at the operatic forms employed during this interval reveals that 23 or nearly 65 percent of the new compositions billed at the turn of the century were operas (16) or lyric tragedies (7). The former compositions were in five (2), four (1), three (7), two (1), or single (5) acts, and the lyric tragedies were mostly in three acts (4). The dancers did execute 13 ballets, however, and they also staged a "pantomime folly" entitled *La Dansomanie*, which proved incredibly popular and brought back to the stage of the Opéra the elegance and refined restraint of former times, a life-style that certain segments of the Paris population regretted in discreet silence. Their new choreographic compositions were divided among the pantomime ballet (8), the opera-ballet (2), the heroic ballet (1), and the regular unmodified ballet (1). Thus, they did not really overshadow the vocalists completely at this time, and they had to share a schedule that also included three oratorios, three *divertissements*, a lyric comedy, and an isolated *intermède* designed for adaptation to longer programs. The real problem was that the Opéra was in a period of mediocrity.

The nearly 20 composers responsible for the music in this array of too often uninspired works included seven musicians who had only a single score performed at the Opéra between 1794 and 1807: Charles-Simon Catel, Nicolas Dalayrac, Mme Devismes, André Eler, Jean-Gaspard de Fontenelle, Daniel Steibelt, and Louis-Emmanuel Jadin. Their contribution to the repertory amounted to four operas in one to three acts, two lyric tragedies, and a *divertissement*, but none of these pieces proved very popular for a variety of reasons. Peter Winter, choir master for the Elector of Bavaria, provided the company with *Tamerlan* in 1802 and a new *Castor et Pollux* in 1806; Luigi Cherubini had been in Paris permanently since 1788, and he and Winter were the only composers to have a pair of titles billed at the Opéra in this period, Cherubini having had *Anacréon* and *Achille à Scyros* represented in 1803-4. Louis Luc Loiseau de Persuis gave the artistes *Léonidas* in 1799 and *Le Retour d'Ulysse* in 1807; his two other additions to repertory were his collaborations with Jean-François Lesueur entitled *L'Inauguration du Temple de la Victoire* and *Le Triomphe de Trajan* of 1807. Jean-François Lesueur was likewise responsible for Napoleon's favorite opera, *Ossian* of 1804, Chrétien Kalkbrenner scored two of the three oratorios, the third being *La Création du monde* by Haydn, while Rodolphe Kreutzer had his *Paul et Virginie* mounted in 1806 after having shared in the collaboration *Flaminius à Corinth* and having created *Astyanax* alone in 1801. Etienne Nicolas Méhul was quite prominent on account of the brilliant success of his *La Dansomanie* in 1800, but he also had *Adrien* and *Daphnis et Pandrose* performed in 1799 and 1803 respectively. F.-C. Lefebvre and Grétry were almost constantly before the public with four and five compositions. It will also be recalled that the work of Mozart returned to Paris with *Don Juan* in 1805, a few years after his *Il Flauto magico* was exploited for the score of *Les Mystères d'Isis* in 1801. The truth of the matter is that the Opéra had decided to return to as undisturbed an existence as possible after the violent days of the Revolution, and nothing seemed more peaceful and comfortable than to revert to the neoclassic manner of an earlier time with an occasional adaptation of the latest hit at the Comédie-Française like Charles-Simon Catel's *Sémiramis* (1802) or a polite invitation to a newcomer like Blangini to participate in the continuing series of revivals and premieres. The remainder of the time could be devoted to the representation of average compositions disturbing nobody. The result of this apathetic attitude was that an artistically lacking work like *Le Triomphe de Trajan* could enjoy more than a hundred performances.

The second and more interesting phase of the history of the Montansier theatre extended from 1807 until 1820, and it began with the premiere of *La Vestale* by Gaspare Luigi Pacifico Spontini at the Imperial Academy of Music on 16 December 1807. It became evident immediately that the composer of *La Petite Maison* (1804), *Milton* (1804), and *Julie ou le pot de fleurs* (1805) at the Opéra-Comique had set up a milestone in the history of the Opéra with this memorable masterpiece. His librettist's skilled use of the traditional rescue motif and his original exploitation of supernatural events, along with a moving presentation of a great love overcoming apparently insuperable obstacles, were supported by Gaspare Spontini's inspired and constantly pertinent music, and this combination of an effective libretto and a dramatic score overwhelmed spectators to the point where they forgot the French invasion of Portugal to discuss the virtues of *La Vestale*. Spontini enforced his position as the leading composer of operatic music by adding four other titles to the repertory before his departure for Berlin in 1820: *Fernand Cortez* (1809), *Pélage* (1814), *Les Dieux rivaux* (1816), and *Olympie* (1819).

The success of *La Vestale* in 1807 renewed interest in ancient subjects once again, and Spontini's work was followed in 1808 alone by four works set in the classical tradition: *Les Amours d'Antoine et Cléopâtre*, *Aristippe*, *Vénus et Adonis*, and *Alexandre chez Apelles*. The artistes accepted 43 new compositions between 1807 and 1820, and no fewer than 21, or nearly half of them, were based upon some episode or situation reported originally in the mythology, legend, literature, or history of ancient Greece or Rome. The Bible was likewise a source of inspiration during this phase of the romantic period after the signing of the Concordat, and it provided material for at least three compositions staged at the Montansier theatre: *La Mort d'Adam* (1809), *Abel* (1810), *L'Enfant prodigue* (1812). French manners and politics afforded the basis for another cluster of short ballets and operas such as *L'Epreuve villageoise* (1815), but the librettists of the time were more inclined to use a single aspect of a foreign culture or an episode from the history of a more exotic civilization as they had done before the premiere of *La Vestale*. They drew upon the lore or legends of China, India, Russia, Babylonia, or Egypt as if to celebrate the adventuresome spirit of the age, but they then turned their attention elsewhere, as if they had exhausted the possibilities offered by the region and culture that had captured their fancy in the first place. François-Charlemagne Lefebvre did an 1816 ballet in one act entitled *Les Sauvages de la mer du Sud*, for example, but none of his other works exhibits his interest in this remote region. Italian and Spanish subjects proved exceptions, and these two

Romance-language countries furnished the setting or characters for at least four pieces.

The other composers providing scores for the company in 1807-20 were often as prolific if not as triumphant as Spontini, and most of them had already had their work performed at the Imperial Academy of Music before the premiere of *La Vestale*. The jury of the Opéra accepted seven new titles by Rodolphe Kreutzer of which *Aristippe* (1808) and *La Servante justifiée* (1818) were the most popular with audiences. Louis Luc Loiseau de Persuis had four original compositions and three collaborations mounted by the company; his ballet *Nina* (1813) was produced nearly 200 times, and his *L'Epreuve villageoise* was danced on almost 100 dates before it was withdrawn. Henri-Montan Berton enjoyed an appreciable measure of success with his ballets, *L'Enlèvement des Sabines* (1811) and *L'Enfant prodigue* (1812), but his opera, *Roger de Sicile*, had to be dropped after only a half-dozen representations in 1817. Charles-Simon Catel's personal success was his opera, *Les Bayadères* (1810), and his *Alexandre chez Apelles* continued for a run of 35 showings after its 1808 premiere, but his *Zirphile et Fleur de Myrte* failed to arouse any enthusiasm in 1818. François-Charlemagne Lefebvre did three scores for the troupe, but only his *Vénus et Adonis* (1808) enjoyed an extended run. Etienne-Henri Méhul was still submitting most of his scores to the Opéra-Comique as he had done in the revolutionary period, but he found time to set *Persée et Andromède* for performance at the Academy in 1810 and to work on the short opera, *L'Oriflamme*, mounted in 1814. Alexandre Piccinni had two dismal failures at the Opéra despite his uncle's success with the company earlier, but Jean-Madeleine Schneitzhoeffer was much more fortunate in 1818 with his ballets, *Proserpine* and *Le Séducteur au village*. Louis-Sébastien Le Brun enjoyed the distinction of having the second most frequently performed work of the period, *Le Rossignol*, included on more than 200 programs. Certain well-known composers like Luigi Cherubini, Louis Emmanuel Jadin, Chrétien Kalkbrenner, and Jean François Lesueur returned to the Opéra with a single score. In all 20 different musicians were responsible for the approximately 50 new titles posted at the Montansier theatre between 1807 and 1820, and 11 of these composers set but a single libretto.

The dramatic works created and mounted at the Opéra included five lyric tragedies and 19 operas in one to five acts with nine of these operas in three acts. The choreographic works amounted to 15 ballets in one, two, or three acts plus a heroic ballet in two acts and an opera ballet in a single act. The trend was away from the lyric tragedy and the variety of ballets developed in the pre-1789 period, and it was the opera in three acts that was coming into favor with ballet retaining its popularity in either a shorter or longer form. The *divertissement* was represented by a single composition, and the public spectacle filled with politico-philosophical symbolism had disappeared completely in favor of restrained salutes to the glory of Napoleon or his Bourbon successor.

The Salle Le Peletier, 1821–1873

When the duke de Berry was leaving the Montansier opera house on the evening of 13 February 1820, he was attacked and wounded mortally by a political assassin named Louvel. Onlookers carried the dying prince into the foyer of the theatre before summoning the archbishop of Paris to administer the last rites of the church to the victim of this savage assault. A persistent legend adds that the prelate arrived on the scene but refused to enter the theatre, which he held to be a profane and immoral place. Acknowledging finally that he could not in good conscience ignore the spiritual needs of his royal ward, he is said to have agreed to administer the sacraments to the duke but only on condition that the theatre be demolished. An accord was reached, and the expiring Bourbon received his viaticum, while the elegant salle Montansier with its 1,300 seats was closed to await its own end. Ironically, it was dismantled with great care, and most of the material in it was salvaged to serve in the construction of the salle Le Peletier. In the interim the artistes moved into temporary quarters in the salle Favart, where they posted their first bill on 19 April 1820; this initial program consisted of Sacchini's *Oedipe à Colone* and the popular ballet by Louis-Jacques Milon and Persuis entitled *Nina*. The company had to share their new stage with the troupe of the Opéra-Comique, but they were able to perform for the public on Monday, Wednesday, Friday, and Sunday, and they did manage to produce six new compositions in the 13 months that they spent in the salle Favart between 19 April 1820 and 11 May 1821.

The performers' next home was the Louvois theatre, built in 1791, but they had scarcely enough time to catch their breath in this facility because their sojourn here lasted only from 25 May until 15 June in 1821: they opened at the Louvois with a concert on 25 May and then mounted programs on only two dates, 1 and 15 June. Curiously enough, Jean-Jacques Rousseau's *Le Devin du village* was on both June bills, and Adalbert Gyrowetz's *La Fête hongroise* had its premiere on the later date. The company was idle for two months between 16 June and 15 August, but on 16 August 1821 they moved into still another theatre in the rue Le Peletier. These quarters were also supposed to be temporary, although they were new and built expressly for the Opéra, but the Royal Academy of Music would remain in them for more than a half century. This opera house had been built of wood and plaster by Debret at a cost of 1.8 million *francs*. The 1821-73 span of the company's residence in the rue Le Peletier is impressive perhaps, but it suggests only fleetingly the number of illustrious artistes, the quantity of famous works, and the array of celebrated composers that contributed to the history and glory of French opera while the corporation was lodged in this provisory theatre that burned down eventually on the night of 28-29 October 1873.

The first two decades that the Opéra was housed in its new facility saw many changes occur in the style of theatrical music in France because the aristocracy and then the middle class exerted pressure on the programs by reason of their social prestige and newly acquired wealth. At first, no truly significant masterpieces were mounted by the Royal Academy of Music in the years between the premiere of Gaspare Spontini's *Olympie* in 1819 and the first performance of Daniel Auber's *La Muette de Portici* in 1828, although it was no less evident that Paris was emerging as the operatic capital of Europe as a result of the activity of Cherubini, Lesueur, Méhul, and Spontini. Yet it was Daniel Auber's *La Muette de Portici* with its mute heroine that gave the first intimation of the new musico-dramatic genre that was about to capture the fancy of the public — grand opera. This type of theatrical composition evolved from the lyric tragedy with its arias, recitatives, and tragic dilemmas, and it was accordingly in the tradition founded and embellished by Lully, Rameau, Gluck, and Spontini. It was represented in 1829-36 by such perennial favorites as Gioacchino Rossini's *Guillaume Tell* (1829), Giacomo Meyerbeer's *Robert le Diable* (1831), Jacques-François Halévy's *La Juive* (1835), and Meyerbeer's *Les Huguenots* (1836). The broad and bold canvasses of passion and sacrifice were in the new romantic style and lacked the aristocratic restraint of the classical manner. The emphasis was placed upon colorful choruses, large ensembles, and grotesque, gothic, or otherwise sensational settings. The stage was populated by lovelorn or rebellious heroes, desperate couples fleeing society and persecution, spectacular crowds proclaiming their convictions and describing their feelings in the midst of crises. The action was longer than necessary, and the ballets were not always completely pertinent. Producing opera on the grand scale involved taking time to do almost everything licit that might create a wondrous effect, even if the effects did not always proceed from perceptible and relevant causes, an incongruity described later by Wagner as "effects without causes."

The liberties taken with previously accepted conventions of composition, the emphasis placed upon emotional content, the growing preference for unusual and exotic settings and the individualistic attitudes of the protagonists were characteristic of the contemporary literature being written by Chateaubriand, Lamartine, and Victor Hugo, and almost the entire repertory of the Opéra between 1829 and 1836 was influenced by the romantic tastes and disposition of the first decades of the nineteenth century. The material that furnished the inspiration for the librettos of the time was especially similar or even identical to the sources providing contemporary authors with their characters, settings, and plots. The historical novel was a favorite literary type in 1820-40, and the national history of France also suggested the protagonists of *Vendôme en Espagne* (1823), *Pharamond* (1825) and *François Ier à Chambord* (1830). Fairy tales and romantic novels were unabashedly the basis for *Cendrillon* (1823), *La*

Belle au bois dormant (1825), and *Manon Lescaut* (1830), and Victor Hugo himself did the libretto for *La Esméralda* (1836). This same poet's preoccupation with exotic figures of the East was repeated in such works as *Aladin* (1822), *Aline* (1823), and *Ali Baba* (1833). English history and literature offered the material for Aumer's *Alfred le Grand* (1822) and Rouget de L'Isle's *Macbeth* (1827), just as Chatterton's biography had suggested itself to Alfred de Vigny as a fit subject for a play. *Moïse* (1827) and *La Tentation* (1832) employed biblical or religious subjects dear to the heart of every romantic writer. Still, contrary to general opinion, the Opéra did not abandon the classical tradition completely at the height of the romantic tide when the company staged *Aspasie et Periclès* (1820), *Stratonice* (1821), *Sapho* (1822), *Virginie* (1823), and even a *Mars et Vénus* (1826) despite the popular trend away from the history and legends of the ancient world.

The entire period of 17 years between 1820 and 1836 saw 54 new titles added to repertory, and the sudden popularity of grand opera is reflected in the fact that only three works in one or three acts were billed as traditional lyric tragedies, whereas six operas in five acts and 17 other compositions in one to four acts were offered simply as operas. One lyric drama, a single tragedy entitled *Macbeth*, a heroic opera, and three "opéra-féeries" comprised the other nonchoreographic compositions. Seven "ballets-féeries" complemented the "opéra-féeries" and proved more popular than the straight ballet represented by three titles, but no fewer than nine pantomime ballets were accepted and staged by the company after the premiere of *Clari* (1820) and before the first representation of *Les Huguenots* (1836). The other two new works were a lyric drama and a *divertissement* in one act.

If the four collaborations of this period and the arrangement by François Antoine Habeneck known as *Le Page inconstant* (1823) are set aside, the 49 other scores played at the Opéra were by 24 composers, and half of these musicians were responsible for only a single work each. A dozen of the other 37 pieces were set by six musicians. Jacques-François Halévy and Adalbert Gyrowetz did the music for three librettos each, but Gioacchino Rossini saw four of his creations produced at the Le Peletier theatre, although two of them were adaptations from the original Italian versions. Only Daniel Auber, L. J. Ferdinand Hérold, and Jean-Madeleine Schneitz-hoeffer managed to have five works each produced here before 1836. The librettists for these titles included a dozen writers who completed only a single work for the troupe in this interval with Adolphe-Charles Nourrit and Etienne Jouy managing to guide five compositions through the vicissitudes of production. The truly striking fact about the men of letters who did dramas or scenarios for repertory between 1820 and 1836 was Eugène Scribe's dominance at the Opéra with three works done in collaboration besides the nine titles he did alone and without having recourse to the texts of the legitimate stage. There were also nine other collaborations by nearly a score of authors whose efforts for the troupe were limited to one text.

The ballets for these works were done by eight choreographers of whom only three created the dances for a single work. Louis-Jacques Milon, Jean Coralli, and Pierre-Gabriel Gardel were charged with the creation of ballets for two, four, and five compositions, but it was Jean Louis Aumer and Filippo Taglioni who made the greatest impact in this area by furnishing the choreography for 19 works with Aumer's 11 contributions heading the list.

The last decade of the Restoration (1820-30) and the early years of Louis-Philippe's reign (1830-36) were not an especially exciting time at the Opéra as far as administrative reforms and managerial innovations were concerned, although gas lighting was introduced for the staging of *Aladin ou la lampe merveilleuse* in 1822. The violinist Habeneck replaced the violinist Viotti as director on 1 November 1821, and, on 26 November 1824, Duplantys took over the directorship. Whatever talents these men had as administrators were buried under the mediocrity of the Superintendent of Theaters, Emile Thimothée Lubbert, who was of noble lineage but without any real knowledge of the theatre. Castil-Blaze noted of this last aristocrat to hold the top position in the theatrical organization of France that he had "all the incapacity of a nobleman." He was the last appointee to assume the directorship under royal aegis, however, and the managerial situation changed drastically after the outbreak of 1830 because the Opéra was now placed under the control of the Minister of the Interior and then reorganized as a private undertaking with the public theatres no longer obliged to subsidize it. The colorful Dr. Louis-Désiré Véron, known for his excessively large cravats and gleaming carriage, was placed in charge of the enterprise still called the Royal Academy of Music; he was given more than 800,000 *francs* to help him launch his newly acquired venture that was to be managed by him as if it were his own business. A born promoter, he gave dinners on a scale recalling Louis XIV's sumptuous repasts at Versailles, and he was generous to a fault with his performers, journalists, and other individuals able to help his cause. He maintained an orchestra of 80 musicians besides 60 odd choristers and 70 dancers of both sexes with whom he was to produce annually a new grand opera, a new grand ballet, and four lesser works in these same two genres. His great success was *Robert le Diable* (1831), but other works also showed a handsome profit, especially those in which Mlle Taglioni had a hand. After a picturesque and profitable career at the Opéra, Dr. Véron relinquished his post to Charles-Edmond Duponchel on 15 August 1835.

A third period in the history of the troupe at the Le Peletier opera house might be said to extend from the premiere of *Les Huguenots* in this theatre on 29 February 1836 until the bourgeois king Louis-Philippe was deposed in the revolution of July 1848. This span of a dozen years saw 23 composers creating 47 new compositions for the Opéra, if Félicien David's oratorio of 1846 and three cantatas offered as "lyric scenes" are not tallied. No fewer than 14 of these nearly two dozen musicians had only a single work performed on the stage of the Le Peletier theatre in 1836-48, but not all of them have been forgotten, and some of them were in fact the most celebrated composers of the time. Meyerbeer had *Les Huguenots* produced in this interval, of course, and this opera was his only new contribution to repertory during the last 12 years of Louis-Philippe's rule, although his *Le Siège de Corinthe* (1826) and *Moïse* (1827) were still bringing him cash and glory with their 100 representations by 1839. He was also enjoying, at the same time, the unquestioned distinction of having his work dominate the stage at the Opéra: Luigi Cherubini was now too old to dispute his laurels; Daniel Auber was busy writing for the Opéra-Comique despite the 1839 performance of his *Le Lac des fées* by the artistes; Gaspare Spontini was occupied in Germany and Italy; Gioacchino Rossini had withdrawn from the Paris scene after *Guillaume Tell* (1831) except for the 1844 production of his *Othello* in translation. Giuseppe Verdi's *Jérusalem* (1848) was similarly this composer's single contribution to the troupe in this period, but, like Meyerbeer and Rossini, he was already known to Paris audiences: his *Nabucodonosar* and *Ernani* had already been mounted in the capital by the Italians in 1845 and 1846 respectively. The other composer of the first magnitude to have a lone work posted at the Le Peletier theatre was Carl Maria von Weber, whose *Le Freischütz* had its premiere in the Berlioz version of 1841 after its previous premiere under the title of *Robin des bois* on 7 December 1824. Hector Berlioz himself, as well as Ernest-Edouard-Marie Deldevez and Louis Niedermeyer, had a pair of works apiece produced in this same pre-1848 decade, and Ambroise Thomas managed to offer three scores to the public of which only *Le Guérilléro* (1842) enjoyed more than 40 representations. François-Adrien Boïeldieu's pupil, Adolphe-Charles Adam, produced eight compositions for the artistes with his facile pen, and two of them went on to attain more than 100 billings: *Giselle* (1841) in which the title-rôle was created by the incomparable Carlotta Grisi; *Le Diable à quatre* (1845) that had already been put into comic opera form by the inexhaustible Eugène Scribe. Yet Adolphe-Charles Adam had to share the spotlight with Casimir Gide, Jacques-François Halévy, and Gaetano Donizetti, each of whom had four new compositions produced by the artistes. Only *Le Diable boiteux* (1836) brought any real success to Gide, and *La Reine de Chypre* (1841) was Halévy's only outstanding work, but Donizetti was more than fortunate with the almost continuous public support given to his *La Favorite* (1840) and *Lucie de Lammermoor* (1846). The most curious feature of the 1836-48 repertory concerned Berlioz's *Benvenuto Cellini* (1838), which had to be rehearsed 29 times before management felt that it was safe and proper to present it to paying spectators. The net result of all this care and concern was that this opera in two acts was performed four times in its entirety.

Victor Hugo's *Les Burgraves* failed on the legitimate stage in 1843, but the majority of the upper-middle-class spectators going to the Opéra continued to favor extravagant spectacles and overpowering music, and librettists lured them to the box office with such promising titles as *La Vendetta* (1839), *Le Vaisseau fantôme* (1842), and *Robert Bruce* (1846) just as their predecessors had promised violence, mystery, and romance with *La Tempête* (1824), *La Révolte au sérail* (1830), or *L'Ile des pirates* (1835). The romantic manner continued full blast at the Le Peletier theatre in 1836-48, therefore, and the quiet melodies and disciplined emotions of earlier times remained forgotten, while composers welcomed librettos inviting the use of horns, trumpets, cymbals, and the novel instruments of wood and metal being made available by Sax. Rossini was well aware of his spectators' tastes and preferences when he placed a military band upon the stage or when he scored for three trombones or four horns. One might almost say that what Berlioz called "the big noises" of romantic music and the concomitant melodramatic librettos featuring exotic settings, picturesque characters, emotional outpourings, and tender or violent confrontations continued throughout the first half of the century, and such a slight but popular opera as Aurélie Marliani's *La Xacarilla* (1839) featured smugglers, a dashing sailor, a girl and her guardian in a Spanish setting and situation recalling Hugo's *Hernani*. Exotic locales included the New World, the Near East, and Tahiti, which furnished the backdrop for *Les Mohicans* (1837) and *Richard en Palestine* (1844) by Adolphe Adam and *Ozai* (1847) by Gide. The Renaissance and its individualistic men of action became a favorite source for authors in search of plots and characters: Meyerbeer's *Les Huguenots* (1836), Berlioz's *Benvenuto Cellini* (1838), and Niedermeyer's *Marie Stuart* (1844). *Le Diable boiteux* by Adolphe Nourrit and *La Esmeralda* by Louise Bertin, both staged in 1836, were suggested by French literary works of a picaresque and romantic sort; the inexhaustible Middle Ages suggested Jacques-François Halévy's *Charles VI* (1843) and a whole array of works indicating their medieval provenance by their titles alone. The geographical and historical settings cherished by the romantics do not tell the whole story, moreover, because librettists also continued to evoke scenes of nature depicting such panoramas as Mathilde's "sombre forêt" in the second act of *Guillaume Tell*. Even more typical was the gothic claptrap of the Inquisition that adorned the stage in Donizetti's *Dom Sebastien, roi du Portugal* (1843). The incidents of stark terror scattered throughout Halévy's *Guido et Ginevra* (1838) were worthy of the pens of Mary Shelley and Matthew Lewis.

The types of operatic composition preferred by librettists for these 1836-48 programs were not as varied as they had been earlier. Exactly 27 works were presented to audiences simply and solely as operas with *Le Freischütz* alone having the distinction of being billed as a "romantic opera." These texts were written in from one to five acts with those in three and five acts accounting for 15 titles; 11 others were in two and four acts. The sole opera in a single act was Aurélie Marliani's *La Xacarilla*. These works were the only dramatic productions billed at the Le Peletier theatre in

1836-48; other additions to repertory were limited to ballets, fantastic ballets, and pantomime ballets. The most favored sort of choreographic composition was the pantomime ballet in two acts, and eight of them were executed, but this same interval of a dozen years also saw six of this same type of ballet in three acts produced by the company.

Scribe was still the outstanding author of librettos for operas with his three titles in five acts and his two works in three and two acts besides his collaboration with Mélesville on Auber's *Le Lac des fées* (1839) in five acts. H. de Saint-Georges did the poem for an opera in five acts besides the librettos for two other operas of two acts each. Théodore Anne wrote the words for *Marie Stuart* (1844) in five acts as well as for *Le Guérilléro* in two acts; Paul Foucher created the poems for one opera in three acts and another in two acts. Collaborations by librettists were frequent but not commonplace, and at least six or seven poems were established by teams including a translator or a pair of creative writers. The choreography created for the ballets was overwhelmingly the work of Jean Coralli and Joseph Mazilier, who were responsible for the dances in 15 compositions. Other choreography for one or two ballets of various sorts included work by Ferdinand-Albert Decombe, Thérèse Elssler, Antonio Guerra, Arthur Saint-Léon, and Filippo Taglioni.

The internal affairs of the Opéra were guided by men of diverse talents and varying degrees of luck during the last 35 years of the artistes' residence at the Le Peletier opera house. After creating sets for *La Juive*, the architect Charles-Edmond Duponchel assumed the directorship of the corporation on 15 August 1835, and he was fortunate enough to have *Les Huguenots* as his first addition to the repertory on 29 February 1836. Matters seemed to be progressing satisfactorily under his leadership in subsequent months, but it became apparent ultimately that he lacked Dr. Véron's flair for publicity and skill in handling the gentlemen of the press. He was in need of help in the area of public relations. As a result, the journalist Edouard Monnais was selected to become his colleague on 15 November 1839. Yet this solution was apparently a makeshift device, because a partnership was formed on 1 June 1841 between Duponchel and Léon Pillet to administer the affairs of the Opéra, while Monnais went on to deal with other governmental matters. M. Pillet was similarly unable to make the Opéra show a profit, but he remained in his position as director with Duponchel until 31 July 1847. He then stepped down from office in favor of his associate and Nestor Roqueplan. There was a deficit of 400,000 *francs* on the books at this time. Roqueplan was an able businessman, however, and the fiscal situation was beginning to improve with the aid of composers like Verdi, singers like Duprez, and dancers like Fanny Cerrito or Saint-Léon when the revolution of 1848 struck Paris and its theatres. The Opéra was closed from 22 to 29 February on account of the fighting in the streets, and it was once again put into the service of politics in April, when it turned its attention to more patriotic productions in the style of 1792. It was renamed the Théâtre de la Nation in February 1848. Duponchel resigned as director on 21 November 1849, and Nestor Roqueplan was left in charge of the troupe and its business. Then, with the coup d'état by Napoleon III, the Opéra became known once more as the Imperial Academy of Music, and Roqueplan resigned in his turn on 30 June 1854 under the onus of a debt of 900,000 *francs*; he was reappointed the following day with the Opéra placed under the control of the government. He was replaced by François-Louis Crosnier before the year was over, however, although the latter's tenure continued only from 11 November 1854 until 1 July 1856 when Alphonse Royer replaced him as general administrator. Finally, on 20 December 1862, Emile Perrin left the directorship of the Opéra-Comique to head the Imperial Academy of Music. After the initial disasters of the Franco-Prussian War and the establishment of the Third Republic, the company was renamed the Théâtre National de l'Opéra on 12 July 1871. Perrin had already agreed to act as provisory administrator of the Opéra between 6 September 1870 and 8 July 1871, and he had turned over his office to Halanzier on this latter date. Unfortunately, the third year of this new regime saw programs at the theatre interrupted by the fire that destroyed completely the Le Peletier opera house on the night of 28-29 October 1873.

The roster of composers contributing to repertory during only these last 25 years of the artistes' sojourn at the Le Peletier theatre furnishes indisputable evidence of the supremacy of Paris in the world of opera in the nineteenth century despite the activity of competent companies in Austria, England, Germany, and Italy. The 1848-73 scores heard in the French capital were not by French composers exclusively, but the alien status of such figures as Verdi or Donizetti did not diminish the effectiveness of their works on the Paris stage: the former's *Louise Miller* (1853) in the Pacini translation was not a great success, but it added to the total impact the composer was to make upon audiences in the rue Le Peletier with *Les Vêpres siciliennes* (1855), *Le Trouvère* (1857), and *Don Carlos* (1867). Ill-starred Donizetti did not write anything for the stage after *Dom Sébastien, roi du Portugal*, which was mounted in Paris on 13 November 1843, but his *Betly* of 1836 also had its premiere at the Imperial Academy of Music in 1853. Charles Nuitter's representation of scenes and acts from Vincenzo Bellini's *Giulietta e Romeo* (1826) and *I Capuletti ed i Montecchi* (1830) was staged in 1859 under the title of *Roméo et Juliette* in 1859, and Rossini brought still another title to the Opéra with his *Sémiramis* of 1860 done in Méry's translation. Meyerbeer remained the spectators' darling during this time, and he added to his already incredible popularity with *Le Prophète* of 1848 and *L'Africaine* of 1865, both in five acts. A cluster of French composers active during the reign of Louis-Philippe continued to have their works accepted by the artistes; especially Jacques-François Halévy, who had his *Le Juif errant* in five acts performed in 1852 and his *La Magicienne*, likewise in five acts, staged a few years later in 1858. Daniel Auber's five act *L'Enfant prodigue* enjoyed its premiere at the Opéra on 6 December 1850, and his *Zerline ou la corbeille d'oranges* was billed as an opera in three acts for the first time on 16 May 1851. But the most enduring full-length opera proved to be Gounod's *Faust* sung initially at the Opéra on 3 March 1869 after having its world premiere at the Théâtre Lyrique of the Boulevard du Temple on 19 March 1859. An impoverished German writer did not have the same good fortune with his *Tannhäuser*, an opera in three acts that had to be withdrawn after its third representation in 1861. The total repertory of dramatic works amounted to 37 of the 68 pieces produced in 1848-73, and 20 of these were in four or five acts; Félicien David, Louis Niedermeyer, and Ambroise Thomas were among the other composers to set librettos of five acts for the artistes, while Auguste Mermet, Eugène-Emile Diaz de la Pena, and Jósef Michal Xavery Franciszek Jan Poniatowski, the future Louis XVIII, limited their creations to three acts. The programs were balanced by a dozen shorter operas in one or two acts. No really new sources of material were tapped extensively by the librettists of the Second Empire, and the dramas developed in the longer or shorter works were based mostly upon Italian, Spanish, French, English, and German history, legend, or literature with an occasional composition calling upon the Bible or ancient history for inspiration. Gothic titles like *L'Apparition* (1848) or *Le Démon de la nuit* (1851) were also posted from time to time to tempt the paying public in search of an evening of chilling entertainment.

There were 28 ballets executed by the company during this same 1848-73 interval in addition to the single opera ballet *Le Cheval de bronze* (1857) by Auber for which Scribe wrote the libretto. The pantomime ballet in one, two, and three acts continued to grow in popularity, and 19 compositions of this sort proved that this type of choreographic work was well on the way to replacing the traditional ballet during the Second Empire: only five scenarios designated simply as ballets were produced, and it was accordingly evident that the pantomime ballet was versatile and effective enough to satisfy performers and spectators alike. Arthur Saint-Léon and Petipa did a "fantastic" ballet apiece, but Jules Perrot's *La Filleule des fées* for which Jules-Henri Vernoy de Saint-Georges did the scenario in 1849 was the sole "ballet féerique." A relatively small number of choreographers created these works, and Arthur Saint-Léon and Joseph Mazilier alone were responsible for 16 of them. Lucien Petipa managed to have four texts produced despite his other duties, but Louis-François Mérante, Marie Taglioni, Auguste Mabille, Henri Potier, Pasquale Borri, Giuseppe Rota, and Perrot did but a single composition each. The most frequently billed title was Arthur Saint-Léon's *La Vivandière* (1848) in which Mme Francesca Teresa G. R. Cerrito created a sensation dancing to Cesare Pugni's music; it was staged on nearly a hundred occasions before the salle Le Peletier burned to the ground. But *Coppélia* (1870) by Charles Nuitter and Arthur Saint-Léon went on to enjoy more than 750 representations by 1962. The other two ballets executed most frequently at the Opéra before 1873 were Joseph Mazilier's colorful *Le Corsaire* (1856) and Saint-Léon's *La Source* (1866) for which Léo Delibes wrote his first ballet music; this pair of compositions was offered by the company on 70 or more dates. The increasing interest shown by the public in the ballet programs can be explained in part by the variety and quality of the programs being produced, of course, but it is also to be remembered that spectators were charmed as usual by the lavish sets that continued to adorn the stage and by the calibre of the stars in the *corps du ballet*, especially the gifted Saint-Léon and Mérante as well as Mlles Fanny Cerrito, Amalia Ferraris Eugénie Fiocre, Angelina Fioretti, Caroline Rosati, Marie Vernon, and the talented friends of the members of the Jockey Club.

The Opéra-Comique, III: 1797–1870

The Opéra-Comique closed down the salle Favart on 19 June 1797 to facilitate repairs on this building, but the troupe returned to their theatre on 25 October 1797 with *Le Secret* and *Guillaume Tell*. The company went on to enjoy a new wave of popularity and prosperity in their refurbished facility during 1798-99, and they added five works to the repertory in this brief interval that saw the premieres of Nicolas Dalayrac's *Alexis* (1798), Mozart's *L'Enlèvement au sérail* (1798), and Henri-Montan Berton's *Montano et Stéphanie* (1799). Representations of works of a similar nature were continuing at the Feydeau, however, and the two rival groups began to undermine each other by attempting to attract the same class of spectators with similar products. This impasse finally moved toward a resolution when Mme Scio left the Feydeau for the Favart, and her admirers among the musicians in the orchestra left with her. A crisis was now in the making, therefore, and it was decided on 16 September 1801 that the two companies should be united under the supervision of the government but with the responsibility for success being lodged with management and the performers. The first program mounted by the new corporation consisted of Méhul's *Stratonice* and Cherubini's *Les Deux Journées*. The scene of this double bill was the Feydeau theatre.

The Opéra-Comique flourished subsequently during the Empire, when Napoleon encouraged the troupe with an annual subsidy of nearly 100,000 *francs*. The box office as well as the government was a dependable source of revenue, because Boïeldieu, Dalayrac, Grétry, Méhul, and Nicolo provided a reliable supply of scores to charm the public into the theatre, although the artistes' address changed from the Feydeau back to the Favart on 23 July 1804 and then to the Olympic on 3 October 1804 before returning to the Favart later in 1804 and to the Feydeau in 1805. Fontaine de Cramayol became chief administrator of the corporation in 1804; Auguste de Talleyrand was named to this post in 1805. The decree of 1806 involved all eight theatres open in Paris at this time, but it singled out the Opéra-Comique as one of the three theatrical groups to enjoy a monopoly on their particular type of production; the governmental edict of 8 August 1807 endowed the company with the rank and title of Imperial Theatre. The Opéra-Comique could no longer be ignored or decried, then, and its position was secured as much by its repertory as by its favored position: Méhul's *Joseph* (1807); the five successes of Nicolas Isouard DIT Nicolo which included his *Les Rendez-vous bourgeois* (1807), *Cendrillon* (1810), and *Joconde* (1814); Boïeldieu's *Jean de Paris* (1812) and *Le Nouveau Seigneur du village* (1813); and Berton's *Ninette à la cour* (1811).

The restoration of the Bourbons to the throne of France in 1815 resulted in the redesignation of the corporation as the Royal Theatre of the Opéra-Comique, and the supervision of all matters pertaining to the troupe was given to the secretary of state for Louis XVIII, the duke d'Aumont. Unfortunately, these administrative innovations did little to prevent or to remedy the financial stress from which the company suffered after 1815, and steps had to be taken to improve the situation: Guilbert de Pixérécourt was appointed director of the organization under the leadership of the duke d'Aumont. The new officer of the company was a prolific dramatist and librettist, but he was not too well suited by temperament to occupy himself with such prosaic matters as receipts, expenses, and budgets, and his managerial problems were compounded by the hostility of the artistes and their complaints to the government about his offensive manner. But the duke favored and supported René-Charles Guilbert de Pixérécourt, doubtlessly because he was earning from 800,000 to more than a million *francs* annually at the box office with the help of such hits as Auber's *Le Maçon* (1825), Boïeldieu's *La Dame blanche* (1825), and Hérold's *Marie* (1826).

Yet if the finances of the Opéra-Comique were in good condition, its walls were in danger of collapsing at this time, and it was decided to transfer the company into new quarters before a tragedy might overtake them and the public. A site and architects were selected; financing was arranged through the millionaire Boursault; ground was broken on 28 November 1826. It was decided to find a new director as well, and the theatre in the rue Neuve-Ventadour was able to open its doors on 20 April 1829 with *Les Deux Mousquetaires* by Berton and *La Fiancée* by Auber. Colonel Ducis had been chosen to head the company and to take care of its affairs in its new quarters. Unfortunately, he found it difficult to handle cash without having it stick to his hands, and authors, actors, and theatrical suppliers were soon clamoring for their money. It was not long before Boursault had to replace the colonel, who resigned his position on 26 July 1830.

But the company had flourished as a theatrical undertaking in these 15 years of the Restoration largely on account of the efforts of an incredibly small group of composers who dominated the stages of the Favart, Feydeau, and Ventadour theatres with their regular if not annual contributions to repertory. *Le Maçon* aside, Auber had given another six hits to the troupe: *Le Testament* (1819), *La Bergère châtelaine* (1820), *La Neige* (1823), *Le Concert à la Cour* (1824), *La Fiancée* (1829), and *Fra Diavolo* (1830). Boïeldieu was almost as prolific with *La Fête du village voisin* (1816), *Le Petit Chaperon rouge* (1818), *Les Voitures versées* (1820), and *Les Deux Nuits* (1829) in addition to *La Dame blanche*. Hérold had *La Clochette* (1817) and *Le Muletier* produced prior to *Marie* (1826). The artistes gave Mozart's *Les Noces de Figaro* for the first time in 1818, and Ferdinand Paër saw the initial performance of his *Le Maître de Chapelle* by the Opéra-Comique in 1821. The theatrical notices in the newspapers and magazines of the day pointed with enthusiasm to the singers of both sexes whose talents enhanced the representation of these works: Boullard, Chollet, Damoreau, Fargueil, Feréol, Lemonnier, Moreau-Sainti, and Ponchard among the men; and Mmes Casimir, Colon, and Lemonnier. And no one had anything but words of praise for the orchestra and the physical structure and appearance of the theatre itself.

But the July 1830 revolution in Paris bringing Louis-Philippe into power had an adverse effect on the theatre, and management not only had to repair the financial damage wrought by Ducis, but the new manager of the troupe from Lyon named Singier was notified that his annual subsidy would drop to 120,000 *francs*. He was similarly aware that he would not receive the yearly rent of 30,000 *francs* that Charles X had paid for his loges. M. Boursault thought it prudent that he should sever connections with the Opéra-Comique, and Lubbert replaced him. Matters were so bad on account of these monetary setbacks and outstanding debts that the payroll was not met at the Ventadour on 14 August 1831 despite the outstanding success of Hérold's *Zampa*, which had had its premiere on 3 May 1831. The theatre closed. The government did not help to improve the situation by threatening Lubbert with the revocation of the company's license if he did not repair the harm done by the company's refusal to pay its debts and to return to the stage. Lubbert tried to rectify matters, but he had to acknowledge total defeat on 8 December 1831 by releasing the personnel of the company from their contractual obligations. Unemployed and angry, the vociferous artistes explained their grievances and described their position in various publications. They proclaimed bluntly, "Paris has to have an Opéra-Comique." The situation seemed beyond repair with negotiations now bogged down in complaints, recriminations, and unheeded suggestions. Laurent assumed control of the theatre for a brief interval at the start of 1832, but nothing came of his presence on the troubled scene. Finally, Paul Dutreich attempted to re-organize the company into a corporation composed of the artistes themselves, but a satisfactory solution was not forthcoming from this arrangement, and François-Louis Crosnier was named director of the Opéra-Comique after the plan for a corporate structure for the group was rejected.

While these changes in management were taking place, the troupe decided to look for a new and more acceptable theatre unencumbered by previous commitments and bitter memories. They moved into the Théâtre des Nouveautés, a facility that had been dark since 15 February 1832, and they gave their first program here on 22 September 1832: Auber's *Le Maçon* (1825) and Boïeldieu's *Les Voitures versées* (1820). The artistes would enjoy a period of brilliant activity at the Nouveautés during their sojourn here in 1832-40. They staged Hérold's popular *Le Pré aux clercs* for the first time on 15 December 1832 and Adam's *Le Chalet* on 25 September 1834. Their subsequent noteworthy hits at their new address included Halévy's *L'Eclair* (1835), Adam's *Le Postillon de Longjumeau* (1836) and *Le Brasseur de Preston* (1836), Auber's *Le Domino noir* (1837), and Donizetti's *La Fille du régiment* (1840). Scribe continued to be the most prolific of the librettists to provide the company with material, and he furnished the words for no fewer than six of the 14 new 1833-40 titles posted at the Nouveautés in the place de la Bourse.

If the fortunes of the company were bright and promising at this time, Crosnier was not content to rest on his laurels, and he began to cast about for a new theatre for the company. His opportunity came when the government decided to rebuild the Favart theatre that had been destroyed completely in a devastating fire on the night of 13-14 January 1838. It took more than two years to ready this new stage, but the artistes were able to present *Le Pré aux clercs* (1832) for the 347th time at the "second" Favart on 16 May 1840. Crosnier had triumphed: the government agreed to grant him an annual subsidy of 240,000 *francs*; the bourgeois king paid 20,000 *francs* rent per year for his loges. Crosnier remained with the troupe until 1845, and these last five years of his tenure saw six successful additions to the repertory, which included *Les Diamants de la couronne* (1841), *La Part du Diable* (1843), and *La Sirène* (1844) by the inexhaustible team of Auber and Scribe. When his good fortune seemed to desert him eventually, he resigned in favor of M. Basset of the Odéon in 1845. The latter became involved in a quarrel with the league of authors before long, and the revolution of 1848 was enough to induce him to relinquish his office to Emile Perrin.

M. Perrin guided the fortunes of the Opéra-Comique during ten golden years, 1848-57. He was able to post nearly a score of new titles at the Favart during this decade, and he could count among his composers musicians like Adam, Halévy, and Meyerbeer. After the revolution was over and the performers had put away their National Guard uniforms, Perrin produced his first new work on 11 November 1848, *Le Val d'Andorre* by Halévy. This piece was an outstanding success, and Perrin was encouraged to undertake 1849 productions of Thomas's *Le Caïd*, Armand-Marie Ghislain, baron Limnander de Nieuwendhove's *Les Monténégrins*, and Adam's *Le Toréador*. The troupe, its writers, and management were so emboldened by the reception accorded to their efforts by the public and the press alike that they undertook to stage no fewer than five new compositions in 1850: *Les Porcherons* by Albert Grisar, *Le Songe d'une nuit d'été* by Ambroise Thomas, *Giralda* by Adolphe-Charles Adam, *La Petite Fadette* by Théophile-Emile-Aimé Semet, *La Chanteuse voilée* by Victor Massé. This surge of activity showed no signs of slackening at the start of 1851 when the premiere of Grisar's *Bonsoir, monsieur Pantalon* was held on 19 February, but events were conspiring to limit the good fortune of the Opéra-Comique: Alexandre Dumas *père* had lost interest in his Théâtre Historique on the boulevard du Temple, and the Théâtre Lyrique organization was moving into it. Then, on 27 September 1851, this latter troupe staged *Mosquita la sorcière* in their new quarters, and the Opéra-Comique under M. Perrin had its first taste of competition from this comic opera in three acts by Xavier Boisselot. This untoward development was accompanied by an inclination on the part of the composers to offer their works to the Opéra in the rue Le Peletier or to the Théâtre Lyrique instead of favoring the Opéra-Comique. Perrin was accordingly obliged to have recourse to newcomers to the Paris musical scene, like the Belgian Armand-Marie Ghislain, baron Limnander de Nieuwendhove, who gave *Le Château de Barbe-Bleue* (1851) to the troupe. Perrin also turned to older texts whose appeal he could restore or even increase with impressive revivals. The two principal works that the resourceful director did manage to bring to the stage of the Favart before the establishment of the Second Empire were Massé's *Galatée*, sung initially on 14 April 1852, and Napoléon-Henri Reber's *Le Père Guillard*, billed for the first time on 7 September 1852.

The Opéra-Comique became the Théâtre Impérial on 2 December 1852 with the establishment of the Second Empire by Napoleon III, and Perrin produced another comic opera by Massé on 4 February 1853, *Les Noces de Jeannette*. He offered another five new compositions to the public before his retirement on 19 November 1857. Meyerbeer's *L'Etoile du Nord* was performed first on 16 February 1854, and it created a sensation among spectators who supported it for three or four performances a week until it reached its hundredth representation less than a year later on 14 February 1855. News of its popularity spread abroad rapidly, and companies in nearly every large city in Europe hastened to rehearse and to perform it. After the premiere of *Les Sabots de la marquise* by Boulanger on 29 September 1854, Grisar's *Le Chien du Jardinier*, with a libretto by Lockroy and Cormon, was posted at the Favart on 16 January 1855 to attract and to amuse the crowds of visitors attending the Exposition Universelle in Paris. Victor Massé's *Les Saisons* closed this spectacular fair on 22 December 1855. François Bazin's *L'Avocat Patelin* (1856) and Ambroise Thomas's *Psyché* (1857) were the last two popular pieces introduced by the troupe during the tenure of Emile Perrin. The first of these compositions was not based upon the well-known medieval farce, but it was well enough received to remain in repertory for 15 years. When Perrin relinquished his office, he could boast that he had left the troupe and the theatre in excellent condition physically and financially. He had refurbished the interior of the opera house between 20 June and 4 July in the summer of 1853; he had supervised activities that had earned the corporation millions of *francs*. He had also placed in the lobby of his theatre marble busts of some of the composers and librettists who had contributed to this success: Berton, Boïeldieu, Dalayrac, Etienne, Favart, Grétry, Herold, Marmontel, Marsollier, Monsigny, Nicolo, Saint-Just, and Sedaine.

Nestor Roqueplan had presided over the affairs of the Opéra between 1847 and 1854 before coming to the Opéra-Comique in the last days of 1857, but he appears in retrospect to have been a politically oriented person more interested in building an attractive and convenient stairway for the emperor and his guests at the theatre than in discovering works with merit enough to convince spectators to leave their money at the box office. Yet it must be admitted that he did not overlook good work and the possibility of profit whenever they came his way, and he was quick to accept Meyerbeer's *Le Pardon de Ploërmel* with a libretto by J. Barbier and M. Carré for production on 4 April 1859. Roqueplan resigned on 18 June 1860, however, and his successor, Alfred Beaumont, was likewise unable to achieve the sustained success enjoyed by Perrin. When the situation became so desperate financially that Beaumont could not meet the payroll and discharge other basic monetary obligations, the government intervened on 26 January 1862 to dismiss Beaumont and to recall Perrin. The latter returned to the Favart on 30 January 1862, and he set about to restore prosperity at the box office by reviving *La Dame blanche* (1825) and billing *Lalla-Roukh* for 12 May. This latter composition in two acts with a libretto by Carré and Lucas that Félicien David set was a typical Perrin success, and it seemed that happier days had returned at last to the Favart. But the director did not remain with the troupe long enough to exercise his administrative talents to the fullest extent for his colleagues: he assumed the directorship of the Imperial Academy of Music on 11 December 1862.

The count de Leuven accepted the responsibility of the directorship of the Opéra-Comique with his associate Eugène Ritt from the Ambigu theatre on 20 December 1862. His first efforts were aimed at improving the lighting system in 1862, expanding his troupe of artistes in 1863, and redecorating the interior of the theatre as well as providing it with a new curtain in 1864. The repertory between 1864 and the outbreak of the Franco-Prussian War included Aimé Maillart's *Lara* of 21 March 1864, François Bazin's *Le Voyage en Chine* of 9 December 1865, and especially Ambroise Thomas's *Mignon* of 17 November 1866 with Mme Miolan-Carvalho and then Mme Galli-Marié in the title-rôle. The box office benefited from the crowds attending the 1867 exposition in the French capital, but it was not until the following year that *Le Premier Jour de bonheur* by Auber had its memorable premiere with the idol of Paris, the twenty-eight-year-old tenor, Joseph-Amédée-Victor Capoul. Inexhaustible, Auber returned to the stage of the Favart once again on 20 December 1869 with *Le Rêve d'Amour* in three acts, and Friedrich Flotow of Mecklenburg had his *L'Ombre* staged on 7 July 1870 just a few weeks before Ritt resigned from management.

The company had arrived at the critical moment of the disintegration of the Second Empire. Yet it was quite evident by now that the comic opera had achieved the variety and sophistication required of it. The middle decades of the nineteenth century had seen its librettists and composers continue to rely upon tales of love in the country or upon the extravagant sets and stories of horror dear to the romantics, but Boïeldieu had shown as early as 1825 in *La Dame blanche* that continuing success came with the dramatic rather than the melodramatic situation, and he had taken care to present his action with sufficient harmony and a suitable combination of gay and touching scenes. Hérold, with his Italian training, and Adolphe Charles Adam appeared in the following decade with an even greater measure of sustained vitality, rhythm, and pertinent orchestration in *Le Pré aux clercs* (1832) and *Le Postillon de Longjumeau* (1836), while Auber pointed to the simple fact that liveliness and gaiety are the proper qualities to grace the course of events in the comic opera. The score also came to have its own musical style too: the music was tonal and could have recourse only to tonic and dominant cadences; the vocal portion of the presentation was limited to the patterns usually found in the traditional forms of the aria, cavatina, duet, quartet, and other groupings suited to the stage. The reign of Louis-Philippe as well as the Second Empire, then, were periods of significant growth for the comic opera and its offspring, the operetta, as it was developed and made popular by Adam, Massé, and Jacques Offenbach above all. The latter's *Les Contes d'Hoffman* was not produced until 1881, it is true, but his *Orphée aux enfers* (1858), *La Belle Hélène* (1864), and *La Vie parisienne* (1866), as well as *La Périchole* (1868), enjoyed immense popularity before the siege of Paris and the fires of the Commune.

The Ventadour Theatre and the Garnier Palace, 1874–1914

M. Halanzier presided over the committee of the society of artistes from 8 July 1871 until the following 1 November, when he was appointed chief administrator of the Opéra, now known as the Théâtre National de l'Opéra. The troupe had not been active between 2 September 1870 and 12 July 1871 on account of the war and the siege of Paris, but they were able to resume performances on this latter date with a representation of *La Muette de Portici*, which returned to the box office the satisfying sum of 8,727 *francs* 69 *sous*. The new regime in the rue Le Peletier seemed to be progressing satisfactorily enough with the premiere of Ernest Reyer's *Erostrate* on 16 October 1871, and a banquet was held to honor Halanzier on 26 March 1872. Receipts for 1871 amounted to nearly 1.7 million *francs*. Suddenly, however, fortune seemed to stop smiling, and the leader of the orchestra, M. Hainel, died on 1 June 1873, while the costume designer Alfred Albert also died on 21 June 1873. Then, in the midst of preparations for the premiere of Auguste Mermet's *Jeanne d'Arc*, the theatre caught fire and burned to the ground on the night of 28-29 October 1873. When the sun rose the following morning, it was obvious immediately that the company would have to seek new quarters, and management turned to the only facility available and suited to their purposes, the theatre being used by the so-called Italian troupe in the rue Ventadour. The artistes had to share this stage, because they could use it only on alternate days in conjunction with the Opéra-Comique.

The artistes' sojourn in the Ventadour theatre was a makeshift, and the corporation remained in its temporary facility for only fifty weeks: they opened with *Don Juan* on 19 January 1874 and closed with *Faust* on 30 December 1874 after staging exactly 166 programs here. Yet despite the knowledge that they would be leaving the Ventadour as soon as possible and although they were alternating their bills with a rival group, the corporation managed to rehearse and to offer to the public one new title, *L'Esclave* by Edmond Membrée. They also took time to give a benefit on 11 October 1874 for Alsace-Lorraine.

Public officials had talked about a special facility for the Opéra since the destruction of the Palais-Royal by fire in 1781, and specific authorization for the creation of a theatre designed exclusively for operatic performances had been given eventually by the government of Napoleon III on 29 September 1860, when a decree had ordered work to begin on a structure capable of meeting the needs of the company. Architects were invited to submit their plans in an open competition won by Charles Garnier. The site was prepared, and the first stone in the outside walls was put in place on 21 July 1862. The builders had encountered trouble at first with underground streams because of the proximity to the Seine, but extra pumps and a vaulted subbasement built to contain the water had overcome the problem. The Franco-Prussian War had brought work to a halt, moreover, and the fighting in the streets during the Commune uprising had caused additional delays. Yet the sumptuous theatre with its incredible decorations executed by thirty painters and more than seventy sculptors, its ample accommodations and sheer size was ready at last on 5 January 1875, when its first spectators climbed the grand staircase to be present at the debut of Mme Gabrielle Krauss and to hear excerpts from such perennial favorites as *La Muette de Portici, Guillaume Tell, La Juive, Les Huguenots*, and Delibes's ballet *La Source*. The only sour note of the evening was Mme Christine Nilsson's refusal to appear for this distinguished audience that included the Lord Mayor of London, Alfonso XII of Spain, and President MacMahon of the Third Republic. It can be said that the glory of the past was combined with the splendor of the present to inaugurate the Palais Garnier.

Halanzier had a unique opportunity and enjoyed remarkable success during his term of office between 5 January 1875 and 16 July 1879. The public was eager to gain admission to his theatre not only to attend operatic performances but also to see how illuminating gas worked on the stage and to satisfy their curiosity about the interior of the incredible opera house. The continuing high receipts at the box office made government officials wonder about the necessity of giving the company a large subsidy on top of the money that the troupe was earning, but the director managed to hold on to his dual income by convincing his superiors that a hot summer, a cold winter, or some unpredictable catastrophe might intervene to change the picture completely by demanding the expenditure of large sums of cash. Also, expenses were truly heavy because so much property had been lost by the Opéra in the fire of 1873, and the new theatre was so much more demanding as far as production was concerned; every revival was tantamount to a premiere in matters involving labor and money. It should likewise be noted that Halanzier was never reluctant to give benefits: he raised nearly 120,000 *francs* on four dates in 1875 alone for such worthy causes as the support of war orphans and to aid flood victims in the south. Other outstanding episodes of his term included the celebration of the centennial of American independence in 1876, the suppression of the claque and the opening of the theatre to sightseers on 14 July 1878, and the restoration of the profitable custom of having masked balls at the Opéra before Lent.

The troupe itself was composed of approximately 40 artistes in 1875, and their efforts during their first year at the new theatre were confined to the ballets *La Source* and *Coppélia* as well as to seven now almost standard pieces, *Don Juan*, *Faust*, *La Favorite*, *Guillaume Tell*, *Hamlet*, *Les Huguenots*, and *La Juive*. The composition to win the distinction of being the first new work billed at the Garnier palace was Auguste Mermet's already rehearsed *Jeanne d'Arc*, sung before the public initially on 5 April 1876. It was followed by Léo Delibes's *Sylvia* on 14 June of the same year, but it was not until 27 April 1877 that a third work was given its world premiere by the company in its new home: *Le Roi de Lahore* of 27 April 1877 by Jules Massenet. Halanzier saw another four titles posted by the corporation before his retirement: *Le Fandango* of 1877, *Polyeucte* and *La Reine Berthe* of 1878, *Yedda* of 1879. His regime was also responsible for reviving *Le Freischütz*, *Robert le Diable*, and *L'Africaine*.

When M. Vaucorbeil took over the directorship of the Opéra in the summer of 1879, he was well aware that it would be folly to risk interfering with the momentum that the public and his predecessor had already imparted to the troupe and their programs. Accordingly, his policy was to proceed in the pattern set by his predecessor: a modicum of revivals, a sprinkling of new titles, the continuing of masked balls, and the staging of benefits for worthy causes. Of course, certain innovations had to be accepted because so many recent departures from former traditions were proving to be quite popular and profitable. Thus, a series of lyric concerts was initiated on 22 May 1880 with *La Vierge* in oratorio form, and electric lighting was introduced on 15 October 1881, five months after the first telephone line was installed in the Opéra to transmit a performance of *Le Tribut de Zamora* to the property warehouse in the rue Richer. When M. Vaucorbeil died on 2 November 1884, he had managed to assure the company of his good will by securing another five calm but successful years at the Opéra, and he had brought *La Favorite* to its 500th representation, besides giving *Aïda* and *Henry VIII* their premieres and bringing to the stage the ballets *La Korrigane, Namouna,* and *La Farandole.*

The log of the Opéra records that Ritt became director of the company with Pedro Gailhard as artistic director on 1 December 1884. Their administration lasted until 1892, and these nine years of their management remain noteworthy at the least for their courage in deciding to return Richard Wagner to their stage after the disastrous experience the corporation had had with *Tannhäuser* at the Académie Impériale de Musique in 1861: *Lohengrin* enjoyed its first representation at the Garnier theatre on 16 September 1891 in the French version by Charles Nuitter. But the success of Wagner's work now pushed the sum of annual receipts to over 3 million *francs*. The second distinctive feature of the 1884-92 repertory was the comparatively large number of new titles it featured: a dozen operas and four ballets including Verdi's *Rigoletto,* Massenet's *Le Cid,* and Gounod's *Roméo et Juliette.* Also, *La Juive* and *Faust* enjoyed their 500th performances in 1886 and 1887 respectively; *Lucie de Lammermoor* and *Sigurd* along with *Coppélia* were among the compositions revived. The special incidents of the 1884-92 interval besides the troupe's excursion to New York included the selection of *Faust* for the first matinee at the Opéra on 22 February 1887 and the celebration of Meyerbeer's centenary on 14 November 1891 with selections from *L'Africaine* (I), *Le Prophète* (IV), *Robert le Diable* (III), and *Les Huguenots* (IV). The theatre was dark on 1 June 1885 on account of Victor Hugo's funeral and again on 13 October 1885 to mourn the death of Emile Perrin, administrator of the Comédie-Française. The doors were also kept closed on 20-25 April 1886 to give the interior of the theatre a thorough cleaning. Benefits were not neglected, and programs were mounted to aid flood victims in France (1886) and famine victims in Russia (1892). Galas were held in 1889 alone for officials of the fair at Paris this year, for the mayors of France, and for French railroad engineers, for whom the artistes sang extracts from *L'Africaine* and *Aïda* besides executing *Coppélia.* Visiting royalty resumed visits to the Opéra now, and the prince of distant Tonga as well as the shah of Persia came to Garnier's palace in 1886 and 1889 respectively.

The company moved into the last decade of the century under the direction of Bertrand, who remained alone at the helm of the Opéra until 1894.

The athlete and singer Pedro Gailhard then returned as codirector of the troupe, and the collaborators Bertrand and Gailhard remained together until the former's death on 30 December 1899. Gailhard continued on alone as director until 1906, when P.-B. Gheusi served with him through 1907.

The many changes taking place in management during these 15 years did not affect the continuing prosperity and the growing prestige of the Paris Opéra, and the repertory of this period was enriched with new titles and a sufficient variety of subjects endowed with enough interest to prompt the public to purchase tickets. The most striking aspect of the artistes' offerings was the growing frequency with which Richard Wagner's works were billed at the theatre. Interest in the German composer grew to such surprising proportions that the phrase "Wagnerian wave" was coined to designate this sudden tide of enthusiasm for a musician whose *Tannhäuser* had proved a fiasco in Paris in 1861 and whose *Lohengrin* had been greeted with spitballs in the capital as recently as 1891 despite the applause it evoked not too much later. Now, between 1892 and 1907, *Tannhäuser* had become a regular feature of the operatic fare being offered in Paris; it was mounted by the troupe 100 times before 1902. As for *Lohengrin*, it had reached its 100th billing at least eight years previously on 28 April 1894. Inevitably, it was not long before management entertained the idea of presenting Wagner's other available works on their stage, and the third composition to swell the cresting Wagnerian wave was *La Walkyrie*, which had its premiere on 12 May 1893 and its 100th staging at the Opéra on 13 March 1899. *L'Or du Rhin* was heard in an audition with two pianos on 6 May 1893, but it was not produced for the public on a full scale until 17 November 1909. Wagner's fourth Paris work was *Les Maîtres Chanteurs de Nuremberg* added to repertory on 10 November 1897; it reached its 100th billing on 28 December 1912. *Siegfried* opened at the Garnier palace on 31 December 1901 after it had been heard at Rouen on 17 February 1900. *Tristan et Isolde* had been mounted in Paris at the Nouveau Théâtre on 28 October 1899 and at the Château d'Eau on 3 June 1902, and it was not given at the Opéra until 11 December 1904.

The 40 other new compositions accepted by the artistes between 1892 and 1907 are quite impressive in retrospect if only on account of their sheer numbers, but it is curious that the lyric works here should have outnumbered the choreographic creations by approximately five to one: only seven ballets were executed for the first time during this interval. The inspiration of all these pieces was quite diverse, moreover, and this variety in the offerings suggests the eclectic tastes of the age. The classical tradition proved to be alive yet, although it was represented almost exclusively by Hector Berlioz's *La Prise de Troie* of 1899, Jules Massenet's *Ariane* of 1906, and Victor Alphonse Duvernoy's ballet *Bacchus* of 1902. Biblical subjects provided the material for Camille Saint-Saëns's *Samson et Dalila* in 1892 and Etienne Nicolas Méhul's *Joseph* in 1899. Contemporary French novels set against ancient Mediterranean backgrounds suggested Ernest Reyer's *Salammbô* of 1892 and Jules Massenet's *Thaïs* of 1894. Medieval romance inspired Victorin de Joncières's ill-starred *Lancelot* (1900), and Shakespeare's presence was felt again in the French version of Verdi's *Othello* in 1894. These works and other lyric compositions were described most frequently by their librettists as operas or lyric dramas, but the terms "musical drama" or "symphonic drama" were used from time to time to designate the genre to which the author had assigned his work.

The steady progression of regular programs was again suspended from time to time to give gala performances designed to honor important visitors to the theatre. Giuseppe Verdi was the only living composer saluted in this fashion; he had just been awarded the Grande Croix of the Legion of Honor, and he was invited to attend the premiere of his *Othello* at the Opéra with the president of the Third Republic on 10 October 1894. The most frequent distinguished guests in the loges were European kings, and the ruling monarchs of Sweden, Spain, Portugal, Norway, England, and Italy were among the special guests now that France was a republic again. The czar of Russia and the American ambassador were accorded similar treatment. These galas did not interfere with benefits, and the artistes made an extra effort to raise money in 1898 for the new statue of Charles Garnier and to bolster the reserve officers' pension fund in 1899. The spirited Automobile Club of France was honored in 1905, and a gala was organized in 1906 to acknowledge the tricentennial of Corneille's birth. Special events not designed to provide money or to show special consideration to individuals or organizations included Weingartner's Berlioz and Beethoven concert of 1906 and the historical Russian concert the following year.

Yet the course of events was not entirely routine in the 1892-1907 period, although these last few decades before the outbreak of World War I would soon make the artistes wish for their return. A new sort of trouble erupted with the electricians' strike of 8 March 1907, the first of many labor disputes to occur in the course of the century. Not much difficulty came of this threat at this time because performances went on without interruption or internal strife for the remainder of the year. More immediately serious was the accident of 20 May 1896 during the ninth representation of *Hellé*, when one of the cast iron counterweights holding up the chandelier fell into the audience: one woman was killed, and two other spectators were injured. Lastly, fire struck the company once again in 1894. Although it was not the theatre but the warehouse for properties and costumes in the rue Richer that burned on this occasion, the losses were by no means trifling. The materials used to stage the popular works in repertory were destroyed and could not be replaced except at great expense. Many less acclaimed operas had to be dropped after this fire because receipts earned by them were not large enough to justify restoring or replacing the required sets and costumes. The second fire that changed the regular course of events at the Opéra was the conflagration of 8 January 1900 that destroyed the Comédie-Française and resulted in the players of this troupe sharing the facilities of the Garnier opera house with the artistes. The actors managed to mount eight programs in their temporary quarters between 1 March and 26 April 1900 and another six bills between 15 July and 11 November 1900. These latter programs were undertaken as joint efforts with the members of the Opéra company.

The internal organization of the Opéra changed drastically again on 1 January 1908 as far as personnel was concerned: André Messager and Broussan assumed control of management; P. Lagarde was placed in charge of the stage; Gabion was made responsible for general administration. This regime headed by Messager and Broussan lasted until 11 June 1914, and certain activities at the theatre during this time continued in the usual manner. Galas were arranged to honor such visiting dignitaries as the king of Sweden in 1908, of Belgium and Bulgaria in 1910, of Serbia in 1911, and of England and Denmark in 1914. Benefits were held to provide aid for victims of disaster in Turkey (1908) and Sicily (1909) and for the Red Cross organization itself (1912). Less humanitarian but perfectly legitimate motives prompted the staging of programs designed to salute Belgian cities and French aviation (1911-12), the Committee of the Republic (1912-13), and the Union of Commerce and Industry (1914). The cause of art was not forgotten: money was raised to finance a monument to Victorien Sardou (1910), and a performance was given to acknowledge the contribution to the theatre made by André Antoine, founder of the Théâtre libre (1914).

Yet while these more or less marginal events were taking place in 1908-14, changes of a more important sort were occurring on the stage because repertory was undergoing certain modifications that are quite manifest in retrospect. First, the Wagnerian wave came to a grand climax, not only because *Tannhäuser*, *Lohengrin*, *Tristan et Isolde*, *La Walkyrie*, and other works by the German composer continued to enjoy almost regular billings, but also because *Le Crépuscule des dieux* enjoyed its premiere in the French version by Alfred Ernst on 23 October 1908, *Siegfried* was revived on 21 May 1909, *L'Or du Rhin* was represented initially for the public on 17 November 1909, and *Les Maîtres Chanteurs de Nuremberg* began its second run at the Opéra on 17 February 1911. But these events did not give the full measure of Wagner's astounding popularity in Paris: his *L'Anneau du Nibelung* was billed for the first time at the theatre in June 1911 with the prologue, *L'Or du Rhin*, being sung on 10 June and with *La Walkyrie*, *Siegried*, and *Le Crépuscule des dieux* being mounted on 11, 13, 15 June respectively. The receipts rose to nearly 30,000 *francs* for the performance of 15 June alone, when *Le Crépuscule des dieux* was offered. The tetralogy was repeated once in June 1911 and twice in June 1912. As a last indication of the extent of Wagner's success, it might be noted that *Tannhäuser* alone enjoyed 17 billings at the Opéra in 1908, while *La Walkyrie* was posted on more than a dozen dates in 1909. Ultimately, *Parsifal* had its Paris premiere on 4 January 1914. Just as Verdi had remarked to count Arrivabene in 1879, Messager could have observed to his codirector Broussan on the eve of World War I, "We've done everything possible to give up our musical nationality; one more step, and we shall be germanized."

Wagner's influence upon the French lyric stage at this time is probably the force that increased the willingness of management not only to approve the appearance of foreign companies at the Opéra with works written in another language but also to accept into the repertory other compositions of alien inspiration made more accessible to French spectators by translation. The Imperial Opera of Moscow with Fédor Chaliapine presented *Boris Godounov* in Russian at the Opéra in 1908, the same year that Nellie Melba and Enrico Caruso sang *Rigoletto* there on 11 June. A special performance of Spontini's *La Vestale* by the La Scala troupe was heard in Italian in 1909; *Mefistofele* with a score and words by Arrigo Boïto along with Giacomo Puccini's *La Fille du Far-West* were offered in their original form by the Monte-Carlo company in May 1912. In fact, ten days in May 1912 were set aside for what management termed an "Italian season" so that the Monte-Carlo artistes might present *Mefistofele*, *Rigoletto*, *La Fille du Far-West*, and *Le Barbier de Séville*: 9, 12, 14, 16, 19, 21, 23, 26, 28, and 30 May. A Beethoven gala had been planned for 23 May 1909, and Verdi shared the program of 19 June 1913 with Saint-Saëns and Beethoven. The new works offered in French translations included Richard Strauss's *Salomé* on 3 May 1910, Umberto Giordano's *Siberia* on 9 June 1911, Ermanns Wolf-Ferrari's *Les Joyaux de la Madone* on 12 September 1913.

But the foreign works that were to have the greatest impact at this time, except for Wagnerian compositions, were neither operas nor lyric tragedies. They were ballets, the score or so of choreographic creations imported into Paris by the Ballets russes and danced at the Opéra as well as at certain other theatres in the capital. This company was headed by Serge Diaghilev, who brought his artistes to the Garnier opera house initially in 1909. Their repertory on this occasion included three new titles: *Le Festin* and *Les Sylphides*, danced on 19 June, and *Danses russes*, presented on 26 June. They had executed *Le Festin* at the Châtelet theatre on 19 May and *Les Sylphides* on the same stage on 30 May, but the 26 June 1909 performance of *Danses russes* at the Opéra constituted this work's world premiere. The troupe created a sensation with dancers like Anna Pavlova and Vaslav Nijinsky executing imaginative choreography by Michel Fokine, and Diaghilev's company was invited to return in 1910 when they staged 12 programs between 4 and 30 June. They brought six new titles with them including Alexander Borodin's *Danses polovtsiennes* and Igor Stravinsky's *L'Oiseau de feu* with choreography once more by Michel Fokine. The dancers did not perform at the Opéra during the 1911-13 seasons, however, although they did mount ten programs here in May and June 1914. Six of their works in these last prewar months had not yet been billed at the

Garnier theatre; one of these novelties was Stravinsky's *Pétrouchka*, created at the Châtelet theatre on 13 June 1911 with choreography by Michel Fokine. As might be expected, this sudden surge of interest in ballets induced management to mount this sort of composition created by French artistes, although they were already quite busy with Wagner, Verdi, and revivals of the perennial favorites by Gounod, Meyerbeer, and Massenet, whose symphonic manner continued to exercise a strong appeal in the theatre. Thus, out of the 41 new titles accepted by the Opéra in 1908-14, no fewer than 21 are clearly ballets. The other score of compositions are described by their authors as lyric dramas (6), musical dramas (3), operas (5), lyric tragedies (2), or some miscellaneous and slightly vague term is used by the librettist in search of an original genre for his poem.

The period of 1871-1914 had been a prosperous time for the Opéra, and many of the composers whose works had been mounted there in this interval had earned a full measure of fame and fortune for themselves and for the new theatre on the place de l'Opéra. Their number included Charles Gounod, Georges Bizet, Ernest Reyer, Camille Saint-Saëns, Edouard Lalo, Emmanuel Chabrier, Léo Delibes, Ernest Guiraud, and Emile Paladilhe. They had turned for inspiration to the myths of antiquity, the Bible, French legends and history, the English Renaissance, modern society, and the contemporary novel; their styles and manner ranged from romantic exoticism to the new realism already evident in the works of dramatists like Emile Augier and the younger Dumas. The foreign composers presented in translation at the Opéra with the greatest success were Richard Strauss, Giuseppe Verdi, and Richard Wagner, already immortal before his death on 13 February 1883, but it was no less evident that the French authors had made their own significant contribution to the lyric theatre in Paris, even if some of them seemed at times too much in debt to Wagnerian scores that preferred orchestral effects to the more traditional *bel canto* manner. Yet despite this array of genius and an ample theatre capable of conveying it to the public, the Opéra-Comique was playing an equally important part in the development and expansion of French opera despite its supposed obligation to limit its repertory to operettas and comic operas. The reasons for the resurgence of the less imposing theatre were quite apparent: new types of musical compositions were not shunned by management; the old distinction between opera and comic opera had disappeared because dialogue was no longer spoken. It had been replaced by the operatic device of the recitative. One could move from Garnier's theatre to the Opéra-Comique without noticing any difference in the performances provided an operetta was not in progress on the latter stage.

The Opéra-Comique, 1874-1914

The defeat suffered by the French in the war of 1871 gave rise to a resurgence of nationalistic sentiments that became manifest in almost all forms of music as well as in other types of expression. Patriotism was once again the order of the day, and the National Society of Music was organized, while the former Imperial Academy of Music was renamed the National Academy of Music as part of the general effort to restore French music to the prominent position it had enjoyed in Europe at the time of the Bourbon kings. All musical efforts derived benefits from this sudden interest shown in them as a facet of national genius, and the lyric theatre was especially favored. However, the Opéra itself did not seek to profit immediately from this new burst of patriotism despite its revivals of Gluck's *Armide* (1777) on 12 April 1905 and of Rameau's *Hippolyte et Aricie* (1733) on 13 May 1908, which seemed to indicate an effort in this direction. It was rather the Opéra-Comique that adapted itself to this situation by undertaking to present more ambitious works that might have been produced with greater esthetic effect and financial profit at the more commodious Garnier theatre. Georges Bizet's *Carmen*, Gustave Charpentier's *Louise*, and Claude Debussy's *Pelléas et Mélisande* were only three of the compositions that were offered to the public at the less prestigious theatre because the Garnier palace continued to be so occupied with the works of Gounod, Verdi, Wagner, and other safely established composers. Indeed, the Opéra had such little need of new or experimental types of musical compositions that on occasion authors had to leave Paris or even France to find an opportunity to set their wares before audiences. Camille Saint-Saëns's *Déjanire* (1911), Jules Massenet's *Roma* (1912), and Gabriel Fauré's *Pénélope* (1913) had their premieres at Monte-Carlo; Vincent d'Indy's *Fervaal* (1897) and *L'Etranger* (1903) as well as Ernest Reyer's *Sigurd* (1884) and *Salammbô* (1890) were created at the Théâtre de la Monnaie in Brussels; Hector Berlioz's *La Prise de Troie* (1891) had its first performance at the Nice opera house.

The war had closed the Opéra-Comique on 3 September 1870, and the disorder of subsequent days as well as unemployment dispersed the troupe. Yet the theatre was able to open again on 3 July 1871, and the artistes were giving regular programs by 1872. They used compositions staged previously at the Théâtre Lyrique, which had just been destroyed by fire during the Commune, and they were already accepting works by composers about to achieve world renown: Bizet's *Djamileh*, Saint-Saëns's *La Princesse jaune*, and Massenet's *Don César de Bazan* were performed in 1872, and Léo Delibes's *Le Roi l'a dit* was billed for 24 May 1873. Yet the director Camille Du Locle was not satisfied with this course of events, and he bought out his codirector de Leuven on 20 January 1874. Free to pursue his own ideas, Du Locle decided to expand the musical horizons at his theatre to attract larger audiences despite the competition he faced from the new opera house opened in 1875 as well as from the Théâtre Italien still in the Ventadour theatre and from the Gaîté now converted into a lyric theatre by Vizentini.

The odds seemed overwhelming, but Du Locle refused to compromise and dared to accept in 1875 a work with an unhappy ending, a heroine for whom fidelity was a myth, and a hero who was quite willing to sacrifice his honor for her. Unfortunately, the public was not ready for this sort of intrigue, and they seemed shocked as well by the unexpected harmonies and bold colors of the music. It would take almost a decade before *Carmen* would begin its ascent to its place alongside *Faust* as one of the two greatest French contributions to the international repertory.

After the retirement of Du Locle from the directorship of the Opéra-Comique and the expiration of Emile Perrin's interim appointment to this office in 1876, Léon Carvalho assumed the responsibility for managing the company from 14 August 1876 until 25 May 1887. He revived several favorites at first to replenish his funds and then staged Gounod's *Cinq-Mars* on 5 April 1877 with new talent that he had invited to join the troupe. Good fortune was with him now. The Théâtre Lyrique and the Théâtre Italien disappeared from the scene with the latter structure being converted eventually into a branch office of the Bank of France. He had only the Opéra as competition, and he could take advantage of the availability of both the artistes and the repertories of the two defunct theatres in planning new programs. His next step was to redecorate his theatre between 30 June and 11 October 1879. He opened his doors with the 1,229th representation of *Le Pré aux clercs* (1832), and in 1880-87 he moved from one success to another with a wealth of stars and works that included *Les Contes d'Hoffman* (1881) by Jacques Offenbach, Delibes's *Lakmé* (1883) with Mlle Van Zandt in the lead, Jules Massenet's *Manon* (1884), which would seem to have only one run lasting forever, and Saint-Saëns's *Proserpine* (1887). Then, on 25 May 1887, when the curtain was going up for a performance of Ambroise Thomas's *Mignon* (1866), a fire broke out suddenly and without warning. A catastrophe of the first magnitude ensued with 400 victims killed in the panic or suffocated by the heavy smoke from burning paint. Carvalho resigned immediately.

The two most pressing needs now facing the company were met by naming Jules Barbier director of the troupe and by persuading the city of Paris to lease to the artistes the Théâtre Lyrique in the place du Châtelet. Barbier stepped aside shortly in favor of Paravey, whose administration lasted only until 1891 but which saw the premieres of Edouard Lalo's *Le Roi d'Ys* (1888), Massenet's *Esclarmonde* (1889), and André Messager's *La Basoche* (1890). Although Carvalho had refused previously to mount Lalo's work, it was praised simultaneously for its Wagnerian orchestration and its Gallic deftness in handling a Breton theme; *Esclarmonde* enjoyed a hundred billings and was to be one of the main attractions of the 1889 exposition in Paris with Sybil Sanderson as its star; *La Basoche* was one of Messager's 40 operettas, but it also ranked among his best 1883-97 creations with *Les Bourgeois de Calais* (1887) and *Les P'tites Michu* (1897). Paravey resigned in 1891, but his regime had been successful, and Carvalho had no troublesome situations to worry him when he returned to the directorship after his exoneration from all guilt in the fire of 1887. His second term of office extended from 1891 until his death on 26 December 1897, and he is to be credited with having brought before the public in this interlude Massenet's *Werther* (1891) and *Phryné* (1893) as well as Alfred Bruneau's *L'Attaque du moulin* (1893) and Benjamin Godard's *La Vivandière* (1895).

Events took an unexpected turn for the company after Carvalho's death, when the new codirectors, Carrel and Porel, had to move their troupe to the Château d'Eau theatre so that the municipal government of Paris could keep its promise to Sarah Bernhardt to allow her to occupy the Théâtre Lyrique. The Opéra-Comique made this move on 30 June 1898 and then transferred on 7 December 1898 to their new theatre.

It had been more than a decade since the second Favart theatre had burned to the ground, but it had not taken all this time to reconstruct it: the inordinate delay had been caused by vociferous planners with expensive plans who could not or would not spend the money to realize their dreams of a second Garnier theatre in the heart of Paris. Compromises were made, however, and work was started eventually. Criticism was directed inevitably at the building for being crowded into its locale or for being in an inconvenient quarter, but the planners did remember to make the exits numerous and accessible, the doors wide, and the staircases open enough to avoid another catastrophe.

The company was host to its first spectators in its new quarters on 7 December 1898, and dignitaries of nearly every description attended the program that included excerpts from *La Dame blanche* (1825) by Boïeldieu, *Zampa* (1840) and *La Part du diable* (1843) by Auber, *Mireille* (1864) by Gounod, *Lalla Roukh* (1862) by Félicien David, and *Carmen* (1875) by Bizet with a symphonic band performing during intermissions. After this impressive inauguration, the third Favart opera house went on to an almost unbroken sequence of triumphs. Massenet created a set of three works for the artistes: *Cendrillon* (1899), *Grisélidis* (1901), *Le Jongleur de Notre-Dame* (1904). Debussy's impressionistic *Pelléas et Mélisande* with Mary Garden hoisted the banner of the revolt against Wagner and went on to establish itself as one of the great compositions of its era despite the plot to discredit it on and after its premiere of 27 April 1902. The realistic "musical novel" entitled *Louise* (1900) and written by Gustave Charpentier on the double theme of Paris and pleasure would have 500 billings by 1921. Camille Erlanger returned to classical inspiration in his *Aphrodite* (1906) based on the work of Pierre Louys; Claude Terrasse developed a second quasi-classical subject in *Le Mariage de Télémaque* (1910). Raoul Laparra added to the variety of the offerings at the Opéra-Comique by turning to Spain for his violent drama of jealousy and fratricide in *La Habañera* (1908), and Maurice Ravel followed his example by selecting Toledo as the setting for his poetic *L'Heure espagnole* (1911). The neoclassic and concomitant impressionistic phases into which French operatic music passed prior to World War I in a revolt against Wagnerism was defined clearly at the Opéra-Comique, where Claude Debussy and Maurice Maeterlinck set the tone, the composer with his gift for what d'Indy calls his "diversely colored musical" ways, and the man of letters with his suspenseful intrigue and mystical characters obedient to the secret impulses of the human soul.

The striking successes scored repeatedly by Albert Carré made him the inevitable candidate for the post of general administrator of the Comédie-Française left vacant by the illness and death of Jules Clarétie in 1913, and he assumed his new office at this latter theatre on 1 January 1914. Pierre-Barthélémy Gheusi then became director of the Opéra-Comique; his assistants were Emile and Vincent Isola of the Gaîté management. Only seven months remained before the outbreak of war, but Gheusi and his company were unaware of what was to come and set about immediately to sustain the pace set by Carré and his associates. They began by mounting Tiarko Richepin's *La Marchande d'allumettes* on 25 February 1914 and what was to become one of their most outstanding hits on 15 May: Henry Rabaud's enchanting *Mârouf, savetier du Caire*.

The Ballet, 1800–1914

The eighteenth century had witnessed the acceptance of Jean-Georges Noverre's thesis that ballet should be expressive and relevant to the drama unfolding on the stage instead of offering the ingenious but unrelated spectacle of geometrical patterns being developed by dancers wearing sumptuous costumes. The triumph of Noverre's ideas had been assured not only by their esthetic merit but also by the emergence of professional artistes in the ballet who had the strength and skill to support this new and more sophisticated doctrine. These more competent performers made simultaneous changes in their costumes on their own initiative so that they might achieve a greater effectiveness on the stage. La Camargo dared to shorten her skirt, and the clumsy *panier* was discarded; she rejected the Greek sandal in favor of a heelless satin dancing slipper to gain greater ease and freedom in her movements. Mlle Sallé clothed herself in a garment resembling an ancient tunic for the same reasons. Charles-Louis Frédéric Didelot paved the way for tights by wearing transparent outer clothing with knit hose beneath it to dance Zéphire in *Corisandre* at the Opéra in 1791. The other innovative and disciplined artistes who appeared on the scene at this time included Gaetano and Auguste Vestris, Jean-Bercher Dauberval, and Madeleine Guimard. These personalities and their contribution to the development of the dance in the Paris theatre were important in their own right, then, but they enjoyed the added significance of preparing the golden age of romantic ballet in France with their conviction that the dance was to be dramatic and pertinent rather than merely kinetic.

The new ballet came to the Opéra, and to opera, with the first performance of *La Sylphide* on 12 March 1832. This work had all the literary accouterments of a poem by Sir Walter Scott or Robert Burns with its humble farmhouse, wild forest, and rocky crags in the highlands of Scotland. This composition had a tremendous impact upon spectators because its action was of an evanescent sort and presented a prima ballerina who was an airy sprite instead of a voluptuous and self-conscious woman given to posturing. Also, this work incorporated another element that was to endure until the romantic ballet was to lose its charm for the public: classical divinities were replaced by a sylphid just as elves, gnomes, and peris of more northern climes would provide the supernatural element in other 1832-60 ballets like *La Péri* (1843), *Eoline* (1845), *Les Elfes* (1856). It established what might be called "the romantic plot" that featured one of these nonclassical sprites consumed by anger because a mere mortal has dared to compete with her for the affections of the man with whom she has fallen in love. This situation was the basis for the intrigue in *Giselle* (1841), *La Péri* (1843), *Ondine* (1843), and *Eoline* (1845). *La Sylphide* was enormously successful, therefore, and its star, Marie Taglioni, was the rage of Paris for days to come not only on account of her revolutionary white muslin skirt, her azure wings, and her unblocked satin slippers that set the pattern of the danseuse's dress for years to come, but also because her ethereal performance made it obvious that new horizons were in store for the ballet. And it is possible to gain a more precise idea of the extent of the growth of the ballet in 1832-60 by recalling that Filippo Taglioni, Jean Coralli, Mazilier, Jules Perrot, Paul Taglioni, and their fellow choreographers produced 40 ballets of various types at the Opéra in this interval. The most enduring of these compositions was *Giselle* of 28 June 1841; it starred Carlotta Grisi as Giselle and Lucien Petipa as Count Albrecht and became the earliest full-length ballet to remain in the repertory despite wars and subsequent changes in taste.

Yet there was a second category of romantic ballets that stood apart in subject matter and mood from the post-1830 works dependent for their interest upon gothic graveyards and the jealousy of an aroused elf, sprite, or Willi. This second group of compositions offered a more realistic view of life and dealt with people and their predicaments in this world. The action and setting did not have to be contemporary, however, since, like *Esméralda* (1836), they might transpire against the background of fifteenth-century Paris; *Paquerette* (1851) was set in France and Hungary during the war of the Palatinate with a brief dream scene serving only as an interlude in the last act to relieve the tone maintained previously by soldiers, peasants, servants, and seventeenth-century officers of the law. Equally free of naiads and gnomes were the works prompted by the success of Coralli's *Le Diable boiteux* (1836) set in Spain to exploit with plausibility as well as with profit the costumes and dances of Iberia. Coralli went on with his original formula for success by placing *La Tarantule* (1839) in Italy and *Ozaï* (1847) on an island in the South Seas. Albert Decombe's *La Jolie Fille de Gand* (1842) moved between Belgium and Venice; *Betty* (1846) unfolded in London.

The production of the grand operas of the romantic period included the staging of ballets too, of course, and the dancers of the corps de ballet were given an opportunity to display their new techniques and costumes in programs featuring vocalists. As early as 1838, Auber's *La Muette de Portici* was set in Naples during the time of the Spanish occupation and contained a guaracca, a bolero, and the popular tarantella that Liszt adapted for the piano. Rossini's *Guillaume Tell* at the Le Peletier theatre in 1829 offered a pas de six in the first act; the long scene in the third act provided the opportunity to execute a pas de trois, the dance of the soldiers, and the Tyrolean dance. Although Donizetti wrote scarcely any ballet music apart from his operas, he felt no reluctance about including passages for the dance in *Les Martyres* and *La Favorite* mounted in Paris in 1840. His subsequent *Dom Sébastien* (1843) incorporated a pas de trois and a pas de deux as well as a picturesque slave dance in its score. The ballet constituted an especially important part of Meyerbeer's lavish productions. The pas de deux in the second act of *Robert le Diable* was developed in six movements. The following act presents the ballet of the apostate nuns raised from their graves to tempt the protagonist, and the bacchanale of the temptation still ranks as one of the most arresting scenes in the nineteenth-century repertory. Liszt thought enough of the *Valse Infernale* in this same act to arrange it for the piano. *Les Huguenots* and *Le Prophète* rely on ballet even more extensively; *L'Africaine* featured an Indian march and ballet in its fourth act.

As the romantic ballet moved through these stages of development and accumulated its own repertory in the process, the importance of the prima ballerina increased, and the contribution of the male dancer to the performance became more passive, while the significance of his rôle diminished. This growing emphasis upon the female protagonist was accompanied in its turn by a greater tendency on the part of the stars to dance *sur les pointes*, on their toes. Shoes were blocked to facilitate this technique that stressed the new lightness that choreographers were creating for their ethereal characters and less earthbound danseuses, who were now leaping across the stage like Undine or even flying above it like the sylphid. The net result of these new directions being taken by choreographers and dancers alike was the emergence of a new group of performers whose names came to shine like stars in the annals of ballet: Marie Taglioni, who changed the course of ballet with her aerial rôle in *La Sylphide*; Fanny Elssler, a few years younger than Taglioni but equally acclaimed for her performance in *Le Diable boiteux*; Fanny Cerrito, who made her reputation in London, but who also took Paris by storm with her shadow dance in *Undine*; Carlotta Grisi, creator of the title-rôle in *Giselle ou les Willis*; Lucille Grahn, who joined with Taglioni and Cerrito to execute the famous *Pas des déesses* in *Le Jugement de Pâris* (1846) after earning the plaudits of London theatregoers for her success in *Le Pas de Quatre* (1845) with Grisi, Taglioni, and Cerrito.

The ballet continued to prosper during the next half century before the start of World War I, and the corps de ballet executed 50 new choreographic compositions during this time in addition to reviving old favorites. Although some librettists insisted upon qualifying their creations with adjectives like "fantastic," the two most popular forms of ballet remained the pantomime ballet and the straight ballet. The former genre had a dozen works to its credit; they were in one, two, and three acts with six of them in a single act, five of them in two acts, and only one in three acts. While the pantomime ballet tended to favor the brevity of a single act, the ten unqualified ballets in two acts demonstrated that this form was the most popular with writers, artistes, and spectators, and there were six ballets in three acts but only three others in one act. The fact that 30 of the pieces were in these two traditional categories reveals that no one seemed inclined now to experiment in the realm of form as long as it remained possible to continue in the new spirit of artistic freedom that the earlier romantics had bequeathed to the following generation.

Two outstanding choreographers active in the 1860-1914 period were already known to Paris theatregoers by virtue of their previous contributions to ballet repertory at the Opéra. Arthur Saint-Léon had the distinction of establishing the dance movements for *Les Papillons* (1861), the only piece for which Marie Taglioni helped to write the book and the first ballet for which Jacques Offenbach created the score. The next two titles that Saint-Léon had billed at the Opéra in the decade prior to the Franco-Prussian War were his *Diavolina* (1863) and *Néméa* (1864). His *La Source* (1866) attracted the public on account of Léo Delibes's score for it, and perhaps because it was so unabashedly in the earlier romantic vein with its forest and enchanted prince whose charms have captured the heart of the powerful and jealous fairy. Finally, when his famous *Coppélia* opened at the Opéra on 25 May 1870, only 55 days before the invasion, it proved to be his greatest triumph in his most prolific decade. The other established choreographer at this time was Lucien Petipa. He had made his Paris debut as a dancer in *La Sylphide* (1832), and he had done choreography for operas as well as for *Sacountala* (1858). It is not surprising, then, that his *Graziosa* (1861), as well as his *Namouna* (1882), suggest strongly the earlier works of the century: they are in the tradition of historical realism and romantic exoticism with their inn scenes, muleteers, fights, picadors, and slaves or aristocrats moving across the stage to the sound of Italian and Spanish music. A third choreographer with an established reputation whose works were posted at the Opéra in 1860-70 was Marius Petipa of Saint Petersburg. His *Le Marché des Innocents* was executed at the Le Peletier theatre on 29 May 1861, although his *Le Roi d'Yvetot* in one act was not performed at the Opéra until the gala of 28 December 1865. And another 17 years elapsed before *Namouna* (1882) was to have its Paris premiere. The famous *Le Lac des cygnes* had to wait until 1935-36 for its first showings at the Opéra-Comique and the Garnier theatre.

Louis Mérante was one of the better known choreographers having works staged at the Opéra immediately after the Franco-Prussian War. A dancer at the age of six and an understudy of Lucien Petipa as early as 1846, he wrote eight pieces for the corps de ballet before his death in 1887. He started his career as a choreographer with *Gretna Green* (1873) and was then fortunate enough to have Léo Delibes do the melodic and picturesque score for *Sylvia* (1876). After turning to a Spanish subject in his less successful *Le Fandango* (1877), Mérante looked to Japan and the Orient for the material in *Yedda* (1879) to profit by the recent surge of interest in Nipponese culture among Parisians. The dancers objected to the headdresses they had to wear in *Yedda*, and they complained about the Breton caps they would have to don for Mérante's next ultraromantic piece about sprites, *La Korrigane* (1880), but their misgivings about appearing like servants were of short duration because it was soon obvious to all concerned that *La Korrigane* was a hit. *La Farandole* (1883) offered a change of atmosphere with its Provençal inspiration, as did *Les Jumeaux de Bergame* (1886), first staged in the Paramé casino (1885); the choreographer's next and last hit was *Les Deux Pigeons* (1886), based upon La Fontaine's fable.

After Mérante's death, his place as *maître de ballet* was taken by J. Hansen, who proved as prolific and as eclectic as his predecessor with more than a half-dozen ballets and other assorted accomplishments to his credit. His Shakespeare-inspired *La Tempête* (1888) and *Le Rêve* (1890) were not sensations at the box office, but *La Maladetta* (1893), with its romantic fairy of the snows and gypsy chief, evoked applause until 1922, when Léo Staats provided it with new choreography. *L'Etoile* (1897) and especially *Bacchus* (1902) were not too enthusiastically received, however, and Hansen finished his tenure at the Opéra with *La Ronde des saisons* (1905) billed on only a score of dates before being dropped. Hansen had likewise compiled three anthology pieces that achieved varied effects by reason of setting the dances to the music of different composers. *Fête russe* (1893) was a *divertissement* using the work of a number of Russian writers; *Danses de jadis et de naguère* (1900) featured passages from Rameau, Berlioz, and nearly 30 other French musicians; *Danses grecques* (1901) used selections from a company of nineteenth-century composers.

Léo Staats did the choreography for *Javotte* (1889) and *España* (1911), but it was Yvan Clustine who accounted for most of the new ballets danced at the Opéra in the decade before the war: he was responsible for the dance element in *La Roussalka* (1911), *Les Bacchantes* (1912), *Suite de danses* (1913), *Philotis* (1914), and *Hansli le bossu* (1914). The first two of these pieces were not especially popular, but his *Suite de danses* to music by Chopin went on to enjoy its 300th billing by 15 December 1954. His last two efforts had almost no success because whatever impression they managed to make upon the public was eradicated almost immediately by the sudden invasion of France.

The operas themselves that continued to constitute the main fare at the Opéra were rich in *divertissements* and ballets, and it is interesting to note that ballets were "created" by separating these dance sections from their matrix and mounting them separately. The operas that provided this sort of orphan ballet included Mozart's *Don Juan* in 1899 (the *divertissement*); Gounod's *Faust* in 1905 (*La Nuit de Walpurgis*); Massenet's *Le Cid* in 1900, *Thaïs* in 1910 (the *divertissements*), *Manon* in 1911 (the minuet); Bizet's *L'Arlésienne* in 1909 (the farandole); Paladilhe's *Patrie!* in 1910 (the *divertissement*); and Saint-Saëns's *Samson et Dalila* in 1911 (the ballet). And it goes without saying that certain elaborate ballets were never separated from their parent work but were no less popular with the public. Ambroise Thomas's *Hamlet* had enjoyed over 300 performances by 1908, and it featured a rural ballet composed of eight numbers. Gounod's *Roméo et Juliette* offered a six-part ballet celebrating the wedding of the heroine and the count de Paris that was a unit by itself.

A number of superb dancers emerged from all this balletic activity, and Rosita Mauri, Carlotta Zambelli, and Rita Sangalli must be counted foremost among them by reason of their mastery of their art and their uninterrupted favor with the public. Yet if these danseuses made a lasting impression individually, they did not have the sudden impact imparted to the ballet in Paris by a newly formed troupe of traveling dancers known as the Ballets russes that visited France under the leadership of the young and wealthy Serge Diaghilev. Their first appearance was on 19 May 1909 at the Châtelet theatre in a suite of dances entitled *Le Festin* and in the *Danses polovtsiennes* from the opera *Le Prince Igor*. The Russians moved over to the Opéra on 19 June 1909 with the second tableau of *Boris Godounov*, *Les Sylphides*, and *Le Festin*. Choreography was by Michel Fokine. *Les Sylphides* was billed as a "romantic revery"; it was in a single act based upon three waltzes, two mazurkas, and a nocturne by Chopin. Mlles Karsavina and Nemtchinova starred opposite Léonide Massine. *Le Festin* was a suite of dances set to music by Rimsky-Korsakov, Glazounov, Glinka, and Tchaikovsky. Anna Pavlova and Nijinsky filled the leading rôles. Receipts amounted to 35,108 francs. The Ballets russes returned to the Opéra for their first extended appearance here in 1910, and they added six new compositions to the repertory of two works presented for the first time at the Opéra in 1909: *Shéhérazade, Carnaval, Danses polovtsiennes* from *Le Prince Igor, Les Orientales, Cléopâtre,* and *L'Oiseau de feu*. Their booking this year at the Garnier consisted of a dozen dates in June. They danced at the Opéra only on 24, 28, 31 December in 1911, but they brought two new titles with them: *L'Oiseau d'or* and *Le Spectre de la rose*. Mlle Karsavina appeared in the former *pas de deux* with Nijinsky; Idzikovsky filled the part of the spectre with Mlle Trefilova as the young girl in the latter tableau. The Ballets russes did not return to the Opéra after New Year's Day 1912 until 1914, when they mounted ten programs in May and June. The company was still led by Diaghilev and produced six compositions that had not yet been offered at Garnier's theatre: *La Légende de Joseph* and *Les Papillons* on 14 May, *Le Coq d'or* and *Pétrouchka* on 24 May, *Le Rossignol* on 26 May, and *Midas* on 2 June.

The Russians had brought a score of new works to the Opéra, but it was not the sheer quantity alone of their contribution that constituted their greatest influence. The importance of their presence in Paris arose rather from the fact that Diaghilev had artistic convictions as well as money, and his company based their entire approach to the ballet on the premise that no one aspect of a production was to be overemphasized or neglected. All elements of the presentation were to be stressed to the point where they stood in balance and in a single and unified representation on the stage. Thus, the artist's work on the set was as important in its way as the costumes, the music, or even the dance itself. Secondly, Diaghilev sought for a change of pace and theme within a program, and an evening of ballet was for him three shorter compositions each in a single act rather than one work in three acts. Unity and variety could be achieved simultaneously in this manner without overlooking any feature of a ballet and without resorting to crass sensationalism or extravagant effects. This attempt to equalize all the components of the ballet also contributed to the restoration of the male dancer to a position of importance with the prima ballerina. Inevitably, of course, the talents of performers like Massine and Nijinsky insured the success and permanence of this development in our time.

War, 1914–1918

The last program to be mounted at the Opéra in 1914 was the performance of *Les Huguenots* on 29 July; *Faust* was scheduled next but not produced on account of the general alarm and the total mobilization ordered by the government. The house remained dark for the remainder of the year and into 1915 until it became impossible for M. Jacques Rouché to control his compassion for the women artistes and other unemployed personnel of his company. On 16 February 1915, he arranged for the troupe to move to the Trocadéro for a concert. The bill opened with the orchestra playing the overture from *Le Roi d'Ys* and closed with *La Marseillaise* after a presentation of selections from a dozen works such as *Rigoletto* and *Thaïs*. The artistes returned to the Trocadéro on 11 March to give *L'Offrande à la liberté* (1792) and *Ma Mère l'Oye* (1912) with Gabriel Grovlez making his debut as leader of the orchestra. The Garnier palace itself had been dark since 28 July 1914, when the lights were turned on again to offer a benefit there on 9 December 1915 for the Belgian Red Cross. Eight bills were arranged for the last three weeks of the year, and one of them was executed by the Ballets russes.

The first eighteen months of the conflict therefore constituted an uneven and hesitant period for the Opéra, but the artistes seemed to recover their resilience when it became apparent in 1916 that Paris was not in immediate danger of siege or occupation. The theatre was closed in 1916 from 29 May until 3 November, but bills were posted during the other seven months of the year. A gala lasting from 2:00 to 7:00 P.M. was arranged for 5 February, moreover, and a surprisingly large number of new compositions was introduced into the repertory, although it is apparent in retrospect that these pieces were selected to provide variety and to enliven the company's offerings in time of war. Thus, while the operatic titles posted at the Opéra in 1916 included four compositions in three acts (*L'Ouragan*, *Les Amants de Rimini*, *Le Roi Arthus* and *Miguela*), two in four acts (*Les Girondins* and *Graziella*), and one in five acts (*Myrialde*), only a single act or one tableau from these compositions was produced. No new ballets were danced and *Le Cortège funèbre*, planned for 9 January, was suppressed at the last moment, probably because management failed to understand how this title might attract the public in a period of long and constant casualty lists. Four concerts were held on schedule during the first half of the year, however, and these programs favored such earlier composers as Cavalli, Lully, and Charpentier.

The international situation continued to shape events on the stage in 1917, and the theatre was again dark between 1 July and 23 November. A matinee was held on 10 January 1917 to benefit the sailors and soldiers of France, and a zeppelin alert at 6:45 P.M. the next day forced the artistes to omit the last tableau of *Guillaume Tell* so that the curtain might be rung down at 11:00 P.M. Employees of the Opéra were the beneficiaries of the premiere performance of Donizetti's *Maria di Rohan* on 22 March, and the Red Cross shared in the profits of 27 June and 24 November. The actors of the Comédie-Française gave a joint program with the artistes in April, and the troupe from La Scala sang *Aïda* on 13 June; Ida Rubinstein starred in the fourth act of Racine's *Phèdre* on 27 June. The new titles posted at the Opéra included Igor Stravinsky's *Les Abeilles* featuring Carlotta Zambelli, Maurice Ravel's *Adelaïde* starring Mme Trouhanova, and Raymond Roze's *Jeanne d'Arc*, which met with little success in Paris.

The last year of the struggle saw much the same pattern of events at the Opéra until the armistice on 11 November. The theatre was dark from 10 June until 2 November. German Gothas interrupted the programs on 17 February and 23 March, but the matinee of 1 April continued as planned despite a bombardment. A benefit was held on 10 February. When the Opéra opened its doors on 3 November, however, the orchestra refused to play *La Marseillaise*. A dispute arose between the chorus and the orchestra. The music not only for the national anthem but also for *Samson et Dalila* and *Coppélia* had to be furnished by a piano. César Franck's *Rébecca* was the only work accepted into the repertory this year. The sole visible trend in events at the Opéra from 1914 to 1918, therefore, lay in the hint of possible labor troubles to come and the growing popularity of ballet.

The Opéra, 1919–1939

When the armistice went into effect at 11:00 A.M. on 11 November 1918, the Opéra made its inevitable contribution to the general celebration: the

Allies' national anthems were sung in the peristyle of the theatre, and the leaders of the victorious countries attended performances at the Garnier as if to indicate by their presence that the season of the arts had returned to Europe with the establishment of peace. The king of Belgium heard *Aïda* on 5 December, Woodrow Wilson was present for the performances of *Monna Vanna* and *Patrie!* on 19 December.

This public rejoicing and the parade of international dignitaries to the Opéra continued into the early months of 1919, when management had the honor of greeting President Wilson and his wife, the prince of Serbia, the queen of Rumania, the queen of Spain, M. and Mme Poincaré, marshals Joffre, Foch, and Pétain, and General Pershing. By the autumn of 1919, however, the crest of public enthusiasm had passed, and trouble arose at the theatre, when a general strike was called by the unions, and a performance of *Thaïs* had to be canceled on 1 October. The problem was resolved finally, and programs were resumed on 8 October. Then, at the beginning of 1920, a second strike erupted on account of complaints voiced by the orchestra, chorus, and ballet; the theatre remained dark from 1 January until the production of *Thaïs* on 19 January 1920. A third work stoppage was approved by the employees in March 1920, moreover, and the government began to fear that friction between labor and management might become a chronic condition when the doors of the theatre had to be closed for a fourth time from 11 October to 3 December 1920. Mediation was possible, however, and it was not until 12 February 1934 that the Garnier was darkened again, but this interruption lasted for only 24 hours. There was no other major labor trouble before World War II because the difficult economic conditions prevailing during the thirties did not encourage job holders to act too independently, and the last labor dispute to erupt at the Opéra under the Third Republic was settled quickly on 7 December 1938.

A series of accidents also interrupted the normal course of programs at the Garnier. They were not all serious. A mishap with the machinery controlling the iron curtain took place on 6 March 1936, and it was not until 30 June that management suspended performances for a month to undertake repairs. The company took a vacation and reopened at the Sarah Bernhardt theatre on 1 August. Then, while the artistes were still at this temporary facility, the Opéra caught fire shortly after midnight on 13 September. The company could not remain at the Sarah Bernhardt, and their own theatre was unavailable now, so they moved to the Champs-Elysées theatre on 30 November 1936. They did not return to their own stage until 21 February 1937, when the extent of the renovations became quite evident to the public. The seats had been reupholstered, the paintings and walls had been cleaned, and a complete job of regilding the woodwork had been undertaken. The stage had been equipped with a three-dimensional screen to permit the projection of color in productions demanding it, and a new curtain weighing twenty tons had been installed for the sake of safety. The only other disruptive episode at the theatre before the war was an accident on the stage on 7 December 1938, but the routine schedule of events was resumed within 24 hours in this instance.

After World War I the administration of the Opéra was liberal and held more cosmopolitan views, and a number of innovations took place in managerial policy. It had been a normal occurrence for artistes from other troupes and independent performers to be invited to the Garnier from time to time, but the score of years after the armistice of 1918 saw an upsurge in the quantity of guest vocalists, instrumentalists, and conductors asked to play or to sing at the Opéra. Feodor Ivanovich Chaliapin gave two recitals in 1924, and Fritz Kreisler performed on violin on seven occasions between 1924 and 1927. Alfred Cortot played piano alone, with the violinist Jacques Thibaud, or as a member of the famous Cortot-Thibaud-Casals trio on seven dates in 1925-27. Jascha Heifetz was the most frequently billed violinist with ten guest appearances in 1925-32. Jacques Thibaud was asked to perform as a soloist in 1926 and with the new French citizen Bruno Walter on two other occasions, when they interpreted three Mozart sonatas. They appeared before the duke and duchess of Windsor on 10 November 1938 at a "soirée exceptionnelle"; they repeated the program on 11 May 1939. Vladimir Horowitz gave two piano recitals in 1926-28; Yves Nat, Dmitri Tiomkin, and Bronsilaw Hubermann made a single guest appearance apiece in 1926.

The receptions extended to these artistes encouraged management to increase programs by invitation in 1927-29. Erica Morini (violin), Artur Rubenstein (piano), Titta Ruffo (baritone), and Mischa Elman (violin) were billed in 1927, and Alexandre Brailowsky (piano), Leopold Godowsky (piano), and Frieda Hempel (soprano) were guest stars in 1928. Artistes asked to perform for the first time in 1929 included Yehudi Menuhin (violin) on two dates, Lotte Lehmann (soprano), and Emil Sauer (piano). The number of invitations extended to concert stars diminished with the deepening of the economic depression in Europe, but André Segovia brought his guitar to the Opéra in 1931, and Tito Schipa (tenor) performed as a soloist in 1931 and 1932. Lily Pons was an unusual case because her exceptional soprano voice provided an excellent vehicle for the rôle of the heroine in *Lucia di Lammermoor*, and she sang at the Opéra three times in 1935, six times in 1936, and twice in 1938. She abandoned the part of Lucia only once to do Gilda in *Rigoletto* on one of these dates. Marian Anderson (contralto) and Kirsten Flagstad (soprano) in 1938 were the last recitalists at the Opéra before the invasion of France.

Guest conductors, orchestras, and other groups to appear at the theatre included the Chorale Tchèque Smetana in 1926, the Gresham Singers in 1927, and the Royal Cambodian Ballet twice in 1931. Mme Ida Rubenstein and Serge Diaghilev were almost constant visitors with their troupes, and Argentina and Loïe Fuller were also seen at the theatre with more than usual frequency. The first guest conductor to appear at the Opéra after the war was Walter Damrosch, who directed the New York Symphony there in 1920. Serge Koussevitzky presided over no fewer than 29 "Concerts Koussevitzky" between 1921 and 1927, and Jan Kubelik was at the podium for six concerts in the opera house in 1924-28. The other orchestras billed at the Garnier after 1920 were the Strasbourg Philharmonic Orchestra once in 1926, the New York Philharmonic under Toscanini in 1930 and 1935, the Concertgebouw of Amsterdam twice in 1932 and once in 1938, and the Vienna Philharmonic Orchestra once in 1934 and twice in 1935. Sir Thomas Beecham accepted two invitations from the Opéra in 1928. The most frequently billed guest orchestra was the Berlin Philharmonic, which played at the Garnier on eight dates under Oskar Fried, and, after observing the 70th anniversary of Richard Strauss at the Opéra in 1934, this same organization returned for another four engagements under Furtwängler in 1937-38. Yet only three operatic companies came to the theatre in the period between the wars: the Royal Opera House of The Hague in 1926, the Vienna Opera Company in 1928, and the Communal Theatre of Florence in 1935. One popular music organization graced the stage of the Garnier when the Jack Hilton orchestra of London gave a concert on 17 February 1931.

An innovation in the presentation of programs was begun in 1921, when a matinee and an evening bill were scheduled for Sundays at the end of the year. In 1922 the policy of posting two performances for Sundays was extended through 14 May. These double programs continued until the end of the decade at the suggestion of the director of the Opéra, Jacques Rouché, and they were designed to keep the classics of the repertory alive by not allowing new works to replace them in production schedules.

Previous directors of the Opéra had already recognized the advantages of modern technology by installing electricity and telephones in the theatre, and they took a third step in the same direction at this time by mounting their first movie shows in 1924. *Le Miracle des loups* was shown on 13, 16, 20, 23, 27 November, but it soon became evident that not everybody welcomed this innovation as a development befitting the Opéra. Jean Marnold wrote a review of this film for the *Mercure de France* (vol. 177), for example, and in his notice he suggested that the large receipts from the film might be used to construct another opera house so that Charles Garnier's palatial edifice might remain a movie house. Yet whatever the objections to projecting films in the Paris opera house might have been, management scheduled another six movies before 1935: *Salammbô* for 25 and 29 October and 1 and 5 November 1925; *La Croisière noire* for 2, 4, 7, 9, and 14 March 1926; *Napoléon* on 7, 12, 14, and 16 April 1927; *Madame Récamier* on 12 June and *Verdun* on 8, 10, 11, 13, and 18 November 1928; *Jeanne d'Arc* on 18 April 1929; and *La Croisière jaune* on 18 March 1934.

A number of other events took place in this period that saw so many diverse programs offered at the Opéra. Fancy dress balls were held for the benefit of all sorts of causes and for victims of a variety of misfortunes.

Railroad employees were helped in 1923, and the French cooks' orphanage received money in 1922 and 1925. "Little White Beds" benefits were promoted frequently for hospitalized children, and even distant victims of famine in Russia were given help in 1922. On the less grim side of human affairs, anniversaries were observed with respect and enthusiasm, for example, the tercentenary of Molière's birth of 17 January 1922. Also, Rose Caron crowned Reyer's bust in the foyer of the theatre on 1 December 1923, and the 50th anniversary of the Garnier palace was celebrated on 6 January 1925. A Debussy festival was scheduled on 12 February 1929, and the first radio broadcast from the Opéra was engineered on 19 August 1932. The 2,000th performance of Gounod's *Faust* was hailed as a special accomplishment on 31 December 1934, although this representation of this perennial work was found to be its 1,809th billing at the Opéra after a more exact tally was made. The Saint-Saëns centenary of 14 October 1935 was followed by the unveiling of the Saint-Saëns memorial in the foyer of the theatre on 21 March 1938. A gala performance to honor George VI and Elizabeth of England was a highlight of 1938. Then, on 1 September 1939, total mobilization was announced by the government, and the doors of the Opéra remained closed until 16 November 1939. The company was billed into the Opéra-Comique 11 times in 1939, while the Garnier was plunged into darkness. The artistes had also performed at the Trocadéro on ten occasions between 1924 and 1934, and they had staged works in the ancient theatre of Orange during the summers of 1938 and 1939.

Yet the prime function of the opera house was to make possible the presentation of operas, and the importance of this activity inevitably outweighed all other individual and collective endeavors at the Garnier in 1919-39 as in all other periods. These lyric compositions were of two sorts because not all works billed at the Opéra during these two decades were produced in the French language. An examination of these works belonging to world repertory reveals that 20 operas by 14 composers using librettos in four languages were responsible for 69 non-French programs. As might be expected, the most frequently performed Italian author was Verdi, who overshadowed Donizetti and Rossini as well as Puccini at this time. German was the second most frequently heard language with 25 operas by four composers of whom the most popular was Wagner. Three of his works were given in their original form on 19 of the 25 German programs, and *Tristan und Isolde* was his most often produced composition by far with 14 representations. The remaining two languages sung at the Opéra in 1919-39 were Russian and Dutch. Mussorgsky's *Boris Godounoff* and Rimsky-Korsakov's *Sadko* were the two works offered in Russian. Only Willem Landré's *Beatrys* was done in Dutch at the Opéra, where it was mounted by the Royal Opera of The Hague on 19 February 1926.

The interchange of operas among the leading theatres of Germany, Italy, and France indicates clearly that these three areas were the sites of most European operatic activity after World War I. This situation is revealed again by the willingness of the Opéra under Jacques Rouché's continuing direction to prepare French translations of the more important works created in other tongues. In 1919-39 five Italian, three Russian, and two German librettos were turned into French for Paris production. Edouard Duprez, Jean Chantavoine, Paul Spaak, and Paul Ferrier were among the bilingual writers to perform this task.

A statistical view of the world premieres of the remaining 47 titles billed at the Opéra for the first time in 1919-39 discloses similarly that not every work given at the Garnier in this interval had its world premiere at the Paris opera house, if it was in this category of nonalien compositions. In fact, only 28 of the 47 works in question enjoyed their world premieres there. Management did not have the opportunity to perform all the remaining 19 operas for the first time, of course, but they had refused to produce some of them originally, and the authors of others had been too discouraged to submit them to the Opéra jury for consideration. Also, producton schedules might have been already filled when the composers were ready to release their manuscripts for possible staging. Yet whatever might have been the reasons for these works having had their world premieres at other theatres, it is a fact that, like *Carmen*, seven of them were taken to the Opéra-Comique for their first performance; *Esclarmonde*, recently revived in New York, and Ravel's *L'Heure espagnole* were among them. Léo Sachs's *Les Burgraves* was produced initially at the Champs-Elysées theatre. Bordeaux, Angers, and Nice had heard three compositions before they were brought to the French capital, and the same situation was true of London, Brussels, and New York. Monte Carlo gave three works their world premieres before they reached the stage of the Garnier theatre: Saint-Saëns's *Hélène* (1919), which had also been billed at the Opéra-Comique with Mary Garden in 1905; *L'Aiglon* (1937) by Honegger and Ibert; and Ravel's *L'Enfant et les sortilèges* (1939), which had also been mounted at the Opéra-Comique (1926). One of the great scandals of the nineteenth century at the Opéra had been the indifference shown to Berlioz and his work, an attitude that led to *Les Troyens* being given in its entirety at Karlsruhe on 6 February 1890, 41 years before it was mounted at the Paris opera house on 10 June 1921.

As an art, however, French musical drama turned largely to experimentation after the close of the war despite a concomitant reluctance to abjure tradition. Thus, while some conservative composers remained content with established forms like the lyric tragedy, the more adventuresome authors created their own types of composition in an effort to find what they considered to be a maximum musical effect. The extent of this 1918-39 preoccupation with experimentation in form may be measured by the fact that only 15 out of 59 compositions of the period were billed simply as lyric dramas or operas, while four were designated as lyric tragedies or tragedies. The other works were announced as belonging to new genres or to subgenres invented by their creators. These latter types included a "romanesque drama" conjured up to describe Massenet's *Esclarmonde* and the "lyric piece" coined to indicate the nature of Canteloube de Malaret's *Le Mas*. "Lyric legend" was applied to *La Vision de Mona* by Louis Dumas and to Jean Poueigh's *Perkain*. Paul Dukas's *Ariane et Barbe-Bleue* was simply a "tale"; Albert Roussel's *La Naissance de la lyre* was an "ancient tale." One of the most puzzling terms was "miracle-fabliau" minted for Jules Mazellier's *Les Matines d'Amour*. These sometimes improbable classifications applied to these works indicated in their fashion the continuing influence of Debussy's impressionism in the twentieth century. The very purpose of such compositions as his *Pelléas et Mélisande* was to assert that the musical or poetic truth or beauty had no precise lines of demarcation to confine its meaning or to limit its charm to one genre.

The composers themselves were mostly of an experimental bent, therefore, and they preferred to remain with the shorter but hopefully more sustained compositions. Berlioz's *Les Troyens* of 1921, Max d'Ollone's *L'Arlequin* of 1924, Henri Rabaud's *Mârouf* of 1928, and *L'Aiglon* of 1937 by Arthur Honegger and Jacques Ibert were in five acts, but they were exceptions to the general tendency. No fewer than 14 new French lyric compositions were in only one or two acts. Another 16 works were in three acts. As for the frequency with which the composers contributed to the Opéra, the brevity of their offerings to the Garnier did not serve to augment the number of titles they had billed there. Only Massenet had four compositions mounted at the Paris opera house in 1919-39: *Esclarmonde*, *Grisélidis*, *Hérodïade*, and *La Navarraise*. All four of these works had been completed before World War I, and it was their effectiveness as opera rather than Massenet's productivity that explains all four of them still being in repertory after 1919. Max d'Olonne saw three of his works in production, but one of them had already been staged in 1913: *L'Arlequin*, *Le Retour*, and *La Samaritaine*. Canteloube de Malaret, Antoine Mariotte, Henri Rabaud, Maurice Ravel, and Albert Roussel each had two scores played at the theatre. Jacques Ibert collaborated on *L'Aiglon* but had no assistance with *Persée et Andromède*. The remaining composers of the period had but a single composition produced at the Opéra. Finally, it is curious to note that the traditional categories of subjects continued to attract the librettists, the artistes, and the public, despite the inclination towards experimentation: early French history (*Vercingétorix*, *Esclarmonde*, *La Fille de Roland*), French romantic literature (*La Chartreuse de Parme*, *Les Burgraves*), classical mythology (*Persée et Andromède*), Shakespeare (*Le Marchand de Venise*, *La Mégère apprivoisée*), Spanish themes (*L'Heure espagnole*), the Bible (*Esther*), and the mysterious and violent East (*Mârouf*). Wagner satisfied the demand for Germanic themes and mythos.

The Opéra-Comique, 1919-1939

The Opéra-Comique resumed its functions after the war not only by casting about for new compositions but also by turning to the production of the better-known titles of the pre-1918 repertory. The management of the theatre, led by Emile Isola, Vincent Isola, and Albert Carré, was rightly convinced that certain proven favorites would return a profit to the box office because the public would support them and because the sets and costumes necessary for their production already existed. They selected for staging three compositions that reached their 1,500th performance at the Opéra-Comique before Louis Masson and Georges Ricou replaced them as directors in 1925. These works were Bizet's *Carmen*, billed for the 1,700th time in 1923; Ambroise Thomas's *Mignon*, which had its 1,500th staging in 1919; and Adolphe Adam's *Le Châlet*, given its 1,500th billing during 1922. Two other compositions might be added to this first group of favorites at the Opéra-Comique on account of the impressiveness of their success: Victor Massé's *Les Noces de Jeannette*, mounted for the 1,200th time in 1921; and *Manon*, that enjoyed its 997th production at the theatre in 1919. Later, in 1925-29, Louis Masson saw no reason for changing this satisfactory policy, and he promoted another four compositions that reached their 500th billing at the Opéra-Comique during his tenure of office. Similarly, seven additional compositions enjoyed their 500th performance at the theatre in 1919-29, when they were brought back to the stage on account of outstanding box-office records in previous years: Massenet's *Werther* (1919), Charles Gounod's *Mireille* (1920), Gustave Charpentier's *Louise* (1921), Puccini's *La Vie de Bohème* (1926) and *La Tosca* (1926), Jacques Offenbach's *Les Contes d'Hoffman* (1927), Puccini's *Madame Butterfly* (1929). One of the most popular of *opéras-comiques* produced during the first decade after the war was the almost perennial *La Dame blanche* by Boïeldieu, which had had its initial performance at the Feydeau opera house on 30 December 1825: it was offered for the 1,669th time on 7 January 1926. Léo Delibes's *Lakmé* had had its premiere on 14 April 1883, and it was brought back to the stage of the Opéra-Comique for its 1,000th billing there on 13 May 1931.

Other older pieces continuing to attract the public in the decade after the war included a cluster of well-known works billed on fewer than 500 occasions at the Opéra-Comique during the course of their history, but they nevertheless left an appreciable imprint upon the contemporary scene with their new costumes, innovative productions, or fresh casts. These compositions included works as familiar as Rossini's *Le Barbier de Séville*, created in Paris at the Odéon on 6 May 1824 and first mounted at the Opéra-Comique on 8 November 1884: it was given its 379th performance on 16 February 1924. Ferdinando Paër's *Le Maître de Chapelle* was on 487 programs between 29 March 1821 at the Feydeau and 13 January 1933 at the Opéra-Comique.

The better-known works that survived for fewer than two hundred productions were more numerous and sometimes equally as well known as the more frequently mounted compositions at the Opéra-Comique. The well-known titles in this group deemed worthy of the large financial investment necessary to guarantee success included such familiar titles as Gluck's

Orphée, Mozart's *Les Noces de Figaro* and *Don Juan*, and Pietro Mascagni's *Cavalleria rusticana*. Massenet's *La Navarraise* (1895), *Sapho* (1897), and *Le Jongleur de Notre-Dame* (1904) were likewise refurbished for revival in this era of satisfying returns at the box office. Camille Erlanger's *Aphrodite* (1906) and Henri Maréchal's *Les Amoureux de Cathérine* (1876) were revived to lend an apparently romantic or exotic note to the repertory along with Henri Rabaud's *Mârouf* (1914) and Claude Debussy's *Pelléas et Mélisande* (1902).

Thus, the decade between the end of the war and the start of the economic depression of the thirties did not witness the creation of a large number of different types of compositions despite the tendency to experiment in the arts that characterized this age of cubism, dadaism, vorticism, and surrealism in painting, poetry, and photography. Librettists were relatively numerous, but they followed the classico-official tenet that the *opéra-comique* as a genre must use spoken dialogue to foster and to support the lyric element. Also, if they respected this basic principle of the *opéra-comique*, the writers felt free to offer their compositions to the Opéra-Comique because they felt that any other type of stage presentation would be performed more properly at some other public or private theatre. Although an occasional author took the liberty to allude to his work as a lyric legend (*Béatrice*, 1917), a musical novel (*La Brébis égarée*, 1923), a lyric fantasy (*L'Enfant et les sortilèges*, 1926), a musical tableau (*Fra Angelico*, 1924), or a musical legend (*Le Poirier de misère*, 1927), the majority of the writers qualified their contributions to the stage of the Opéra-Comique as *opéras-comiques*.

What is more significant here is the fact that the reliable hits of pre-1914 vintage constituted only a relatively small portion of the 1919-29 repertory, which contained no fewer than 51 new titles. The peak period for the billings of these new compositions at the theatre was 1922-24, when 19 compositions were added to the repertory, and 1923 was the only calendar year to see as many as eight works accepted for production by the company at the Opéra-Comique in the 1918-28 interval. These 51 additions to the repertory were provided by 44 composers. None of these composers had three titles posted at the theatre during the period in question, but seven of them had two works apiece performed there within this decade: Alfred Bachelet (1864-1919), Alfred Bruneau (1857-1934), Gabriel Fauré (1845-1924), George Adolphe Hüe (1858-1948), Charles Lévadé (1869-1948), and Darius Milhaud (1892-1974). Jacques Offenbach (1819-80) should be counted in this group because his *Le Mariage aux lanternes* of 1857 was mounted at the Opéra-Comique for the first time in 1919, and his *Les Bavards* of 1863 was done initially in this same theatre in 1924.

Yet 30 of these 51 new works had their world premieres at the Opéra-Comique, and four of them had been given for the first time in Paris but on another stage: one of the latter group had been produced privately before it was offered to the public; two had been mounted at the Théâtre des Bouffes-Parisiens; Alfred Bachelet's *Scémo* had been billed at the Opéra on 6 May 1914. Two others had been created in Lyon and Rouen, while three of them had been heard initially outside France in Munich and Baden-Baden. Mozart's *Così fan tutte* was one of the new operas at the Opéra-Comique after World War I, but, of course, it had been performed for the first time as early as 26 January 1790 in Vienna and under the direction of Mozart himself long before it was brought to the Opéra-Comique on 26 June 1920. Smetana's *La Fiancée vendue* had had its world premiere in Prague on 30 May 1866 in two acts before its version in three acts was done at the Opéra-Comique in 1928. Also, it may come as a surprise to learn that three cities in the United States offered three works before they were picked up by the Opéra-Comique: Boston (*La Forêt bleue* by Louis Aubert, 1911), New York (*Gianni Schicchi* by Giacomo Puccini, 1918), and Chicago (*Gismonda* by Henry Février, 1919). Brussels could boast of the addition of two works to the repertory (*La Fille de Madame Angot* by Charles Lecoq, 1872; and *Résurrection* by Franco Alfano, 1906), while Barcelona had produced *Pepita Jimenez* (1896) before this work by Isaac Albeñiz made its way to Paris in 1923 in a French version by J. de Marliane. Monte Carlo was the most prolific supplier of texts by reason of the four titles its opera house provided for the Paris theatre at this time. As for the relative popularity of all these productions that had their premieres at the Opéra-Comique before 1930, they accounted for approximately 1,200 performances during this decade, although there were 16 of them given on fewer than ten occasions, and only one of them was produced on more than 100 dates, Fauré's *Masques et Bergamasques* (1920). The second and third most profitable pieces at the box office were Marcel Samuel-Rousseau's *Le bon roi Dagobert* (1927) and Fauré's *Pénélope* (1919), which were given on 72 and 63 programs respectively.

The Opéra-Comique was hurt financially by the economic crisis of 1930-36, of course, and the theatre felt pressure from two theatrical sources throughout 1930-40, although the extent of the influence of these two competitive forces was not recognized immediately. As a "live" theatre, the Opéra-Comique suffered from the growth of the cinema because a private citizen caught in the grips of the growing depression could still afford to rent a seat for two or three hours in a movie house, but he could not spend five or even six times that amount to occupy a place at the Opéra-Comique, where a single audience gathered for a solitary performance provided the receipts for the entire day. On the other hand, a movie house could run one film six times for six audiences and therefore charge one-sixth as much for admission as a legitimate theatre. This simple mathematical fact gave the movies an appreciable advantage in the struggle for spectators. In the second place, there was a proliferation of theatres in the provinces after World War I, and they specialized in films and in the production of *opéras-*

comiques by hiring one star for box office appeal and filling the remaining rôles with whatever talent was available locally. The large opera houses of Bordeaux, Lyon, and Marseille were not involved in this amateurish sort of undertaking, but there were enough stages in smaller cities and towns to give the *opéra-comique* as a theatrical genre the reputation of being a sort of poor cousin to the lyric tragedy and opera. When the genre endured this sort of degradation throughout the country, therefore, it was inevitable for the theatre known as the Opéra-Comique to suffer a decline in prestige in Paris, where Cocteau's latest film gradually became more important than the most recent production of *Les Pêcheurs de perles*. *Pelléas et Mélisande* was billed on 98 dates at the Opéra-Comique in Paris between 9 May 1919 and 30 January 1930, but it was billed on only 30 programs between 29 September 1933 and 12 September 1940. Yet the Opéra-Comique did not receive its truly fatal blow until the beginning of 1940, when the amalgamation of the national lyric theatres of France began to have an effect. A single administration was placed in charge of the Opéra and of the Opéra-Comique, and the latter theatre began to assume slowly but surely the appearance of a branch of the main office.

Still, the venom acted slowly, and the company was able to add 43 titles to its repertory in 1930-40, although only 23 of them were created at the theatre. But it was becoming apparent that management was not only losing its major performers to the world circuit, but the administrators were finding themselves obliged to borrow from the repertories of the Gaîté-Lyrique, the Théâtre des Variétés, the Trianon Lyrique, and the Théâtre-Lyrique du Vaudeville for material to use with the old favorites from Italy, Germany, and Austria. They gave for the first time in Paris compositions that had been created in Nice, Monte Carlo, Rome, Milan, Venice, Vienna, and Saint-Petersburg months or even years before. There was this hard core of 23 compositions created at the theatre, but these 23 new texts were contributed by as many composers who never appeared tempted to make a second effort to submit a text to the Opéra-Comique. As for the 23 works themselves, it is significant that 13 of them never had more than ten billings at the theatre, while seven of the remaining ten titles never reached their 20th performance. The three remaining works were the most valuable compositions in this group from a financial point of view, therefore, and they were Raoul Lappara's *Le Joueur de viole* with 36 billings, Franz Lehar's *Frasquita* with 51 stagings, and Omer Letorey's *Le Sicilien* with 82 performances. The less successful titles included such compositions as Roger Ducasse's *Cantegril*, Emmanuel Bondeville's *L'Ecole des maris*, and Daniel Lazarus's *La Chambre bleue*.

This lack of suitable creativity and leadership seemed simultaneously a cause and a symptom of the decline of the Opéra-Comique after the completion of M. Albert Carré's 25 years of service to this theatre. His successors were unable to sustain the pace and the tone that he had set during his tenure of office, and no measures were instituted to counteract the growing popularity of the movies and the lack of an exciting new repertory. Rabaud's *Mârouf* and Fauré's *Pénélope* especially stood out as examples of forceful production, but, as the saying goes, a few swallows do not a summer make. Also, the former work was billed on 78 dates between 1919 and 1928, but it was then shifted to the Opéra on 22 June 1928; the latter composition had been brought to the theatre on 20 January 1919 by M. Carré, but it too was transferred to the Opéra on 14 March 1943. This situation would have been discouraging enough by itself, but the problem of an inadequate repertory was compounded by falling receipts and insufficient subsidies from the government. Finally, let it be repeated, the death blow was delivered with the decision to form the Réunion des Théâtres Nationaux so that the administration of the Opéra could direct the affairs of the Opéra-Comique.

The Opéra, 1940–1950

A restless and disturbed mood was evident in the French capital in 1939 on account of the threat to peace posed by a belligerent Germany, but events at the Opéra followed a more or less normal pattern this year until a governmental order for total mobilization was issued on 1 September and war was declared on 3 September. The changes wrought by the outbreak of hostilities were not of the most drastic sort, however, and, as journalists had predicted, Paris organized a musical season at the Garnier and other theatres even while young electricians and tenors were being called into military service.

The artistes did not give any performances at the Opéra between 21 September and 16 November 1939, but, if this theatre was dark, the Opéra-Comique was alive with activity and accommodating the troupe from the Opéra as well as its own company. Performances were usually but not always scheduled for Saturdays and Sundays, and the curtain rose at 6:00 P.M. and fell no later than 9:00 P.M. to allow spectators to observe the curfew. The Opéra-Comique was selected over the Opéra as a wartime theatre because it presented a less conspicuous target for enemy missiles, and it provided room for more people in the bomb shelters of the area. The house was packed whenever a program was announced, and no one complained about Carmen's performance when Europe was about to go up in flames. The artistes from the Opéra performed at the Opéra-Comique on 21 and 28 September; 5, 12, 14, 21, and 28 October; and 1, 4, 9, and 11 November. They sang *Faust, La Damnation de Faust, Thaïs, Rigoletto,* and *Samson et Dalila* in representations that were broadcast as well as offered to a live audience. The staging of *Roméo et Juliette* on 9 November was the 500th performance of this work by the Opéra.

It was decided finally that no good purpose was being served by keeping the Garnier closed, and the troupe returned to their own theatre on 16

November to celebrate the start of their wartime schedule with Albert Roussel's *Le Festin de l'araignée*, the second act of *Alceste*, and Ravel's *Daphnis et Chloé*. The administration decided to give Sunday matinees for the remainder of the year. Jacques Rouché continued to function as general administrator with Philippe Gaubert as director.

If management and personnel might have hoped that they would escape the more terrible effects of the war in the coming months, they spared no effort to join in the war effort. The troupe was called upon to promote a concert for the benefit of the "Franco-Polish Wings," which was given on 12 January 1940 to provide support for the pilots put into the air by these two countries. The Finnish victims of the struggle in the north were the beneficiaries of the program on 8 February featuring music by Sibelius. The evening of music on 16 March was arranged to assist needy French and British soldiers. Yet it was not until the bombardment of Paris on 3 June 1940 that the full significance and impact of the war became evident. Then, on 10 June the Germans entered Paris. The city fathers placed the Garnier theatre in the custody of the ballet master Serge Lifar because he was a Russian, and the nonaggression pact was still in force between Germany and Russia. The Opéra had already been evacuated and closed earlier in the day. Nothing happened at the Garnier until 23 June, when the janitor-caretaker is supposed to have heard a knock on the door. He went running to tell Lifar that they had a visitor. It was 6:00 A.M.; the visitor was Hitler. A week later, on 1 July, another knock was heard at the door. This time, it was Goebbels and his staff who were ushered into the library by Lifar. Nothing resulted from these visits, which appear in retrospect to have been purely touristic, if not mythical, although Goebbels's interest suggests that some propaganda coup might have been in the offing. The theatre reopened on 24 August 1940 with the staging of *La Damnation de Faust*, and a regular schedule of performances was established for three or four days of the week with emphasis on such compositions as *Rigoletto*, *Samson et Dalila*, and *Le Vaisseau fantôme*.

The influence of the Occupation upon the Opéra became more manifest in 1941 because an even greater emphasis was placed upon Wagnerian programs in particular and German oriented works in general this year. *Die Walküre* had been available in a French version since 1887, but the revival of this work on 11 March 1941 was undertaken in German in a production by the Manheim Opera under the direction of Friedrich Brandenburg with Fraulein Zwingenberg as Brunnhilde and Herr Schmitt as Guerhilde. Four days later *Tristan und Isolde* was presented in German in a collaboration by the Staatsoper Berlin and the Festspielhaus Bayreuth under the direction of Herbert van Karajan. The Deutsches Opernhaus of Berlin gave *Die Fledermaus* on five dates in September under the auspices of the Occupation authorities, and these performances were reserved exclusively for the military and civil personnel stationed in Paris. The other direct influence of the politico-military situation became apparent in the organization of programs for the benefit of victims of the war, especially for the families of prisoners of war.

The Germanic aspect of 1941 activities at the Opéra continued into 1942-43 with the importation of Bertil Wetzelberger to lead the Munich orchestra at the Paris premiere of Hans Pfitzner's *Palestrina* (1942), a German production of *Der fliegende Holländer* (1942), a Berlin Philharmonic concert led by Hans Knappertsbusch (1943), Rudolph Krasselt leading the Hanover Opera orchestra at the 50th anniversary celebration of *Die Walküre*, and the observance of the 150th anniversary of Wagner's birthday (1943). Finally, on 23 July 1944, the Opéra had to close its doors on account of a lack of electric power, and no programs were mounted from this date until 23 October 1944. Paris had been liberated on 24 August 1944.

The Opéra passed through a difficult period between 1 September 1939 and 31 December 1944, but the company found time nevertheless to add 14 new pieces to the repertory, despite shortages in every category of necessary supplies from paint to food. Marcel Samuel-Rousseau's brief choreographic piece entitled *Entre deux rondes* and Darius Milhaud's *Médée* were billed in 1940, and no fewer than four new compositions were mounted in 1941; the ballets *La Princesse au jardin*, *Le Chevalier et la demoiselle*, and *Jeux d'enfants* were introduced during 1941, but only one opera was given, *Le Roi d'Ys*, which had had its world premiere at the Opéra-Comique on 7 May 1888 in a Charles Ponchard production. *Joan de Zarissa* of 10 July 1942 and *Les Animaux modèles* of 8 August 1942 with choreography by Lifar were both ballets, but *Le Drac* was offered as an *opéra féerique* in three acts on 29 June 1942. *Le Jour* by Maurice Jaubert and *Suite en blanc* by Edouard Lalo were the new ballets of 1943, when André Coeuroy's French version of Werner Egk's *Peer Gynt* was also brought to the Garnier palace. The sole new composition of 1944 was André Jolivet's *Guignol et Pandore*, for which Lifar did the choreography. It is interesting to see that the subject matter of these wartime ballets is drawn generously from the areas where the imagination is the dominant creative force and interest: chivalrous love, fairy tales, the antics of animals and children, and Punch and Judy. It is likewise significant that the majority of these new compositions are ballets, a theatrical form that can be staged with economy.

These works were produced only by virtue of great ingenuity and sacrifice on the part of the workers and artistes, therefore, and the public supported this effort with a willing spirit. Even wealthier opera-goers had been reduced to shoes with wooden soles that beat a rough tattoo on marble stairs; few evening clothes were without patches by 1943, and there were only two modes of transportation available for making the trip to the Opéra or any other theatre: a bicycle-powered sort of rickshaw or walking. Once at the theatre, the spectators had to endure interruptions by German, American, or British bombers. Then, on the way back home, there were the "string beans" hanging around almost every corner in their green uniforms and enforcing the curfew. Of course, a ticket had to be obtained first of all, and the Germans usually accounted for at least half of them, while most of the others were bought up by poor speculators willing to sit in line all morning and afternoon to make a few *francs* on the black market. If a melomaniac were fortunate enough, however, he might save himself from all this fuss and intrigue by persuading the man in the box office to part with a ticket or a scarce libretto for a bit of bacon or a few eggs.

Many distasteful but unavoidable compromises had to be accepted by the vanquished in 1939-44 lest the theatre be suppressed or perhaps destroyed. The authorities in charge of the Opéra had to assume this unpleasant responsibility with the knowledge that there would always be overly zealous accusers ready to charge them later with collaboration with the enemy or moral treason despite the fact that they had nothing personal to gain by assuming the responsibility of making these compromises. Almost inevitably, charges of collaboration were filed against M. Jacques Rouché and M. Serge Lifar by a committee formed to ferret out war guilt in the organization directing affairs at the Opéra. In a savage stroke of irony, the two men who had done most to preserve and to protect the theatre were charged with betraying it. M. Rouché had become director of the Garnier theatre at the start of World War I, and he had done everything possible to keep his facility intact and his staff employed during both conflicts. M. Lifar had made the Opéra his home during the Occupation at the request of the city of Paris, and he had taken every precaution to protect it until the German withdrawal from the capital. M. Rouché along with his musical director Marcel Samuel-Rousseau were acquitted of the charge of collaboration by the Paris Civic Court. Yet the newly established government of the Fourth Republic was obviously displeased with the conduct of affairs at the Opéra during the Nazi occupation of Paris, and this official disapproval was quite apparent in two government decrees issued in the first half of 1945. On 21 February, M. Rouché was relieved of his duties as director of the Opéra, and M. Gadave became the temporary administrator. Then, on 28 June, it was ordered that permanent officials be installed: Maurice Lehmann was named administrator of the Réunion des Théâtres Lyriques Nationaux, and Reynaldo Hahn was appointed director of the Opéra-Comique. Serge Lifar did not appear to defend himself in the 1945 trial in the Paris Civic Court, and he was condemned to expulsion from France in this first verdict. He was later cleared of the charges lodged against him, and he returned to his successful career at the Opéra as ballet master and choreographer.

Yet the demands of labor provided more problems at the Opéra after 1944 than had been caused by managerial difficulties. The first inkling of the trouble to come was furnished as early as 23 May 1945 with a strike that was settled immediately. The year 1946 was more unsettled and began with a strike on 9 January by the musicians, who refused to play for the scheduled performance of *Faust* on 11 January in addition to remaining idle on 9 January. The company settled back into routine, but the situation was not stable, and the strike broke out again on 20 April and lasted until 3 May. In the meantime, M. Lehmann had resigned on 20 April. The stage-hands refused to work on 24 September, 1 and 24 October 1948 and on 13 November 1948, but the sequence of programs was not disturbed until 1949, when the musicians defied management again and called a general strike. There seems to have been a period of deliberation or hesitation on 26 and 27 November, when performances were restored after a cancellation of *Die Meistersinger von Nürnberg* on 25 November, but the theatre was closed on 28 November and remained dark until 10 January 1950. Although 32 programs had been suppressed by this 1949-50 work stoppage, the end of labor troubles at the Opéra was not yet in sight: stagehands and electricians of all five national theatres walked off the job on 3 March 1950, and this new strike continued until 4 April, when it was decided to meet the workers' demands for higher pay by increasing ticket prices by 35 percent. The 14 programs announced for the 3 to 20 March interval had to be canceled. Still, the opera house had not yet seen the last disruptive episode of the year: a fire broke out in the theatre at 40 minutes past midnight of 24-25 December. Some of the loges and balcony seats were damaged, and programs had to be discontinued. The period of suspension lasted from 25 to 30 December on this occasion, and the doors of the theatre were opened for a production of *Faust* on New Year's Eve.

The end of World War II in Europe inspired a number of galas and celebrations for and by musical figures or organizations and personalities that had contributed to the victory. A special night for the Allies was scheduled for 14 April, but it had to be postponed until 21 April on account of the period of national mourning declared in observance of President Roosevelt's death. *Pénélope* was staged for the Gabriel Fauré centenary on 14 May, and general de Gaulle and the sultan of Morocco presided over an evening in honor of the Resistance on 18 June. The French aviators of World War II were saluted at a special party for the Normandie-Niemen squadron on 28 June. The Resistance was honored again on 18 June 1946, when Lily Pons and Reynaldo Hahn headed a program saluting general Leclerc that had already been given for the benefit of his division on 13 April. Politics intruded on 11 May with an evening in honor of the delegates to the conference of Ministers of Foreign Affairs in Paris. The delegates to UNESCO were honored on 9 December. Then, on 23 January 1947, president de Gaulle returned to the theatre on an unofficial visit to attend a gala for the aviators of France, while "a night of fire" was scheduled for the firemen of Paris on 22 May 1947. Still another evening celebrating the Resistance was arranged for 10 December 1948, and Serge Lifar came back to the stage of the Opéra on 2 February 1949 to dance *Prélude à l'après-midi d'un faune*. The Congress of Esperantists had the 3 August 1949 performance of *Rigoletto* reserved for their group, although Verdi's work was sung in Italian on this occasion. In the autumn, a salute to Serge Diaghilev took place on 5 October. The death of Vaslav Nijinsky in London on 9 April 1950 moved Serge Lifar to dance again in *Prélude à l'après-midi d'un faune* on 12 April as a tribute to his deceased colleague. A second act of homage was paid to the dancer in the library of the Opéra on 13 April with A. Haskell, P. Michaut, L. Vaillat, and S. Lifar in attendance. On 21 June a memorial performance was dedicated to Nijinsky and Auguste Vestris. An exhibition commemorating their achievements was arranged on this occasion, and the orchestra opened the program in the theatre by playing *Le Spectre de la rose*.

Visiting artists as well as visiting dignitaries graced the opera house with their presence in 1945-50, and Lily Pons and Grace Moore were among the first performers to appear on its stage, although they attended galas and concertized instead of singing entire rôles in 1945 productions. The first artiste to give a "full" performance after the liberation of Paris was in fact an instrumentalist rather than a vocalist, Yehudi Menuhin, who played with the Conservatory orchestra under the direction of Charles Munch. The other guest orchestra to play in concert at the theatre was the American jazz band organized by the late Glenn Miller and billed into the Garnier theatre on 18 February 1945 under the leadership of Ray McKinley and Jerry Gray, Miller's arranger. The house vocalist, Joseph Luccioni, had the honor of singing *La Marseillaise* at the Opéra on 14 July 1945.

After the Opéra and the country had became better organized and things had returned to a more normal basis, the pattern of performing artistes at the Opéra became more regular and reminiscent of prewar practices, a condition that was ratified by management's decision to restore the rules relating to formal dress at the theatre in 1946. Marjorie Lawrence returned to sing Amnéris in 1946, and the company from La Scala presented *Rigoletto* in Italian on 30 May and 1 June 1947. Lily Pons and Libero de Luca filled the leading rôles in *Lucia di Lammermoor* on 28 May 1948, and the Covent Garden Opera gave an "hors repertoire" performance in English of *Peter Grimes* on 11, 12 June of the same year. Three weeks later, on 23 and 26 June, Kirsten Flagstad and Max Lorenz did *Tristan und Isolde*. The cycle was now complete again: French audiences were hearing English, German, and Italian repertory, but, unfortunately, the artistes themselves were not French. This perpetual coming and going at the Garnier was not long in evoking the criticism that management was allowing the Garnier to become a stopover where foreign vocalists could replenish their funds between more important engagements. In the meantime, the Vienna Philharmonic Orchestra performed under the direction of Furtwängler on 8 and 9 October 1949, the same year that H. Konetzni did La Maréchale and E. List filled the rôle of the baron Ochs of *Der Rosenkavalier* in German on 30 May. Furtwängler returned to the Opéra in 1950 to give concerts with the Berlin Philharmonic Orchestra on 3, 4 June.

Management followed the prewar policy of offering films from time to time in 1945-50, when they presented *Autant en emporte le vent* (26 May 1945), *Le Combattant* (24 July 1945), *La Bataille de l'eau lourde* (12 February 1948), *Jeanne d'Arc* (13 October 1949), *Stromboli* (12 October 1950), and *Agent X23* (23 October 1950).

The Opéra-Comique, 1940–1950

The war had an impact on the Opéra-Comique as it did on everything else after 1939, and the theatre relied heavily upon the revival of old favorites to provide material for its current programs because neither manpower nor materials were required to prepare new costumes and sets for these older works. In the 1940-43 period especially, 13 almost perennial hits were exploited again with a satisfactory measure of success: *Les Noces de Figaro* and *Pelléas et Mélisande* in 1940; *L'Enlèvement au sérail* in 1941; *Les Noces de Jeannette* in 1942; and *Cavalleria rusticana* and *Lakmé* in 1943. Charpentier's *Louise* never really disappeared from the repertory after its premiere on 2 February 1900 at the Opéra-Comique, and it reached its 943d representation by 28 February 1950 with Geori Bori in the title-rôle.

These eight works did not suffice to support the theatre and its staff after the war despite their popularity, of course, and management found another 16 supportive compositions to produce in 1945-50 under more favorable conditions. As might be expected, the peak period for the revival of these less popular but still quite reliable works was reached immediately after the war in 1945-46, when no fewer than 13 of the 16 postwar revivals were scheduled. These included Massenet's *Don Quichotte*, Puccini's *La Tosca*, Raoul Laparra's *La Habañera*, and André Messager's *Fortunio*. Also, a certain degree of variety and change of pace were gained by borrowing from the repertories of other theatres whenever it was imperative to find new material: the Trianon Lyrique (*La Chanson de Paris*, 1941), the Gaîté-Lyrique (Février's *Carmosine*, 1941), Les Bouffes-Parisiens (Offenbach's *Mesdames de La Halle*, 1940), and the Théâtre-Lyrique de la Porte Saint-Martin (Pierné's *Fragonard*, 1946). On 20 September 1949, management went back as far as 1759 in their revival of Danican Philidor's *Blaise le savetier* created at the Foire Saint-Germain.

The war years were not without fresh compositions, however, and the first half of the 1940-50 decade boasted more creations at the Opéra-Comique than the last five years of this period despite the Occupation and its concomitant restrictions. Eight works were given their premieres between the initial representation of Antoine Mariotte's *Nele Dooryn* on 17 October 1940 and the introduction of Paul Spaak's version in French of Richard Strauss's *Ariane à Naxos* on 30 April 1943. Also, six compositions were mounted for the first time between the premiere of Reynaldo Hahn's *Malvina* on 12 July 1945 and this same composer's *Le Oui des jeunes filles* on 21 June 1949. Yet seven of these 14 creations were billed on fewer than a dozen dates, and three of the seven other works never reached their 20th production at the Opéra-Comique. The most popular among them were Henri Busser's *Le Carosse du Saint-Sacrement* (24 performances), Francis Poulenc's *Les Mamelles de Tirésias* (27 performances), and Emmanuel Chabrier's *L'Etoile* (38 performances).

The Opéra-Comique seemed to exhibit all the signs of a healthy organization in the first half of the twentieth century. It had survived two wars; it had courted and won a faithful public by virtue of a strong and constant effort to achieve an autonomous existence. It had proven its merit by presenting 401 works to audiences in 1900-1950: 68 compositions created before 1 January 1900, 86 other titles added to the repertory between 1 January 1900 and 31 December 1950, and 111 ballets. The company could boast of having presented 136 works in their world premieres. Yet time was now beginning to run out for the second most important lyric theatre in France. A strong and uninterrupted leadership such as M. Rouché had provided for the Opéra was needed for the Opéra-Comique at this crucial moment after the war. Yet a change in the directorate was now taking place every few years after the 1944 departure of Max d'Ollone from this office: a committee of four in 1944 was followed by Albert Wolff in 1945-46; he was succeeded in 1946 by Henry Malherbe, who yielded to Emmanuel Bonde-ville in 1948; Louis Beydts replaced Bondeville in 1952. If stability in management was lacking when it was needed most, it is also true that the company itself suffered similar afflictions because it was larger, more amorphous, and certainly less independent on account of its increasing subordination to the Opéra after the consolidation of the national lyric theatres. There would be moments in the next score of years when it would seem that the Opéra-Comique was on its way to recovery, but this impression was an illusion because there was another and less visible cause for the decline of the theatre in the rue Favart: money. In the meantime, however, the company had managed to survive the decade of 1940-50 by reviving old favorites, by borrowing works from other Paris theatres, and by filling in with new works that were more numerous than they were adequate.

The Opéra after 1950

The second half of the twentieth century began at the Opéra with changes in the administrative personnel of the national lyric theatres on 26 September 1951, when Georges Hirsch failed to receive a renewal of his contract as chief administrator of the theatres. He was replaced by Maurice Lehmann on 28 September 1951, and M. René Gadave was appointed to serve for M. Lehmann until the latter was able to assume the duties of his office on 17 November 1951 with Emmanuel Bondeville as director of the Opéra. The Lehmann-Bondeville administration lasted until late in 1955, but it was not long before it became evident that management was hoping to satisfy the public and to hold down the annual deficit simultaneously: Rameau's *Les Indes galantes* was produced on a lavish scale on 18 June 1952. Paul Dukas and Henri Busser had revised the score; spectacular sets and costumes had been prepared by the most competent artists and designers available. The production was a glorious success, and money poured into the box office. It seemed as if a substitute for the great spectacles of the nineteenth century had been found at last: dazzling revivals. Accordingly, when M. Jacques Ibert of the French Academy of Rome was named administrator of the national lyric theatres on 1 October 1955, he found that new sets and costumes had been planned for *Faust* by Georges Wakhévitch. This production of Gounod's work on 13 April 1956 was also highly profitable and was followed by a revival of Berlioz's *La Damnation de Faust* on 10 December 1956.

This renewed interest at the Opéra in older and better-known compositions was accompanied by an influx of foreign companies that lent an international flavor to the repertory, a quality that helped to restore the Paris opera house to its standing as a world center, although the singers on the house staff could scarcely be considered adept in singing English, Italian, Russian, and German. The San Carlo company of Naples staged Verdi's *Giovanna d'Arco* at the Opéra on 30 June and 3 July 1951; they offered this same composer's *Ballo in maschera* on 1 and 4 July. The Vienna Opera presented Richard Strauss's *Elektra* on 16 and 17 May, *Die Liebe der Danae* on 16 May, and Mozart's *Die Zauberflöte* on 18 May in 1953. The Stuttgart Opera Company brought *Parsifaal* to the Garnier on 24 March 1954, when they used their own sets and costumes done by Heinrich Wendel. This same group returned to the Opéra on 9, 11, and 12 March 1955 to mount *Fidelio* with new sets and costumes by Wieland Wagner. The fifth and sixth productions of *Der Ring des Nibelungen* were billed at the theatre in May 1955 with the usual emphasis on sets that Wagner directors reserve for their productions. These May 1955 representations of Wagner's tetralogy were undertaken under the aegis of Karl Schmidbloss.

Georges Hirsch was named general administrator of the two national lyric theatres for a period of three years beginning on 30 September 1956, but he assumed office on 13 April 1956 because Jacques Ibert had decided suddenly in favor of an early retirement. Foreign companies appeared only slightly less frequently under his leadership. Hans Knappertsbusch conducted performances of *Tristan und Isolde* on 11, 13, and 16 May 1956, while the artistes and the orchestra of the National Opera of Ljubljana collaborated on *L'Amour des trois oranges* on 27 and 29 June of the same year. *Der Ring des Nibelungen* was billed twice in 1957 with Hans Knappertsbusch again conducting in these productions by Karl Schmidbloss. In 1959 the only group to visit the theatre was the Stuttgart Opera, which sang *Jephta* in German on 10 and 12 October with Ferdinand Leitner conducting the orchestra, Josef Traxel filling the title-rôle, and Friederika Sailer as Iphis.

Concomitantly with these performances by operatic companies, three ballet groups accepted invitations to dance at the Garnier: the New York City Ballet (1952, 1956), the Sadler's Wells Ballet (1954), and the Bolchoi Ballet (1958).

A. M. Julien had become director of the national lyric theatres on 12 April 1959, and his tenure extended over three years, but he does not seem to have altered the course of events at the Opéra, which continued to function as if sustained by its own momentum rather than as a result of a deliberate and canny policy evolved to enhance its prestige as a world center for operatic activity. It had become almost imperceptibly a matter of custom to extend invitations to troupes whose custom it was to travel, and this policy was not ignored in 1959, because it was a convenient device for whetting interest in programs and raising money. Also, it was obviously a procedure pleasing to French audiences, who are traditionally attracted to performers from other climes and cultures. The ballet of the Kirov theatre in Leningrad visited the Garnier in 1961, and they were followed later by the Moiseyev dancers (1966), the Royal Ballet of Denmark (1969), the Royal Ballet of Stockholm (1972), the Bolchoi Ballet (1969-70, 1972). Yet no operatic companies were billed into the theatre because the financial rewards did not compensate for the logistic and financial problems of moving an entire company. Also, managers had begun to understand that it is the name of the star, not the name of the company, that fills the theatre and the till. Then too, it was now becoming more usual to hear French artistes sing in Italian and even in German, and a host of individual and independent guest artistes were beginning to appear at the theatre in such works as *La Tosca*, *Tannhäuser*, and *La Traviata* between 1960 and 1965.

The individual guest vocalists appearing at the Opéra after 1950 were far more numerous than the number of groups invited to perform there, not only because individuals could move more easily and more rapidly, but also because the airplane had facilitated travel between the major cities of the world after World War II. Kirsten Flagstad and Max Lorenz appeared in the leads of *Tristan und Isolde* in 1951; Lorenz starred in *Siegfried* this same year and in Richard Strauss's *Salome* with Inge Borkh in 1952, the year that Vittoria de Los Angeles sang Marguerite in *Faust* at the Opéra on 9 May. Boris Christoff filled the lead in the Russian version of *Boris Godounov* in this same year on six dates, while Lily Pons did Gilda on 29 June 1953 with Gianni Raimondi and Raymondo Torres both making their debuts on the stage of the Opéra at the same time. Yvan Petrov made his initial appearance at the Garnier as Boris in *Boris Godounov* in 1954, the year that Gino Penno made his second trip to the Opéra to sing Rhadamès in *Aïda* on 4 June. Windgassen did Parsifal opposite M. Modl as Kundry on 24 March 1954, while Nicolas Rossi-Lemeni sang Boris on 4 August 1954. Thus, as in the case of foreign companies, singers from other countries offered comparatively little to the enrichment of the 1951-54 repertory at the Garnier. They shared in the production of one Russian work and one Italian work and three German compositions by two composers in the course of a score of appearances spread over four years. Yet it was not only the infrequency of programs presenting works in world repertory by top stars that inspired adverse comment about the offerings at the Opéra. Visiting artistes seemed to have a casual air about them, and some of the best-known performers in the operatic world were nowhere in sight at curtain time on more than one occasion. Too often they came to the theatre to perform because they found Paris in the middle of their European itinerary or because it offered a convenient pause in a schedule made heavier than necessary by efficient airplanes. In fact, opera singers had emerged as a jet set in their own right, and at least one critic referred to them as "the globe-trotters."

The number of invitational billings remained more or less constant in the second half of the fifties. In 1955 Lily Pons performed once more as Gilda on 24 June, and Yvan Petrov repeated his interpretation of Boris on 18, 20, and 28 November; he added Méphisto to his Paris repertory on 25 November. Virginia Zeani made an appearance on 31 May 1957 after Hans Beirer had filled his first rôle in Paris as Tannhäuser in 1956. Rita Gorr had done Venus in this latter production; she was billed as Brangaine of *Tristan und Isolde* on 18 April 1958 and as Waltraute in *Götterdämmerung* on 5 May 1958. Miroslav Cangalovic did Boris in his Garnier debut on 12 December 1958. The following year, 1959, Liane Synek filled the part of Elisabeth in *Tannhäuser*, and Flaviano Labo made his debut on the stage of the Opéra as Rhadamès on 11 December 1959. Joan Sutherland sang for the first time at the Garnier as Lucia in Donizetti's *Lucia di Lammermoor* on 25, 30 April and 7 May 1960. Hans Hotter and Arnold van Mill starred in a German production of *Der fliegende Holländer* the same year on 3 May. Once again, therefore, guest artists had appeared in the same sort of programs: Wagner, Verdi, and *Boris Godounov*.

The relative paucity of visiting companies and unattached stars at the Opéra in the decade of 1950-60 leads to the inevitable question of how many compositions were staged by the house artistes at this time. This inquiry reveals that there were 47 new works produced by the staff of the Garnier, and 39 of them were ballets. The need for money explains the preponderance of ballets, of course, because they were more profitable to produce. The lyric works mounted in 1950-60 included Sergei Prokofiev's *L'Amour des trois oranges* (2), Henri Tomasi's *L'Atlantide* (20), Henry Barraud's *Numance* (9), Darius Milhaud's *Bolivar* (22), Samuel-Rousseau's *Kerkeb* (26), Francis Poulenc's *Dialogues des Carmélites* (27), and Arthur Honegger's *Jeanne au bûcher* (93). Carl Maria von Weber's *Obéron* (6) was also presented to audiences at the Garnier for the first time in this decade.

Still, management continued to exploit the world repertory in their search for operatic material. Rosanna Carteri made her debut at the Garnier as Violetta on 30 October 1961, and Hans Beirer returned on 19 and 22

January 1962 to appear in Saint-Saëns's *Samson et Dalila*, while Elisabeth Schwarzkopf filled the rôle of La Maréchale in the German version of *Der Rosenkavalier* produced on four dates in 1962. Gertrude Grob-Prandl reappeared at the theatre on 6, 9, and 14 April 1962 to sing Brunehilde in *Götterdämmerung* with Thomas Stewart and Grace Hoffman. Regina Resnik sang Carmen in 1964, the year that Giaourov appeared in *Don Juan* on 5 June and in *Don Carlos* on 15 June, while Maria Callas was billed for eight performances of *La Tosca* with Tito Gobbi and Cioni between 19 February and 13 March 1965. Mlle A. Silja sang in the German version of *Salome* on 12, 15, and 17 March 1965, and Rita Gorr was invited to star again in *Tannhäuser* on 28 May 1965. Birgit Nilsson and Wolfgang Windgassen did *Tristan und Isolde* on 25 February 1966, and Tito Gobbi headed the cast of *Otello* on 25 April 1966. The same period saw the Garnier artistes do Cherubini's *Médée* (1962), Berg's *Wozzeck* (1963), and a cluster of ten ballets among which were the *pas de deux* from *Sylvia* (1964) and from Minkus's *Don Quichotte* (1964).

The tendency to call upon foreign artistes and companies diminished in the following decade because labor troubles made it increasingly difficult to plan ahead and to honor contractual agreements. In May 1968, for example, striking workers had gone so far as to occupy the Opéra and the Opéra-Comique. Also, financial troubles had been brewing since as early as 1950, when M. Hirsch had cited a lack of money as the cause of his problems: only 15 percent of his three-million-dollar subsidy was left for costumes, sets, electricity and all the other purely theatrical expenses after he had paid out the other 85 percent of the government grant in salaries. The remaining bill had to be met with the income from the 3,800 seats and standing-room-only tickets that could be sold. After M. Auric took over the administration in the spring of 1962, it became clear that even President De Gaulle was disappointed in the failure of the "march to cultural grandeur" that had been promised to the country by the minister of Cultural Affairs, André Malraux. The subsequent strikes and riots that broke out among workers outside as well as inside the theatre culminated in a disaster for the Fifth Republic in general and for the national lyric theatres in particular, and it was not until 1971 and the interim direction of M. Daniel that an effort was made to establish a balanced and cosmopolitan repertory offered by French artistes as well as by foreign stars. Specific steps were taken to avoid scheduling a work if management did not yet have any idea of which vocalists would head the cast. A frantic or even an indifferent director would not have to grab for a phone to catch a soprano or a tenor passing through Paris.

The first step in the projected reform at the Opéra was to find a new director, and Rolf Liebermann was invited by Marcel Landowski, director of music and dance in France, to become head of the National Lyric Theatres. It was June 1971. Liebermann selected as music consultant Georg

Solti, director of the Paris orchestra. Roland Petit was placed in charge of choreography with Paul-Emile Deiber as stage director and Georges Prêtre as conductor of the Garnier orchestra. A chorus of one hundred voices was established, and an agreement was reached in the troublesome matter of rehearsal schedules. Programs were set up in the pattern employed at La Scala and Covent Garden: one or two operas alternating with ballets for a month. This permitted ten or so billings of a given opera within a month, and foreign or domestic artistes, known for their skill and familiarity with the selected compositions, could be expected under normal conditions to accept invitations, rehearse, and then perform instead of hurrying for a taxi at the airport, singing a part, and then reembarking for Milan, Moscow, or New York. M. Liebermann's contract ran from 1 January 1973 to 31 July 1976, but he was quite successful from the beginning largely because he worked on the realistic principle that contracts calling for at least a dozen appearances in the same rôle within a short time would be too attractive for stars of the first magnitude to ignore.

He offered the following works during the initial phase of his directorate: *Les Noces de Figaro* given first at Versailles on 30 March 1973 in a striking production by Giorgio Strehler before it was mounted in Paris on 7 April 1973; Arnold Schoenberg's *Moïse et Aron* in French and directed by Raymond Gérôme with choreography by Dick Price on 27 September; the ballets *Hommage à Varèse* and *Coppélia* on 9 June 1973 and 18 December 1973 respectively. The third opera of the year was *La Bohème* with Gian-Carlo Menotti in charge of production on 23 November 1973. He also did Gluck's *Orphée* in its Paris version, *Il Trovatore* with the final scene that Verdi wrote for Paris, *Don Quichotte*, *I Vespri Siciliani*, and *Così fan tutte*. Later, he added *Elektra*, *Manon*, *Les Contes d'Hoffman*, and *Faust* to his accomplishments. Audiences were especially enthusiastic over *I Vespri siciliani*, but his greatest success remained his *Figaro*.

The vocalists whom Liebermann had convened to help him in this splendid resurrection of the Opéra included a number of performers making their debuts at the Garnier theatre and Versailles: Francine Arrauzau, Martina Arroyo, Piero Cappuccilli, Viorica Cortez, Placido Domingo, Robert Dumé, Fernand Dumont, Mignon Dunn, Nicolai Ghiaurov, Gwyneth Jones, Tom Krause, Kurt Moll, Jeannette Pilou, Margaret Price, Anna Ringart, Renata Scotto, Teresa Stratas, Kiri Te Kanawa, Hélia T'Hézan, and Shirley Verrett. Yet all performers and productions were not perfection itself in every respect. Critics found the premise of Peter Ustinov's *Don Quichotte* flawed, and they were not profoundly impressed by the portrayal of Monforte in *I Vespri siciliani*. Still, it was unanimously agreed that there was nothing mediocre or slovenly about the new programs at the Opéra. The public was pleased. One melomaniac confessed that he had decided to tear up his train tickets to Bordeaux because he no longer had a reason to patronize the opera house in this southern city; another wit observed that he had stopped gazing at Chagall's ceiling to look at the stage. Also, aside from his administrative and artistic success, M. Liebermann had performed a financial feat that was not to be overlooked. A decade previously, management under M. Auric had not achieved 70 percent attendance in 1964-65, but the house was filled in 1973 for all but one of the new director's programs, although the cost of tickets had doubled since 1965 to a $15.00 top for opera and a $10.00 top for ballet. It is quite difficult to overestimate the importance of M. Liebermann's regime to the Opéra when it is recalled that he was managing to fill the theatre at these prices after the Garnier had been closed for almost two years before his arrival in Paris.

In retrospect, it is clear that the decline of the Opéra was caused as much by the disruptive influence of strikes as by the desultory treatment of performances and of repertory that inspired dismay in the public and provoked quarrels among the artistes, staff, and management. Originally the situation had seemed quiet enough until the stagehands at the Comédie-Française went on strike on the evening of 16 October 1953, and M. Cornu, secretary of Fine Arts for the government, responded by ordering a lockout at all national theatres. The technical and artistic personnel of the Opéra were forbidden to enter the theatre, the museum, and the library early on the morning of 17 October. The interdict remained in force for 25 days, and the Opéra was dark until 11 November, with many individuals at the Garnier palace feeling that they had been subjected to unfair treatment. The matter was settled nevertheless, and there was only a brief hint of the trouble to come in the strike of 28-30 April 1954, which forced the cancellation of performances by the Leningrad and Moscow ballets in May 1954. A brief work stoppage then occurred again on 14 March 1956, but matters reached a serious stage in 1957, when the stagehands refused to work on 15 October, and the progam marking the opening of the restored theatre at Versailles had to be postponed. The regular schedule of performances was restored on 25 October, but the embers of dissension were still smouldering, and the stagehands walked out on 15, 20, and 24 November; they were joined by the dancers on 2, 4, 8, and 18 December; all theatrical activity ground to a halt on 22 December for the remainder of 1957.

It was now certain that the situation had deteriorated to an alarming degree, although the workers returned to their tasks on 3 January 1958. The corps de ballet was not satisfied with the settlement, and *Faust* had to be substituted for three subsequent ballets because the dancers would perform only in the *divertissements* of operas. The stagehands struck again on 14 February because programs were given through 19 February despite the growing bitterness of the conflict. A stalemate had been reached, and the minister of National Education reacted by suspending all activity at the Opéra and at the Opéra-Comique and by dismissing the stagehands and dancers at these two theatres. The former responded by accepting a ten percent increase in wages, and they were reinstated on 3 March. Then, on 5

March, programs were restored through the willingness of the star dancers and leading vocalists to perform in costume. It was a makeshift solution, and management admitted it by lowering prices. Finally, on 26 March, Yvette Chauviré and the other dancers still in revolt agreed to return to the stage. Thus, the entire first quarter of 1958 had been marred by the dispute, although it appeared that everybody was happy to be back at work as of 1 April 1958. Then, on 3 February 1961, the chorus struck in the middle of rehearsals for Berlioz's *Les Troyens*. The theatre did reopen its doors on 8 February, but it was apparent once again that the situation was going to be resolved only with patience. The impasse continued until 24 February, when it was decided to limit performances to concerts and to excerpts from operas with the artistes appearing in costume. This was a solution that solved nothing, but it kept the theatre open until 27 March 1961, when the regular format of programs was resumed with a production of *Faust*.

Once again affairs settled into a more or less normal pattern at the Opéra, where the facade was repaired and cleaned during August 1963, and Marc Chagall's ceiling was presented to the press at 9:00 P.M. on 21 September 1964 before its formal unveiling two days later to the accompaniment of extracts from the *Jupiter* symphony. Then, on 11 December, the calm was broken by a brief labor dispute, and an electricians' strike closed the theatre on 27 January 1965. Another work stoppage on the following 10 December postponed the premieres of *Notre-Dame de Paris* and *Adage et variations* for 24 hours. These one-day rumblings were portents of more disturbing events to come. After the electricians' strike of 23 March 1966, five more strikes interrupted scheduled programs in 1967: an undisclosed cause of trouble prompted the first confrontation on 1 February; the members of the chorus filed a list of their grievances on 14 May; a general strike was called for 17 May; the musicians staged an independent work stoppage on 28 May; the electric company had to suspend service to the Opéra on 13 December on account of their own strike.

The cork was out of the bottle now, and labor troubles continued to plague the Garnier palace in the spring of 1968. The chorus refused to perform on 23 and 27 March, and a general strike was called on this latter date. Programs were resumed as scheduled on 30 March, but the chorus was responsible for a second disruption on 19 April, when they declared their unwillingness to sing in *La Tosca*. This episode proved to be of minor importance, but the latent conflict at the Opéra between management and personnel erupted violently on 17 May. On this date a general meeting was called to discuss mutual problems, and the confrontation lasted from 2:00 P.M. on 17 May until 1:20 A.M. on 18 May. The result of the meeting was the declaration of a general strike "with the places of work to be occupied." The artistes and technical personnel participated in the picketing, but they opposed any attempt by outside laborites to occupy the theatre, although one group gained entrance to the loggia by surprise and broke five large mirrors there. The struggle continued until an accord was signed on 7 June by all the personnel except the chorus. The pickets disbanded the next day, and the chorus agreed to resume their services on 11 June. The Garnier palace remained dark through 14 June. *Carmen* was performed on 15 June, and a regular pattern of representations was maintained until the opera house was closed for repairs and renovations on 27 May 1969.

The company returned to their cleaned and redecorated home on 19 November 1969, and the first half of 1970 passed without apparent trouble except for a brief strike by technicians on 3 January. Then, on 30 July 1970, it was announced that the theatre would be closed for an indefinite period of time because the general administration of the national lyric theatres had repudiated the 1962 collective agreement between management and personnel. The employees refused to work without a contract, but they did not take steps to resolve their predicament until 19 September, when the personnel of the Opéra-Comique met with the direction of the lyric theatres to discuss the situation. The artistes and technicians of the Opéra-Comique objected to a proposed settlement because they found the suggested hours of work unacceptable. Management responded by suspending the recalcitrant performers for one, three, or eight days. This countermove did nothing but aggravate the impasse because the Opéra-Comique was obliged to close down on account of a lack of performers on 19 and 20 September. A twenty-four-hour strike was declared on 23 September by way of retaliation, but the theatre remained closed for the remainder of the month. The Opéra also remained dark throughout September because both it and the Opéra-Comique were involved in the dispute.

October 1970 did not bring a solution. A continuing attempt to negotiate was made at the start of the month despite bitter disagreements leading to interruptions in the talks by both parties. Then, on 7 October, a group of malcontents invaded the offices of the administration, and it appeared that matters might go from bad to worse. The company of the Opéra moved to the Palais des Sports on 13 October to give extraordinary performances, although the Opéra-Comique opened its doors on 21 October. Yet affairs were in a delicate balance: the Opéra was performing at the Palais des Sports; the Palais Garnier was closed; the Opéra-Comique declared strikes of four hours duration from 8:00 P.M. to 12:00 P.M. from 20 to 24 October. The work to be mounted on these dates was Roberto Rosselini's production of *L'Annonce faite à Marie*.

The situation worsened during the final months of the year. The Opéra-Comique declared a 15 minute strike on 6 November to signal their unabated discontent. A day of national mourning on 12 November suspended programs on this date, and the orchestra refused to play in a supplementary performance designed to compensate for the missed day. Finally, the musicians were warned on 30 November that their unwillingness to cooperate would result in their suspension until 31 May 1971. While these events were taking place at the Opéra-Comique, the Opéra performed the same bill between 3 and 15 November at the Palais des Sports. M. Autin, inspector of finances, was summoned on 8 December to reorganize the National Lyric Theatres Corporation, and the Garnier remained dark until the end of the year. The corps de ballet had been performing at the Palais des Sports since autumn, but it left this facility to dance *Coppélia* at the Théâtre des Champs-Elysées on 9 dates between 22 and 31 December. The doors of the Garnier theatre had been closed from 30 July until 31 December in 1970.

The situation was precisely the same at the start of 1971 as it had been at the end of 1970: the Garnier was closed, the corps de ballet was appearing at the Théâtre des Champs-Elysées, and reconciliation was not in sight. The dancers abandoned their programs at the Champs-Elysées after the bill of 5 January, and they remained idle for the rest of the month. Georges Prêtre decided to resign on 25 January, and the dancing examination scheduled for 3 February was postponed indefinitely. All personnel connected with the Opéra spent February and March in the doldrums. Then, on 2 April, the corps de ballet reopened at the Théâtre des Champs-Elysées. They staged a series of varied compositions during the first and second weeks of the month, and, before their first number on opening night, Mlle Brigitte Lefèvre stepped forward in street dress to explain the dancers' situation to the audience. At the raising of the curtain on 7 April, a minute of silence was observed as an act of homage to Igor Stravinsky, but no programs were executed for the rest of the month after 12 April. There was only a concert held at Saint-Louis des Invalides on 29 April with Mlle Andréa Guiot as vocalist, M. B. Garoty at the organ, and M. M. Quéval conducting the orchestra and chorus of the Opéra.

Still another discordant note was struck when the talks between the minister of Cultural Affairs and the personnel of the lyric theatres broke off on 7 May. The technicians and the musicians had signed a proposed agreement, but the singers, dancers, and choristers refused to accept the working conditions offered to them. The minister responded to their obduracy by announcing that the Opéra would not reopen in October. Discouraged, M. Autin announced his retirement, although he had been charged only the year before with reforming the organization of the National Lyric Theatres. It seemed impossible that matters could deteriorate further, but the Opéra-Comique added to the confusion and acrimony by closing after the matinee performance of *Werther* on 20 May. The exiting spectators joined the protesting personnel of the theatre in a public demonstration, and the merchants of the quarter closed their shops to follow the angry parade to the Ministry of Cultural Affairs. The corps de ballet made a move toward peace the next day, 21 May, when its members decided to sign the new contract. But their return to the stage was accompanied by the sudden death of M. René Nicoly at about 1:30 P.M. on 22

May, and the organization of the National Lyric Theatres was left without a general administrator at the very moment when he was needed most. Yet his death did not prevent the definitive dismissal of the choristers on 27 May, the day before René Nicoly's funeral at the Madeleine.

The chief concern in June was the finding of a new general administrator for the lyric theatres, and no programs of any sort were attempted. On 2 June, however, Daniel Lesur was named interim administrator of the theatres. M. B. Lefort was his representative at the Garnier, and L. Erb was his executive assistant at the Opéra-Comique. It was decided that the Opéra would open its doors again on an undetermined date during the coming winter, and that the Opéra-Comique would resume programs in August. M. Lesur received his chiefs of service on 3 June, and the entire personnel of the two companies was presented to him on 10 June. Then, on 18 June, the news broke that M. Rolf Liebermann, director of the Hamburg Opera, had accepted an invitation to serve as director of the Opéra. His term would begin in 1973, but he would arrive in Paris at an earlier date to lay the foundation for his administration. M. Georg Solti would assist him in musical matters. M. Liebermann granted an interview to *Le Figaro* to explain his plans to the French people and to announce his appointment of M. Hugues Gall to assist him at the Garnier. M. Liebermann was to be virtual czar of the lyric theatres, although he could not hold the position of director of the National Lyric Theaters because he was not a French citizen. In fact, he was the first citizen of a foreign country chosen to guide the fortunes of the Opéra since Jean-Baptiste Lully had served as head of the Royal Academy of Music in the seventeenth century.

Curtain: The Opéra-Comique, 1952–1972

After 1950 the Opéra-Comique continued to produce the same sort of works that had made up its repertory in previous decades, but the fate of the theatre was more immediately bound to the fortunes of the Opéra now that the Réunion des Théâtres Lyriques Nationaux had been formed. The inevitable result of the formation of this latter organization was the ultimate weakening of the Opéra-Comique because administrators came to favor the Opéra to the detriment of the less prestigious theatre. Whenever artistes showed promise at the opera house in the rue Favart, they were transferred to the Garnier; whenever a work enjoyed a longer run or returned more money than expected, it was taken over to the Opéra. Examples include *Le Roi d'Ys*, *Ariane et Barbe-blue*, *Mârouf*, *Pénélope*, *La Tosca*, and *Carmen*. This situation was quite discouraging, and one of the directors of the theatre in the 1960s, M. Hervé Dugardin, threw up his hands in despair and walked out of the theatre convinced that nobody could save the Opéra-Comique. His successor, Eugène Germain, believed that he might restore the vitality of the theatre by lowering prices to a level within the reach of the common people who could not afford the current range of admission prices, which ranged to a top of 16 *francs* 50 *centimes*. He was partially successful and managed to collect enough extra money to repair costumes and sets; he even made an effort to enlist the aid of singers like Michel Roux, but it was an uphill struggle despite his determination. Unfortunately, there was no real permanency to his gains on account of the basic instability of the situation from which the Opéra-Comique could find no escape.

Some critics blamed the shortcomings of the company upon a shortage of competent singers, a lack of proper stage direction, or the persistent notion in the theatre in the rue Favart that the Comique could do whatever was done at the Opéra, and, what was worse, that it could be done in the same style and on the same scale. Theatregoers saw the deficiencies of the troupe as the result of a lack of support from the administration, a fault that M. Giraudeau promised to remedy in August 1968 by taking charge personally of rehearsals in addition to finding new performers capable of singing in Italian and German as well as in French.

These declarations and resolutions were as noble as they were sincere, but they were also unrealistic because strikes of lesser or greater magnitude were interrupting plans as quickly as the hard-pressed directors were making them: every strike affecting the Opéra and the organization of National Lyric Theatres involved the Opéra-Comique. Most importantly, money was an obstacle that was apparently insuperable. There was a deficit of 50 million *francs* despite a paid attendance of 296,620 spectators, who left only 16 percent of the annual budget at the box offices of the lyric theatres. Thus, when the singers and technicians of the Opéra-Comique went on strike for higher wages in 1969-70, the state was already paying 84 percent of their salaries and could afford to pay them no more. Even De Gaulle lost his temper because he knew that some of the performers were singing only once or twice a year.

The situation exploded on 4 February 1972, when the minister of Cultural Affairs announced the abolition of the Opéra-Comique. His decree provided for the creation of the Opéra-Studio of Paris, a national center for the musical and lyric theatre that would be founded on 1 January 1973 to replace the Opéra-Comique. The orchestra of the theatre would be transformed into a traveling unit that would serve Paris and the 11 departments contiguous to the capital. The personnel of the Opéra-Comique objected vociferously, but the die was cast, and the press pointed out that M. Jacques Duharnel had hinted as early as June 1972 that these changes were being contemplated. The public as well as the artistes and technicians regretted the disappearance of the old theatre covered with glory and filled with memories, but it was admitted generally that the Opéra-Comique had been dying slowly for a number of years. Its devotees and audiences had been declining relentlessly; the minister of Finance had accused it constantly of extravagance; musical circles had suggested too frequently that the results produced by the company left much to be desired professionally. M. Jacques

Duharnel expressed his disappointment privately, especially after the 1970-71 season. Thus, everyone not connected with the theatre directly was agreed that it was a tragedy to have to close the theatre, although financially the Opéra-Comique itself was nothing short of a catastrophe. The announcement by M. Duharnel added that the Opéra-Comique theatre would close its doors on 1 April 1972 so that the building might be transformed into a facility suitable to the purposes of the Opéra-Studio.

The Ballet after 1920

The 1920s proved to be another period of sustained interest in the ballet at the Opéra, and foreign companies were quick to profit by this enthusiasm for theatrical dancing by accepting bookings at the Garnier palace. The Ballets russes continued to appear upon the scene with colorful costuming, exciting decor, and an energetic manner that made their presence felt immediately, and the influence exerted by Serge Diaghilev and his troupe was apparent not only in the theatre but in the Russian color and style of everyday dress and household furnishings. Gradually, however, it became obvious after World War I that there was nothing really genuinely Russian about the orange satin pillows, the variegated silken costumes, and the shining boots featured in compositions like *Pétrouchka*, even if the admiralty spire in Saint Petersburg was visible in the background. Spectators were beginning to realize that these quasi-Russian textiles, these lurid and luminous colors, and even the Oriental look of the dancers had originated on Léon Bakst's sketch pad.

Yet this brilliant misrepresentation did no harm, and the true contribution made by Serge Diaghilev and his associates lay in another direction. Their basic aim was not exclusively visual because their premise as performers was to put the scenario, the music, and the choreography of their productions on an equal footing. At times, it is true, the Russian impresario seemed to lose himself in trivia, or he might appear to err by attempting to force Chopin's or Stravinsky's already structured and defined compositions to serve another purpose. Conversely, he might fall into the error of trying to convert an athletic activity into a balletic performance. Yet these miscalculations disappeared before the effectiveness of his total production, and Diaghilev's work was still relevant and persuasive after the war. It is easy to understand why he remained active and significant in the theatre until his death in 1929.

It is not incongruent, then, that Diaghilev made no pretense of bringing Russia or any aspect of this country's culture to the stage of Western Europe in his initial postwar programs of 24, 27, and 30 December 1919. He began by producing *La Boutique fantasque* and *Les Femmes de bonne humeur*; the first of these works was based upon Ottorino Respighi's arrangement of music by Rossini, and the second was designated as a "choreographic comedy" derived from Carlo Goldoni with music by Alessandro Scarlatti. His company presented five new compositions at the Garnier in 1920 for which Michel Fokine and Léonide Massine had done the choreography, and they returned to the theatre in the spring of 1922 to mount another four works that had not yet been produced at the Opéra. They added two more titles to their balletic repertory at the Garnier on 27 December 1927, when they performed works by George Balanchine and Léonide Massine, and in 1928 they were back on the stage of the Paris opera house to do *Les Dieux mendiants* and *Apollon Musagète*. It is true that some of these compositions were derived from the myths of the East or from the literature of Russia, but it is also evident that the company did not feel obliged by any means to confine their stage offerings to works derived from East European history or culture. They turned to Italy for their material in 1919, and they displayed subsequently an even greater degree of eclecticism by presenting *Le Tricorne* with music by Manuel de Falla, *Astuce feminine* derived from Pietro Metastasio, and *Pulcinella* based upon Giovanni Pergolesi with sets by Pablo Picasso. In 1921 Diaghilev exploited the classic tradition with *Daphnis et Chloé*. His appearances at the Garnier continued until 1929, when his death halted the activity of his company at the Opéra. The final program offered by the Ballets russes at the Garnier was billed on 3 January 1929; it included *L'Oiseau de feu*, *Apollon Musagète*, and *La Chatte*.

One of Diaghilev's greatest gifts to the French stage had been the number and the calibre of the artistes whom he had assembled in Paris but who left him subsequently to pursue their own careers. Ida Rubinstein was one of these so-called defectors. She had been with Diaghilev for his initial Paris season of 1909, but she had decided to embark upon a program of producing her own spectaculars based upon the dance and highlighting her own talents. Accordingly, she remained in Paris after the newly formed Ballets russes left France to honor the remainder of their schedule, and, when Léon Bakst and Alexandre Benois separated from Diaghilev, she enlisted their aid to provide the scenery and costumes for her ballets. She had staged *Le Martyre de Saint-Sébastien* at the Châtelet theatre as early as 1911, and she was relatively well known in the French capital when she did *La Tragédie de Salomé* at the Opéra on 1 April 1919. Encouraged by her success, she revived *Le Martyre de Saint-Sébastien* at the Garnier in 1922 with costumes and sets by Bakst. Then, after filling the rôle of the heroine in Ildebrando Pizzetti's *Phaedre* on 7 June 1923, she brought *Istar* to the Opéra on 10 July 1924.

A note of protest against Mme Rubinstein's performances was heard almost immediately, when a Paris journalist objected to her appearing in a theatre supported by public funds. The writer was not upset by a private citizen using the opera house for personal profit but by the ludicrous spectacle he alleged her to be making of herself on its venerable stage. Mme Rubinstein was unmoved by these hostile assertions, and she returned to the Garnier in 1927 to do the title-rôle in *L'Impératrice aux rochers*. Then, as if to silence her enemies for all time, she created seven parts at the Garnier in

1928: the lead in *La Bien-Aimée*, Psyché in *Les Noces de Psyché et de l'Amour*, the danseuse in a new version of Ravel's *Boléro*, the fairy in *Le Baiser de la fée*, the girl in *Nocturne*, the title-part of *La Princesse Cygne*, and the protagonist of *David*. Yet time was takng its toll, and one of her less charitable colleagues remarked in a moment of insight that, whenever she went on her points, her knees kept separating. More invulnerable than ever, Mme Rubinstein refused to yield, and she appeared in the title-rôles of *Perséphone*, *Diane de Poitiers*, and *Sémiramis* as late as 1934.

These ballets brought to the Garnier by the guest troupes of Diaghilev and Mme Rubinstein were billed with other compositions mounted at the Opéra by the resident corps de ballet in the same interlude. Not all of them had their world premieres at the Opéra, although they were presented to the public for the first time in Paris theatres as well as outside the French capital. Ravel's *Daphnis et Chloé* had already been billed at the Châtelet theatre in 1911, for example, and André Fijan's *La Lime* had been seen at Aix-les-Bains in 1913. Strangely enough, no single composer provided scores for three of these compositions, and only two provided the music for two ballets: Chopin (*La Nuit ensorcelée*, 1923; *Les Feuilles d'automne*, 1925) and Gabriel Pierné (*Cydalise et le chèvre-pied*, 1923; *Impressions de Music-Hall*, 1927). As for the choreographers, Léo Staats dominated this aspect of ballet production in 1920-29: his name is affixed to 13 of the 27 works billed initially at the Paris opera house during this decade.

A former dancer and ballet master at the Opéra, Léo Staats had a career as a choreographer that extended beyond 1930, and he became one of the most prolific choreographers to contribute to repertory. He had 15 compositions produced in the score of years before World War II, and he must have set some sort of record by doing the choreography for all seven ballets given their premieres at the Garnier between and including his *Padmavâti* of 1 June 1923 and his *Soir de fête* of 30 June 1925. The best-known work of his postwar period is doubtlessly *Cydalise et le chèvre-pied*, an elegant and graceful synthesis of the attitudes of Greek antiquity and the regency of Philippe d'Orléans toward love and sex. It starred Carlotta Zambelli and Albert Aveline, two of the leading dancers of the day at the Opéra now that Pavlova had turned globetrotter and Nijinsky was in the United States. The striking characteristic of Staats's ballets was the range of their inspiration. *Les Abeilles* was suggested by Maeterlinck's work on bees and was set to a score that Stravinsky denied writing, for example, while *Soir de fête* was based upon another ballet, Delibes's *La Source*. The diversity of Staats's compositions was probably promoted to some degree by the number of librettists associated with his work: Funck-Brentano (*Taglioni chez Musette*, 1920), André Gérard (*Maimouna*, 1921), Léon Bakst (*La Nuit ensorcelée*, 1923), Henry Ferrare (*La Lime*, 1924) among others.

Léonide Massine was likewise one of the more creative contemporary choreographers. Although he had done his first ballet entitled *Le Soleil de minuit* as early as 1915, he was still active after the war and had eight titles posted at the Opéra by 1931. His most successful compositions in the first years after World War I included *La Boutique fantasque* (1919), *Le Tricorne* (1919), *Pulcinella* (1920), *Le Chant du rossignol* (1920), and *Le Sacre du printemps* (1920), which he choreographed during his association with the Ballets russes. He was influenced strongly by painters who plied their craft in the theatre or who were his compatriots from Russia. His *Jeux d'enfants*, produced at the Garnier theatre as late as 1941, gave ample evidence of having been shaped by the surrealist school, and it constituted a striking example of the mutual influence that ballet and painting can exert upon each other. Americans in large numbers saw Massine's work on the stage, perhaps unaware of his importance at the time, when he directed the enormous ballets and deployed the huge sets used in the production of spectacles in the now defunct Roxy theatre in New York during 1926-29.

Mme Bronislava Nijinska, sister of the famous Vaslav Nijinsky, would have been a more productive choreographer if she had not devoted so much time and energy to dancing with Diaghilev's troupe and later to teaching in Kiev until her return to Paris. Eventually she had nine titles billed at the Opéra, although the majority of these pieces were mounted by visiting companies. After a few preliminary efforts, she choreographed *Le Renard* (1922) for production at the Garnier palace by the Ballets russes, and in 1928 she created the choreography of *Nocturne*, *La Bien-Aimée*, and *Le Baiser de la fée* for staging at the Opéra by Mme Rubinstein and her troupe.

Still another member of the Ballets russes to break albeit temporarily with Diaghilev was Mikhail, or Michel, Fokine, who had come to Paris with the impresario at the beginning of the great venture in 1909. They had shared the uncertainty, labors, and triumphs of the company from the beginning, but they had finally fallen into a series of arguments over the production of *Daphnis et Chloé* at the Châtelet theatre, and it was not long before they parted. They were reconciled later, and Fokine resumed creating ballets for the company in his customary style. His two most important postwar compositions were *Thamar* (1920) and *Daphnis et Chloé* (1921). His work came to have a more enduring influence, and many of his pre-1918 titles were revived after the return of peace: *Les Sylphides* (1909) was brought back to the stage in 1920, *L'Oiseau de feu* (1910) in 1927, the Diaghilev *Giselle* (1910) in 1924, *Le Spectre de la rose* (1911) in 1922 and 1931, and *Pétrouchka* (1914) in 1919, 1922. Serge Lifar would consider *Pétrouchka* and *L'Oiseau de feu* significant enough to present them again in 1948 and 1954, respectively, with revised choreography. The Fokine *Giselle* was revived not only in 1924 but also in 1932, 1935, and 1939. Thus, Fokine exerted a strong influence in his time through his large authorship consisting of more than 50 ballets, some of which have become near classics, if not classics. Also, he is remembered as a guiding force in the art of ballet on account of his convictions about gesturing, miming, and dancing as balletic functions.

As for the ballets themselves, their subject matter, and their relative popularity, it is possible to discern in them certain characteristics that distinguish the growth of theatrical dancing after World War I in France. Most striking is the tendency of librettists and performers to prefer works with a classical or neoclassical flavor, and Maurice Ravel's *Daphnis et Chloé* (1921), Paul Paray's *Artémis troublée* (1922), Roger Ducasse's *Orphée* (1926), and Serge Lifar's *Les Créatures de Promethée* (1929) had an evident relationship with mythic antiquity that was characteristic of the decade. The Renaissance provided a modicum of inspiration and was represented by Massine's *Pulcinella* (1920), which relied upon the *commedia dell'arte* for the structure of its intrigue, while Pierné's *Cydalise et le chèvre-pied* (1923) recreated the atmosphere of Versailles after the death of Louis XIV. Literature of the earlier nineteenth century and the romantic tradition in the arts suggested the moods and material for *Taglioni chez Musette* (1920), *Les Feuilles d'automne* (1925), and the Poesque *Le Diable dans le beffroi* (1927). Also, the exotic appeal of distant lands remained one of the essential elements of post-1920 ballet in *Maimouna* (1921) and *Siang-Sin* (1924). The apocalyptic symbolism becoming more and more fascinating to the public was obvious in *Istar* (1924), Léon Bakst's last colorful effort at the Opéra. An attempt to tie the ballet to the contemporary scene was made in *Impressions de Music-Hall* (1927), while the influence of such unalike composers as Mozart and Debussy was apparent in *Le Rêve de la marquise* (1921) and *Petite Suite* (1922). This variety of themes, subjects, and inspirations along with the new topics and fresh techniques proffered by Loïe Fuller, Mme Nijinska, Igor Stravinsky, Diaghilev, Ravel, Mme Rubinstein, and their associates provided a variety that could have left little room for complaints about lack of inventiveness and creativity at the Opéra in 1920-30.

Yet the question of the relative popularity of these works remains, although it is easy enough to resolve this problem if the number of billings enjoyed by a composition may be used as a gauge of its importance and as a measure of the degree to which it was approved by audiences. If this scale is applied here, the four outstanding works of the period and the number of times they were performed were Léo Delibes's *Soir de fête* (300), Maurice Ravel's *Daphnis et Chloé* (108), Vincent d'Indy's *Istar* (107), and George Hüe's *Siang-Sin* (105). Two unquestionably popular ballets that did not reach a hundred billings were Bakst's *La Nuit ensorcelée* and Pierné's *Impressions de Music-Hall*, included on 98 and 82 programs, respectively. As many as 11 ballets of the 1918-29 period never managed to enjoy more than ten representations at the Garnier, and yet only 11 others were produced on from 13 to 80 dates. Also, it is interesting to find that 17 of the ballets of this first post-World War I decade were in a single act, while only six were in two acts. Roger Ducasse's *Orphée* (1926) was the sole composition in three acts. Yet other divisions were made in the texts by their authors. *Petite Suite* (1922) by Mlles Howarth and Pasmanik was billed as a "ballet en 4 images"; Léonide Massine described his *Pulcinella* (1920) as a ballet "avec chant en un tableau"; Mme Nijinska's *Le Mariage de la belle au bois dormant* was all of one piece without structural divisions of any sort. Also, works were often posted simply as ballets, although such terms as "fantasy ballet" or "choreographic symphony" were used from time to time. *Fresques* (1923) was described by its creator as a "choreographic suite," but the most original coinage seems to have been "lyric mimodrama" minted for *Orphée* (1926).

Also, there was a young man in the corps de ballet named Serge Lifar, who had been called from Russia in 1923 to join the Ballets russes. He had demonstrated unusual ability, and, after Diaghilev's death on 19 August 1929, M. Jacques Rouché had suggested to Lifar that he might be interested in producing and dancing Beethoven's *Promethée*, created by Vigano in Vienna in 1801. Lifar was flattered by this offer from the director of the Opéra and accepted. Rehearsals were not without problems and friction, and the original composition was so altered that its title had to be changed, but *Les Créatures de Promethée* was ready for its premiere on 31 December 1929. A strong and spontaneous dancer, Lifar's performance was charged with drama: Prometheus was a rôle announcing the dancer's character and taste on an esthetic level; the part demanded boldness, if not bravado; it was a fit vehicle for an imaginative and aggressive performer. The production was so successful that Lifar was named ballet director and premier danseur étoile without delay. The young star was about to begin his impressive career at the Opéra at the very moment when the Great Depression of the 1930s was lurking in the wings.

The economic crisis saw the disappearance of visiting companies from the stage of the Garnier except for two short programs mounted by Mme Ida Rubinstein's dancers. The only new choreographer of significance to have any appreciable number of works performed at the Opéra during this time was Albert Aveline, who had become ballet master at the Garnier in 1917. He had been acclaimed many years previously as the partner of Carlotta Zambelli and Olga Spessivtzeva, but it was not until 1935 that his first composition was billed at the Opéra. *La Grisi* was a gratifying success on account of its lively and spirited pace, and Aveline was encouraged to produce *Un Baiser pour rien* (1936) and *Elvire* (1937), but these two ballets seemed to disappoint the public. In *Les Santons* (1938) Aveline returned to his *con brio* manner and resorted to the irresistible genre of the doll ballet. Lastly, he entered the insect world by writing fresh choreography for *Le*

Festin de l'araignée (1913), which was presented for the first time at the Garnier theatre on 1 May 1939. Later, in 1941, he also created new choreography for the premiere of *Jeux d'enfants* at the Opéra.

Lifar was in a position to dominate the creation and the production of ballets at the Opéra, and he did precisely this until he left his position there in 1945. In fact, he took care of the darkened opera house itself with the help of the janitor during the early days of the Nazi occupation of Paris. Later he would return to the Garnier as guest choreographer in 1947-58. In 1930, he had to deal with the depression, and, perhaps to his surprise, he found that conditions were favorable for the production of ballets on account of shrinking budgets and decreasing revenue: new works were needed to maintain a note of freshness in the repertory, and it was considerably less expensive to mount a new ballet in a single act than to produce an elaborate opera in four or five acts. Thus, 59 new titles were posted at the Garnier in 1930-39, and 37 of them were ballets. Managerial sensitivity to the relatively low cost of producing ballets is evident again in the fact that 28 of the 37 choreographic compositions in question here were created specifically for the Opéra, where they had their premieres. Also, when *Le Lac des cygnes* was brought to the Opéra from Moscow (1877) via the Opéra-Comique (1935), it was given in its entirety on only 56 programs, whereas extracts from it were billed on 97 evenings. As for the ballets themselves, they were briefer than usual on the average: no new compositions in three acts were mounted in 1930-39, while 12 of the 28 pieces created for the Garnier opera house were in a single act, and only eight were in two acts. The remaining eight ballets were not divided into acts but were presented simply as "a poem" or "a farce" or even as "a choreographic epic," and it is easy to believe that the production of these compositions was neither lavish nor extravagant.

The scores for these ballets were provided by 28 composers of whom 24 did but a single text for the Opéra during the ten years before World War II. Arthur Honegger did two ballets in a single act for the Garnier repertory, *Amphion* (1931) and *Le Cantique des cantiques* (1938), but neither of them was an overwhelming success. The only other individual composers to have two titles billed at the theatre were Tchaikovsky and Henri Tomasi. Serge Lifar did choreography for the former's *Le Lac des cygnes* (1936) and for the *divertissement* of 8 June 1932 offering *La Belle au bois dormant*. Tomasi created the scores for *Les Santons* (1938) in one act and for the extremely popular *La Grisi* (1935) in two acts. Only Albert Roussel had as many as three ballets staged by the dancers in this interval: *Bacchus et Ariane* (1931), *Aenéas* (1938), and *Le Festin de l'araignée* (1939). His last work of 1939 was well received not only at the opera house but also in the Théâtre des Arts, where it had its world premiere in 1913, and at the Opéra-Comique, where it was mounted for the first time in 1922. Laura de Santelmo did the choreography for *Danses espagnoles* (1931) and *Danses d'Espagne* (1936), but she used selections from different composers for her scores, a procedure that was also adopted for *Soirée romantique* (1934) by Henri Busser and for *Fluorescences* (1938) by Loïe Fuller.

As for the major choreographers themselves during the 1929-39 period, it has already been indicated that Léo Staats had been active as a choreographer since the end of World War I, that Albert Aveline was the only other new choreographer besides Lifar to make an appreciable impression on the balletic scene in 1930-39, and that Lifar dominated the situation with his outstanding productivity. Specifically, these three men were responsible for 29 of the 37 ballets: Léo Staats, 5; Albert Aveline, 5; and Serge Lifar, 19. Lifar's influence on the ballet as an artistic medium of communication as well as upon the repertory of the Opéra is to be noted especially because it was he who managed to demonstrate with conclusive force that the music must follow the will of the dancer rather than dictate the dancer's actions and moods. His genius was eclectic, moreover, and he drew his inspiration from wherever he found it without compromising his conviction that the stage and orchestra were in the theatre on account of the performer, not vice versa. *Les Créatures de Promethée* (1929), *Prélude dominical* (1931), *Bacchus et Ariane* (1931), *Jeunesse* (1933), *Icare* (1935), and *Aenéas* (1938) all derived in one way or another from ancient mythology. His *divertissement* of 1932 was a reworking of Petipa's choreography for the fairy tale ballet entitled *La Belle au bois dormant*; *Sur le Borysthène* (1932) was a village comedy set in Russia; *Jeunesse* (1933) satirized in gentle fashion the beach athletes, heliophiles, and bathing beauties of the flapper era trying vainly to amuse themselves. *La Vie de Polichinelle* (1934) and *Salade* (1935) were set in the tradition of the *commedia dell'arte*.

In 1936-38 Lifar did the folkloric *Harnasie* (1936), set in the Tatras mountains and featuring the primitive ways and violent dispositions of the inhabitants of the region. *Le Roi nu* (1936) was inspired by an Andersen fairy tale; *Promenades dans Rome* (1936) told a story of banditry and kidnaping in the villa d'Este. These three 1936 compositions filled with intrigue, action, and color were followed by a cluster of works in which Lifar exhibited a philosophical disposition not seen in his previous creations. *David triomphant* (1937), *Le Cantique des cantiques* (1937), *Alexandre le Grand* (1937), and *Aenéas* (1938) were based upon biblical or pagan antiquity and focused upon a single protagonist faced with his destiny unfolding in a solitude that recalls the loneliness in which Alfred de Vigny's heroes confronted death or God. The physically demanding choreography established by Lifar in these ballets pointed to the superhuman efforts required of the central figures if they were to cope successfully with their predicaments. *Oriane et le prince d'Amour* (1938) expounded a medieval subject set in fourteenth-century Avignon and depending upon a Maeterlinckian brand of symbolism for its effect. Thus, Lifar felt free in his choice of subjects or themes, and he turned without hesitancy to antiquity, the Middle Ages, the Renaissance, or modern times for his settings. His manner ranged from light satire or lively intrigue to philosophical seriousness. Most importantly perhaps, he and Nijinsky restored the male dancer to the position of prominence that he had occupied before the ballerinas of the romantic era had reduced him to the status of a catcher.

A curious feature of the balletic repertory as a whole in 1919-39 was the diverse and relatively large number of musicians and librettists who collaborated with the choreographers at this time. Igor Stravinsky created the music for nine compositions, but he was an outstanding exception to the general pattern of the composer remaining satisfied to have provided one or two pieces for performance at the Opéra. Even Arthur Honegger, with his three original pieces and an orchestration of Bach, was an exceptional case, as was Albert Roussel with his scores for *L'Eventail de Jeanne* (1929), *Bacchus et Ariane* (1931), *Aenéas* (1938), and *Le Festin de l'araignée* (1939). Such composers as Sergei Prokofiev (2), Manuel de Falla (2), Jacques Ibert (2), Darius Milhaud (1), Paul Paray (1), Gabriel Pierné (2), Claude Debussy (2) established the prevailing status of affairs by furnishing one or two but certainly not three compositions for the corps de ballet. Thus, there were enough compositions to meet current needs, but they came from every possible source, and it is a tribute to Lifar's administrative and artistic ability that he was able to maintain a fresh and sufficient repertory throughout the first ten years of his tenure as ballet director.

It should be observed that a surprising number of these ballets produced on limited budgets proved to be quite successful if box office returns may be used as an indication of audience approval. While it is true that two dozen 1930-39 ballets enjoyed no more than ten billings at the Opéra, five of them went on for 20 to 45 representations, and no fewer than seven of them enjoyed more than 50 billings at the Garnier even if *Le Lac des cygnes* be excluded from this count on the grounds that it was not an indigenously French composition. The four works mounted on 50 to 100 dates with the number of times they were performed at the Paris opera house were as follows: *Alexandre le Grand*, 52; *Les Santons*, 78; *Le Festin de l'araignée*, 83; and *Icare*, 84. The three most popular ballets were *La Grisi*, 106; *Elvire*, 139; and the *divertissement* from *La Belle au bois dormant*, 170. Albert Aveline was responsible for the choreography of four of these last seven pieces, while Serge Lifar choreographed the other three, including the *divertissement*.

The outstanding danseuses appearing in these ballets included Camille Bos, Rosita Cérès, Lycette Darsonval, Marie-Louise Didion, Paulette Dynalix, Suzanne Lorcia, and Jacqueline Simoni. The male performers cast almost constantly with them were Serge Peretti, Martial Sauvageot, Nicolas Efimoff, Paul Goubé, and Serge Lifar.

The countless dislocations attendant upon World War II seemed designed to hasten the conversion of the Paris Opéra into a theatre for the ballet as far as new works were concerned in the 1940s because only nine operatic compositions were produced at the Garnier for the first time between 1940 and 1949, and they came from other theatres in Germany and in France. Thus, the same shortage of materials and money that had caused the ballet to flourish in the economically depressed 1930s continued to favor it during the 1940s, and 23 of the 32 new works given at the Garnier in this decade were ballets. It is similarly significant that only nine of these 23 ballets were produced before 1 January 1945 and that Serge Lifar did the choreography for all of them, a fact that prompted charges of collaboration with the enemy to be lodged against him despite the fact that he had been placed in charge of the Opéra by the municipal government of Paris with instructions to preserve the theatre from abuse or even physical destruction. Eight of these ballets were created for the Opéra, and only Edouard Lalo's *Suite* had already been staged elsewhere; it had been given its world premiere by the corps de ballet on a visit to the opera house in Zurich. In retrospect, it seems clear that the theatre would have been closed and left to deteriorate physically, or it would have been made to serve as an overt instrument of enemy propaganda if Lifar had not made a diplomatic effort to preserve the Opéra by keeping it in operation.

In 1945-49 the previously described strikes and money troubles returned to hamper the operation of the Opéra, but the corps de ballet was able to offer 14 new compositions to a critical public demanding greater efforts from the company. Thirteen ballets had their world premieres at the Opéra, while Maurice Ravel's *Pavane pour une infante morte* was borrowed from the repertory of the Opéra-Comique in 1946.

These 23 works billed at the Garnier for the first time in 1940-49 were offered during an especially troubled time, and a lack of uniformity in their themes and the effects they created reflected the unsettled era of their genesis. Although the ballet in a single act was the favored form with nine compositions in this format, the compositions were presented as belonging to a wide variety of subgenres. One work was listed as a tableau, and three others were presented simply as pieces in three tableaux. Three "danced" or "choreographic" poems contained no division by acts. *Lucifer* (1948) was billed as a mystery in three episodes; *Suite en blanc* (1943) was announced tersely as a ballet excerpted from another ballet, *Namouna* (1882).

A similar taste for novelty and variety is found in the range of subjects treated in the ballets. The predilection for classical subjects diminished with only *Endymion* (1949) drawing upon the myths or legends of Hellenic antiquity, and *Lucifer* (1948) returned to the romantic preference for the Bible with its treatment of the story of Adam, Eve, Abel, and Cain. *Entre deux rondes* (1940) presented a fanciful choreographic exchange between a dancer from a Degas painting and an ancient statue of Apollo in the closed Louvre; Gaubert's *Le Chevalier et la damoiselle* (1941) related the tale of the errant knight endowed with great powers and winning the hand of his lady fair despite apparently insuperable obstacles. This imaginative note had been found in the ballets of every age, of course, but it had not been stressed so stunningly in recent programs. It was again present in generous measure in *Les Animaux modèles* (1942) and in *Le Jour* (1943), where stars and the sun parade across the stage, and man meets the object of his quest near a prairie river. Yet sombre and striking portraits of death personified as well as "escape" works were likewise inevitable at this time, and *Les Mirages* (1947) by Henri Sauguet fell into this category. Also, as if to contradict the device of personalizing objects and concepts, George Balanchine tried to sublimate his dancers into hard and abstract light in *Le Palais de cristal* (1947), and the members of the corps de ballet reached for Mallarmean purity in *Suite en blanc* (1943). Once again, Mallarmé's influence asserted itself in *La Mort du cygne* (1948), perhaps the greatest synthesis of the new attitudes toward beauty, love, and death that were becoming discernible in the ballet.

The musicians who provided the scores for the librettos of the war decade were not disposed apparently to write more than one work apiece for the Opéra during this period, although Arthur Honegger proved to be an exception with his *L'Appel de la montagne* (1945) and *La Naissance des couleurs* (1949). Also, Tchaikovsky's music was used on two occasions because Serge Lifar created new choreography for a portion of *Roméo et Juliette* (1945) and George Balanchine revived his work for *Sérénade*. As for the choreographers, George Balanchine had *Le Palais de cristal* (1947) as well as his *Sérénade* (1947) billed at the Opéra, but he, Aveline, and Lifar were the only choreographers to have more than a single work mounted at the theatre. Once again, as ballet master at the Garnier, Lifar dominated the situation as far as choreography was concerned: he did the dance movements for 17 ballets. Robert Quinault and Serge Peretti were the remaining choreographers with *Les Malheurs de Sophie* (1948) and *L'Appel de la montagne* (1945), respectively. As for the comparative success of the works by these five choreographers, seven of their 23 ballets earned ten or fewer representations, and another six were billed at the Opéra between 11 and 30 times. Four of the five compositions mounted on 60 to 100 occasions between 1940 and 1960 were by Lifar: *Roméo et Juliette* (1945), 60; *Les Animaux modèles* (1942), 78; *Guignol et Pandore* (1944), 91; and *Le Chevalier et la damoiselle* (1941), 93. The four most popular works were Lifar's *Entre deux rondes* (1940), 118; Lifar's *Les Mirages* (1947), 129; Balanchine's *Le Palais de cristal* (1947), 175; and Lifar's *Suite en blanc* (1943), 306.

The danseurs cast most frequently in these ballets at this time included Max Bozzoni, Pierre Duprez, Nicolas Efimoff, Alexandre Kalioujny, Lucien Legrand, Serge Peretti, Serge Lifar, Michel Renault, Roger Ritz, and Martial Sauvageot. The danseuses appearing with them were most often Yvette Chauviré, Lycette Darsonval, Paulette Dynalix, Micheline Bardin, Madeleine Lafon, Suzanne Lorcia, and Marianne Ivanoff.

The ballet had an extraordinary resurgence of popularity in the second half of the twentieth century on account of the growing interest shown in it by the public at large, and perhaps the most obvious aspect of the popularity of the ballet was the reappearance of a relatively large number of guest companies at the Garnier. The New York City Ballet was billed at the theatre on 10 May 1952 to mount *Valse*, which was based upon Ravel's music; Alexis Emmanuel Chabrier's *Bourrée fantasque*; and Igor Stravinsky's *La Cage*. George Balanchine also led the company in his choreography for *Le Lac des cygnes* on this program. Two years later, in 1954, the Sadler's Wells Ballet of London appeared at the theatre from 27 September to 10 October. The English artistes brought with them several compositions that Parisians had not yet seen. Extracts from Tchaikovsky's *La Belle au bois dormant* had been given as ballet at the Opéra-Comique on 23 January 1947, but it was not until 27 September 1954 that Tchaikovsky's work was produced in its entirety at the Opéra in a production by the Sadler's Wells company. The second new work by the visitors was the skating ballet from Meyerbeer's *Le Prophète*, which had new choreography by Ashton, and to which the separate title of *Les Patineurs* was given. *Hommage à la reine* was a ballet created in 1953 on the occasion of the coronation of Elizabeth II, but its 1 October 1954 representation at the Garnier palace was the first time that Parisians saw it. The other new compositions offered by the British troupe were *Tirésias* in three scenes and *Mam'zelle Angot* in three acts, both produced initially on 4 October 1954.

A delegation of Russian dancers would have appeared at the Opéra in 1954, when the three weeks between 8 to 31 May had been reserved for them, but the Soviet government canceled their trip to Paris, although specific invitations had been sent by French officials to such distinguished performers as Mlles G. Oulanova, Stoutchkova, Moisseieva, and Doudinskaia and MM. Bregvadzi, Idanov, Makarov, and Sergueiev. The New York City Ballet returned to the Garnier for a billing from 17 to 21 October 1954, and they had an almost completely new repertory for spectators at the Garnier: Benjamin Britten's *Fanfare* (17 October), Balanchine's *Divertissement No. 15* (17 October) with music by Mozart, Balanchine's *Pas de dix* (17 October) with a score by Glazounov, Hershy Kay's *Western Symphony* (17 October), *Les Quatre Tempéraments* (19 October) with music by Hindemith and choreography by Balanchine, and the latter's *Allegro brillante* (19 October) employing music by Tchaikovsky. Lastly, Aaron Copland's *Pied Piper* with choreography by Jerome Robbins was mounted on 19 October.

The Russians compensated in 1958 for their enforced inactivity in 1954: the Bolchoi Ballet appeared at the Opéra from 30 May until 16 June on 16 programs that offered 20 new compositions ranging from a *pas de trois* from *Le Cheval bossu* entitled *Drigo* to *Mirandoline* by Vassilenko in three acts presented on 1 June 1958. In fact, their programs featured no fewer than eight *pas de deux*, four of which starred the teams of Mlle Bogolomova-Vlassov and Mlle Stroutchkova-Khokhlov. Russian dancers were not seen again at the Opéra until the spring of 1961, when the artistes of the Leningrad Opera Ballet brought four new titles with them: Igor Stravinsky's *La Troika*, Vassili Vainonen's *La Valse rose*, Minkus's *Les Ombres* presented on 19 May, and Sergei Prokofiev's *La Fleur de pierre* with choreography by Youri Grigorovitch.

George Balanchine and the New York City Ballet were back at the Garnier to enjoy an engagement of six days and five programs between 28 June and 3 July 1965. The indestructible Balanchine had done the choreography for all nine ballets he staged at the theatre this time, although Martha Graham had collaborated with him on the *Episodes* of 29 June, for which Anton Webern had done the music. The offerings were quite varied and included such diverse pieces as Sousa's *Stars and Stripes* (28 June), Gottschalk's *Tarentella* (28 June), and *Bugaku* (28 June), for which Toshiro Mayuzumi had written the score. The other new pieces on Balanchine's programs were *Liebeslieder Walzer* (29 June) with music by Brahms and *Donizetti Variations* (3 July). Perhaps the most interesting ballet that Balanchine brought with him in 1965 was his *Raymonda Variations* (29 June), which avoided all narrative. Other ballet groups to visit the Garnier more recently included the Moiseyev dancers, who were billed at the theatre on 5 October 1966 before transferring to the Palais des Sports for the remainder of their programs. The Royal Ballet of Denmark performed on 26 and 28 February and 1, 2, and 3 March 1969. Their repertory was composed of a cluster of distinctly exotic compositions that had not yet been billed at the Garnier: *Le Mandarin merveilleux* on 26 February; *Le Conservatoire, Graduation Ball*, and *La Renne de lune* on 1 March; and *Auréoles* on 3 March.

The widening interest in ballet along with a shortage of money for larger operatic compositions had an almost exaggerated influence on the repertory of the Opéra in 1950-70: 58 of the 74 new works produced there in this score of years were ballets, and the ballets in a single act outnumbered the ballets in two acts by two to one, while only three ballets in three acts were selected for presentation. This preponderance of works in a single act allowed once again for a greater variety in the material selected by the Opéra for representation in ballets. It was inherent in the situation that greater variety had to be achieved when 37 new titles were posted in 1950-59 and 21 new compositions were mounted in 1960-69.

Strangely enough, the services of 46 composers were required to provide the scores for these 58 ballets, which depended upon Frédéric Chopin, César Franck, Franz Liszt, and Felix Mendelssohn as well as upon more contemporary musicians for their scores. In fact, Bach supplied the music for *Dramma per musica* (1950) and for *Concerto barocco* (1963), while Hector Berlioz's work was used for *Symphonie fantastique* (1957) and *Arcades* (1964). Tchaikovsky alone among all 46 composers performed this same service for three ballets: *Casse-noisette* (1952), *Pas de deux* (1958), and *La Princesse Aurore* (1964). The musicians to supply two scores included Béla Bartók (*Concerto aux étoiles*, 1956; *Sarracénia*, 1964), André Jolivet (*L'Inconnue*, 1950; *Concerto*, 1958), Sergei Prokofiev (*Roméo et Juliette*, 1955; *Symphonie classique*, 1958), and Knudage Riisager (*Etudes*, 1952; *Qarrtsiluni*, 1960). Works by older composers were revived in whole or in part for a single composition in six instances: Brahms for *Grand Pas* (1953), Chopin for *Suite romantique* (1958), Couperin for *Pastorale* (1961), Debussy for *Pas et lignes* (1957), Mendelssohn for *Symphonie écossaise* (1963), and Liszt for *Constellations* (1969). A number of living musicians who collaborated upon the creation of certain ballets accepted into the repertory during 1950-69 had not had their music played previously at the Opéra, despite their fame in other countries and in France. George Gershwin's *Pas de dieux* (1960) was his first contribution to the company, and *Extase* (1968) was the occasion of Alexander Scriabin's initial booking at the theatre. Jacques Chailly, Raffaelo de Banfield, and Jacques Castarède made their debuts at the Garnier with *La Dame à la licorne* (1959), *Combats* (1957), and *But* (1963), respectively, and other works could be added to this list, for example, Marius Constant's *Le Paradis perdu* (1967), Raymond Loucheur's *Hop-Frog* (1953), and Karlheins Stockhausen's *Zyklus* (1968).

A relatively large group of choreographers was responsible for the creation of the dancing in these ballets, and Serge Lifar continued to be prominent among them, despite his troubles with the committee organized to investigate 1939-44 activities at the Opéra. In 1950-53 he collaborated on a dozen ballets, and he also created the choreography for *Nautéos* (1954), which had had its world premiere at Monte Carlo in 1947. He worked on Prokofiev's music for *Roméo et Juliette* and Marcel Delannoy's *Les Noces fantastiques* in 1955. He did two other pieces in 1957 before doing the book as well as the choreography for *Symphonie classique* in 1958. In this 1950-58 interval, when Lifar was still active, the Opéra likewise billed *La Grande Jatte* (1950), with movements by Albert Aveline; *La Belle Hélène*, upon which John Cranko had collaborated; and five works for which Harald Lander had supplied the dance. These compositions and a Russian *pas de deux* by Lev Ivanov constituted the additions to the ballet repertory at this time except for Hector Berlioz's *Symphonie fantastique* (1957). Thus, Lifar continued to dominate the situation at the Garnier until his retirement, which proved temporary when he returned to the stage for a year on 30 September 1962.

After 1957 a number of choreographers appeared upon the scene with varying degrees of success and frequency. George Skibine's *Idylle* was revived on 5 March 1958 and followed by his three works created for the Garnier during the same year: *Annabel Lee* on 12 March, *Concerto* on 22 October, and *Conte cruel* on 16 December. George Balanchine and Michel Descombey also had three compositions booked at the Opéra, but the latter's *Zyklus* on 8 March 1968 was hissed and provoked a shower of pamphlets demanding the appointment of a new ballet master. The most active choreographer after Lifar proved to be Roland Petit, whose five ballets for the Opéra were posted between 1965 and 1969: *Adage et variations* (1965), *Notre-Dame de Paris* (1965), *Le Paradis perdu* (1967), *Extase* (1968), and *Turangalîla* (1969). Anton Dolin was the creator of the dancing in *Pas de quatre* (1959) and *La Princesse Aurore* (1967), but the eight remaining choreogaphers, including Gene Kelly, Lycette Darsonval, and Yvan Clustine, collaborated on only a single work.

These 1950-70 compositions were sometimes well rooted in the balletic traditions of the Opéra, but others among them struck a completely novel note. Literary masterpieces continued to supply a generous measure of inspiration for scenarists, for example, and Cervantes's famous protagonist was resurrected to furnish the action for *Le Chevalier errant* (1950). *Phèdre* (1950) depended upon Racine's tragedy and upon D'Annunzio's *Fedra* (1915), and at least two other ballets were indebted to the classical literature of France: *L'Astrologue* (1951) was modeled upon La Fontaine's astrologer, who kept looking at the sky until he fell into a well to find the truth there; *Les Fourberies* (1952) was based upon the humor found in Molière's *Les Fourberies de Scapin* and *L'Etourdi*. On the other hand, *Dramma per musica* (1950) was a tale of hunting and love in the style of the eighteenth century, and *Les Caprices de Cupidon* (1952) was a composition of Danish origin recreating the atmosphere of Marie-Antoinette's Versailles. Literary figures of the nineteenth century were recalled in *La Grande Jatte* (1950), which presented a gallery of Maupassant characters enjoying an outing on the Seine as Manet might have seen it, and *La Dame aux camélias* was clearly derived from the play of the same name by Dumas fils, despite its failure to grip its audiences at the Garnier in 1960. *Le Roi David* (1960) by Honegger was biblical in tone, of course, but *Qarrtsiluni* (1960) depended upon sorcery in its rituals celebrating the glory of the midnight sun in the land of the Lapps. This representation of foreign and unfamiliar lands had already been undertaken in Balanchine's *Western Symphony* on 17 October 1956, but the novelty of setting ballet movements to tunes like "On Top of Old Smokey" had failed to impress spectators in Paris.

Yet traditional themes and unusual settings in a different land at different times did not constitute the exclusive inspiration of ballets at the Garnier after 1950 because the philosophical element in balletic representations was becoming more and more pronounced. Concomitantly, less stress was being placed upon intrigue, although stage decorations and costuming were not yet losing their importance on any great scale. Balanchine's *Concerto barocco* had had its world premiere at the Hunter College Playhouse in New

York on 28 May 1941, but it was still important enough to be accepted into Paris repertory on 18 February 1963 because, like Massine's *Les Sylphides* (1956), it opened up new vistas for the ballet by avoiding any trace of a plot in order to pay individual and undistracted attention to the ballet itself. Similarly, *Septuor* (1950) was an abstract ballet; it presented seven hanged men and was devoted to a philosophical allegation concerning man's inhumanity to man. *L'Inconnu* (1950) by Vaillat was likewise based upon a moral statement suggested by the figure of a soldier wandering through the ruins of a shell-torn city only to find his destiny in the cruel and brutal power surrounding him. Thus, no precise or academic limits were placed upon the functions or modes of the ballet, which could now be devoted to pure dancing as in *Les Quatre Tempéraments* or to a philosophical observation about the human condition. One of the compositions to take advantage of this new freedom was *Pas de dieux* (1960), which featured a bit of antiquity and a touch of modernism simultaneously with Venus descending to earth to bring the good word to bathing beauties, boys in tee-shirts, and a gaggle of beatniks. Unfortunately, it was not an impressive production despite Gershwin's music and Gene Kelly's dancing.

This freedom to experiment also encouraged the creation of a large number of ballets at the Opéra in 1950-70, but only *Etudes* (1952) has enjoyed more than a hundred representations since its premiere. Three other ballets were billed appreciably more than the other compositions in this score of years: *Les Caprices de Cupidon*, 70; Serge Lifar's *Variations*, 72; and Jean Cocteau's *Phèdre*, 77. At least 15 of the 58 new ballets of 1950-70 never managed to enjoy five performances despite the services of such distinguished performers as Mlles Josette Amiel, Claude Bessy, Yvette Chauviré, Lycette Darsonval, Liane Daydé, Margot Fonteyn, Madeleine Lafon, Noëlla Pontois, Antoinette Thibon, and Christiane Vaussard and MM. Jean Babilée, Max Bozzoni, Attilio Labis, Serge Lifar, Rudolf Nureyev, Michel Renault, Peter Van Dijk, and George Skibine.

The circumstances leading up to the appointment of Rolf Liebermann to head the administration of the Opéra have already been described, and the corps de ballet and repertory were inevitably affected in parallel fashion by this chain of events. The first important development for the organization of the corps de ballet had taken place on 30 September 1963, of course, when Serge Lifar had left the Garnier for the third and last time. His strong personality had been influencing the tone of every balletic production, whether the program featured Claude Bessy in *Les Noces fantastiques* or Yvette Chauviré in *La Mort du cygne*, but it was now suddenly possible to break away from the Lifarian neoclassic style that was beginning to bore audiences. As often happens, however, it was easier to bid farewell to Lifar than to replace him. Only two candidates seemed qualified to succeed him, Maurice Béjart and Roland Petit. The former refused even to consider becoming dance director at the Opéra, and Roland Petit accepted the invitation twice only to withdraw on both occasions. The strikes, quarrels, and closings plaguing the Garnier theatre were too constant to allow these performers to pursue their art without interference or frustration. M. Petit purchased the Casino de Paris, where he proceeded to direct reviews with his wife, and he accepted the directorship of the Ballets de Marseille, which he had formed; Béjart took a plane to Brussels to sign a contract with the Théâtre de la Monnaie.

Yet the management of the Opéra did keep the ballet alive at the Garnier by establishing the repertory just described and by inviting to Paris the companies already named as having danced on the Garnier stage in the 1960s. The old régime at the Opéra gave as its last program before the installation of Liebermann's staff three works well known to Parisians: *Apollon Musagète*, *Pétrouchka*, and *Les Sylphides*. Nureyev starred in the presentation of these three titles taken from the old Diaghilev repertory of 30 years standing. The new management at the Garnier palace decided to present several pieces set to music by Edgard Varèse in *Hommages à Varèse*, a special program mounted on 24 May 1973 by the Americans Merce Cunningham and John Cage. Liebermann did not wish to foster a spate of new offerings at first lest he arouse opposition, however, and his initial balletic production was a complete ballet executed as the conclusion of Gluck's *Orphée*. A revival of *Coppélia* was the result of this same policy. The year was a success, and it was marred only by Natalia Makarova's refusal to dance in *Le Lac des cygnes* with Nureyev because she felt that he was not equal to the task of performing as her partner. Other highlights of the first year of Liebermann's directorate at the Opéra included an invitation to Roland Petit to appear at the theatre. Petit still had a large following in Paris, and he brought his Marseille troupe to the capital in 1973 with great success, but it was not until 28 February 1974 that he had them dance in a performance at the Opéra, where they executed the recently recovered *Shéhérazade* by Ravel. The composer John Cage and the choreographer Merce Cunningham also had their work performed again on the stage of the opera house on 6 November 1973 when they created *Un Jour ou deux*, a work that required an entire evening to present. Other outstanding attempts made to arouse and to sustain interest in the Opéra included: Jerome Robbins's first trip to Paris in 1973 to produce *Scherzo fantastique*, *L'Après-midi d'un faune*, and *Circus polka*; Balanchine's productions of his own works; revivals of Béjart's *Webern Opus V*, *Le Sacre du printemps*, and *L'Oiseau de feu*; the mounting of *Le Lac des cygnes* (1973) and *La Belle au bois dormant* (1975) in the Cour Carrée of the Louvre; the creation of ballets like *Jeux* (1973), *L'Apprenti Sorcier* (1973), *Il y a juste un instant* (1974), *Tristan* (1974), and *Le Loup* (1975).

The Opéra Today and Tomorrow

In retrospect it is easy to see what caused the present state of affairs at the Garnier palace. In May 1970 the theatre entered a dark period that lasted for a year and a half, and this lengthy closing was simultaneously and ominously a sign and a result of its ailing condition: the Opéra could not continue to function in the presence of the many threats besieging it. The unrelieved mismanagement of the artificially created Réunion des Théâtres Lyriques Nationaux was stifling both the Opéra and the Opéra-Comique by forcing these two companies into a single organization. Also, there was a social crisis born of the sociopolitical conflicts within these two theatres as well as persistent inflation and a lack of artistic values in certain quarters. Eventually the Opéra became an overstaffed unit assigned to perform an impoverished repertory whose productions were paralyzed by the lack of money, talent, and internal harmony.

M. Auric's administration (1962-68) had managed to hold back the flood for a while, but nothing could be done to halt the eventual exodus of international stars from the ranks of the performers at the Garnier, and it was only too obvious that an irreversible deterioration was taking place. The politicians and the administrators called an emergency meeting at the last moment, and their desperate efforts resulted in the appointment of M. René Nicoly to stave off disaster. Unfortunately, M. Nicoly lacked the strength necessary to accomplish this formidable task, and he died in office. M. Edmond Michelet, director of Cultural Affairs, was now obliged to close the Opéra because he could not escape from the appalling fact that the theatre was consuming 40 million *francs* annually and accomplishing little or nothing.

It was at this point that M. Liebermann, director of the Hamburg opera house, was appointed to guide the fortunes of the Opéra in January 1973. The unavoidable interim period was handled by Bernard Lefort and Daniel Lesur.

As has already been noted, M. Liebermann chose to take seriously his commission to restore the Garnier as a recognized center of operatic activity, and he persuaded the government to give him a budget of 60 million *francs* to reach his goal. His policy was expensive: he relied upon the lavish production of great works already in the repertory, and he was determined to cast international stars in the leading rôles. The public responded immediately by returning to the Garnier theatre in large numbers to hear Nicolai Gedda in *Orphée et Eurydice* (1973) or Placido Domingo in *I Vespri siciliani* (1974).

Yet even this new success inspired objections, and Liebermann found himself facing charges that he was neglecting French singers and spending too much money. Then, in 1975, he exceeded his budget of 96.4 million *francs* by 17.8 million *francs*. He protested that salaries paid to foreign singers were not the cause of the deficit, and he replied to his detractors by organizing a successful tour of the United States for the American bicentennial in 1976. Also, he reminded his critics that he wished to use French performers exclusively at the Opéra-Comique, an idea that had not borne fruit because the government had refused to give him permission to open this theatre. Instead, M. Jacques Duhamel, minister of culture, had given the facility on the place Favart to M. Erlo for the Opéra-Studio project that was now costing the taxpayers of France eight million *francs* annually.

The struggle at the Opéra between artistic success and money, between artistes and politicians, came to a head on 19 March 1976. Mozart's *L'Enlèvement au sérail* was billed for performance at the theatre on this evening, and the president of the Republic planned to attend with his guests, but a strike was called at the last moment. The issue was money. The prime minister, M. Jacques Chirac, was now obliged to scrutinize the budget in force at the Garnier, and he was shocked to learn the cost of operating the theatre. He ordered M. Liebermann not to spend more than the 125 million *francs* allotted to him, and he directed the unions to explain to their members that they would have to work longer hours and adhere to more realistic production schedules. There had to be more tours and broadcasts to increase income. M. Chirac entrusted Jean Salusse with the implementation of these innovations.

The situation had now progressed to a critical stage, but M. Salusse's skill as a negotiator, along with the prime minister's threat to close the Opéra, was effective in persuading the unions to moderate their demands. Unfortunately, however, tension arose between M. Liebermann and M. Salusse over the question of finances, and the situation became quite awkward at the opening of the 1976-77 season. Also, this period saw huge sums invested in new productions of *L'Or du Rhin*, *La Walkyrie*, and *La Flûte enchantée*, and these standard works of the repertory failed on this occasion to justify the confidence placed in their box-office appeal. Then, at the end of the season, M. Jean Salusse took his own life for reasons yet unknown.

It was also in 1977 that M. Liebermann announced his decision to retire from the Opéra at the end of his current contract, and he suggested that his successor be chosen as soon as possible. The post of administrator was offered to M. Bernard Lefort, 55 years old and a former baritone and director of the Marseilles opera house in 1965-68. M. Lefort had already served as interim director of the Paris Opéra in 1971-72, and he was currently in charge of the Aix-en-Provence festival. As had been anticipated, M. Lefort accepted the appointment.

Meanwhile M. Liebermann continued in office for the remainder of his term, but the 1977-78 season saw only two new productions at the Opéra: *Le Couronnement de Poppée* by Monteverdi in March 1978 and *La Dame de pique* in July 1978. There were five new titles posted between September 1978 and June 1980: Verdi's *Simon Boccanegra* and *Nabucco*, Berg's *Lulu*, Ravel's *L'Enfant et les sortilèges* paired with Stravinski's *Oedipus rex*, and a new work by Olivier Messiaen.

The seven years after 1973 saw a number of highly successful programs staged at the Opéra, and no operagoer in Paris will forget the Liebermann representations of Wagner, *Les Contes d'Hoffman*, or the world premiere of Berg's posthumously produced *Lulu*. And there were memorable revivals of *Les Noces de Figaro*, *Don Juan*, and *Pelléas et Mélisande*, as well as a reawakening of interest in Verdi. As a director, M. Liebermann's successes were surprisingly constant and certainly merited. Inevitably, he made enemies, but this was not the reason for his retirement in 1980. He explained to his friends and foes alike, "I shall be 70 in 1980. I have worked all my life. I can't do any more. It is the turn of the younger generation to fight for the Opéra."

A number of documents, pronouncements, and interviews have provided insights into the plans that had been made for the future of the Opéra after M. Liebermann's retirement on the evening of 31 July 1980, but the most detailed projection is to be found in the Bloch-Lainé report that stressed a new policy of "simplicity and efficiency" for the Opéra. First, the organization of the Réunion des Théâtres Lyriques Nationaux was dissolved, and the Opéra-Studio was abolished as a separate and independent unit. Henceforth the Opéra was to be the only establishment performing and presenting opera, and the Opéra-Studio would function under its aegis. As for the Opéra itself, it was placed under the authority of a single administrator answering to the administrative council. He was totally responsible for all artistic activity. The first man to occupy this post was M. Bernard Lefort. Secondly, the post of secretary general was created with the understanding that he report directly to the head administrator. M. Jean-Pierre Leclerc filled this office initially and was charged with supervising the management of financial, administrative, and technical services. Lastly, M. Jacques Harmon was named inspector of finances.

These organizational details offered in the Bloch-Lainé paper shed little light on the artistic policy and programs to be pursued, but M. Lefort's own announcements upon assuming office filled this lacuna. He declared as early as 1978 that a School of Lyric Art would replace the Opéra-Studio directed by M. Erlo, and he specified that this school would concern itself primarily with the formation of French singers. Subsequently he revealed his intention to enlarge the repertory at the Opéra in every possible way while featuring works from the eighteenth and twentieth centuries. Thus, it became clear immediately that the new regime did not intend to ignore works like *Turandot*, *La Femme sans ombre*, and *Wozzeck* produced in the Liebermann and pre-Liebermann periods. Also, it was promised that an effort would be made to unearth unusual talent and artistic ability so that the casts for these works might be rejuvenated and strengthened.

Nor did M. Lefort forget the ballet: he decided to keep busy as many dancers as possible by using the other theatres of Paris as well as the Opéra for dance programs, and he asserted that he intended to maintain a high quality of performance wherever the company appeared. He appointed Rosella Hightower as his ballet director, and he engaged Mikhail Baryshnikov to stage a major classical work each year. Contemporary choreographers of the calibre of Jennifer Muller, John Neumeier, and Alwin Nikolais were invited to create works for the Opéra.

M. Lefort began his formal tenure as general administrator at the Opéra in September 1980 with *Die Frau ohne Schatten*, a work that had had its premiere at the Paris opera house on 11 October 1972, when Lefort had been serving as interim head of the Opéra while waiting for M. Rolf Liebermann to assume command. Problems arose in connection with this 1980 revival of Strauss's composition, but the performances by Walter Berry, Gwyneth Jones, Mignon Dunn, and René Kollo along with Christoph von Dohnanyi's conducting provided sufficient reason to nourish high hopes for the immediate future of the Opéra. M. Lefort turned next to *Dardanus* in October 1980, but this production by Jorge Lavelli and Max Bignens of Rameau's neglected composition failed to win audience approval. While Strauss and Rameau inaugurated M. Lefort's regime at the Garnier theatre, the company of the Opéra also presented Jean-Michel Damase's *L'Héritière* at the Salle Favart and Claude Prey's *Les Liaisons dangereuses* at the Salle du Conservatoire. The following month, on 14 November 1980, Sir Charles Mackerras directed the Opéra orchestra in a production of Janáček's *Jenůfa* with Rachel Yakar in the title-rôle of this Götz Friedrich production. The attempt to present this work in French diminished the effectiveness of its music, however, and the ensuing representation of *Der fliegender Holländer* on 5 December with José Van Dam and Hildegard Behrens also proved to be a competent but unimpressive performance that did little to enhance M. Lefort's reputation as general administrator. Few theatregoers paused to take the full measure of M. Lefort's accomplishments during his first four months in office.

The following year, M. Lefort did not relax in his attempts to please his traditional audiences and to attract new spectators by offering a mixture of new and older works at the Opéra and other suitable theatres in the capital. He staged an almost Hollywood-style production of *Carmen* at the Palais des Sports, and he cosponsored the staging of Peter Brook's *La Tragédie de Carmen* at the Bouffes du Nord. Nor did he forget the Champs-Elysées theatre, where he promoted revivals of *Der Rosenkavalier* with Kiri Te Kanawa and *Semiramide* with Montserrat Caballé. He selected the Georges Pompidou Center as the setting for three shorter works by modern composers. In the meantime, the task of refurbishing the Garnier theatre was reaching completion and plans to re-open the opera house with Rameau's *Platée* were moving ahead, when labor disputes arose. Then, only days before opening night, stage director Henri Ronse and designer Beni Montrésor decided that they did not wish to remain involved in the production of Rameau's work, and they walked off the job. M. Lefort was now obliged to cancel his opening night. He filled in with ballets, and the public and press complained. Unfortunately, a new production of *Lohengrin* in January 1982 and a revival of *Fidelio* in February 1982 furnished no consolation either for management or audiences, when these works encountered a cool reception despite conductor Seiji Ozawa's presence in the pit. Jean-Claude Auvray's *Tosca* of 22 March 1982 fared no better than the compositions by Beethoven and Wagner despite Jean-Paul Chambas's striking sets and an enthusiastic ovation accorded to Kiri Te Kanawa. Another bitter pill had to be swallowed the following month: spectators at the Salle Favart rejected Auvray's *Così fan tutte*, when they found this latest version of Mozart's classic boring or even vulgar. Subsequently, the Opéra gave Antoine Vitez's *Orfeo* at the Palais de Chaillot on 2 April and Daniel Lesur's *Ondine* at the Champs-Elysées theatre on 26 April. M. Lefort became even more bitterly discouraged, when certain critics continued to describe his efforts as ineffective and disappointing.

Yet more sympathetic theatregoers began to hope in 1982 that M. Lefort's luck would change at least to the point of allowing him to use his own theatre and of not having the members of his production staff or casts fall ill or resign before opening night. Thus, everybody was looking forward to the new productions of *Eugène Onéguine* and *Roméo et Juliette* at the Garnier palace, when rumors of M. Lefort's resignation began to circulate. Articles appeared in the press. One newspaper of stature observed cautiously that these rumors had not been confirmed at the Ministry of Culture or at the Garnier palace, but some reporters recalled that the minister of culture, Jack Lang, had not renewed Lefort's contract in October 1981. Reasons for M. Lefort's alleged resignation were identified in the press: a lack of harmony among the members of the staff at the Opéra; financial and professional disarray within the Opéra; the incompetence of the orchestra assigned to play for the representation of *Der Rosenkavalier* at the Champs-Elysées theatre; personnel overworked as the result of staging multiple programs at a variety of theatres within a short time; the financial fiasco caused by the lavish staging of *Carmen* at the Palais des Sports; the limited success enjoyed with *Lohengrin*, *Fidelio*, *Tosca*; and the outright failures of *Le Barbier de Séville* and *Orfeo*. Ominously, a press conference was called for 23 June 1982 at the Opéra.

The story broke during the first week in June, when the minister of culture announced that M. Lefort would leave his post at the Opéra on 10 June 1982, although his appointment was not scheduled to expire until 1 July 1983. In the meantime, the Opéra would be managed by a committee composed of M. Paul Puaux, president of the administrative council; M. Jean-Pierre Leclerc, general director; M. Alain Lombard, director of music; and M. Georges Hirsch, dance administrator. M. Lefort would transfer to another position in the Ministry of Culture, and his successor at the Opéra had already been chosen, M. Massino Bogianckino, formerly director at La Scala in Milan.

M. Lefort canceled his 23 June press conference, but he did indicate that he had resigned, because he had come to the conclusion that his position at the Opéra was a thankless and burdensome task. Also, he spoke of the acrimony of certain artistes who resented working full time for their money, and who had done their best to make his stay at the Garnier palace quite unpleasant. There was likewise a cluster of waspish individuals outside the Opéra who made every effort to be a constant source of irritation for reasons best known to themselves. Most depressing was the hostile atmosphere within the opera house where a resentful mood stood in marked contrast to the happy attitudes the director had encountered in the other theatrical environments where he had worked.

Yet it was a real consolation for M. Lefort to be able to recall that he had proven himself to be abreast of the times with his operatic and balletic programs even if every undertaking had not been a total and resounding success. He had brought Janáček's *Jenůfa* and Ligeti's *Le Grand Macabre* to Paris at great risk to his reputation in 1980-81, and in ballet he had scheduled Alwin Nikolais's *Schema* for 1980 as well as Neumeier's *Le Songe d'une nuit d'été* and Rudolf Nureyev's *Don Quichotte* for 1981.

The Opéra was able to offer programs in the second half of 1982 despite M. Lefort's abrupt departure from the theatre inasmuch as he had played an important part in arranging for the productions of *Il Tabarro* and *La Paillasse* in July, *Eugène Onéguine* in September, Aribert Reimann's *Lear* in November, and *Falstaff* in December. A schedule of ballets continued until the end of 1982, when the Opéra contributed to the spirit of the Advent season with a performance of *Cassenoisette* after its production of the fragile but indestructible *La Sylphide* at the Opéra-Comique, where *Les Contes d'Hoffmann* had also enjoyed another revival.

M. Lefort's sudden resignation was a shock to many people, but it caused only a minor upheaval compared to the reaction to the 1982 announcement that plans were being formulated to build a new opera house to replace the grand old structure erected by Charles Garnier at the head of the avénue de l'Opéra. As when the Garnier palace had been projected at the close of the nineteenth century, architects throughout the world were invited to submit plans for the new opera house to be located on the site of the present place de la Bastille. These plans were to be filed by December 1982. The minister of culture, Jack Lang, explained that an international jury would select the winning set of plans without knowing the identity of the author of the plans. Architects were urged to pay attention to the milieu in which the building would stand, and they were informed that the theatre must contain 2,500 to 3,000 seats (the Garnier theatre has 1,710 seats of which 300 are acknowledged to be partially or totally obstructed). The new structure should contain in addition to the theatre itself a rehearsal hall that would be a duplicate of the theatre itself so that scenery and lighting might be in proper placement and alignment for rehearsals. Room had to be made available for tryouts, television filming and recording, and other functions expected of a modern theatre, while the usual space for the fabrication and storage of scenery and costumes had to be similarly provided. These requirements were rigid, because it was planned to mount four or five works in close rotation during each of the 25 units of performance time to be established every year. The government did not publish a suggested budget for this project.

Future developments in this ambitious building program are being awaited with mixed emotions in Paris, but no one has yet had the courage to assess the impact of a new opera house on future generations of opera lovers. Yet it is already possible to see here and there a pedestrian crossing the place de l'Opéra with a wistful look in his eye.

ABBREVIATIONS

ACD: Anatole Chujoy, *The Dance Encyclopedia* (New York: A. S. Barnes & Co., 1949).

ACPM: Anatole Chujoy, *The Dance Encyclopedia*, ed. Anatole Chujoy and P. W. Manchester (New York: Simon and Schuster, 1967).

AEM: *Die Musik in Geschichte und Gegenwart: allgemeine Enzyklopädie der Musik*, ed. Friedrich Blume, 17 vols. (Kassel u. Basel: Barenreiter, 1949-79).

AM: *L'Art musical*, Paris, 1860-70, 1872-94, 1935-36, 1938-39.

BBD: *Baker's Biographical Dictionary of Musicians*, ed. Nicolas Slonimsky, 6th ed. (New York: Schirmer Books, 1978).

Bio univ: *Biographie universelle ancienne et modern* (Paris: Delagrave, n.d.), 40 vols.

Brenner: Clarence O. Brenner, *A Bibliographical List of Plays in the French Language, 1700-1789* (Berkeley, California: Assoc. students' store, 1947).

CBCM: David Ewen, *The Complete Book of Classical Music* (Englewood Cliffs, New Jersey: Prentice-Hall, Inc., 1965).

CDHS: Alexandre Cioranescu, *Bibliographie de la littérature française du dix-huitième siècle*, 3 vols. (Paris: Editions du Centre National de la Recherche Scientifique, 1969).

CDSS: Alexandre Cioranescu, *Bibliographie de la littérature française du dix-septième siècle*, 3 vols. (Paris: Editions du Centre National de la Recherche Scientifique, 1965-66).

CG: Cuthbert Girdlestone, *La Tragédie en musique, 1673-1750* (Genève: Droz, 1972).

Chouquet: Gustave Chouquet, *Histoire de la musique dramatique en France* (Paris: F. Didot, 1873).

CL: Félix Clément and Pierre Larousse, *Dictionnaire des opéras*, 2 vols. (reprint ed., New York: Da Capo Press, 1969).

CODB: Horst Koegler, *The Concise Oxford Dictionary of Ballet* (London: Oxford University Press, 1977).

DBF: *Dictionnaire de biographie française*, 14 vols. (Paris: Letouzey et Ané, 1933-).

DDO: Félix Clément and Pierre Larousse, *Dictionnaire des opéras*, 2 vols. (reprint ed., New York: Da Capo Press, 1969).

EC: Emile Compardon: *L'Académie royale de musique au XVIIIe siècle*, 2 vols. (reprint ed., New York: Da Capo Press, 1971).

EDB: *The Encyclopedia of Dance and Ballet*, ed. Mary Clarke and David Vaughan (New York: G. P. Putnam's Sons, 1977).

EDS: *Enciclopedia dello spettacolo*, 9 vols. (Roma: Casa editrice Le Maschere, 1954-62).

EFC: Jean Gourret, *Encyclopédie des fabuleuses cantatrices de l'Opéra de Paris* (Paris: Editions Mengès, 1981).

ELM: *Encyclopédie de la musique*, ed. François Michel, 3 vols. (Paris: Fasquelle, 1958-61).

Fétis: F.-J. Fétis, *Biographie universelle des musiciens et bibliographie générale de la musique*, 8 vols. and 2 suppl. (reprint ed., Brussels: Culture et civilisation, 1963).

GDHS: Georges Grente, *Dictionnaire des lettres françaises: Le dix-huitième siècle*, 2 vols. (Paris: Arthème Fayard, 1960).

GDSS: Georges Grente, *Dictionnaire des lettres françaises: Le dix-septième siècle* (Paris: Arthème Fayard, 1954).

GE: *La Grande Encyclopédie*, 31 vols. (Paris: H. Lamirault et Cie., 1886-1902).

Grove: *Grove's Dictionary of Music and Musicians*, ed. Eric Blom, 5th ed., vols. 1-9 and suppl. (New York: St. Martin's Press, 1955).

Lajarte: Théodore de Lajarte, *Bibliothèque musicale du théâtre de l'Opéra*, 2 vols. (Paris: Librairie des bibliophiles, 1878; reprinted in Georg Olms Verlag, Hildesheim, 1969).

LXIX: Pierre Larousse, *Grand dictionnaire universel du XIXe siècle*, 15 vols. and 2 suppl. (Paris: Larousse et Boyer, 1866-90).

MOTO: Louis Biancolli and Herbert F. Peyser, *Masters of the Orchestra from Bach to Prokofieff* (New York: G. P. Putnam's Sons, 1954).

MQ: *Musical Quarterly*, 68 vols. 1915- .

NBG: *Nouvelle biographie générale*, ed. Hoefer, 46 vols. (Paris: Didot, 1853-66).

NEO: David Ewen, *The New Encyclopedia of the Opera* (New York: G. P. Putnam's Sons, 1971).

ON: *Opera News*, New York, 47 vols., 1936-   .

PJ: Arthur Pougin, *Un ténor de l'Opéra au XVIIIᵉ siècle: Pierre Jélyotte et les chanteurs de son temps* (Paris: Librairie Fishbacher, 1905).

RdM: *Revue de musicologie*, 68 vols. 1922-   .

RGO: *Recueil général des opéras*, 3 vols. (reprint ed., Genève: Slatkine Reprints, 1971).

RHL: *Revue d'histoire littéraire de la France*, 83 vols. 1894-   .

RHS: *Revue d'histoire des sciences et de leurs applications*, 35 vols. 1947-   .

RHT: *Revue d'histoire du théâtre*, 34 vols. 1948-49-   .

RM: *Revue musicale*, Paris, 1920.

SDLD: *Saisons de la danse*, 16 vols., Paris, 1967-   .

Sonn: Oscar George Theodore Sonneck, *Catalogue of Opera Librettos Printed before 1800* (Washington, D.C.: Government Printing Office, 1914).

SS: Riccardo Mezzanotte, ed., *The Simon and Schuster Book of the Ballet* (New York, N.Y.: Simon and Schuster, 1980).

SVEC: *Studies on Voltaire and the Eighteenth Century* (Banbury, Oxfordshire: Voltaire Foundation).

SW: Stéphane Wolff, *L'Opéra au Palais Garnier, 1875-1962* (Paris: L'Entr'acte, 1962).

TdT: Évrard Titon du Tillet, *Le Parnasse français* (Paris: Coignard fils, 1732; reprint ed., Genève: Slatkine Reprints, 1971).

Thompson: *The International Cyclopedia of Music and Musicians*, ed. Oscar Thompson, 6th ed., ed. Nicolas Slonimsky (New York: Dodd, Mead, & Co., 1949).

Thurner: A. Thurner, *Les reines du Chant* (Paris: A. Hennuyer, n.d.).

WT: Walter Terry, *Great Male Dancers of the Ballet* (Garden City, New York: Anchor Press-Doubleday, 1978).

The
Paris
Opéra

A

Achille et Polyxène, which was produced for the first time at the Palais-Royal* on 7 November 1687, was the creation of five artists. Jean-Baptiste Lully* wrote the overture and the first act of the score, which was completed by Pascal Colasse* after the former's death on 22 March 1687. Jean Galbert de Campistron* did the libretto for this lyric tragedy in five acts, and the ballet was created by Lestang* (I, IV) and Pécourt* (prologue, II, III).

The prologue of *Achille et Polyxène* employs the usual seventeenth-century device of developing a spectacle through the presentation of gods and goddesses gathering together to sing the praises of the king and to announce the subject of the forthcoming performance in the course of their divine celebration. The comparatively brief prologue here begins in a slightly different manner because the Muses of tragedy, comedy, and music have met to lament the sadness in the land and their rejection by a king bent upon new conquests. Yet this reference to the current national predicament is in the vein of Lully to some degree because this composer had pointed to current events in his previous compositions, for example, *Cadmus et Hermione.** The more confident and laudatory tone of the Lullian prologue is restored without too much delay when the scene is returned to "its first magnificence" to match the renewed joy of the Muses and their retinues, who sing and dance with delight in their anticipation of a more joyous day at hand. The conclusion of the prologue, with its description of "the valor, goodness, and profound wisdom" of "the greatest King," is sheer stereotype. Jupiter is responsible for this revival of spirits and renewal of optimism, and his arrival in his celestial chariot enforces a stage effect that was almost a convention at the Palais-Royal by 1688. Campistron had already written the poem for Lully's *Acis et Galathée,** and Colasse had been his secretary charged with filling in certain portions of his scores. The similarity of *Achille et Polyxène* to Lully's other works makes it imperative to describe this last composition upon which Lully worked as being totally bound to his manner and concepts.

The main action in the work itself does not call upon a secondary plot for support and relief, however, and its involvement of four characters in the love affair recalls Racine's techniques with plots and Campistron's admiration for this playwright and his work. Just as the author of *Andromaque* had presented the story of Hector's widow, her maternal love for Astyanax, and the portrait of the woman scorned in Hermione, Campistron depicts his own Andromaque as a grieving mother, and he develops the situation of Briséis calling upon Junon to avenge her rejection by Achille, now in love with Polyxène. The phase of the intrigue wherein Agamemnon loves Briséis, who loves Achille in love with Polyxène, echoes Racine's arrangement of Oreste in love with Hermione, who loves Pyrrhus in love with Andromaque, but this involvement is not maintained to the end by Campistron. He introduces Briséis as the captive of Agamemnon and indifferent toward a resentful Achille (I), but the Trojan king returns her to her suitor when the latter consents to do battle with Hector (II). He then introduces Achille's sudden love for Polyxène and his fickle rejection of Briséis (III). The marriage of Polyxène and Achille is arranged (IV), but Paris kills him, and Polyxène stabs herself with the arrow that has killed Achille (V).

The plot adheres to the course of Homeric events, but the presentation of these episodes is not always satisfactory. The major weakness of the libretto is its unprepared use of Paris as the agent responsible for Achille's death, and its failure to establish a link between Paris and Junon's wrath is an inadequacy that leaves one wondering why Junon was summoned to appear in the first place. A seventeenth-century audience might reasonably be expected to know the principle figures of Homeric legend and their destinies, and detailed explanations were not a rigid regulation for musical compositions at the time, but it seems that a careful librettist might have afforded his listeners at least a hint of what was in the offing without destroying suspense. The team of Lully and Quinault* had not found it necessary to call suddenly and at random upon gods and goddesses merely to assure the use of machines.

But, like the prologue, the tragedy does recall Lully at nearly every other turn. The recitative promotes the progression of the intrigue, and arias are introduced at crucial points in the evolution of the plot to underline and to exploit moments of emotional stress. The course of events in each act except the last is interrupted by the spectacle of a goddess descending from the skies, for example, Vénus entering to console Achille (I, 4) and Junon appearing with her Furies (III, 7), or by choruses offering hymns to martial prowess (II, 2) or to pastoral joy (III, 9). Since the fifth act concludes with the dramatic suicide of Polyxène, the equivalent of a grand finale is included but placed at the end of the fourth act, where Priam orders the marriage celebration, and the bands of Trojan men and women oblige the king in a series of solos, duets, and choruses praising love, peace, and abundance. Lully's preoccupation with the rules of regular tragedy is reflected in two allusions to the unity of time (III, 7; IV, 2), but the usual casual attitude toward the unity of place prevails, and each act unfolds in a different location: Achille's secluded refuge (I), Agamemnon's camp (II), Achille's camp (III), Priam's palace (IV), the temple of Apollon (V). Thus, the action takes place inside and outside the walls of Troy.

Parisians were awaiting the premiere of *Achille et Polyxène* with impatience after Lully's death because they were wondering about the calibre of future programs at the Palais-Royal. The dauphin remembered Campistron's *Acis et Galathée* given in his honor at Anet, and he attended its premiere. But the work was a disappointment, and the log of the Opéra suggests that it was dropped sometime between 23 November and 14 December 1687. It was brought back to the stage in the capital on 11 October 1712, but it had to be dropped permanently from the repertory on 30 October 1712 after only six billings. The *Mercure* for November 1687 seems to imply that the cause of its failure was its inadequate music and its inability to adhere to the standards set by Lully for lyric tragedies. The leading female rôles were created by Mlles Le Rochois* (Polyxène), Moreau (Andromaque), and Desmatins* (Briséis) opposite Du Mesny as Achille and Dun as Agamemnon. Priam was sung by Beaumavielle.* This work enjoyed the services of the foremost members of the company, therefore, and its unhappy fate can scarcely be attributed to the performers who appeared in it.

BIBLIOGRAPHY: CDSS I, 510-11; GDSS 222-23; Lajarte I, 56, 71; Parfaict brothers, *Dictionnaire des théâtres de Paris*, 6 vols. (Paris: Rozet, 1767) I, 10-13; L. Travenol and Jacques Durey de Noinville, *Histoire du théâtre de l'Opéra en France*, 2 vols. (Paris: Joseph Barbou, 1753) I, 188-90.

Acis et Galathée is Jean-Baptiste Lully's* last completed work. Since Philippe Quinault* had withdrawn his services as librettist to Lully after the completion of *Armide*,* the composer requested Jean Galbert de Campistron* to supply him with a written text for his new heroic pastoral. *Acis et Galathée* had been commissioned by the duke de Vendôme, who desired to stage a festival at the Château of Anet in honor of the dauphin. This celebration took place on 6 September 1686, and Lully's composition was well received with Mlle Le Rochois* and Du Mesny in the title-rôles. The unpublished log of the Opéra asserts that it was staged five times in all at Anet on 6, 7, 9, 10, and 18 September, but Lully's secretary has left a report that it "was played every evening at Anet from the sixth to the thirteenth of September." It was also applauded with enthusiasm in Paris, where it was given for the first time at the Palais-Royal* on 17 September 1686.

The prologue of *Acis et Galathée* presents an abstraction, L'Abondance, and a group of gods and goddesses who have gathered at the château of Anet to honor the son of "the most just and powerful of kings." The leading rôle is assigned to Diana because the château was built for Diane de Poitiers and is laden with artistic references to the goddess of the same name. The celebration is to be in the form of singing and dancing with all the joy and merriment that L'Abondance can inspire with the aid of Comus. Apollon appears on a cloud to approve all this festivity and to provide the inevitable eulogy of Louis XIV and his son. This prelusive section of *Acis et Galathée*, then, is in the tradition of *Pomone** and *La Grotte de Versailles* insofar as it is set in a real place recognized by the spectators. It employs both groups of characters usually found in prologues, allegorical figures and divinities, and it strives for a more than perfunctory interest by arranging for the spectacle of a god suspended in the sky.

The libretto of the work itself is based upon three love affairs apparently established to provide the composer with a wide range of moods and sentiments. The Tircis-Aminte involvement is presented as the perfect pastoral love, which is free from all perils and obstacles. It is introduced in I, 6 and is neither prepared nor revived. This pair of lovers serve only to lead a chorus singing the charms of untroubled love. The Télème-Scylla affair is endowed with the status of a subplot, but its relevance to the main intrigue is achieved almost exclusively by Télème's friendship for the protagonist and by his sympathetic interest in Acis's predicament. Obviously developed to run parallel to the main plot, this love affair provides moments of despair and frustration created by Scylla's adamant refusal to entertain her lover's suit. This couple is never on stage alone, and they appear in the company of Acis or Galathée in three scenes (I, 5 and 6; II, 2). This hopeless and impossible love is also dropped early in the composition, when Scylla exits for the last time in II, 3. Thus, these minor love affairs are introduced and abandoned in the first half of the work.

The principal intrigue changes its structure from act to act and even within the acts themselves on account of the shifting attitudes of the characters involved in the triangle. The first six scenes of the opening act present Acis in love with Galathée but apparently rejected by her. This unusually simple love situation is made more complex in I, 7 by the disclosure that the monster, Poliphème, is a second suitor of Galathée. The triangle is then complicated further by Galathée's subsequent encouragement of Poliphème's suit to prevent harm from befalling the land and its people (I, 8). Thus, by the end of the first act, the heroine rejects one suitor only to accept a second suitor under duress. Failing to understand Galathée's ploy, Acis threatens to seek death by doing battle with the unconquerable giant. Galathée is obliged to explain her motives to Acis, and the triangle is apparently resolved by her admission to the hero that she loves him, not Poliphème (II, 4-5). Yet Galathée's fear of the giant induces her to encourage him to seek her father's consent to their marriage (II, 7). Once again, therefore, the plot is simplified only to be complicated by Galathée's fear of Poliphème. Yet the marriage of Acis and Galathée has been planned, and it is only a question of time before Poliphème is aware of being betrayed and falls into a murderous rage (III, 3). He crushes Acis to death with an enormous boulder (III, 5-6). Galathée finds her lover's lifeless body (III, 7) and calls upon Neptune (III, 8) to restore him to life as a river. The curtain falls amidst general rejoicing and the reminder that love triumphs over all obstacles (III, 9-11).

The use of peripeteia is almost constant in this work, therefore, and the element of surprise so cherished in operatic productions is furnished at least twice in each act. The divinity of Galathée (I, 3; III, 8) and Neptune (III, 9) promotes the spectacle of this nymph and god emerging from the sea on three occasions. As an added fillip, Galathée also disappears into the waves in III, 6. Acis is a mere mortal, but he is subjected to death, resurrection, and metamorphosis, three devices dear to audiences at the Palais-Royal.* The awesome sight of Poliphème slaying him with a huge boulder constitutes an episode of bloody violence not matched since the slaughter of Medusa in *Persée*.* And the chorus in the grand finale provides the necessary lesson that fear, hatred, and anger pale before insuperable Amour.

The unpublished journal of the Opéra indicates that *Acis et Galathée* was the only work performed at the Palais-Royal* between 17 September and 29 December 1686, but this document is not complete for these last four months of 1686. After its first run, it was revived for 17 representations between 13 June and 21 July 1702 and for another 15 billings from 3 September to 6 October 1709. It had a fourth run of 23 performances in the interval of 8 August to 7 October 1718. After the regency, it was returned to the stage again in 1734, 1744, 1752, and 1762. It had the distinction of being the first foreign opera presented in Hamburg (1689).

The chorus of *L'Amour dans ces beaux lieux* in I, 6 and the passacaglia in III, 9 were the two musical passages in *Acis et Galathée* that evoked the greatest response among spectators.

BIBLIOGRAPHY: CL I, 6; DDO I, 6; Lajarte I, 54-55; Lionel de La Laurencie, *Lully* (Paris: Alcan, 1919), 71-72; Henry Prunières, *Lully* (Paris: Henri Laurens, n.d.), 64-67; RGO III, 179-212; R.H.F. Scott, *Jean-Baptiste Lully* (London: Peter Owen, 1973), 114-15; Sonn I, 29-30.

Alceste was mounted initially at the Palais-Royal* on 19 January 1674, and it has the distinction of being the first work to have its premiere in this theatre under the auspices of the Royal Academy of Music. Philippe Quinault* did the libretto, and Lully* wrote its score. *Alceste* was the second composition by these collaborators; its origin in Greek tragedy underlines Lully's intent to develop the new genre designated as "lyric tragedy."

Like *Pomone*,* *Alceste* is endowed with a prologue set in the Tuileries,* and the mood of the text is sad and langorous to match the spirit of the idea developed in the prologue to *Cadmus et Hermione**: the king's absence has saddened the country. No connection exists between the prologue and the tragedy itself, and one of the principal virtures of this requisite homage to Louis XIV is its brevity.

Quinault and Lully seem to have agreed to use Euripides' account of Hercules and Alceste for two reasons: it was based upon a god's intervention in human affairs; and it provided an opportunity to demonstrate the validity of the concept that opera should be dramatic as well as musical. But *Alceste* is also a *tragédie galante* appealing to the "precious" audiences of the day. Hercule is a pining lover; Admète is a faithful and attentive suitor; Céphise is a constant flirt. The love element dominates all else in *Alceste*, then, since no character escapes the wiles of Venus. Moral maxims about love, life, and the pursuit of the opposite sex abound.

The French version of the story presents Admète, Lycomède, and Alcide as suitors of Alceste, who is already pledged to Admète. The subordinate plot depicts Lichas and Straton as rivals for the hand of frivolous Céphise. The scene of events varies freely enough to offer with plausibility the spectacles of an escape across the sea, a besieged city, and a sojourn in the underworld. Lully takes advantage of these opportunities to compose a musical picture of a storm at sea and of a battle announced with trumpets and violins. It is evident that Lully has already found his formula for martial scenes. He relies heavily upon the recitative as he had done before in *Cadmus et Hermione*,* however, and one of the most striking passages in the score is Lycomède's declamation in D minor (I, 5), where his voice blends with two violins. The affinity of the music for the words is one of the truly prominent features of the score, moreover, and Lully never stops the action simply to exhibit his talents in a burst of Italianate virtuosity. One of his most interesting airs in *Alceste* is Caron's "Il faut passer tôt ou tard" (IV, 1).

Alceste was presented twice at Court in 1677: at Fontainebleau in September and at Saint-Germain en Laye in December. It was given once again at the latter royal residence in the first week of January 1678. The prologue and first act were mounted for the Queen's Concert at Marly on 14 February 1703, and the second and third acts were done there under the same auspices two days later. *Alceste* was revived in Paris in 1678, 1682, 1706, and 1707.

BIBLIOGRAPHY: CG 60; CL I, 26; DDO I, 27; Etienne Gros, *Philippe Quinault* (Paris: Champion, 1926), 529-30, 555-65, 597-99; Lajarte I, 24-25; Lionel de la Laurencie, *Lully* (Paris: Alcan, 1919), 39-41, 149-52; Jean-Baptiste Lully, *Alceste . . . reconstituée et réduite pour piano et chant par Théodore de Lajarte* (Paris: T. Michaëlis, 18?); idem, *Oeuvres complètes: les opéras*, ed. Henry Prunières, 10 vols. (New York: Broude Brothers, 1966) II, VII-XXXIX and 1-349; RGO I, 205-72; Sonn I, 49-51.

Alcide is a lyric tragedy in five acts and a prologue for which Jean-Galbert de Campistron* did the libretto and the team of Louis de Lully* and Marin Marais* wrote the score. The poem was criticized for being poorly composed, but the work was revived as *La Mort d'Hercule* on 23 June 1705 and under the third title of *La Mort d'Alcide* on 18 August 1716. It was returned to the stage of the Palais-Royal* for the last time on 15 October 1744. The first run of *Alcide* extended from 3 February to 15 May 1693; it enjoyed another 34 representations between 23 June and 8 September 1705, and the 1 to 27 September 1716 revival saw only a dozen billings of the composition. The records for 1744 are incomplete, but they imply that this last revival was quite brief, perhaps three or four stagings at most.

The prologue of *Alcide* is based upon the rather ingenious idea of presenting Victoire refusing to listen to the frantic pleas of the enemies of France, since the causes for which this nation goes to war are so just that they cannot be denied. As in *Coronis** and *Astrée*,* the prologue of this work is brief and sings the praises of the dauphin while alluding only fleetingly to the coming "spectacle of pomp" that has been made possible by royal valor in the current war of the League of Augsburg.

The interlocking of political and love interests in *Alcide* recalls the constant use of this technique in regular tragedy, and the status of the heroine as a captive loved by her captor suggests Racine's *Andromaque*, although Iole is not a bereaved widow. In the opera, Iole is the prisoner of Alcide, who has slain her father and confiscated her kingdom (I, 1), but her enemy's love for her leads him to offer her his hand in marriage, the return of her kingdom, and the liberty of her people (I, 5). This proposal fills Iole with deep misgivings (I, 6) because she is in love with Philoctète (I, 3, 7). The second act brings the added complications of Déjanire's arrival in the kingdom of Iole (II, 1) and her discovery that her fickle husband has fallen in love with his latest captive (II, 3). L'Amour pledges his aid to Iole and Philoctète in a rapturous interlude (II, 6), and Déjanire's decision to punish Iole, not her husband, leads to the third act set in the grotto of the sorceress Thestilis. The latter recalls to Déjanire the magic power of Nessus' shirt, which she still has in her possession, and which will help Alcide forget Iole (III, 1-3).

A series of four short scenes at the start of the fourth act presents Alcide's discovery that Iole and Philoctète are in love (IV, 1-3) and his subsequent determination to destroy his rival (IV, 4). The remainder of the fourth act is devoted to Alcide's last offerings to Iunon (IV, 5-7) and Déjanire's resolution to use Nessus's shirt to prevent the Alcide-Iole wedding (IV, 8-9). The conclusion of the legend recounting Hercules' death was too well known for Campistron to dare change it, of course, and the last act of the opera presents Alcide in the torments of a fiery death after donning Nessus's garment poisoned with the centaur's blood (V, 4). This episode occurs after the completion of preparations for his marriage to Iole (V, 1-3). When Déjanire beholds what she has wrought, she dies of grief (V, 5). Alcide then casts himself into the flames of the pyre in a desperate act of self-immolation (V, 6). The tragedy comes to an abrupt and sudden halt because it is complete: nothing remains except for Iole and Philoctète to wed.
BIBLIOGRAPHY: CG, 139; CL I, 28; Lajarte I, 60-61; RGO IV, 229-80; Sonn I, 52.

Alcine is a lyric tragedy in five acts and a prologue with music by André Campra* and a libretto by Antoine Danchet.* It had its premiere at the

Palais-Royal* on 15 January 1705, and its first run extended for 16 performances, but it was dropped from the repertory on 16 February 1705. Mlle Desmatins* created the title-rôle with Mlle Maupin* as Mélanie and Thévenard* in the part of Athlant.

The prologue presents the followers of La Gloire urging their warriors to new feats of arms, but Le Temps resolves to eradicate their glory. La Gloire refuses to surrender to Le Temps, and she suggests that the story of Alcine be retold.

The opera begins with Alcine wandering through a desert and finding a soldier washed ashore in the recent storm. When she admits to Nérine that she loves this unknown victim of Neptune, her companion reminds her that Athlant is still her suitor (I, 1). Alcine comes upon Astolphe lamenting the death of his beloved (I, 2); she encourages him to take heart and raises an enchanted palace for his pleasure (I, 3). She beautifies the countryside to distract him further, but he refuses to be consoled for losing Mélanie at sea. Alcine confesses her love for him and urges him to forget his grief, but he rejects her proposal (I, 4-5). Alcine summons her demons to protect him (I, 6).

The set of the second act deserves separate mention: it features several of Alcine's former lovers transformed into trees, and it is against this background that Athlant insists that he has lost interest in cruel Alcine (II, 1). Mélanie arises suddenly from the sea accompanied by a chorus of Néréides (II, 2), and Athlant assures Alcine that he has found a new love in Mélanie. Alcine adds that her beloved Astolphe also loves Mélanie. He suggests that they join forces to disrupt the Astolphe-Mélanie relationship by persuading Alcine to announce her marriage to Astolphe (II, 3-4). Alcine falls in with the plot (III, 1-3). Mélanie laments her lover's inconstancy (III, 4), and Athlant tries to win her hand by consoling her, but she rejects him (III, 5). He entertains the idea of retaliation for an instant but then decides to deceive Alcine and to help Astolphe escape (III, 6).

Astolphe plans to sail away with Mélanie (IV, 1). He prays for fair weather and disappears (IV, 2) before returning to hear Mélanie upbraid him for his sudden love for Alcine. He denies the charge, and they are reconciled only to have abysses open at their feet and flames shower down upon them. Evil magicians and monsters add horror to their perils (IV, 3-5). Yet despite this pyrotechnical attack, Alcine is still pondering whether to destroy or to spare Mélanie and Astolphe (V, 1). Athlant is determined to slay Astolphe, however, although Alcine shudders at the prospect of his death (V, 2). In fact, she interferes when he attacks Astolphe. Athlant allows Astolphe and Mélanie to marry, and the exasperated enchantress attacks Mélanie bodily in her fury to provide the first physical struggle between female characters in the history of French opera (V, 3). Mélisse intercedes to stay Alcine's hand while liberating her captives and leaving the happy couple free to wed (V, 5).

BIBLIOGRAPHY: CG, 197; CL I, 28; Lajarte I, 104-5; RGO VIII 333-92; Sonn I, 54.

Alcyone, **or** *Alcione*, is a lyric tragedy in five acts and a prologue with a musical score by Marais* and a libretto by Houdard de La Motte.* This work has been remembered by musicologists for its musical description of a storm in the fourth act; this portion of its score is credited with being one of the earliest instances of descriptive music in French opera. *Alcyone* was revised many times, but the storm music remained intact. Its first run lasted from 18 February until 27 April 1706 at the Palais-Royal,* and its initial revival extended for 17 representations between 17 April and 14 May 1719. Its third run at the Palais-Royal lasted from 9 May until 11 July 1730 with additional billings on 28 September and 8 October of this same year. The prologue was dropped on this last date so that the *divertissement** entitled *Le Caprice d'Erato* might be given with it. Marais's work was revived with many changes in 1756 and 1771. The rôle of Alcyone was created by Mlle Journet,* and this part was sung later by Mlles Pélissier (1730) and Chevalier (1756). Ceix was sung first by Murayre and then by Tribou with the rôle of Pélée being filled by de Chassé and Le Page in 1730 (for Mlle Pélissier, Chassé, Le Page and Tribou, see eighteenth-century volume). It might be recalled that Alcyone provides the English word halcyon, as in halcyon days, an etymology remembered by Neptune at the end of the opera.

The prologue of *Alcyone* is based upon Pan and Apollon competing in a song contest; Echo, wood sprites, and birds gather to hear their performances. Pan sings the praises of war, but Apollon prefers a hymn to peace. Apollon is the winner, and he suggests that the story of Alcyone be sung next.

The first act of the tragedy is set in Ceix's palace, and the action starts with Pélée lamenting the impending wedding of Alcyone and Ceix: he loves Alcyone, but he cannot oppose her marriage because the groom is his friend and has protected him generously in his time of need (I, 1). Alcyone and Ceix join the chorus celebrating their wedding (I, 2), and the high priest is marrying them when the Furies emerge from Hades to interrupt the ceremony (I, 3). Phorbas and Ismène are plotting to aid Pélée (II, 1), when Ceix enters in despair. Phorbas suggests that he renounce Alcyone. When Ceix rejects his proposal, Horbas evokes Proserpine, Pluton, and the Fates to lend authenticity to his false pronouncement that Ceix and Alcyone will perish (II, 2). Phorbas reveals to Pélée that he is sending Ceix away (III, 1-2), and a crew of sailors offers a celebration to Neptune to protect him on his voyage to Claros (III, 3). Ceix entrusts Alcyone to Pélée at the moment of his departure (III, 4), but she faints at the shock of his leaving (III, 5).

The second half of the tragedy deals initially with what transpires between Alcyone and Pélée in the absence of Ceix. The fourth act begins with grieving Alcyone's consent to participate in a sacrifice to Junon (IV, 1-2); she falls asleep (IV, 3) and dreams of Ceix perishing at sea (IV, 4). Pélée, Céphise, and Doris keep Alcyone from suicide. Pélée confesses his love to Alcyone; he offers his life in retribution for Ceix's death, but she attempts to kill herself (V, 1). Phosphore announces the return of Ceix (V, 2), and Pélée exits in despair (V, 3). Ceix's body is washed up on the shore; Alcyone kills herself with his wet sword (V, 4). Neptune announces the death of Phorbas and explains that Alcyone and Ceix will have immortal life together. The reunited couple appear on stage amidst general rejoicing by the gods of the sea who will remain calm henceforth on Alcyone's days (V, 5).

BIBLIOGRAPHY: CG 189, 192; CL I, 28; Lajarte I, 106-7; Antoine Houdard de La Motte, *Oeuvres complètes*, 11 vols. (Genève: Slatkine Reprints, 1970) II, 243-55; RGO IX, 65-114.

Amadis is the first opera by Jean-Baptiste Lully* and Philippe Quinault* that was not based upon ancient legend or mythology. It was presented for the first time at Paris, not Versailles, although its medieval subject is supposed to have been suggested by Louis XIV. It started its initial run at the Palais-Royal* on 15 January 1684 because the French and Italian troupes were holding the attention of the Court at this time with comedies and tragedies mounted under the direction of the dauphine. The dauphin and then the dauphine in the company of the dauphin went to Paris to hear it on 23 June and 7 July 1684, however, and it was taken eventually to Versailles on 5 March 1685.

The prologue of *Amadis* presents the enchantress, Urgande, and her husband, Alguif, who must remain under a magic spell until they are liberated from it by a hero. Their rescuer appears without delay, and they profit from their freedom by delivering Amadis from the darkness to which he has been consigned. Strangely enough, it is not specified that the protagonist in this action is Louis XIV, but the tenor of the laudium makes it clear beyond doubt that he is the king of France. The allusions to Louis XIV and to the forthcoming production of *Amadis* recall the use of this same device in Lully's previous work, *Phaéton*,* but there is an innovative feature in this prologue: one of its characters reappears in the opera. Otherwise it is similar to most Quinault-Lully prologues in its use of song and dance, its praise of the king, and its fleeting reference to the coming program. It is to be placed among the simple and brief prologues of Lully rather than among those that are more monumental and regal.

The composition of *Amadis* is deficient by the regular classical standards of tragedy if only because it lacks unity and direction by reason of its double exposition and the multiple events it presents to produce theatrical effects rather than to move the intrigue rapidly and suspensefully toward its conclusion. In a word, the story meanders. It is impossible to know in which direction it will turn in any one of its five acts. This is especially true of the first two acts. As in *Alceste*,* and *Cadmus et Hermione*,* there are a plot and a subplot. The principal involvement presents Amadis in love with and loved by Oriane, who, like the heroine of *Isis*,* is pledged by her father to another man; Oriane accepts this second suitor because she believes Amadis to be in love with Briolanie (I). The second affair between Corisande and Florestan is without obstacles until the enchantress Urgande puts Florestan under her spell. These two situations are described carefully in the first act, but they are forgotten completely at the start of the second act, which opens with Arcabonne standing near a bridge and amidst trees hung with trophies. Her brother Arcalaus enters, and the second exposition is launched with the explanation that Arcabonne and Arcalaus are sworn to pursue Amadis, who has killed their brother. It is added that Arcabonne has fallen in love with a handsome stranger who has rescued her from a dragon. This second act of *Amadis* is probably the most heavily laden act in the repertory of the Royal Academy of Music before 1685 because it not only presents the vengeance to which Arcalaus and Arcabonne are bound and the latter's love for a stranger but it also depicts Arcalaus's twice calling up the demons of the underworld to help him in his quest for revenge. And other developments include Amadis's lamentation over his fate, Corisande's report that Florestan has been whisked away by an enchantress, a quarrel between Arcalaus and Amadis, Corisande's kidnaping, and Amadis being charmed into surrendering his sword to a nymph. Florestan's disappearance is especially disconcerting because he was quite self-sufficient and unthreatened at the moment of his last appearance on the stage.

The first act of *Amadis* is set in the palace of Oriane's father. The second act is laid near a bridge in a forest. The third act transpires against the romantic setting of a ruined palace wherein the slain Ardan Canile is entombed. Here the enemies of Arcalaus and Arcabonne are held captive: Florestan, Corisande, and countless other mourning souls who deplore their condition in a memorable chorus with their jailers. The highlight of the act occurs at the moment when Arcabonne recognizes Amadis as the man whom she loves, and this development endows the third act with a certain unity. But the fourth act returns to an almost hopelessly complicated pattern. In the first scene alone, Arcalaus holds Oriane captive and learns that his sister has spared Amadis; he swears to punish Oriane and Amadis. He then produces the bloody and lifeless form of Amadis. Having killed him, he suggests to Arcabonne that they revive him so that they may increase their hatred of him. But Oriane is now dead, and Amadis is recalled to life only to mourn the passing of his beloved. These rapid deaths and cruel resurrections are the apparent reason for the sudden entrance of the enchantress Urgande, who is pledged to reward and to preserve virtue. The Demons of the Air and the Demons of Hades fight, and the former are victorious in the name of Urgande and virtue. Amadis and Oriane are left in peace after the defeat of Arcalaus and Arcabonne (IV). It is a strange fact, but all these events and changes in individual fortunes may be construed simply as the victory of Amadis over Arcalaus, but a simple triumph scarcely constituted an opera at this time. The work comes to an end eventually with the total reconciliation of Amadis and Oriane, the only couple worthy to pass under the Arch of Loyal Lovers and into the Forbidden Chamber (V).

The superabundance of incidents in the plot is matched by the proliferation of spectacles: the fight of the warriors (I, 4), the arrival of the magicians (II, 2) and of the demons (II, 6) from the underworld, the prisoners in the ruined palace (III, 1), Urgande's entrance with the Serpent (IV, 6), and the grand finale before the Forbidden Chamber. Such unusual sights as the appearance of Amadis's bloody corpse might be added to this catalogue.

It is not surprising that this deluge of incidents and spectacles was disconcerting to some theatregoers and a source of dissatisfaction for the more conservative members of contemporary audiences. *Amadis*, they said, was too extravagant and too disjointed; it violated the rules of unity and probability; the minor characters were more effectively developed than the colorless principals; sympathy was attracted to the less admirable figures in the story. The fifth act did nothing to support the work, which was based upon an unreal and irrelevant tradition. Strangely enough, no one seems to have insisted that the great problem with *Amadis* is the rapidity with which new events and fresh characters are introduced before it is possible to orient one's self to the flow of action.

The great contribution that Lully and Quinault made in this curious work is its bold innovation in subject matter. For it is obvious that an effort was made here to enlarge the sphere of opera beyond its customary boundaries of ancient mythology. *Amadis* was in the medieval and chivalrous manner, which was suggested as another lode to exploit in the enrichment of opera. The novel which inspired *Amadis* was well known and read frequently in the seventeenth century. As indicated above, Louis XIV himself is supposed to have suggested the subject as worthy of an opera. Readers of the romances by Mlle de Scudéry and La Calprenède applauded the choice of this tale of gallant love for an opera. The popularity of the work itself attests to its acceptance by the public despite its critics. In short, it became evident once again that the average purchaser of a ticket to the Palais-Royal* before 1700 was much more interested in moving music, breathtaking spectacles, and picturesque episodes than in appraising works on the basis of codified principles of esthetics.

Amadis was revived in Paris in 1687, 1701, 1707, 1709, 1718, 1731, and 1759. It can be said, therefore, that it remained in the repertory for nearly ninety years. But perhaps the greatest argument for the validity of Lully's choice of a medieval subject is to be found in the fact that his next work was entitled *Roland*.*

The artistes who appeared in the premiere of *Amadis* included Du Mesny* in the title-rôle, Dun as Florestan, Mlle Moreau as Oriane, Mlle Le Rochois* as Arcabonne. Women appeared regularly in the ballet now, and the principal danseuses in *Amadis* in 1684 were Mlles La Fontaine,* Carré, and Pesan. They performed with Beauchamp,* Pécourt,* Lestang.* The most enduring air from *Amadis* has proven to be the hero's "Bois épais, redouble ton ombre" in II, 4.

Lully's *Amadis* came to be called and known as *Amadis de Gaule* to avoid confusing it with Destouches's *Amadis de Grèce.**

BIBLIOGRAPHY: CG 98; CL I, 38; DDO I, 38; Etienne Gros, *Philippe Quinault* (Paris: Champion, 1926), 537-39, 565-69, 625-29, 673; Lionel de La Laurencie, *Lully* (Paris: Alcan, 1919), 65-66, 158-61; Jean-Baptiste Lully, *Oeuvres complètes: les opéras*, ed. Henry Prunières, 10 vols. (Paris: Editions Lully, 1939) III, 1-251; Henry Prunières, *Lully* (Paris: Henri Laurens, n.d.), 101; RGO II, 431-91; Sonn I, 71.

Amadis de Grèce is a lyric tragedy in five acts and a prologue with music by André-Cardinal Destouches* and a libretto by Houdard de La Motte.* It had its premiere on 26 March 1699. The royal musicians played it before the dauphin and Court at Fontainebleau in the "grande galerie des cerfs" this same year on 24 October according to the *Journal de l'Opéra* and perhaps a week earlier according to the *Mercure*. Mlles Moreau and Journet* appeared opposite Thévenard* and Du Mesny* in its initial representation at the Palais-Royal.* It was brought back to the stage for 15 billings between 3 November and 1 December 1711; it was revived again on 2 March 1724 and 7 March 1745. Mlle Fel, Jélyotte, de Chassé sang in its last run starring Mlle Camargo and Carville in the ballet (for Fel, Jélyotte, and Camargo, see eighteenth-century volume).

The prologue to *Amadis de Grèce* is not long, but its set boasted sumptuous monuments, a pyramid, and pedestals along with other signs of the protagonist's courage and strength. The action is limited to the enchantress Zirphée's announcement that "the great conqueror" whose "name fills the universe" is to be fêted presently.

The intrigue starts with Amadis planning to flee Mélisse to rejoin his beloved Niquée (I, 1). Shepherds and Mélisse oppose his departure (I, 2-5), and Amadis finds himself confronted with the porch of flame through which only "the most generous lover" may pass. The prince of Thrace challenges him to mortal combat, but Amadis steps through the blazing barrier unharmed (II, 1). Niquée appears with her Court to declare her love to Amadis (II, 2-3), but Mélisse enters on a dragon to threaten him and to kidnap Niquée (II, 4). Amadis comes upon the Fountain of Love's Truth in which he thinks that he sees the prince of Thrace and Niquée happy in each other's company. He faints (III, 1), but Mélisse revives him only to inform him falsely of Niquée's infidelity. He attempts suicide, and Mélisse interferes, but this is to no avail since he spurns her advances. Enraged, she summons her demons, magicians, and monsters to ravage the landscape and to serve her fury by torturing Amadis with the spectacle of Niquée and the prince of Thrace happily in love (III, 2). Mélisse disguises the prince of Thrace as Amadis, and Niquée declares her love to him in this disguise (IV, 1). The jealous prince vows to slay Amadis (IV, 4), but Amadis intervenes to kill the prince (IV, 5). Mélisse evokes the shade of the prince to help her destroy Niquée and torture Amadis, but she kills herself upon learning that she is powerless (V, 1-3). Amadis and Niquée are free to marry after the suicide of despairing Mélisse (V, 4-6).

BIBLIOGRAPHY: CG 189, 193; CL I, 38; Lajarte I, 88; Antoine Houdard de La Motte, *Oeuvres complètes*, 11 vols. (Genève: Slatkine Reprints, 1970) II, 145-56; RGO VI, 355-412; Sonn I, 72.

Amarillis is a pastoral in a single act that was substituted for the original *La Pastorale* in *Les Muses** shortly after the staging of the latter work in 1702. It was written in four brief scenes and began with the heroine about to die because Diane has decreed her death. Mirtil volunteers to die in her place, but Montan arrives to comply with Diane's order to sacrifice Amarillis. Touched by the lovers' plight, Montan cannot execute his mission, and Diane revokes her decree. The original *divertissement** at the end of the first *La Pastorale* was retained to conclude *Amarillis*.

BIBLIOGRAPHY: CL I, 42; Sonn I, 80, 780.

Les Amours déguisés was billed as a lyric ballet in three entrées and a prologue. Its subject was borrowed from one of the fourteen entrées in the ballet that Lully* had produced for Louis XIV at the Palais-Royal* on 13 February 1664. It had been performed by the actors of the hôtel de Bourgogne. The idea that Louis Fuzelier* developed in this 1713 opéra-ballet* had also been used by him for a work that he had presented previously at one of the Paris fairs. Louis-Thomas Bourgeois* did the musical score for this third libretto with words by Fuzelier again. The composition was not overly popular, but it was mounted 24 times between its premiere on 22 August 1713 and 15 October 1713. It was returned to the Palais-Royal on 12 September 1726 for a brief run; it was produced in its entirety for the last time on this occasion. Its third act, entitled *L'Estime*, formed part of the "fragments" of 10 September 1748.

Fuzelier explains in the printed version of his ballet that love takes many forms and that he wished to show three of the disguises it assumes. He adds that his first entrée does not seem to adhere to this plan, but in this act, if love is not disguised, it is unmasked. As for the sequence of the entrées, he reveals that he has chosen their present order of presentation because it provides the best pattern for allowing the actors and actresses to change costumes.

The prologue presents Vénus assembling lovers of all nations into a chorus singing her praises. The vocalists set sail for Cythère, and Vénus explains that love can be disguised as "sensitive friendship" or "cruel hatred" or "peaceful esteem."

Entitled *La Haine*, the first entrée takes place in a desert before an ancient temple of the sun with the sea in the distance. Diomède is obliged to hide his love for Phaétuse, who is about to offer up the Greeks to her father, the sun. Her first victim is to be Diomède, who has rejected her charms (I, 1-2). Phaétuse orders the sacrifice to begin, and Diomède asks that he alone be slain. He proclaims his love for Phaétuse, and she halts the sacrifice while proclaiming her love for him (I, 3-4). The entrée ends on a festive note celebrating L'Amour (I, 5).

L'Amitié, its second act, is pastoral in tone because the authors felt that love could don its most innocent disguise among "hamlets and thickets." Paris complains to Ismène of Oenone's indifference, but she reminds him that L'Amour often passes for L'Amitié. She suggests that Paris should make Oenone jealous to ascertain her true feelings (II, 1-2). Paris pursues Florise in Oenone's presence, therefore, and the latter accuses him of ingratitude and inconstancy. She admits her love for him (II, 3). Paris notes to Oenone that they were friends, but Oenone's confession of love for him results in their reconciliation (II, 4). The final scene offers a celebration in honor of spring and love (II, 5).

L'Estime opens with Julie curious about Ovide's secret love, Corine, because she loves the Roman poet. Albine warns her to be discreet because she is the daughter of the emperor Auguste (III, 1). Ovide determines to keep his love concealed (III, 2), but Julie asks him to disclose the identity of Corine. Ovide remains silent, but Julie hints to his delight that she has penetrated his secret (III, 2). The games planned to salute Julie present inhabitants from the far reaches of the Roman Empire singing her praises (III, 4), but no conclusion is provided for the love intrigue.
BIBLIOGRAPHY: Lajarte I, 118-19; RGO I, 2-48.

Les Amours de Momus was the thirty-fifth title added to the repertory since the foundation of the Royal Academy of Music, but it was only the fifth composition offered to the public as a ballet or opéra-ballet in this period of two dozen years between 1672 and 1695. The decision to present a work featuring the dance might well have been fostered by the fact that the six previous works billed at the Palais-Royal* had been lyric tragedies like *Céphale et Procris** and *Médée*,* works that had never enjoyed any substantial measure of success and had not been returned to the stage. The musical score for *Les Amours de Momus* was written by Henri Desmarets,* and its libretto was done by Duché.* It was in three acts and a prologue, but it was not revived after its initial run at the Palais-Royal from 25 May 1695 until sometime in the autumn of the same year.

After the usual prologue featuring a laudium of Louis XIV, the first act of *Les Amours de Momus* presents two ballets growing out of the situation evolving on the stage: Momus and Palémon in love with Mélitte, Comus in love with Hébé, Hébé in love with Comus, and Mélitte indifferent toward both her suitors. The conclusion of this series of emotional involvements is the wedding of Hébé and Comus. The plot, then, may be described as moving through a labyrinth of deceit to reach a conclusion that was at hand in the first place and is really too simple in view of the knotty problems that had to be considered before it was reached. Its principal feature is the joviality with which Momus greets both victory and defeat and his ability to make the best of any situation. It is his retinue that dances the two ballets in the last act (III, 5, 7), and his "loves" are Mélitte and Hébé.

BIBLIOGRAPHY: Lajarte I, 64; RGO V, 135-84; Sonn I, 108.

Les Amours de Vénus, also called *Les Amours de Mars et de Vénus,* is an opéra-ballet in three acts and a prologue with a libretto by Antoine Danchet* and a score by André Campra.* It had its premiere on 6 September 1712, and its first run lasted until 9 October 1712 for a total of 15 billings. It was never revived in its entirety, but its prologue was mounted with *Les Festes vénitiennes* on 15 October 1712. Lajarte reports that the prologue was included among the *Nouveaux Fragments* of 29 July 1729 and the *Fragments* of 10 September 1748. The date of 29 July 1729 may be an error, however, because *Le Journal de l'Opéra* gives 19 July 1729 as the date of the billing of the *Nouveaux Fragments.*

In the prologue that survived for more than thirty-five years, the Court of Hébé sings and dances to express its joy with its happy condition, and, as in the prologue to *Manto la feé,** Les Amours have left the world ravished by war to find security and calm with Hébé. But La Victoire discloses that she has returned peace to the earth with the help of a king skilled in using victory to promote peace. The prologue, then, is in the Lullist tradition of offering a laudium to Louis XIV and of alluding to the international situation.

The first entrée is set in a pleasant wood where a celebration is to be held in honor of the victory that Vénus has won over Junon and Pallas. Hébé sets the scene for the festival wherein Faunes and Silvains dance and sing (I, 1-2). Mercure suggests to Hébé that she is more attractive than Vénus, but she dismisses his flirtatious flattery (I, 3). Vénus and Mars declare their mutual love (I, 4), and a cosmopolitan chorus sings their praise (I, 5). Vulcain is absent from the forges of the Ciclopes, who have turned from their labors to games (II, 1). Mercure relays to them Jupiter's order that they resume their tasks, even if Vulcain has left Lemnos (II, 2). When he returns to the forges, he directs his workers not to forge any more arrows because Jupiter and the other gods are determined to protect faithless Vénus. Mercure and Hébé defend Vénus (II, 3). Momus enters leading a group of dancers and instrumentalists who offer a *divertissement** to divert Vulcain (II, 4), and Silène suggests that the god of fire abandon Vénus for the joys of Bacchus (II, 5).

The last act opens in a removed corner of the earth where Silène and Vulcain have decided to celebrate Bacchus. Vulcain is still asleep, and Vénus congratulates Silène on his ability to subdue her jealous husband (III, 1). Silène orders his attendants to remove from Vulcain's mind the disturbing memory of Vénus's infidelity (III, 2-3). Vulcain awakens and dismisses his recollections of Vénus and Mars as troubled dreams. The married couple are reconciled, but Vénus warns her hot-tempered husband against jealousy (III, 5). Jupiter descends to give them his blessing, and the grand finale is executed by the retinues of Vulcain, Vénus, Silène, and Momus (III, 6).

BIBLIOGRAPHY: Lajarte I, 115-16; RGO X, 447-80; Sonn I, 109.

Antier, Marie (b. 1687, Lyon; d. 3 December 1747, Paris), singer, arrived in Paris in about 1710 and made her debut at the Royal Academy of Music almost immediately. She was applauded enthusiastically from the start of her career, which lasted for thirty years, and there was scarcely an important work in the entire repertory of the Opéra in which she did not play a rôle at one time or another. Tradition repeats that she was especially effective when she was representing the enchantress or magician in Lully's works.

Only a catalogue of the operas in which Mlle Antier sang can give the true measure of her activity at the Opéra. She made her debut with the Royal Academy of Music in 1710 or 1711, and she withdrew from the stage in 1741. She appeared in approximately 60 compositions during this period of 30 years, and in some works she was billed in two and even three parts. She was cast in nearly 80 rôles before retirement.

The following list of operas gives the titles of the revived works in which Mlle Antier performed. The date in parentheses after the title of the work indicates the date of the premiere of the composition in question. The date or dates after the names of the characters in the works are the years of Mlle Antier's appearances in the piece. Of course, the characters named here were interpreted by Mlle Antier in the revivals noted:

Alceste (1674): La Nymphe de la Seine and Thétis, 1716
Thésée (1675): Médée, 1729
Atys (1675): Cybèle, 1725 and 1738
Bellérophon (1679): Sthénobée, 1728
Proserpine (1680): Cérès, 1715 and 1727
Persée (1682): Cassiope, 1722 and Mérope, 1737
Phaéton (1683): Théone, 1721 and 1730
Amadis (1684): Arcabonne, 1718 and 1731 and 1740
Roland (1685): Angélique, 1727
Armide (1686): Armide, 1724
Zéphyre et Flore (1688): Flore (?), 1715
Thétis et Pélée (1689): La Nuit, 1712 and Thétis, 1723 and 1736
Vénus et Adonis (1697): Cydippe, 1717
L'Europe galante (1697): Vénus and Doris, 1715 and Octavio [sic],
        Doris and Roxane, 1724
Issé (1697): Issé, 1721 and Première Hespéride, 1733

Amadis de Grèce (1699): Mélisse, 1724
Hésione (1700): Vénus, 1729
Omphale (1701): Argine, 1733
Tancrède (1702): Clorinde, 1717 and 1738
Iphigénie en Tauride (1704): Iphigénie, 1720
La Vénitienne (1705): Isabelle and Léonore, 1711
Philomèle (1705): Progné, 1723
Alcyone (1706): Ismène, 1711

This second list furnishes the titles of the works in which Mlle Antier created one or more characters at the time of the premieres of the compositions. A date after the name of the character signifies the year when Mlle Antier also appeared in one of its revivals:

Idoménée (1712): Dircé
Médée et Jason (1713): Melpomène, 1727
Les Amours déguisés (1713): Minerve and second entrée (?)
Télèphe (1713): La Pythonisse
Le Festin de Thalie (1714): Iphise (see *Les Fêtes de Thalie**)
Télémaque (1714): High Priestess of Minerve
Les Festes de l'été (1716): Vénus and Doris (see eighteenth-century
        volume for post-1715 works)
Camille (1717): La Nymphe de la Seine
Le Jugement de Pâris (1718): Doris, 1727
Les Ages (1718): Vénus and Silvanire
Les Plaisirs de la campagne (1719): Terpsichore, Lisette, and Agathine
Polydore (1720): Ilione
Les Amours de Protée (1720): Pomone
Les Eléments (1721 at Court): Emilie
Pirithoüs (1723): Hermilis, 1734
Festes grecques et romaines (1723): Erato, Cléopâtre, Délie in 1733
La Reine des Péris (1725): ?
Télégone (1725): Circé
Pyrame et Thisbé (1726): Zoraïde, 1740
Les Amours des dieux (1727): Niobé
Orion (1728): Minerve and Diane
Tarsis et Julie (1728): Julie (?)
Les Amours des déesses (1729): Diane
Le Caprice d'Erato (1730): Minerve
Pyrrhus (1730): Eriphile
Jephté (1731): Almasis in 1733 and only La Vérité in 1740
Hippolyte et Aricie (1733): Phèdre
Les Grâces (1735): Eudoxe
Les Indes galantes (1735): Phani-Palla

Scanderberg (1735): Roxane
Les Voyages de l'Amour (1736): Julie
Les Romans (1736): ?
Les Génies (1736): principal nymph
Castor et Pollux (1737): Phoebé
Les Caractères de l'Amour (1738): Elmire
La Paix (1738): Philis

BIBLIOGRAPHY: DBF II, 1509; EFC 133; Fétis I, 117; GE III, 198; Arsène Houssaye, *Princesses de comédie et déesses d'opéra* (Paris: Henri Plon, 1860), 406-7; Lajarte I, 24-31, 34-38, 42-49, 52-54, 56-58, 67, 83-87, 90-91, 93-94, 102-3, 105-7, 114-15, 117-19, 121-23, 125, 127-35, 137, 140-51, 171-72, 174-75, 178-86; PJ 45-51; TdT, 796; Thurner 17-18, 20; L. Travenol and Jacques Durey de Noinville, *Histoire du théâtre de l'Opéra en France*, 2 vols. (Paris: Joseph Barbou, 1753) II, 67-69.

Aréthuse is an opéra-ballet* in three acts and a prologue. Its score was written by André Campra*; Antoine Danchet* created its libretto and entitled its three entrées *Les Enfers*, *La Mer*, *La Terre*. It was billed initially at the Palais-Royal* on 14 July 1701. Its first run of 28 performances closed on 13 September of the same year. It was brought back to the theatre in 1758 with a revised libretto by Danchet and new music by Dauvergne.

The prologue of Campra's work is set in the gardens of Marly, where a ballet of gardeners and a chorus of shepherds help the nymph of the Seine to beautify the landscape for "a king whom the universe adores."

Based on the legend of Alphée and his love for a member of Diana's retinue, *Aréthuse* begins in the dark avenues of Hades, where Alphée confronts infernal obstacles and hellish creatures in his pursuit of Aréthuse (I, 1). Pluton promises Alphée protection (I, 2) just as Proserpine comforts Aréthuse (I, 3). Pluton transforms his dismal realm into a pleasant retreat, where l'Amour prevails (I, 4), but Aréthuse continues to flee from Alphée (I, 5-6).

The second entrée transpires in Neptune's subaqueous palace with Alphée still in pursuit of his beloved (II, 1). Neptune invites Aréthuse to the celebration of Vénus's birthday, but she is shocked to learn that she has sought refuge in the home of the goddess she seeks to avoid (II, 2-3). After the festivities in honor of Vénus (II, 4), Alphée and Aréthuse meet, but the latter explains to her suitor that Diane has forbidden her to remain in his company (II, 5-6).

Diane herself falls in love with Endimion (III, 1), to whom she confesses her love (III, 2-3). Alphée and Aréthuse are now free to wed, and L'Amour gives his blessing to both couples (III, 4-6).

Mlle Maupin* filled the part of the nymph of the Seine in 1701, while Mlles Moreau and Desmatins* sang Aréthuse and Diane respectively. Thévenard* created the rôle of Alphée.

BIBLIOGRAPHY: CL I, 70; Lajarte I, 91-92; RGO VII, 167-214; Sonn I, 136.

Ariadne et Bacchus is a lyric tragedy in five acts and a prologue based upon a legitimate tragedy by Thomas Corneille* and a heroic comedy by Donneau de Vizé. Its libretto was written by Saint-Jean,* and its music was composed by Marin Marais.* The unpublished log of the Opéra dates its premiere performance as 23 February 1696 and records no representation for it after 8 March of the same year. It is agreed that *Ariadne et Bacchus* was never revived, but there is some dispute over the starting date of its first run, which the Parfaict brothers give as sometime in February 1696 while La Vallière posts it as 8 March 1696. The failure of this composition at the Palais-Royal* is rather difficult to understand if it is remembered that the most effective artistes of the Royal Academy of Music appeared in it: Mlles Le Rochois,* Desmatins,* and Moreau as Ariadne, Corcine, and Dircée respectively, opposite Du Mesny* (Bacchus), Dun (Aenarus), and Hardouin* (Adraste).

Some prologues of previously produced lyric tragedies had been set on the banks of the Seine, near the Louvre, or close to the Tuileries, but no librettist had yet thought of selecting "the City of Paris in one of its finest vistas" as the site for his prologue. Yet the introductory section of *Ariane et Bacchus* is even more striking by reason of being the perfect example of all the prologues written during the war of the League of Augsburg: its characters include nymphs, muses, divinities, even a personification; the main theme is that "the fury of war cannot penetrate into . . . this happy empire" protected by Louis XIV; this king of France is referred to as "our august hero" who "flies from victory to victory" while guaranteeing peace within his own borders. It is exact to say that by 1696 the prologue of the lyric tragedy had become stereotyped, although the poet was apparently still free to decide whether or not he wished to make a fleeting allusion to the forthcoming representation by pointing to its relevancy to the contemporary scene.

In *Phèdre* Jean Racine had chosen to dramatize the moment when Thésée returns home to Phèdre; in *Ariadne et Bacchus* the poet builds his composition on events that transpired after Thésée had just abandoned Ariadne to flee with Phèdre. Thus, the latter work opens with Ariadne complaining of fickle Thésée and with Adraste encouraged to press his suit for the heroine's hand because she has been ignored by her lover (I, 1). Dircée reproaches Adraste for his waning interest in her, but he protests her doubts about his constancy (I, 3). King Aenarus, brother of Dircée, announces Bacchus's approach and orders a sacrifice to appease Neptune so that he may arrive safely in port (I, 4). Junon interrupts the sacrifice on account of her hatred of Bacchus (I, 5-6), however, and Aenarus is filled with dismay (I, 7). The second act is pointed toward the first encounter between Bacchus and Ariadne, and it starts with the sudden turmoil in the harbor leading Ariadne to believe that errant Thésée has returned (II, 1). L'Amour enters to explain to her that Bacchus has disembarked and that she must allow him to fall in love with her (II, 2). Ariadne rejects Adraste (II, 3-4), and Bacchus proclaims his disdain for love (II, 5) only to fall in love with Ariadne during the festive celebration held to honor him (II, 6-7).

The rather complicated third act affords a perfect example of the extent to which lyric tragedy relied upon divine interference in human affairs to promote a spectacular representation of the struggle between love and jealousy with love triumphant at the end. Adraste asks Junon for aid in his now hopeless quest for Ariadne's hand (III, 1), and the goddess reassures him that she will comply with his request. Junon assumes the appearance of Dircée and orders Iris to carry Dircée herself off to another island (III, 2). Still in the guise of Dircée, Junon allows Ariadne to overhear her decision to reject Bacchus but to make Adraste jealous by telling him of Bacchus's love for her (III, 3-4). Misled by this misinformation that she has garnered through eavesdropping, Ariadne is furious at being deceived twice in so short a time, but she manages to fall asleep to forget her cares (III, 5). A group of Songes dances and sings about her (III, 6) before L'Amour awakens her to explain that Bacchus loves her and that the entire deception has been the work of angry Junon (III, 7). Ariadne is convinced (III, 8). The fourth act begins with a complete reconciliation between Bacchus and Ariadne, therefore, but this touching scene of trusting love angers Adraste (IV, 1) to the point where he persuades Géralde to summon up the demons of Hades to help him gain revenge (IV, 2-3). When the dancing devils from the netherworld acknowledge their inability to deal with Bacchus (IV, 4), Géralde calls upon Alecton to fan the dark flames of jealousy in Ariadne's heart (IV, 5-6).

This tug-of-war between love and jealousy, truth and deception, could have continued on without interruption apparently, but the fifth act does terminate it, even if the resolution of the intrigue is tortured. Dircée is angry with Adraste's continuing coolness toward her, and Elise warns her that Ariadne still thinks that she has stolen her lover (V, 1-2). Ariadne then upbraids Bacchus and tries to kill herself on account of his inconstancy. When Bacchus takes the knife away from her (V, 3), Adraste enters and attacks his rival because he believes that he is trying to slay Ariadne with the knife. A general fight breaks out between the followers of the two suitors (V, 4), and Adraste is slain (V, 5). Jupiter, Junon, and Mercure appear to restore Ariadne's reason and place her crown among the stars while her marriage with Bacchus is being celebrated (V, 6). This concluding act is weak from an esthetic point of view, therefore, if only because Dircée never appears to reach a stable situation but slips off into limbo after lodging still another complaint against fickle Adraste. The latter's death seems cruel and superfluous because it adds nothing to the drama. More importantly, however, one wonders why and how this lyric tragedy came to be considered tragic. It does not terminate in any unfortunate fashion but rather in the tragicomic style of the happy ending. Bacchus and Ariadne are wed at the end, and there is no reason to believe that they will not live happily and forever.

BIBLIOGRAPHY: CG, 126, 128; CL I, 72-73; Lajarte I, 66; RGO V, 291-352; Sonn I, 139, 140.

Aricie is catalogued as a ballet or an *opéra-ballet** in five entrées and a prologue for which La Coste* composed the music and the abbé Jean Pic wrote the libretto. It had its premiere at the Palais-Royal* on 9 June 1697 and may have been billed until August of the same year. The work was never very popular, and it was never returned to the stage after its first and only run in the summer of 1697.

The prologue presents the satyr Marsias asserting to three Muses that he sings more beautifully than Apollon. Displeased, the god orders him punished for his presumptuous words and directs the Muses to sing the praises of "the greatest king of the universe," who does not allow war to ravage the banks of the Seine. Like the prologues of *Ariadne et Bacchus*,* *Méduse*,* and all the other lyric tragedies composed during the war of the League of Augsburg, the prefatory section of *Aricie* is a laudium of Louis XIV depicting this monarch going to war only to preserve peace for his fortunate subjects.

It will be seen from the following account of its libretto that *Aricie* is scarcely a ballet or even an *opéra-ballet* if only because there is no central notion or theme in it to which each entrée contributes as in the case of *Les Saisons** or *L'Europe galante*.* The characters move in the pattern of the lyric tragedy, where there is but a single intrigue, and this intrigue is more important to the composition than the configurations of the dance. If *Aricie* were to be accepted as a genuine *opéra-ballet*, moreover, it would have to have as many separate plots as it has entrées. Yet the love story of Fernand-Aricie continues throughout the entire work. It starts in the first act with Fernand, prince of Spain, being presented as the rejected lover of Aricie, princess of the Unknown Isle, and it concludes with a festival celebrating Aricie's final acceptance of her suitor.

The exposition begins with the Spanish prince lamenting the sudden indifference shown to him by Aricie, whom he still loves (I, 1), but he refuses obstinately to attend a festival she is preparing (I, 2-3). After the heroine regrets her unrequited love in her turn (I, 4), the two lovers admit their love for each other (I, 5). This first act is in the nature of a playlet, then, but the second act is decidedly in the tradition of the Lullian lyric tragedy, because it adds a subplot to the intrigue by introducing Elise complaining of the irony of her loving a man impervious to her charms while she remains indifferent to Arcas, who is in love with her (II, 1). Elise explains to Arcas that she has lost interest in him because he has been paying less attention to her (II, 2). Alcipe assures Arcas that he, Alcipe, is not concerned with Elise's opinion of Arcas because she is in love with him (II, 3). Aricie and Elise attend the festival in honor of love and lovers (II, 4-5). The intrigue of

Aricie, then, is composed of two love affairs: the Aricie-Fernand situation, which is complicated by the lovers' own suspicions and then resolved through the force of their love; the Arcas-Elise-Alcipe involvement, which affords essentially the same problem since Alcipe and Elise are in love and Arcas is taken seriously only when Alcipe remains aloof.

This apparently settled condition in which the characters find themselves cannot be tolerated at the end of a second act, of course, and the result of this awkward development is that the third act becomes quite busy on account of the almost unstable emotions of the lovers. It all begins again when Fernand and Alcipe pause in front of a temple. They await Aricie (III, 1), but, when Elise appears, Alcipe explains to her that he has no desire to be a victim of love and lose his liberty (III, 3). Aricie resolves to admit her love to Fernand until she sees him approaching (III, 4-5). Fernand assures Aricie once more that he loves her, but she remains unresponsive (III, 6). Elise urges Fernand not to be discouraged since Aricie loves him, and she reassures Aricie that Fernand thinks only of her (III, 7-9). The fourth act is quite brief, strangely enough, and it does nothing to promote the action, although it does provide a stage spectacle by having recourse to the standard device of calling upon devils and demons. It begins abruptly with Aristandre's sudden announcement that he is a magician who can control lovers' hearts (IV, 1). Aricie consults him to determine whether or not Fernand is really sincere (IV, 2). Aristandre summons up a quartet of demons and a magic robe to aid Aricie (IV, 3-4).

The last act ties these still loose threads together with dispatch but not without additional demonstrations of inconstancy, suspicion, and fear. Fernand now decides that it is time for him to consult Aristandre (V, 1), and Alcipe tells Elise that he remains impervious to love (V, 2). Arcas reveals to Elise that she is indifferent toward him (V, 3). Aricie is still unwilling to admit to Fernand that it is he whom she loves (V, 4). Fernand makes it absolutely clear that the action has not moved at all since the first scene of the first act: he complains of his fate (V, 5). The conclusion is at hand, however, because Aricie is a witness to Fernand's attempted suicide prompted by despair (V, 6), and this act of self-destruction inspires her to confess her love for him (V, 7). The curtain falls on a celebration in honor of love (V, 8).

BIBLIOGRAPHY: CL 1, 73; Lajarte I, 68; RGO VI, 63-120; Son I, 143.

Arion is a lyric tragedy in five acts and a prologue. Jean-Baptiste Matho* wrote its musical score, and Louis Fuzelier* did its libretto. It was never revived, but it did enjoy 28 performances during its only run from its premiere at the Palais-Royal* on 10 April 1714 to its final representation on 29 May 1714.

The prologue is simple and opens with Venus encouraging her idle Amours to sleep as long as Mars continues to trouble the world. La Victoire announces that peace has been restored, however, and Venus returns her charges to their duties.

The tragedy is based upon a triangle with Arion admitting his love for Irène, the daughter of Périandre and the future bride of Eurilas (I, 1). This situation is complicated when Eurilas confesses to Arion that he loves Orphise (I, 2). Arion plays his lyre for the pleasure of Périandre's Court, and a band of shepherds and shepherdesses joins him to honor Venus, to applaud his musical genius, and to celebrate the coming wedding of Irène and Eurilas (I, 3-4). Orphise perceives that Arion has fallen in love with Irène, but she admits her love to him (I, 5).

After it is established that Eurilas loves Orphise who loves Arion in love with Irène, whose emotional entanglements are unknown, Arion hesitates to accept Palémon's advice to flee Corinth (II, 1), and Irène also tells him to leave because she senses that he is about to declare his love to her openly (II, 2). Yet she admits her love for Arion while complaining of her impending marriage and Arion's departure (II, 3-4). Les Amours, Les Grâces, and Les Plaisirs celebrate the approaching wedding of Irène and Eurilas; L'Amour announces that Irène must crown the son of the god coming to visit Corinth (II, 5-6).

The pace of the action quickens when Orphise urges Eurilas to prevent Arion from perishing at sea by keeping him in the city (III, 1-2); jealous Eurilas calls upon Borée and his icy blasts to sink Arion's ship (III, 3). Orphise reproaches Eurilas for not restraining Borée (III, 4). Eurilas tells Irène that Orphise loves Arion, who has been killed at sea (IV, 1-2). Irène bewails his death (IV, 3), but he arrives on the scene in the company of sailors and marine gods singing of his triumph over the storm (IV, 4-5). Orphise expresses her displeasure to Arion because he loves Irène, and she threatens suicide (IV, 6). Périandre mourns the deaths of Orphise and Eurilas; he orders the arrest of Arion, whom dying Eurilas has accused of plotting against him (V, 1). Irène fears for Arion's life and urges him to flee V, 2-4). Despairing, Arion attempts suicide, but Périandre intervenes to consent to the Arion-Irène marriage (V, 5-6).

BIBLIOGRAPHY: CG, 177; CL I, 73; Lajarte I, 120; Sonn I, 143.

Armide is the last lyric tragedy in five acts created by the partnership of Jean-Baptiste Lully* and Philippe Quinault* because the latter's health was failing. As in the case of *Amadis*,* Louis XIV had suggested the subject of *Armide*, and the plan had been to present it initially at Versailles, although it had its world premiere at the Palais-Royal* on 15 February 1686.

The prologue of *Armide* presents La Gloire and La Sagesse disputing about whether glory or wisdom is dearer to the heart of the king, but these two characters suspend their argument to consider their love for him. This debate is an excuse to introduce the usual laudium of Louis XIV, but it also serves as a pretext to call attention to the coming representation of Armide's escape from the Enchanted Palace. The prologue is little more than a conversation, therefore, and there is no use of machines to produce a spectacle sensational enough to increase its impact and leave spectators awed. A singular feature of the text here is a fleeting reference to the revocation of the Edict of Nantes in two lines speaking of Louis XIV's victory over "a monster that was thought to be invincible."

The action of *Armide* may be described in a few words: Armide's sorcery enables her to capture but not to hold Renaud. The episodes upon which this slight narrative is based are more suited to a legitimate drama, moreover, since they are psychological for the most part. Renaud incurs Armide's anger (I), but the heroine cannot prevent herself from falling in love with him. She casts a spell over Renaud so that she may carry him off to her enchanted palace (II). Armide tries to overcome her love a second time (III), and two of Renaud's companions escape from the wiles of her hostile demons (IV) to wrest Renaud from Armide's domination (V).

The intrigue was taken from Tasso's *Jerusalem delivered*, and a comparison of the French opera with the Italian epic reveals that the later work owed much to its source. The first two scenes of the opera, for example, derive directly from *Jerusalem delivered* IV, V, X. The second act of the Lully-Quinault version presenting Armide's vain decision and fruitless efforts to kill Renaud in his sleep are a faithful duplication of events in canto XIV as is the determination of Armide to kidnap her enemy with whom she has fallen in love. Armide's desperate struggle to overcome her desires (III) is indicated in Tasso XIV and XV, but the extent to which this psychological development is expanded in the opera endows it with the freshness of an original feature. The fourth act of the tragedy, with its shield of diamonds, golden sceptre, and liberating sword, are found in the Italian poem, and Tasso also provides the two warriors bent upon rescuing Renaud (XIV, XV). The presentation of the two nymphs as temptations to delay the rescuers is found in the earlier text, but disguising them as the knights' beloved damsels is an innovation. The final act presenting the beguiled hero first charmed by Armide and then delivered from her wiles is largely an adaptation of Tasso's narrative, and the progressive steps taken to depict the rupture between the two main characters are parallel in both texts.

Lully's work was not without its critics, of course, and the fourth act was described by some carping spectators as superfluous. But this group of detractors was decidedly in the minority. Lully himself pointed with satisfaction to the success which *Armide* enjoyed from the moment of its premiere, and Mlle Le Rochois* enjoyed the greatest triumph of her career as Armide. The effect of the fifth act upon audiences was almost indescribable; Parisians wept openly at the climactic moments on the stage.

Armide remained in repertory for nearly eighty years. It was done only once in 1703, on 1 January, when it was replaced by Destouches's* *Le*

*Carnaval et la Folie,** and it ran only from 26 to 31 December 1713, but it appears to have been mounted from 9 November to the end of the year in 1724 according to the unpublished log of the Opéra. It was billed as *Armide et Renaud* on 7 January 1746, and it was heard on 29 dates by 27 March of this year. It was revived again in 1761 and 1764. The title-rôle was filled by such stars as Mlles Armand, Journet,* Antier,* and Chevalier, while Dumoulin and Mlle Camargo (for Mlles Armand and Camargo, see eighteenth-century volume) appeared in its ballet in the course of its eighteenth-century productions. Its musical moments that inspired applause included the duet by Hidraot and Armide, "Esprits de haine et de rage" (II, 2) as well as Armide's triumphant "Enfin il est en ma puissance," sung before Renaud's sleeping form in II, 5. "Voici la charmante retraite" (executed by Lucinde and the chorus in IV, 2) and Armide's closing solo, "Le perfide Renaud me fuit" (V, 4), provide two other memorable passages.

BIBLIOGRAPHY: CG, 112 ff.; CL I, 76-78; DDO I, 78-80; Lajarte I, 52-54; Lionel de la Laurencie, *Lully* (Paris: Alcan, 1919); Robert Lawrence, "*Armide* Restored," *ON* 44 no. 16 (15 March 1980), 1820; Jean-Baptiste Lully, *Armide, . . . reconstituée et réduite pour la piano par Théodore de Lajarte* (Paris: T. Michaëlis, 188?); RGO III, 121-78; R.H.F. Scott, *Jean-Baptiste Lully* (London: Peter Owen, 1973), 109-11; Sonn I, 152-54; SW 41-42; Fausto Torrefranca, "La prima opera francese in Italia? *l'Armida* di Lulli, Roma, 1690," *Festschrift für Johannes Wolf* (Berlin: Breslauer, 1929), 191-97.

Astrée, with a libretto by the famous poet Jean de La Fontaine,* was Pascal Colasse's* fourth contribution to the repertory of the Royal Academy of Music, but it enjoyed little success and was never revived after its first run lasting only from 11 to 28 November 1692. It was offered as a tragedy in three acts and a prologue.

Each of the three acts is inspired by a particular aspect of d'Urfé's pastoral novel in five thousand pages. The first act corresponds suitably enough to the opening scene of the fiction where Astrée banishes Céladon from her presence, because she believes that he is in love with Aminte. The stage version of *Astrée* for the Royal Academy of Music shows an immediate parallelism with the earlier narrative, and both compositions include Sémire (I, 1) and Hilas (I, 2) as well as offering instances of Druid worship (I, 6) and using Céladon's supposed drowning as the basis for the central intrigue. La Fontaine builds his second act upon the love affair of Galatée and Céladon, and his last act returns the hero to Astrée. The grand finale is executed in Italian, however, and the spectator is left with the feeling that he is witnessing a Lullian *intermède* for a comedy-ballet by Molière rather than the conclusion of an opera,

BIBLIOGRAPHY: CG, 128; CL I, 89; Lajarte I, 59; RGO IV, 155-205; Sonn I, 177.

Atys is the fourth lyric tragedy in five acts and a prologue created by Jean-Baptiste Lully* and Philippe Quinault* for the Royal Academy of Music. It had its premiere at the Palais-Royal* in August 1675, and it was performed for the king at Saint-Germain en Laye on 10 January 1676. *Atys* was one of Louis XIV's favorite works, and it came to be known as the king's opera. It was returned to Saint-Germain en Laye in 1677, 1678, and 1682. The lords and the ladies of the Court took part in its ballet along with the regular artistes during its performance of 7 January 1682. Its prologue and first two acts were mounted at Fontainebleau on 5 October 1703.

The prologue of *Atys* is brief, and its music follows the French pattern of a joyous introduction followed by a martial passage terminating in a peaceful conclusion. The music is designed to follow the action, which opens with the announcement by the god Time that Louis XIV has surpassed all heroes of the past and that his greatness is evident in his ability to make the flowers of happiness bloom in the peaceful but chill season of winter. Time's twenty-four Hours and Flore's colorful retinue begin to dance, therefore, but they are interrupted by the arrival of Melpomène. The Muse of Tragedy reveals that she has been dispatched to earth to retell the story of Cybèle, but the members of her train fall to fighting among themselves: Hercules against Antée, Castor and Pollux against Lyncé, Etéocle against Polynice. Iris restores calm by ordering Melpomène and Flore to set aside their differences. The librettist's increasing effort to unify his composition is apparent in the allusion to the subject of the opera in the prologue. The presence of the legendary warriors of antiquity relieves the banality of the customary eulogy of the king, which is introduced carefully instead of being proclaimed blatantly. The prologues of *Alceste** and *Thésée** had been set at the Tuileries and Versailles, but Quinault avoids a repetition of this obvious device by placing the scene in the palace of Time. It is certain here that Quinault attempted to provide Lully with varying fare, lest his composer lack opportunities to use the full range of his talents.

The lack of any effort to achieve comic effect and the absence of a subplot in *Atys* mark the beginning of the second period in the collaboration between Lully and Quinault. On the positive side, it is the tightening of the dramatic composition and the concomitant discipline in the score that make this opera different from its predecessors. The resemblance of the libretto to a legitimate tragedy is real, moreover, and the closing couplet of the last scene is almost a direct allusion to Aristotle's principle of catharsis. Yet Quinault's text provided Lully with ample opportunity to pause long enough to exploit his gift for descriptive music. A composer could hardly complain, for example, about a finale that featured thunder, lightning, and an earthquake contrasting with rustling trees and murmuring waters.

Only four characters are involved in the intrigue, and they are joined in a chain of mutual and unrequited love: Cybèle loves Atys, who loves and is loved by Sangaride, who is pledged in her turn to marry Célénus. The plot, then, is parallel to the basic situation in *Thésée** since each of the lovers has an unwelcome suitor. Also, Médée plays a prominent part in *Thésée* just as

Cybèle dominates sizable stretches of the action in *Atys*. But Cybèle is an integral part of events in *Atys* by reason of her humanity. She does not hover like a monster of evil ready to pounce upon the other personages.

Quinault distributed the material of his narrative over five acts in the following fashion: Atys and Sangaride declare their love for each other (I); Cybèle admits her love for Atys (II) and informs him of her feelings for him in a dream (III); Atys prevents the marriage of Sangaride and Célénus by kidnapping his beloved (IV); Cybèle destroys Atys's sanity so that he kills Sangaride and himself (V). The related episodes contribute to this tale of suspense and horror, and scenes of a varying nature are interspersed with sufficient frequency to remind the spectators that they are at the Opéra, not the Comédie-Française. The scene where Atys and Sangaride declare their undying love to each other in I, 6, the moments when Cybèle is moved to jealousy and suspicion at the end of the third act, Sangaride's arguments with Atys at the start of the fourth act, and the madness scene at the conclusion of the tragedy are obvious instances of the librettist pausing long enough to allow his composer to make the most of his art. Yet the really striking portions of Lully's score occur in the air he created for Cybèle's descent to earth (I, 8) and Sangaride's "Atys est trop heureux" (I, 4).

The principal rôles of *Atys* were filled by Mlle Saint-Christophe (Cybèle), Mlle Aubry* (Sangaride), and Clédière (Atys). Beaumavielle* did Temps in the prologue with Mlle Beaucreux as Melpomène.

Atys was returned to the stage of the Palais-Royal in 1677, 1678, 1689, 1690, 1699, 1700, 1709, 1738, 1739. The famous artiste Jélyotte (for Jélyotte, see eighteenth-century volume) made his debut with the company as Morphée in the 1738 revival.

BIBLIOGRAPHY: CG, 73; CL I, 98; DDO I, 98-99; Etienne Gros, *Philippe Quinault* (Paris: Champion, 1926), 533-34, 553-55, 603-7, 672; Lajarte I, 29-31; Lionel de la Laurencie, *Lully* (Paris: Alcan, 1919), 49-50, 153-54; Jean-Baptiste Lully, *Atys . . . reconstituée et réduite pour piano et chant par Théodore de Lajarte* (Paris: T. Michaëlis, 188?); Henry Prunières, *Lully* (Paris: Henri Laurens, n.d.), 99-100; RGO I, 371-444; Sonn I, 183-84.

Aubry, Marie (b. ?; d. 1704, Paris), singer, was a member of Philippe d'Orléans's private musical staff, and her first stage appearance was in Cambert's* *Les Peines et les plaisirs de l'amour.** She was obviously talented and Lully* retained her as a member of his troupe when he was organizing the Royal Academy of Music. She retired from the stage in 1684 after having figured prominently during the first decade of public opera in France. Tradition records that she withdrew from the theatre not on account of age, but because she had grown so rotund that it was impossible for her to move around the stage. She was involved in the famous litigation arising from Lully's charge that Guichard* had tried to poison him.

Mlle Aubry was a participant in another six world premieres during her association with the Opéra after she had created the rôle of Philis in *Les*

Peines et les plaisirs de l'amour during 1671. She sang Aeglé of *Thésée** in 1675, Sangaride of *Atys** in 1675, Io of *Isis** in 1677, and Philonoé of *Bellérophon** in 1679. She did the title-rôle of *Proserpine** at the premiere of this work in Paris on 15 November 1680 after the elder Mlle Ferdinand had filled the same part at Court on 3 February of the same year. The singer appeared in only one other premiere during her last five years at the Palais-Royal,* *Persée** of 1682, in which she was cast as Andromède.

BIBLIOGRAPHY: DBF IV, 276-77; EFC 131; Fétis, Suppl., I, 30-31; Lajarte I, 20, 25-26, 29-32, 34-37, 42-43.

B

Bach, Johann Sebastian (b. 21 March 1685, Eisenach; d. 28 July 1750, Leipzig), composer, became an orphan at age ten and went to live with his elder brother, Johann Christoph, who taught him to play the keyboard instruments. The boy showed remarkable promise almost immediately, and he moved to Luneburg in 1700 to sing there at St. Michael's Church. He now studied the organ, and in 1707 he was named organist at St. Blasius Church in Muhlhausen. Bach's ability was common knowledge by this time, and he was invited to Weimar in 1708. Here, he became concertmaster in 1714, and his duties required that he visit important musical centers like Kassel, Halle, Leipzig, and Dresden. After the death of his first wife in 1720 and his second marriage in 1721, Bach moved to Leipzig in 1723 to become organist at the Thomaskirche and Nicolaikirche. He remained in Leipzig until his death.

Most of Bach's work went unpublished during his lifetime, and his importance as a composer was generally ignored until Mendelssohn resurrected his *St. Matthew Passion* in Berlin in 1829. Further impetus was given to a Bach revival by the celebration of the Bach centenary in 1850, and the subsequent establishment of a number of Bach societies resulted almost in a Bach cult, while the twentieth century saw its own resurgence of the master's music in the "Back to Bach" movement. The Opéra has shared modestly in this constant homage to the composer, and his music has been heard during the performances of a trio of ballets employing his music in their scores:

Les Noces de l'Amour et de Psyché	22 November 1928
Dramma per musica	28 June 1950
Concerto barocco (for these works, see twentieth-century volume)	18 December 1963

BIBLIOGRAPHY: BBD 76-79; MOTO 1-29; Thompson 88-96.

Ballet de cour was a type of ballet performed during the *ancien régime* by members of the aristocracy instructed in the art of dancing by a professional dancing master. The kings of France and the members of the Court participated in these ballets during and after the reign of Louis XIV, when

Isaac de Benserade* created a number of them for execution in Paris, Fontainebleau, and Versailles. These included *Le Ballet de la nuit* (1653) and *Le Ballet royal des saisons* (1661).

Ballet de cour was also the name of a ballet extracted from Rameau's *Les Paladins* as late as 7 July 1949 for performance at the Queen's Theatre in the Petit Trianon at Versailles. Roger Desormière provided the musical arrangement for this single representation of the work, and Serge Lifar (for Lifar, see twentieth-century volume) created fresh choreography for it. Lifar, Roger Ritz, Michel Renault, and Max Bozzoni performed in this composition alongside Micheline Bardin, Madeleine Lafon, Jacqueline Moreau, Paulette Dynalix, and Denise Bourgeois (for these performers, see twentieth-century volume).

BIBLIOGRAPHY: Marie-Françoise Christout, "The Court Ballet in France, 1615-1641," *Dance Perspectives* 20 (1964) 4-25; CODB 42; Margaret M. McGowan, *L'Art du ballet de cour en France, 1581-1643* (Paris: Centre National de la Recherche Scientifique, 1963); Jean Roy, *Présences contemporaines: musique contemporaine* (Paris: Debresse, 1962), 42; C. Silin, *Benserade and His "Ballets de cour"* (Baltimore: The Johns Hopkins Press, 1940); SW 243.

Le Ballet de Villeneuve-Saint-Georges was composed of three entrées by Banzy* with music by Pascal Colasse.* It was produced for the first time on 1 September 1692 at Villeneuve-Saint-Georges before the dauphin and was mounted initially in Paris the following month at the Palais-Royal.* It was never revived.

The first of the three entrées depicts Aminte and Mirtil leading a chorus singing the praises of the dauphin and announcing the joys that his return from the battlefield and his inevitable victories in the current war of the League of Augsburg will inspire. Pan leads a special celebration in the second entrée, and the dauphin is once again the recipient of a laudium citing all the perils and torments he has endured in the present struggle to restore peace. A love affair between Tircis and Climène is added to the composition at this point to increase the interest of the presentation, and Faune sings the praises of unfettered love in an interlude reminiscent of the pastoral manner. The last entrée introduces Silène filled with anger because he has not been invited to the celebration. He recovers his composure after bring asked to serve as a judge in the dispute between Faune and Tircis for Climène's hand. Silène's return to good spirits is accompanied by a celebration in honor of the harmony existing between Bacchus and L'Amour, and these festivities conclude with a general ballet in which all the celebrants participate.

BIBLIOGRAPHY: CL I, 111; Lajarte I, 60; RGO IV, 207-28; Sonn I, 196.

Ballet héroïque came to be barely distinguishable from the *opéra-ballet** because it was similarly composed of acts joined by a common concept appearing in each act under a different form. It also had as many intrigues and as many sets of characters as it had acts because each act was likewise an independent unit as far as its narrative was concerned. The *ballet* *héroïque* was distinct from the *opéra-ballet*, however, because its intrigues were more dramatic, and its recitatives carried a greater burden. Thus, the emphasis was more on the plot and the conflicts in the heroic ballet, and the stress moved in the direction of the dance in the *opéra-ballet*. It was also more surprising to find humor and realism in the heroic ballet, which allowed gods and goddesses to figure in its prologues.

Ballets finding their way to the stage of the Opéra in Paris derive from a number of sources including the already established repertories of companies from other countries, the current repertories of other troupes active in Paris or the provinces, and even the creative imaginations of members of the corps de ballet at the Garnier (for the Garnier palace, see nineteenth-century volume) theatre itself. Yet there is still another origin for ballets created at the Paris opera house: the operas that have been produced at the Opéra and that contain *divertissements** and ballets popular enough to justify separate production. This category of ballets has rarely been examined as a separate class of composition, and the list of such compositions given below should provide an idea of their prevalence and growth at the Opéra. They are listed here in chronological order, and the name of the parent opera is supplied whenever it differs from the name of the ballet. A double asterisk after a title indicates that the titles of the ballet and the opera are identical:

Ballet	Composer (Parent Opera)	Premiere
Alceste**	Gluck	1 August 1786
Bal Masqué	Auber (*Gustave III*)	27 April 1834
Hamlet**	Thomas	30 April 1870
Les Fleurs	Rameau (*Les Indes Galantes*)	11 June 1878
La Vie Pour Le Tzar**	Glinka	19 May 1892
Don Juan**	Mozart	18 March 1899
Le Cid**	Massenet	15 July 1900
Nuit de Walpurgis	Gounod (*Faust*)	3 June 1905
Farandole	Bizet (*L'Arlésienne*)	26 June 1909
Danses polovtsiennes	Borodin (*Prince Igor*)	7 June 1910
Thais**	Massenet	1 July 1910
Patrie!**	Paladilhe	20 October 1910
Bacchanale	Saint-Saëns (*Samson et Dalila*)	18 November 1911

Menuet	Massenet (*Manon*)	10 December 1911
*La Favorite***	Donizetti	24 May 1917
*Le Cobzar***	Mme Ferrari	27 June 1917
*Roméo et Juliette***	Gounod	9 March 1918
*Henry VIII***	Saint-Saëns	5 July 1919
Le Chant du Rossignol	Stravinsky (*Le Rossignol*)	2 February 1920
*Ascanio***	Saint-Saëns	28 June 1922
La Chasse Royale	Berlioz (*Les Troyens*)	12 July 1922
La Princesse Cygne	Rimsky-Korsakov (*Tzar Saltan*)	29 November 1928
*Castor et Pollux***	Rameau	5 October 1936 (Sarah-Bernhardt Theatre)
Bacchanale	Wagner (*Tannhäuser*)	29 July 1939
Ballet de Cour	Rameau (*Les Paladins*)	7 July 1949 (Versailles)
Ballet Romantique	Ibert (*L'Aiglon*)	15 May 1953
Les Patineurs	Meyerbeer (*Le Prophète*)	1 October 1954
Mam'zelle Angot	Lecoq (*La Fille de Mme Angot*)	4 October 1954
Polonaise et Cracovienne	Glinka (*Ivan Soussanine*)	8 June 1958

Thus, 21 composers enjoyed the distinction of having 30 operas plundered for the ballets that they contained. Only six of them could boast that two or even three of their lyric compositions had had their scores accepted for balletic as well as operatic programs. Thirteen of these musicians were French, but their numbers did include Russians (Borodin, Glinka, Rimsky-Korsakov), Germans (Meyerbeer, Wagner), and an Italian (Donizetti) as well as Austria-oriented Gluck and Mozart. Rameau, Saint-Saëns, and Massenet (for these composers, see nineteenth- and twentieth-century volumes) were the three composers who contributed three ballets apiece to this constellation of ballets derived from operas.

Similarly, a smaller but no less interesting cluster of 23 ballets constitutes a category of works cognate to the foregoing ballets derived from operas: they were extracted from operas. These works were not viewed as acts, scenes, or *pas* taken from specific ballets; they were billed as ballets possessing their own identity, and the average spectator usually accepted them as original artistic units in their genre. In a word, they were offered to the public as shorter balletic compositions unrelated to their origins. Thus, on account of their brevity, their attraction for audiences had to be at least as strong as that of their matrix works inasmuch as they had less time to capture public fancy.

Note that 14 of the 23 compositions listed are of Russian origin, a surprising fact explained by the peculiar circumstances of their production: they were brought to the stage of the Opéra by Serge Diaghilev's Ballets russes (3), the Bolchoi Ballet of Moscow (7), and the corps de ballet of the Leningrad Opera (3). The Diaghilev ballets were given before 1929, because this impresario's troupe disbanded in this year after his death. Yet if the relatively early productions by the Ballets russes come as no surprise, it is a striking fact that eleven of these Russian compositions are taken from three Tchaikovsky works: *Le lac des cygnes*, *Casse-noisette*, and *La Belle au bois dormant*. Also, this last work provided the material for seven of the ballet-derived ballets:

Ballet	*Composer (Opera)*	*Premiere*
La Sabotière	Widor (*La Korrigane*)	24 December 1907
L'Oiseau d'or	Tchaikovsky (*La Belle au bois dormant*)	31 December 1911
La Princesse enchantée	Tchaikovsky (*La Belle au bois dormant*)	29 December 1915
Le Mariage de la belle au bois dormant	Tchaikovsky (*La Belle au bois dormant*)	18 May 1922
Soir de Fête	Delibes (*La Source*)	30 June 1925
Divertissement	Tchaikovsky (*La Belle au bois dormant*)	8 June 1932
Trépak	Tchaikovsky (*Casse-noisette*)	8 February 1938
L'Oiseau bleu	Tchaikovsky (*La Belle au bois dormant*)	20 December 1940
Suite en blanc	Lalo (*Namouna*)	19 June 1943
Le Cygne noir	Tchaikovsky (*Le Lac des cygnes*)	1 March 1951
Pas de deux	Tchaikovsky (*Casse-noisette*)	6 July 1952

Pas de deux	Delibes (*Sylvia*)	16 June 1956 Dijon
Suite Romantique	Chopin (*Suite de danses*)	12 March 1958
Don Quichotte**	Minkus	8 June 1958
Danses Kourdes	Khatchatourian (*Gayane*)	8 June 1958
Pas de deux	Tchaikovsky (*La Belle au bois dormant*)	8 June 1958
Les Variations d'Ostap	Soloviev-Sedoi (*Tarass-Boulba*)	8 June 1958
Drigo	Minkus (*Cheval bossu*)	11 June 1958
Danses d'acrobates	Glière *(Fleur rouge)*	11 June 1958
Variation	Alexandre Krein (*Laurentia*)	11 June 1958
Cosaques zaporogues	Soloviev-Sedoi (*Tarass-Boulba*)	19 March 1961
Les Ombres	Minkus (*La Bayadère*)	19 May 1961
La Valse rose	Tchaikovsky (*Casse-noisette*)	19 May 1961
La Princesse Aurore	Tchaikovsky (*La Belle au bois dormant*)	9 December 1964

BIBLIOGRAPHY: Mary Clarke and Davis Vaughan, *The Encyclopedia of Dance and Ballet* (New York: G. P. Putnam's Sons, 1977), 260-62; GM 102-10.

Ballet School. The Ballet School attached to the Opéra is presently designated as the École de Danse de l'Opéra de Paris. It has enjoyed an uninterrupted tradition of service for more than 300 years and dates back to 1672, when it was founded by Jean-Baptiste Lully,* who nominated his ballet-master Beauchamp* as its director. Originally all candidates for positions as singers or dancers could take lessons under its programs because the distinction between dancer and singer was not as clearly and as constantly defined during the reign of Louis XIV as it is today. There were no tuition charges at the school in the beginning, and in 1713 the institution was granted official status through special action on the part of the king.

Initially the school was housed in the Opéra storehouse in the rue Saint-Nicaise, where classes were held on Tuesday, Thursday, and Saturday mornings. Discipline became rigid as time progressed, and it was not long before applicants for admission were required to pass a physical examination.

The Second Empire saw a growth in the importance of the Ballet School that boasted an enrollment of 23 pupils of both sexes in 1860. Instruction now included elementary level classes for boys and girls, and the teacher of the advanced class was responsible for the discharge of his duties as a teacher and as Director of the School. Studies lasted five years and did not include general education courses, but students had to attend a regular school until age 12 or 13. Ultimately, in 1919, Jacques Rouché (see twentieth-century volume for Rouché) opened a school reserved for Opéra children in the rue de la Ville-l'Évêque.

Today, children will not be admitted to the Ballet School unless they are between 8 and 13 years old and of French nationality, although 5 percent of an entering class may be the children of aliens. Passing a physical examination is still necessary. If the young candidate meets all entrance requirements, he is assigned to an orientation course consisting of a single dancing class that meets every evening in April, May, and June. There are no further admissions during the regular school year except in the case of the winners of certain dance contests held in France. The total number of girls and boys accepted depends upon the number of vacancies existing at admissions time. At the start of the 1979-80 school year, enrollment consisted of 47 girls and 32 boys.

At the end of the students' training in the school, the graduates submit to competitive examinations and execute a repertory solo like the bolero from *Coppélia* or the variation from *Castor et Pollux* to decide their relative positions in the class. The pupils in the terminal class are admitted to the corps de ballet of the Opéra according to the number of vacancies in the ballet at the moment. A sampling discloses that four students, three of them girls, were accepted into the corps de ballet of the Paris Opéra in 1976, while four boys and four girls were chosen in 1979.

Recently, the faculty of Ballet School has consisted of the following teachers conducting courses in the subjects indicated:

Classical Ballet: Liliane Garry, Jacqueline Moreau, Claire Motte, Christiane Vaussard, Christiane Vlassi, René Bon, Lucien Duthoit, Daniel Franck, Gilbert Mayer
Adagio and preparation for jumps: Max Bozzoni
Repertoire: Lucien Duthoit
Pointwork: Lycette Darsonval and Christiane Vlassi
Character dance: Irina Grjebina
Folk dance: Michelle Blaise
Variation: Jacqueline Moreau, Serge Peretti
Artistic preparation: Serge Perrault

Jazz dance: Molly Molloy
Mime: Yasmine Piletta
Gymnastics: Jean-Paul Sereni
Music and rhythm: Marie-Thérèse Baubion
Anatomy applied to dance: Germaine Bordier
History of dance: Germaine Prudhommeau
History of the theatre: Jean-Marie Villegier

Claude Bessy has been director of the Opéra Ballet School since 1972, and fifty of her pupils have been accepted into the corps de ballet of the Opéra since the start of her tenure in this position. Uniquely suited for this office, Mlle Bessy has distinguished herself at the Opéra as danseuse étoile, choreographer, and creative administrator (see twentieth-century volume for Claude Bessy).

Balon or Ballon, Jean (b. 20 February 1676, Paris; d. 1712 ?, Paris), dancer, has left very little information about his life outside the theatre, but his activities on the stage of the Royal Academy of Music point to a competent and energetic performer. He appeared in the revivals of three of Lully's* works before the death of Louis XIV: *Acis et Galathée** in 1702, *Armide** in 1703, and *Roland** in 1705. Also, he danced in the premieres of no fewer than 17 compositions produced for the first time between 1697, the date of his debut at the Opéra, and 1710, the year of his disappearance from the musical scene in France. He danced in *L'Europe galante** and *Issé** in 1697, and he was assigned to the ballet of *Marthésie, reine des Amazones** in 1699 and of *Canente** and *Hésione** in 1700. In the eighteenth century he executed dancing rôles in *Omphale** (1701), *Médus, roi des Mèdes** (1702), *Tancrède** (1702), *Le Carnaval et la Folie** (1704), *Iphigénie en Tauride** (1704), *Télémaque** (1704), *Alcine** (1705), *Cassandre** (1706), *Bradamante** (1707), *Méléagre** (1709), *Sémélé** (1709), and *Diomède* (1710). It has been suggested that Jean Balon may be the dancer seen in as many as five portraits, one by Bérain that was engraved by Le Pautre on the occasion of the mounting of *Le Carnaval et la Folie.** He danced most frequently with Françoise Prévost* and Marie Subligny.*

BIBLIOGRAPHY: ACPM 112; CODB 53; DBF IV, 1516-17; EDB 50; Lajarte I, 48-49, 52-55, 83-87, 90-91, 93-95, 97-99, 100-105, 108-9; J. Lawson. *A History of Ballet and Its Makers* (London: Sir Isaac Pitman & Sons, 1964); André Levinson, "Notes sur le ballet au XVIIIᵉ siècle: Les danseurs de Lully," *RM* VI (janvier, 1925), 53-54; TdT 800; Marian Hannah Winter, *The Pre-Romantic Ballet* (Brooklyn, N.Y.: Dance Horizons, 1975), 48-50, 52-53, 56-57; WT 13.

Banzy, or Banzi, librettist, has left no information to provide subsequent generations with even a sketchy knowledge of his origins and artistic activity, but his name has come to be associated with the music provided for

Molière's *Mélicerte*. His sole contribution to the repertory of the Royal Academy of Music was the libretto he wrote for *Le Ballet de Villeneuve-Saint-Georges** of 1692.

BIBLIOGRAPHY: Marcelle Benoît, *Musiques de Cour, Chapelle, Chambre, Ecurie* (Paris: A. et J. Picard, 1971), 162; Jules Bonassies, *La Musique à la Comédie-Française* (Paris: Baur, 1874), 9; Lajarte I, 60; *Oeuvres de Molière*, ed. Eugène Despois et Paul Mesnard, 10 vols. (Paris: Hachette, 1873-1927), VI, 125-86 and 277-302; Julien Tiersot, *La Musique dans la comédie de Molière* (Paris: La Renaissance du livre, n.d.), 90.

Batistin (b.?, Florence; d. 9 December 1755, Paris), composer, whose complete name was Jean-Baptiste Struck, was called Stuck incorrectly according to Fétis, who insists upon the spelling of his name as Struck. He was born in Florence of German parents, but France was the scene of his musical career, which included a position in the household of the duke of Orléans and the post of first violoncellist at the Royal Academy of Music. Louis XIV had given him an income to persuade him to stay in France, and this sum of money was increased in 1718 on account of the effectiveness of his work for the programs and balls held at the Palais-Royal* during the regency. He composed the score for *Méléagre** in 1709 and for *Manto la fee** in 1711. His third and last title for the repertory of the Opéra was *Polydore* (for *Polydore*, see eighteenth-century volume) in 1720. He did a number of other operas and ballets for the Court that were not mounted at Paris, for example, *L'Amour vengé, Céphale, Thétis, Lérida*. His publications include four books of cantatas.

BIBLIOGRAPHY: Bio univ III, 261; CG 169, 181, 252; DDO II, 729; Fétis I, 269; Lajarte I, 157.

Beauchamp, Pierre (b. 1639, Paris; d. 1705, Paris), dancer, was born into a musical family, but his own interests lay in the direction of the dance, and he served as Louis XIV's personal dancing master for more than 20 years while performing his other duties at Court or in Paris. He was named head of the Academy of the Dance by the king when this institution was founded in 1671 at the time of the establishment of the Opéra. His major responsibility at Court was to create and supervise the ballets to be performed before royalty, and he is credited with having done the choreography for *Les Fâcheux* and *Psyché* in 1670. He danced in these compositions, and his skill along with his influence at Court induced Perrin* and Cambert* to employ him to write and to manage the choreography for their operas, a function Beauchamp also performed for Lully.* He was considered a strong and brilliant dancer by his contemporaries, and he was the favored choice of professional artistes in search of a coach. Pécourt* was his most outstanding student. As a performer himself, Beauchamp was known for his flashy pirouettes, and as a teacher he indicated the five basic positions of the classic ballet.

Beauchamp danced in the ballets at the premieres of seven compositions by Lully between 1673, the first year of the Florentine's reign at the Opéra, and

1687, the date of the dancer's retirement: *Cadmus et Hermione** (1673), *Alceste** (1674), *Thésée** (1675), *Atys** (1675), *Isis** (1677), *Bellérophon** (1679), and *Amadis*, (1684).

BIBLIOGRAPHY: ACD 65; CODB 60; DBF V, 1054; EDB 53-54; R. Kunzle, "Pierre Beauchamp: The Illustrious Unknown Choreographer," *Dance Scope* 8 (Spring, 1974), 33-42, and 9 (Fall, 1974), 30-45; Lajarte I, 22-32, 34-35, 46-47; André Levinson, "Notes sur le ballet au XVIIe siècle: Les danseurs de Lully" *RM* VI (janvier 1925), 48-52, LXIX II, 431; TdT 800; Marian Hannah Winter, *The Pre-Romantic Ballet* (New York: Dance Horizons, 1974), 4, 15, 41, 45-46, 108, 149, 260; WT 13.

Beaumavielle, François (b. ? Languedoc; d. 1688 ?), a singer whose birth and death are shrouded in mystery, appeared on the stage first as a chorister in Molière's *Psyché* at the Tuileries in January 1671. He was chosen to fill the part of Vertumne in *Pomone*,* when the newly formed Opéra mounted this work in the rue Mazarine two months later in March 1671. Cast as Faune in *Les Peines et les plaisirs de l'amour** in the autumn of this same year, he was still active as a vocalist at the time that he joined Lully's* Royal Academy of Music in 1672. His flair for acting and his strong voice made him a favorite in his day, and he created such important parts as Alcide in *Alceste*,* Cadmus in *Cadmus et Hermione*,* and the title-rôle in *Roland*.* He was posted for the part of Neptune in *Thétis et Pélée** in 1688, when he disappeared suddenly and completely from the operatic scene, although he had also been singing Egée in *Thésée** at the time.

BIBLIOGRAPHY: DBF 5, 1128-29; Fétis I, 286; GE V, 1040; Lajarte I, 19-20, 22-23, 25-26, 29, 31-32, 42-43, 48, 56-58; TdT 797; L. Travenol and Jacques Durey de Noinville, *Histoire du théâtre de l'Opéra en France*, 2 vols. (Paris: Joseph Barbou, 1753), II, 54.

Bel-Air. After Jean-Baptiste Lully* purchased Pierre Perrin's* monopolistic license to produce operatic programs, he refused to have anything to do with the salle de la Bouteille,* where Perrin's unscrupulous partners were continuing to operate for their own profit. He opened a new facility at the Béquet tennis court located on a piece of property known as Bel-Air and situated in the rue de Vaugirard* opposite the Luxembourg palace. Thus, his theatre came to be known as the salle du Bel-Air during its brief existence. His newly formed Royal Academy of Music offered its first program here on 15 November 1672, when *Les Fêtes de l'Amour et de Bacchus** was given its premiere. Lully mounted a second work in the Bel-Air theatre, *Cadmus et Hermione*,* but the deteriorating physical condition of the structure obliged him to seek new quarters almost immediately. After Molière's death on 17 February 1673, he acquired the Palais-Royal* for his troupe and transferred *Cadmus et Hermione* there on 15 June 1673.

Bellérophon is the second and last work composed by Thomas Corneille* and Jean-Baptiste Lully* after the latter had been obliged to dismiss Philippe Quinault* for offending Mme de Montespan in *Isis*.* Bernard de Fontenelle* also played a substantial rôle in the writing of the libretto, although it was not until 1741 that he published a letter in the *Journal des Savants* to claim that he had had an active part in its composition.

The subject of *Bellérophon* had already been used by Quinault in a legitimate tragedy, but the opera is quite different from this earlier treatment of the story. Sténobée is now the rival, not the sister, of Philonoé, and she is the widow, not the fiancée, of Proteus. Thus simplified, the action is spread evenly over the five acts to allow for the production of a spectacle in each act. The exposition presents the unencumbered triangle of Sténobée in love with Bellérophon, who loves and is loved by Philonoé (I). Rejected and wrathful, Sténobée profits by Amisodan's love for her by prevailing upon him to evoke a monster from Hades to spread havoc throughout the kingdom (II). Bellérophon determines to fight Chimaera even at the cost of his life and despite the Oracle's pronouncement that the son of Neptune will be the hero to slay the monster and marry Philonoé (III). Bellérophon slays the Chimaera with Pallas's help (IV), and he wins Philonoé as his bride after it is recognized that he is the son of Neptune (V). *Bellérophon*, then, is another musical illustration of the thesis that love triumphs over evil, although it may itself engender evil on occasion.

Bellérophon enjoyed immense success, and its popularity was enhanced by the patriotic appeal it made by suggesting that the protagonist slaying the tripartite monster was Louis XIV defeating the triple alliance of the Empire, Spain, and Holland. It was given for the first time on 31 January 1679, and the *Mercure* announced immediately that Lully had outdone himself and that all Paris was at the Palais-Royal* to see the new production. *Le Journal de l'Opéra* notes that public interest was increased by the "débuts of Mlle de Rochois* and of Louison Moreau" in it. Lully's work ran from 31 January to 27 October 1679. It was mounted at Court before the dauphin on 31 May; he was enthusiastic about *Bellérophon* by virtue of Louison Moreau's presence in the cast. It was taken to Saint-Germain en Laye for several performances before the king between 3 and 26 January 1680 after it had been staged for Marie-Louise d'Orléans, queen of Spain, on 6 September 1679. It was also part of the program celebrating the marriage of the prince de Conti and Mlle de Blois, natural daughter of Louis XIV, in 1680. The records of the Opéra indicate that it was also represented at the château d'If in Marseilles, but without machinery, at a party given for the countess de Grignan by the duke de Vendôme. At the Palais-Royal, *Bellérophon* was revived in 1706, 1718, and 1728 for a total of 56 billings after its first run.

At its premiere, Clédière played the title-rôle with Mlles La Prée and Saint-Christophe as Pallas and Sténobée respectively. Boutteville, Lestang,* Noblet, and Pécourt* danced in the ballets.

BIBLIOGRAPHY: CG, 130-31; CL I, 142-43; DDO I, 142-43; Lajarte I, 34-35; Lionel de La Laurencie, *Lully* (Paris: Alcan, 1919), 53-56, 154-55; Jean-Baptiste Lully, *Bellérophon . . . reconstituée et reduite pour piano et chant par Théodore de Lajarte* (Paris: T. Michaëlis, 188?); RGO II, 135-96; Sonn I, 212-13.

Benserade, Isaac de (b. 1613, Normandy; d. 20 October 1691, Gentilly), writer, was considered one of the greatest poets of his time by his contemporaries, and he was favored by nobles and king alike at Versailles. His verse employed all the usual poetic forms of the post-Malherbe period, but Benserade is remembered almost exclusively as the author of the court ballets in which youthful Louis XIV danced. Lully incorporated his work into *Les Festes de l'Amour et de Bacchus** and adapted part of his *Le Carnaval, mascarade royale* (1668) to the overture of *Le Carnaval** of 1675 besides using his words for the seventh entrée of this latter composition, *Les Nouveaux Mariés*. Benserade's other piece for the Royal Academy of Music was the text he supplied for *Le Triomphe de l'Amour* of 1681, a libretto upon which he collaborated with Philippe Quinault.*

After nearly three centuries, Benserade returned to the Opéra with *Le Triomphe de l'Amour* on 6 January 1925, when this "royal ballet" enjoyed its 256th performance. It was billed for seven programs with choreography by Léo Staats and costumes as well as scenery by Maxime Dethomas (see twentieth-century volume for Staats). Its success led to a second twentieth-century revival on 16 December 1932 with a cast that included Mlles Didion and Simoni among the dancers and the vocalists Mmes Campredon, Laval, and Renaux. Gabriel Grovlez led the orchestra during this 263rd staging of Benserade's most enduring ballet.

BIBLIOGRAPHY: Isaac de Benserade, *Poésies*, ed. Octave Uzanne (Genève: Slatkine Reprints, 1967); CDSS I, 332-34; GDSS 150-51; Lajarte I, 21, 28, 38; Charles Silin, *Benserade and his "ballets de cour"* (Baltimore: The Johns Hopkins Press, 1940); SW 333-34.

Bérain, Jean (b. 1640, Saint-Mihiel, Lorraine; d. 24 January 1711, Paris), stage designer and costumer, moved to Paris as a small boy. In the French capital, he studied to be a gunsmith and an engraver, but he began to earn a livelihood as a decorator and fashion designer. He was talented and industrious, and he became attached to the Court before long. Here, he worked for the Crown under the guidance of Henry Gissey. After Gissey's death in 1673, the young man assumed the responsibilities of his master's office, and he was charged accordingly with organizing the festivals, entertainments, funerals, and theatrical productions undertaken at the Court of Louis XIV.

Bérain stepped into his master's shoes at a time when Court spectacles were frequent and lavish. In fact, the Royal Academy of Music had just been founded, and Lully* had ambitious plans for it. Bérain's talents were employed for the representations of *Hermione,** *Atys,** *Proserpine,** *Phaëton,** *Armide,** and he continued to contribute to operatic productions sponsored by the Opéra until the staging of Campra's *Les Fêtes vénitiennes** in 1710 on the eve of his death. One of his major efforts was exerted for *Le Triomphe de l'Amour,** the ballet in twenty entrees given at Saint-Germain en Laye in 1681.

Recently, a large number of costume designs have been recovered that are the work of Jean Bérain and his son, Jean Bérain II (1674-1726), who succeeded his father as Court decorator. These precious sketches were presented to the public at the Hôtel Drouot on 26 April 1982. They included such fascinating items as the original sketches of the costumes worn by Armide and Proserpine in Lully's operas by the same names.

BIBLIOGRAPHY: Grove (1980) II, 514-15; Vladimir Hofmann, "Bérain aux enchères," *SDLD* 143 (10 avril 1982), 48.

Bertin, T. de La Doué (b. 1680, Paris; d. 1745, Paris), composer, was master of the harpsichord in the Orléans household and organist at the Théatins church in Paris. He entered the orchestra of the Royal Academy of Music about 1714 to play the violin and the harpsichord. He retired on a pension in 1734. His works for the Opéra included *Cassandre** with Bouvard in 1706, *Diomède** in 1710, *Ajax* in 1716, *Le Jugement de Pâris* in 1718, *Les Plaisirs de la campagne* in 1719 (for Bertin's post-1715 works, see eighteenth-century volume).

BIBLIOGRAPHY: CG, 158, 181, 238; *Encyclopédie de la musique*, ed. François Michel, 3 vols. (Paris: Fasquelle, 1958-61), I, 406; Fétis I, 383; Lajarte I, 158; NBG V, 730; L. Travenol et Jacques Durey de Noinville, *Histoire du théâtre de l'Opéra en France*, 2 vols. (Paris: Joseph Barbou, 1753), II, 27.

Blondy (b. 1677, Paris; d. 13 August 1747, Paris), dancer, was the son of a dancing master and a nephew of Beauchamp,* ballet master for Louis XIV and the Royal Academy of Music directed by Lully.* Inevitably, he took instruction in the art of ballet from his uncle, and, after the death of Pécourt,* he became ballet master at the Opéra in 1729. His conduct of the affairs of his office was beyond reproach, and he remained in his position until his death at age 70 after a short illness.

Blondy's versatility is reflected in the variety of works in which he appeared. At the start of his career, he danced in the ballet for the early revivals of Lully's works, for example, *Cadmus et Hermione** in 1690, *Armide** in 1713, and *Amadis** in 1718. He also was billed for the return to repertory of *Thétis et Pélée** in 1712 in addition to participating in the premieres of four new lyric tragedies: *Télémaque** in 1704, *Camille, reine des Volsques* in 1717, *Polydore* in 1720, and *Télégone* in 1725. He was cast in only one heroic pastoral, *Le Jugement de Pâris* of 1718, but he performed in three ballets: *La Vénitienne** of 1705 by La Barre,* *Les Amours déguisés** of 1713 by Bourgeois,* and *Les Stratagèmes de l'Amour* of 1726 by Destouches* (for the post-1715 works in which Blondy danced, see eighteenth-century volume).

BIBLIOGRAPHY: CODB 78; GE VI, 1173; Lajarte I, 22-23, 46-47, 52-53, 57-58, 104-5, 118-19, 127-28, 130-31, 140-41; TdT 800; Marian Hannah Winter, *The Pre-Romantic Ballet* (New York: Dance Horizons, 1974), 45, 50, 53, 86, 108, 162, 260; WT 13-15.

Boullay, Michel du (b. ?, Paris; d. 1691, Rome), librettist, was secretary to the duke de Vendôme, but the duties of this office did not prevent him from collaborating on two compositions for the Opéra. He did the libretto for the ballet, *Zéphyre et Flore,* for which Louis and Jean-Louis Lully* did the score in 1688, and two years later he provided the words for Louis Lully's *Orphée** of 1690.

BIBLIOGRAPHY: CDSS 771; DDO II, 820, 1176; Lajarte I, 56-58, 69.

Bourgeois, Louis-Thomas (b. 1676, Fontaine-L'Evêque in Hainaut; d. January 1750, Paris), composer, entered the Opéra initially as a vocalist in 1708 but left the troupe as early as 1711. He did not sever relations completely with the Royal Academy of Music, however, and he had his *Les Amours déguisés** presented at the Palais-Royal* in 1713. Two years later, on 29 April 1715, his *Les Plaisirs de la paix** was billed at the same theatre. In about 1716 he left the capital to go to Toul, where he had been named chapel master; he went from here to Strasbourg to hold the same position in this city. Restless, he returned to Paris to die in poverty despite his talents. He published two books of cantatas and a third volume entitled *Cantates anacréontiques* besides composing various ballets never represented at the Opéra, for example, *Les Nuits de Sceaux* (1714), *Diane* (1721) with Aubert, and a *Divertissement pour le Dauphin.*

BIBLIOGRAPHY: Fétis, II, 43; Lajarte, I, 158.

La Bouteille was an indoor tennis court built during the reign of Henri IV in the rue Mazarine. When Louis XIV granted the abbé Perrin* permission on 28 June 1669 to stage operas in his kingdom, the entrepreneur and his confident associates bought and remodeled the *jeu de paume de La Bouteille* to serve as their theatre. The corporation opened their opera house in March 1671 with *Pomone.** This work was quite successful, but the members of the company fell to arguing among themselves, and Lully* managed to gain control of Perrin's monopolistic license. The Florentine installed his troupe in the *jeu de paume du Bel-Air* in the rue Vaugirard* near the Luxembourg palace on 15 November 1672.

BIBLIOGRAPHY: Jacques Hillairet, *Dictionnaire historique des rues de Paris* (Paris: Les Editions de minuit, 1963), II, 116; André Lejeune and Stéphane Wolff, *Les quinze salles de l'Opéra de Paris* (Paris: Librairie théâtrale, 1955), 8-15; Charles Nuitter, *Le Nouvel Opéra* (Paris: Hachette, 1875), 1-3.

Boutelou, singer, has left no record of his birth, death, or complete name, although his bellicose disposition led him into troubles with the police after he had consumed too much wine. He was attached to the chapel of Louis XIV, who took a special interest in him on account of the effectiveness of his voice. The king saw to it that his singer was well supplied with food and money whether he was in or out of prison.

Boutelou appears to have made his debut as a shepherd in *Issy* in 1698, and he filled many other minor parts in such works as *Canente*,* *Le Carnaval*,* *Hésione*,* and *Iphigénie en Tauride** before being cast in a major rôle like Amadis in Lully's *Amadis** in 1707. He then reverted to singing minor parts in *Bradamante*,* *Tancrède*,* *Atys*,* and *Thétis et Pélée* in 1707-8.

BIBLIOGRAPHY: EC I, 75-79; Fétis II, 46; GE VII, 866; Lajarte I, 24-25, 33, 36-37, 46-47, 64-65, 94-95, 100-101, 108.

Bouvard, François (b. 1670, near Paris; d. after 1757, ?), composer, entered the Opéra as a child, but he was obliged to abandon his rôles to women after he lost his voice at the age of sixteen. He then gave himself over to the study of composition and spent some time in Rome. He returned to Paris at the turn of the century and had his *Médus, roi des Mèdes** represented at the Palais-Royal* in 1702. His next contribution to the Royal Academy of Music was *Cassandre*,* produced in 1706. He wrote *Ariane et Bacchus* for the Court in 1729, the year of the staging of his *divertissement** entitled *Le Triomphe de l'Amour et de l'Hymen* (for Bouvard's post-1715 works, see eighteenth-century volume).

Bouvard enjoyed the favor of Madame, dower of Monsieur, brother of Louis XIV, and she honored him at this time not only with her protection but also with a pension of 400 *livres* for the pleasure he had afforded her with his music. This money allowed Bouvard to travel, especially in Spain, Italy, and Portugal. The king of this last country also recognized his talent as a musician in a tangible way. He returned to France to write the idyll *Diane et l'Amour* (1730) and *L'Ecole de Mars* (1733) during the reign of Louis XV.

In addition to his theatrical music, Bouvard has left four collections of airs to be sung to the accompaniment of the flute, a group of violin sonatas, and a paraphrase of a psalm done in the style of Italian oratorios. Bouvard was married twice; his first wife was the widow of Noël Coypel, director of the Royal Academy of Painting and Sculpture.

BIBLIOGRAPHY: CG, 126, 158; Fétis II, 47; Lajarte I, 94-95, 108, 158-59.

Boyer, Claude (b. 1618, Alby; d. 22 July 1698, Paris), dramatist, was known to his contemporaries as the abbé Boyer. After his ordination as a priest, the abbé went to Paris, but his academic success as a student of theology did not carry over into his pulpit in the capital: the satirist Furetière remarked that the only reason that the abbé did not put his listeners to sleep with his preaching was his lack of a congregation. But he did become well known through his work for the theatre, and he was elected to the French Academy in 1666 after having had more than a dozen plays accepted for performance by legitimate actors. He continued to write for the regular stage in Paris after becoming a member of the French Academy, moreover, and Chapelain remarked of him that he was second only to

Corneille* as far as dramatic compositions were concerned. In all, he did seventeen tragedies, three tragicomedies, two heroic dramas, and a straight pastoral for the legitimate stage, but his only text for the Royal Academy of Music was *Méduse** in 1697.

BIBLIOGRAPHY: Bio univ V, 376-77; Clara Brody, *The Works of Claude Boyer* (New York: King's Crown Press, 1947); CG 155-57; DBF VII, 96-97; Lajarte I, 70; H. C. Lancaster, *A History of French Dramatic Literature in the Seventeenth Century*, 9 vols. (Baltimore: The Johns Hopkins Press, 1940) IV, 217-22; TdT 472-73.

Bradamante is a lyric tragedy in five acts and a prologue with a musical score by La Coste* and a libretto by Pierre-Charles Roy.* Although Garnier had dramatized the Bradamante story in 1582, Roy's work was derived from Ariosto's *Orlando furioso*. The principal departure from the Italian version is Roger's deception of his friend.

The two previous lyric tragedies at the Palais-Royal,* *Cassandre* and *Polyxène*,* were not too well received by the public, and La Coste's composition was mounted only 18 times between its premiere on 2 May and 31 May 1707, when it was dropped.

The prologue presents the magician Athlant casting a spell over the arms that he intends to distribute among his favorite knights so that they might rid the earth of giants, monsters, and tyrants. Mélisse descends from the sky to announce that a just and powerful hero now rules France. Four spirits whisk away the statue of Roger to offer it to this "wisest of kings" in a gesture indicating that the forthcoming tragedy is being offered to Louis XIV.

The exposition of the opera presents Bradamante complaining that her father has ignored her love for Roger by promising her hand to the prince of Greece (I, 1). When the latter enters the harbor of Marseilles (I, 2), Mélisse suggests that Merlin might help her. The enchantress evokes the magician's palace (I, 3), and his statue foretells that only the warrior who defeats Bradamante is worthy to wed her (I, 4). The heroine interprets this oracle as meaning that she will slay Roger and marry the prince that her father has chosen for her, but Mélisse assures her that Merlin would never countenance such cruel events. Mélisse leaves to persuade Aymon to consent to the duel for his daughter (I, 5).

After the establishment of the triangle involving Bradamante and her two suitors, Roger refuses to oppose the prince's marriage to Bradamante because his rival saved his life when they were enemies (II, 1). Roger then disguises himself in Greek armor to avoid embarrassing Bradamante or arousing her father's anger by appearing at Court (II, 2). Aymon consents to Bradamante's fighting a duel with Roger. If she is defeated, she will become his bride (II, 3-4). Roger reveals his presence and declares his love to Bradamante (II, 5-6).

The duel constitutes the basis for the action of the next two acts, which present Roger saddened by the prospect of Bradamante doing battle (III, 1) and the prince puzzled by the necessity of defeating his beloved to win her heart (III, 2). Roger is seeking a proper course of action (III, 3), when Mélisse gives him a suit of armor identical to that worn by the prince. She urges him to do combat in disguise (III, 4). The prince has discovered Roger's presence in Marseilles by the start of the fourth act, and he decides to slay him for his treachery (IV, 1). He challenges him as soon as he sees him (IV, 2), but he does not yet know that Roger has already defeated Bradamante in his duplicate armor (IV, 3). The deceived populace hails the prince as the victor in the duel because they have been duped by the two sets of identical armor. A public festival continues until nightfall despite this misunderstanding; Bradamante is disconsolate and threatens suicide (IV, 4-5). The prince arms his troops when he discovers that another claimant for the hand of Bradamante has defeated her (IV, 6).

The deception is continued into the last act, which begins with the heroine lamenting the "prince's" victory over her (V, 1). Mélisse saves her from suicide and reveals to her that she was defeated by Roger (V, 2). The latter saves the day by disarming the angry prince and returning his sword in the name of friendship, a gesture which the disappointed suitor of Bradamante accepts. The bleak landscape matches the joyous mood of the moment by changing into a blooming garden (V, 3-4), and the opera closes amidst an eager celebration (V, 5).

BIBLIOGRAPHY: CG 222, 223; CL I, 169-70; Lajarte I, 109; RGO IX, 227-78; Sonn I, 231.

C

Cadmus et Hermione is a lyric tragedy in five acts and a prologue. Its libretto was by Quinault,* and its musical score was the work of Lully.* It was the last of the two operatic works produced at the Bel-Air* tennis court, and its authors presented their first active collaboration as a lyric tragedy to meet the need for an entirely new sort of composition to replace the pastiche pastoral entitled *Les Fêtes de l'Amour et de Bacchus.** The success of *Cadmus et Hermione* was helped by the presence of the king, his brother, and a number of nobles at its premiere on 27 April 1673, and the king's brother returned to see it again with the English ambassador on 30 July 1673. Louis XIV was so pleased with the libretto that he awarded Quinault a pension of 2,000 *livres*. Lully was delighted enough to hire him as his regular librettist at a salary of 4,000 *livres* annually in return for one text a year.

Lully dedicated his work to Louis XIV, but he gave some relief to the usually tedious laudium by suggesting that there was room for certain improvements in the conduct of national affairs. In his 38 alexandrine lines, he exhorted his monarch not to sadden his subjects by leaving the country and waging war abroad. He expressed the wish that the Sun King remain at home to warm the hearts of his people and to bring "love and pleasure" to the human race.

The authors of *Cadmus et Hermione* wrote a prefatory note to their work in which they revealed that the idea for the prologue derived from the story of the monstrous serpent, Python, recounted in Ovid, *Metamorphoses* I, 8. The Roman poet relates how Python was born of the great postflood slime and how he presented such an overpowering threat that he had to be slain by Apollo, god of the sun. Thus, the note continues, the subject of *Cadmus et Hermione* is so patently allegorical that explanations are superfluous. The spectators were thereby invited to see Louis XIV in the sun and the enemies of France and happiness in the monstrous dragon slain by Apollo, and the idea of this allegory was repeated in the body of the opera itself. In the prologue, however, the sun god is described as the source of all contentment, the reason for all gaiety, the glory of all nature. The only dark note is Envie, borne in on winds to summon Python from his foul fen. A fearsome concert arises on the stage at this point, and only the flaming breath and eyes of rearing Python are visible. Suddenly, a rain of fire falls, and the light of the sun returns to disclose the remains of the slain serpent. The singers take up the refrain of "The sun is conqueror" and "Let us profit from good days"; the sun descends in triumph to reassure all humans. The central personages of the prologue are taken from Ovid, but all else is the invention of the librettist: the pastoral scenes and lyrics, the scenario for the ballet, and the opportunities for machine episodes.

The five acts are set in regular dramatic form except for the variations in verse. There is an early exposition of the basic situation to be evolved. The action moves forward with a reversal in the fortunes of the characters until a crisis occurs to precipitate the conclusion. The intrigue begins with the establishment of the Cadmus-Hermione-Draco triangle, which is complicated further by the gods, who ally themselves with Draco or Cadmus (I). Cadmus is determined to slay Draco, and he bids a sad farewell to Hermione before setting out to accomplish this mission (II). Draco is slain (III), but Hermione is kidnaped by Junon (IV). Cadmus laments the disappearance of Hermione, but she is returned to earth after Junon and Jupiter resolve their differences to bring joy to all (V). As in the case of the prologue, Quinault uses only the central episode in Ovid: the birth and the slaying of the monster who has now become Draco, the giant. The librettist creates a triangle to provide the requisite love interest, and he adds Pallas, l'Amour, Mars, Junon to his cast to allow ample exploitation of machine displays. He adds a subsidiary love affair between Abas and Charité to offer legitimate comic relief. *Fêtes* are supplied to enhance the ballet, and the choreographer was given the opportunity to animate statues of gold and to petrify demons and furies in the middle of their flights. But it was the composer who was rewarded most amply by the libretto, and Lully took full advantage of the text. His "Suivons l'amour" (I, 4) for a trio and chorus, his minuet (V, 3) in the last act, and the chorus of "O Mars! Reçois nos voeux" (III, 6) were all applauded, but the farewell scene between Hermione and Cadmus in II, 4 created the greatest impression upon audiences. An innovative excellence was likewise quite apparent in Lully's handling of the recitative and his combining the movement of his score with the texture of the verse presented to him.

The leading rôles were created by Mlle Bigogne as Hermione, Mlle Cartilly as Charité, and Beaumavielle* as Cadmus. MM. Clédière and Miracle did l'Envie and Le Soleil, respectively, in the prologue. Beauchamp* continued in the ballet in which Lestang* made his debut with the company.

The unpublished log of the Opéra records that part of the prologue of *Cadmus et Hermione* was mounted for Colbert in the presence of the king in July 1677. It had its second production for the Court at Saint-Germain en Laye in 1678. It was revived at the Palais-Royal* in 1674, 1678, 1679, 1690, 1691, 1703.

BIBLIOGRAPHY: DDO I, 183; Etienne Gros, *Philippe Quinault* (Paris: Champion, 1926), 526-29, 542-44, 592-97, 666-70; Lajarte I, 22-23; Lionel de La Laurencie, *Lully* (Paris: Alcan, 1919), 37-38, 148-49; Jean-Baptiste Lully, *Oeuvres complètes: les opéras*, ed. Henry Prunières, 10 vols. (New York: Broude Brothers, 1966) I, 1-196; Henry Prunières, *Lully* (Paris: Henri Laurens, n.d.), 96-97; RGO I, 143-204; Sonn I, 241.

Callirhoé is a lyric tragedy in five acts and a prologue for which André-Cardinal Destouches* created the musical score. Pierre-Charles Roy* wrote the libretto. Along with *Philomèle** and *Bradamante,** produced in 1705 and 1707, *Callirhoé* established Roy's reputation as one of the foremost lyricists and librettists in the closing years of Louis XIV's seemingly endless reign. It was given without interruption no fewer than 39 times between its premiere on 27 December 1712 and the close of its first run on 9 March 1713. It was billed a single time on 16 March 1713, when it was produced with considerable changes, particularly in the fifth act. It was returned to the stage of the Palais-Royal* on 3 January 1732, and *Le Journal de l'Opéra* infers that it was scheduled until the end of the second week in February. Its second revival started on 22 October 1743, and it was mounted alone until 14 November and without interruption. It was alternated subsequently with other works between 15 November and 26 December 1743. Mlle Journet* played the title-rôle during its initial run with Thévenard* as Corésus.

The prologue presents La Victoire honoring her warriors. Astrée proclaims that the universe is about to enjoy a peace that "the wisest of heroes" has established. This portion of the libretto is brief, but it does return to the Lullist-Quinault tradition by offering a laudium of Louis XIV and a reference to the contemporary situation in Europe.

The curtain rises on the opera at the moment when princess Callirhoé of Calydon is lamenting her marriage to a man she despises (I, 1). Her mother reminds her that she must wed Corésus, minister of Bacchus because her people wish him for their king. She regrets this duty and the death of her beloved Agénor, who might have saved her from this union, but she consents to do her mother's bidding (I, 2-3). Suddenly, Agénor appears, but she insists upon following her "too fatal duty" (I, 4). A chorus of citizens of Calydon celebrates the Callirhoé-Corésus wedding as the groom greets his bride. She glimpses Agénor during the ceremony and faints. She is carried off unconscious before she is wed officially (I, 5).

The intrigue is still bound to the triangle of Corésus-Callirhoé-Agénor at the start of the second act: Agénor hopes that his beloved is not married to his rival (II, 1), but she assures him that she will become Corésus's wife. Emotion overcomes them both, and they declare their mutual love (II, 2). Corésus surprises Agénor at Callirhoé's feet; he is aghast and calls upon Bacchus to destroy Calydon and its inhabitants (II, 3-5). Callirhoé and her mother are overcome by the slaughter and ruin in their land. The queen directs her daughter to try every ruse to persuade Corésus to lift the curse

(III, 1). The latter asks Bacchus to desist (III, 2). The queen and the princess then witness a celebration that ends with the Oracle's pronouncement that peace can be restored only if Callirhoé's blood is shed, or if a substitute can be found for her (III, 4).

The heroine bewails her destiny (IV, 1) and relates the message of the Oracle to Agénor. The latter attributes this turn of events to Corésus and swears vengeance (IV, 2); Callirhoé fears for Agénor's death, and a chorus of shepherds and shepherdesses prays for peace (IV, 3-4). Resigned to her fate, the heroine prepares for the sacrifice, and Agénor offers himself as a substitute (IV, 5-6). The theatre now represents the temple of Bacchus with its sacrificial altar and with Corésus making ready for the sacrifice. He realizes that Agénor will be cherished even more highly by Callirhoé after his rival dies in her behalf (V, 1). Callirhoé offers herself at the altar, however, and she upbraids Corésus for daring to sacrifice Agénor (V, 2). Agénor insists that he die despite Callirhoé's protests, and Corésus proclaims that he will decide who is to be sacrificed. He stabs himself (V, 3). Bacchus removes the curse he has placed upon the land and names Agénor as successor to Corésus in his temple (V, 4).

It will be seen from this account of the intrigue of *Callirhoé* that no minor characters or confidants are included in the action. This was a deliberate omission by the authors, who expressed their opinion that such personages only slowed down or otherwise interfered with the main course of the plot. It is strange that this striking feature of *Callirhoé* is so little noticed.
BIBLIOGRAPHY: Lajarte I, 116; RGO X, 481-544.

Cambert, Robert (b. *circa* 1628, Paris; d. 1677, London) holds the distinction of being the first composer of French operatic music in an official capacity. He started his career by taking harpsichord lessons from Chambonnières and obtaining the position of organist at the collegial church of Saint-Honoré. He was later named superintendent of music for Anne of Austria, mother of Louis XIV. He became the first French musician to compose a score for an opera when Perrin* had the idea of promoting a new stage spectacle in the manner of *Orfeo ed Euridice* that Mazarin had ordered staged by an Italian troupe in 1647; he entitled his composition *La Pastorale, première comédie française en musique.* Cambert was commissioned to create the music for the work, and it was given at Issy in April 1647. This venture was so successful that Louis XIV directed *La Pastorale d'Issy* to be repeated at Vincennes.

Mazarin continued to encourage the Cambert-Perrin team, and they wrote a second work, *Ariane, ou le mariage de Bacchus*, which was rehearsed at Issy in 1661 but never staged on account of Mazarin's death. Cambert's third opera, *Adonis*, was never mounted, and it has been lost. Then, on 28 June 1669, letters patent were issued Perrin to stage musical dramas, and Cambert helped him create the first formally sponsored French opera, *Pomone*,* given at Paris in 1671 under the auspices of the Académie d'Opéra. The next year Cambert did the music for *Les Peines et les plaisirs de l'amour*.* But it was at this moment that the license to perform opera was taken from Perrin and given to Jean-Baptiste Lully.* Irritated, Cambert quit France and went to England in 1673 to become musician for the king at the Court of Charles II. He died of resentment and aggravation in 1677 without realizing the importance of his position in the history of French opera.

BIBLIOGRAPHY: Bio univ VI, 455; DBF VII, 953; Norman Demuth, *French Opera: Its Development to the Revolution* (Sussex, England; Dufour, 1964), 100-117; Fétis II, 161-62; Lajarte I, 70; Arthur Pougin, "Les origines de l'opéra français: Cambert et Lully," *Revue d'art dramatique* XXI (1891), 129-55; idem, *Les vrais créateurs de l'opéra français: Perrin et Cambert* (Paris: Charvay, 1881); TdT 387-88; André Tessier, "Robert Cambert à Londres," *RdM* IV (December, 1927), 101-22.

Campistron, Jean Galbert de (b. *circa* 1636, Toulouse; d. 11 May 1723, Toulouse), dramatist, was born of a noble family of Armagnac origin that had settled in Toulouse in the sixteenth century. He was involved in a scandal and wounded in a duel at the age of seventeen, and his family sent him to Paris to avoid further complications. In the capital he came to know not only the theatrical family of Jean-Baptiste Raisin and his wife but also Racine, who inspired him to write for the stage. He had a series of two comedies and nine tragedies produced between 1683-1709: *Virginie* (1683), *Arminius* (1684), *Amante Amant* (1684), *Andronic* (1685), *Tiridate* (1691), *Aëtius* (1693), *Le Jaloux désabusé* (1709). He joined the retinue of the duke de Vendôme in 1691 and was present at the battle of Steenkerke (1692) with him. He was the recipient of a series of honors bestowed upon him by the king of Spain and the Academy of Toulouse, and he was elected to the French Academy in 1701. He returned to his native city in 1710 to marry Mlle de Maniban, sister of the archbishop of Bordeaux. Six children were born of this marriage.

Campistron had entered the service of the duke de Vendôme because he had successfully executed the duke's commission to write a libretto, *Acis et Galathée*,* for an entertainment planned for the dauphin at Anet. Lully* did the music for Campistron's text. The performance at Anet delighted the duke's guests, and the work was taken to the Palais-Royal* for public representation. Lully was in the process of collaborating upon a second composition with Campistron when death overtook the composer. But Lully had finished the music for the overture and the first act of *Achille et Polixène*,* and his secretary, Pascal Colasse,* completed the score. This lyric tragedy was the object of some criticism, but it was greeted with enough applause in the theatre to encourage Campistron to undertake a third opera, *Alcide*,* for which Louis Lully* did the score. It was performed for the first time on 3 February 1693 in Paris, and it was revived as *La Mort d'Hercule* in 1705 and as *La Mort d'Alcide* in 1716. Yet it was never a popular work, and it was criticized so mercilessly in some quarters that Campistron returned to writing comedy and tragedy for the legitimate stage without ever attempting a fourth title for the Royal Academy of Music.

BIBLIOGRAPHY: Bio univ VI, 513-14; CG 137-42; DBF VII, 1002-3; V. Fournel, "Contemporains et successeurs de Racine; les poètes tragiques décriés: Le Clerc, l'abbé Boyer, Pradon, Campistron," *RHL* I (1894), 251-58; Curt Hausding, *Jean Galbert de Campistron in seiner Bedeutung als Dramatiker für das Theater Frankreichs und des Auslandes* (University of Leipzig: Diss., 1903); Lajarte I, 71; H. C. Lancaster, *A History of French Dramatic Literature in the Seventeenth Century*, 9 vols. (Baltimore: The Johns Hopkins Press, 1940) IV, 243-77, 527-33; idem, *Sunset: A History of Parisian Drama in the Last Years of Louis XIV, 1701-1715* (Baltimore: The Johns Hopkins Press, 1945), 194-98.

Campra, André (b. December 1660, Aix-en-Provence; d. 14 June 1744, Versailles), composer, became a choirboy at Saint Sauveur church in his native city in 1674. He completed his formal musical studies in Aix-en-Provence and became choir master at Sainte-Trophîme in Arles on 22 August 1681. He then moved on to Saint Etienne in Toulouse on 11 June 1683. Finally, in 1694, he came to Paris to assume the duties of music master at Notre-Dame, where he introduced violins into sacred music on solemn occasions and was responsible for the numerous *Te Deums* that were executed here at the end of the seventeenth century.

But Campra had already begun his career in profane music discreetly and under the name of his brother, Joseph. He did *divertissements** for the duke de Sully in 1697 and for the duchess de La Ferté in 1698. More importantly by far, he contributed *L'Europe galante** to the Royal Academy of Music on 24 October 1697. After the success of this latter work, a tragedy in music that broke the classical form of French opera, Campra did one more composition for the Palais-Royal* before he left his post at Notre-Dame — *Le Carnaval de Venise** of 1699. In December 1700 he had *Hésione** produced by the Opéra only two months after his resignation from Notre-Dame. *Hésione* was the first composition that he did with Danchet* as his librettist, and in it he showed the influence of Lully* in his recitatives, while his originality as a composer was apparent in the arias. Still, Campra's previous success in the ballet had proven so rewarding that he returned to this form with *Aréthuse** in 1701.

After this first period of alternating between ballet and tragedy, Campra and Danchet realized that Lully's popularity was far from diminishing with the passage of time inasmuch as *Phaéton** and *Acis et Galathée** were enjoying a substantial revival. They decided to do an opera-ballet with extracts from the Florentine's work, and the result was *Les Fragments de Lully** in 1702. This reliance upon another composer was only a temporary device, however, and Campra pursued his own inspiration for the next two decades: *Tancrède*,* 1702; *Les Muses*,* 1703; *Iphigénie en Tauride*,* 1704;

*Alcine,** 1705; *Hippodamie,** 1708; *Les Festes vénitiennes,** 1710; *Le Triomphe de la folie,* 1711; *Idoménée** and *Les Amours de Vénus et Mars,* 1712; *Télèphe,** 1713; *Camille, reine des Volsques,* 1717; *Les Ages,* 1718; *Achille et Déidamie,* 1735 (for Campra's post-1715 works, see eighteenth-century volume).

Campra's success increased with his many contributions to the repertory of the Palais-Royal. He became "batteur de mesure" for the Royal Academy of Music as early as 1702 with *Tancrède,* and Louis XV gave him a pension of 500 *livres* in 1718. He was attached to the household of the prince de Conti in 1722 and was made Inspector of Music for the Academy in 1730 with a salary of 1,500 *livres.* Campra dominated his era with his impressive fecundity, and Voltaire considered him the leading figure of his time in the field of music.

BIBLIOGRAPHY: Maurice Barthélémy, *André Campra: sa vie et son oeuvre, 1660-1774* (Paris: Picard, 1957); Bio univ VI, 516; DBF VII, 1004-5; Fétis II, 170-71; Lajarte I, 159-60.

Canente is a lyric tragedy in five acts and a prologue with music by Pascal Colasse* and a libretto by Houdard de La Motte.* Its only run extended for 27 performances between its premiere on 4 November 1700 and its last representation on 19 December 1700. Mlles Desmatins,* Maupin,* and Moreau with Thévenard,* Dun, and Hardouin* appeared in the singing rôles; the dancers included Mlles Dangeville and Subligny* opposite Balon,* Desplaces, and Pécourt* (for Mlle Dangeville and M. Dun, see eighteenth-century volume).

The prologue of *Canente* is set in Fontainebleau, where L'Aurore hails the approach of Diane, Flore, and Vertumne coming to beautify the gardens of the royal château. The occasion of all this activity is the return of Louis XIV.

The intrigue is based upon a situation involving four characters, and it begins with Circé making Picus king on account of her love for him and despite his love for Canente (I, 1). After Saturn's announcement that his son's victories will be countless (I, 2), Picus insists to Circé that he will wed Canente despite Le Tibre's love for her (I, 3), and the sorceress resolves to destroy her rival (I, 4). Canente has momentary fears that Picus's regal rank may diminish his love for her (II, 1), but he and devious Circé reassure her (II, 2-3). A magnificent palace appears filled with minor divinities loyal to Le Tibre (II, 4-5), who presses for Canente's hand in vain. Rejected, he threatens ruin to the kingdom, and Circé warns Canente to renounce Picus before disaster strikes. Canente refuses and Circé summons her demons to kidnap her (II, 6).

The plot continues to be laden with incidents even after the librettist has developed it to the point where only a solution is needed to achieve a complete action. Canente refuses to renounce Picus in favor of Le Tibre (III, 1-2), and Circé's demons prepare to torture her only to be disarmed by Grâces and Amours (III, 3). Circé counterattacks by transforming her harmless demons into "furious monsters" bent on devouring her rival, but Le Tibre cannot countenance this horror and intervenes to save her (III, 4-5). The third act, therefore, is largely an exercise in terror that adds little to the drama because it presents the already well-demonstrated fact that Circé and Canente are obdurate.

Now desperate, Circé lies to Picus by telling him that Canente has been unfaithful to him, and she casts a spell over him so that he will fall in love with her (IV, 1). La Nuit arrives at her call, but L'Amour refuses to do her bidding to make Picus forget Canente (IV, 2). Circé acknowledges defeat by admitting to Picus that she lied about Canente. She promises to arrange his wedding to her, but a vicious "aside" by Circé reveals that the sorceress is preparing another trap (IV, 3). Circé calls up the Eumenides from Hades to sacrifice Canente while sparing Picus (V, 1). Alecton assumes the identity of Hymen, the Furies disguise themselves as Jeux and Plaisirs, and the stage set becomes a dazzling palace in preparation for the Canente-Picus marriage (V, 1). Circé explains to puzzled Le Tibre that she is planning to punish the two lovers by having dying Picus see Canente in Le Tibre's arms (V, 2). The Furies perform their wedding dance (V, 3), and Alecton poisons Canente. After her death, Circé transforms Picus into a woodpecker so that he cannot follow his beloved to the underworld (V, 4).

BIBLIOGRAPHY: Lajarte I, 90; Antoine Houdard de La Motte, *Oeuvres complètes*, 11 vols. (Genève: Slatkine Reprints, 1970) II, 192-204; RGO VII, 49-108.

Cariselli was offered as a comic entertainment based upon an alleged episode in the life of an Italian composer by the same name who considered his musical attainments so impressive that he came to France to replace Lully.* The latter composer is supposed to have heard of this plan and to have rehearsed three vocalists to sing *Bondi Cariselli* as soon as his rival appeared at Court. The anecdote ends with the assertion that Cariselli was so upset by this greeting at Saint-Germain en Laye that he returned to Italy forthwith.

Lully had created *Bondi Cariselli* especially for this occasion, then, but he decided apparently to exploit his work by writing both the Italian words and the music of his trio. He took advantage of the fact that Cariselli stammered, and he presented a situation that evoked laughter whenever it was produced as part of *Les Fragments de Lully.** It was not a long piece and was composed of scenes wherein Cariselli lamented Vafrina's indifference, the three Pantalons greeted him, and Vafrina and Garbini mocked him. These rôles were sung initially by Mlle Maupin* (Vafrina), Boutelou* (Cariselli), and Hardouin* (Garbini).

BIBLIOGRAPHY: Lajarte I, 95.

Le Carnaval is a pastiche in ten entrées that Lully* put together in 1675 while *Thésée** was being sung at Court, and the Palais-Royal* was seeking a new work. It was brief and designed to serve as a curtain raiser, if the need arose, but the records of the Opéra show that it was produced alone on occasion. There was no real unity in the composition, and none was intended, since it was presented in whole or in part as a suite of entertaining interludes; for example, the entrée of *Les Espagnols* and the Turkish ceremony from *Le Bourgeois Gentilhomme*. The music was entirely by Lully, but the words of the various units had been written by Benserade,* Quinault,* and Molière.* It was staged at Court and at the Palais-Royal in 1675. It was produced at the Palais-Royal again in 1692 under the title of *Le Carnaval mascarade*, when it was billed with the ballet that had been danced before the dauphin at Villeneuve Saint-Georges on 1 September of the same year. The artistes performed it for the last time at their own theatre with *La Grotte de Versailles* on 11 July 1700.

BIBLIOGRAPHY: Lajarte I, 28-29; Jean-Baptiste Lully, *Le Carnaval: selections*, ed. Karel Huse (Kassel: Nagels Verlag, 1968); RGO I, 347-70.

Le Carnaval de Venise reflects the post-Lullian trend away from mythological subjects: it is set in an Italian locale, and its characters are citizens of Venice. Like *Aricie** and *Les Fêtes galantes*,* this composition by Campra* with a libretto by Regnard* was a continuous ballet, and its plot and its characters developed but did not change from act to act like the regular *opéra-ballet** that was growing from *Les Saisons** and *L'Europe galante.** The conclusion of the third act of *Le Carnaval de Venise* presents a separate opera-within-an-opera entitled *Orfeo nell'Inferni*, however, although this latter subordinate composition ends in a ball and is linked to the return to Venice of the principal personages of the main plot. Campra's ballet had its premiere at the Palais-Royal* on 20 January 1699; its first and only run extended until 29 February 1699.

Prologues produced previously to the premiere of *Le Carnaval de Venise* were set most often on the banks of the Seine, in some bucolic corner of Europe, or in a more remote location inhabited by the gods and goddesses of antiquity. The prologue of Regnard's libretto was laid in "a room where a theatrical performance is to occur. Everything is still in disorder; the place is full of pieces of wood and unfinished sets. A group of workers strives to put things in place." This sudden touch of realism in a seventeenth-century prologue is a surprise, but the situation becomes normal when Minerve complains of the chaotic condition of the stage. She refuses to appear in such a disordered environment and summons the deities presiding over the arts to build a "magnificent theatre."

The situation on which *Le Carnaval de Venise* is based is presented with dispatch. Léonore suspects that Léandre has fallen in love with Isabelle, although he has pledged his heart to her (I, 1), Isabelle reveals to Léonore that she is also in love with Léandre (I, 2). Léandre admits his preference for

Isabelle, and Lénore swears vengeance (I, 3). After a lengthy interlude of music and dancing (I, 4), Isabelle describes her fears of what Léonore might do, but Léandre reassures her that her apprehension is groundless (I, 5).

Rodolphe describes his jealousy (II, 1), and Léonore persuades him to join her in punishing Isabelle and Léandre for their duplicity (II, 2). Night falls after the powers of Fortune are celebrated by a ballet and chorus (II, 3), and Rodolphe hides (II, 4) to overhear Léandre serenading Isabelle (II, 5). Enraged by the tender scene that transpires between the two lovers (II, 6), Rodolphe emerges from his hiding place to find vengeance before sunrise (II, 7). Isabelle mistakes him for Léandre in the darkness, and she explains her dislike for Rodolphe (II, 8). The latter's anger mounts to new heights (II, 9).

Léonore renews her vows of vengeance (III, 1), and Rodolphe tells her that Léandre is dead. Léonore is repulsed by Rodolphe's suggestion that they marry (III, 2). After a carnaval held by the citizens of Venice (III, 3-4), Isabelle attempts to kill herself (III, 5) at the moment when Léandre enters alive and with the explanation that Rodolphe killed the wrong man. The reunited couple leave Venice to wed after hearing the opera, *Orfeo nell'Inferni*.

BIBLIOGRAPHY: Lajarte, I, 87; RGO VI, 291-354.

Le Carnaval et la Folie is a comedy-ballet in four acts and a prologue with music by André-Cardinal Destouches* and a libretto by Houdard de La Motte.* Its prologue and first act were performed before the king at Fontainebleau on Sunday, 14 October 1703, but it did not have its world premiere at the Palais-Royal* until 3 January 1704. Its first run extended for 24 billings until 12 February 1704. It was revived for 38 representations between 16 May and 8 August 1719 and for another run in the summer of 1730. It was produced with *Cariselli** and *Monsieur de Pourceaugnac* on 5 February 1731 and was brought back to the theatre in 1738, 1739, 1748. Mlle Maupin* created the rôle of La Folie, a part which Mlle Pélissier sang in 1738 (for Mlle Pélissier, see eighteenth-century volume). Thévenard* appeared as Le Carnaval in the premiere. Boutelou* executed the rôle of Le Professeur de Folie when the *divertissement** from the third act was mounted under the title of *Le Professeur de Folie* on 17 September 1706. This *divertissement* was revived again in 1711 and 1722. It was given at the end of Lully's *Les Fêtes de l'Amour et de Bacchus** in 1706, but it formed part of the *Fragments* of 1711 and 1722.

Destouches admits in the preface to his work that Erasmus suggested "the setting and almost all the personages of my composition." He adds that he made La Folie the daughter of Plutus and La Jeunesse because the earlier writer had done so.

The prologue presents distraught Momus upraiding the gods and goddesses for their irresponsible behavior, although the divinities point out to him that love is the key to eternal happiness. Jupiter silences Momus, and Mercure orders him to descend to earth.

Momus tries to warn humanity that their gods are to be respected or adored (I, 1). When Le Carnaval enters singing the praises of Bacchus and L'Amour, Momus tells him of the shocking state of affairs in heaven. Le Carnaval invites Momus to attend his marriage with La Folie (I, 2). Plutus and La Jeunesse are so happy over their own successful union that they raise a dazzling palace for the celebration of their daughter's wedding (I, 3). La Folie orders her parents to leave and then changes her mind so that the festivities may continue (I, 4). La Folie continues to follow her caprices and rejects Le Carnaval at the start of the second act, and the remainder of the composition is devoted to demonstrating the validity of La Folie's impertinent observation that her actions and decisions are always contrary to her parents' wishes (II, 1-2). La Folie calls upon Neptune to raise such a severe storm at sea that it drives a band of sailors ashore (II, 2-3). The sailors drink from Lethe to forget their misfortunes, and La Folie charms them into staying ashore (II, 3). Le Carnaval turns to Bacchus when La Folie once again rejects him (II, 4-5).

The second half of *Le Carnaval et la Folie* revolves largely about the jester's cap worn by La Folie. Additional complications occur when Momus reproaches La Folie for her cruelty and tells her that Le Carnaval has ceased to love her. Angered, she throws down her cap, which Momus retrieves (III, 1-2). She then summons her musicians, and Le Professeur de Folie emerges to sing "Son Professor di pazzia" with them (III, 3). Momus assures Le Carnaval that La Folie has sworn her love to him and has given him her jester's cap as a sign of her fidelity. Le Carnaval swears vengeance and calls upon the winds of winter to ravage the island (III, 4). La Folie construes this damage as a sign that Le Carnaval still loves her, an opinion that he confirms. La Folie remains indifferent, however, and plucks her cap from Momus's hands. After the latter confesses to Le Carnaval that he has lied to him about the cap (VI, 1-3), La Folie's parents enter to disapprove of the marriage between their daughter and Le Carnaval. When La Folie hears their verdict, she insists upon becoming the wife of Le Carnaval. Jupiter prepares a throne and palace for the couple. The grand finale features music, dancing, singing, and the approbation of the gods, who are not above folly (IV, 4-5).

BIBLIOGRAPHY: Antoine Houdard de La Motte, *Oeuvres complètes*, 11 vols. (Genève: Slatkine Reprints, 1970) II, 219-32; Lajarte I, 100-101; RGO VIII, 181-232.

Cassandre is a lyric tragedy in five acts and a prologue. The libretto was the work of La Grange-Chancel*; Bouvard* and Bertin de La Doué* collaborated on the music. The work enjoyed a dozen performances at most after its premiere on 22 June 1706. Bouvard is said to have insisted that only the fifth act was applauded because he composed it. Other critics blamed the hot weather of the summer of 1706 for its failure. One writer suggested that the public, women especially, did not take kindly to the tragedy, because "it exalted marriage at the expense of love." In any event, the opera did not fail on account of lack of talent: Mlles Desmatins,* Journet,* and Poussin* appeared in it with Boutelou,* Dun, and Thévenard.* Mlles Guyot and Prévost* danced its ballets opposite Balon* and Blondy.*

The picturesque prologue of *Cassandre* is set in the ruins of Troy with the divinities of the three Trojan rivers pondering the fate of their city. Apollon reassures them that Pâris is alive and about to found a new city named after him. This metropolis will be rich in the arts, and Vénus will foster love and joy there because Parisians will find peace and abundance in their shining city. A Trojan survivor suggests that it is time to please Apollon by retelling the story of Cassandre in a "pompous spectacle."

The tragedy opens with Arcas assuring Egiste that Clitemnestre will acknowledge the death of absent Agamemnon and will share her rule with him, but he protests that she has turned her attention to Oreste, Agamemnon's son (I, 1). Clitemnestre reveals that she has seen Agamemnon in a dream: he was about to slay her and Egiste when he stopped to place a crown upon Cassandre's head; the king and Cassandre then disappeared in a deluge of blood. Egiste reveals his love to Clitemnestre, but she must prepare a memorial sacrifice to dead Agamemnon (I, 2). Clitemnestre admits to Céphise that she is troubled by Oreste and his love for Cassandre. She adds that she will marry Egiste if her son does not reject Cassandre (I, 3). A tomb is raised to Agamemnon (I, 4), and Oreste is revering the memory of his father when "subterranean fires" blaze forth to consume his offerings and the tomb (I, 5).

Clitemnestre is now bound to all three male personages: Egiste, her suitor; Agamemnon, her husband; and Oreste, her son. The second act brings Cassandre to the fore, however, when she laments her unhappy love in the temple of Junon, where Ilione informs her that Clitemnestre wishes to sacrifice her to the shade of Agamemnon. Cassandre sees her death as a liberation from her shameful love for Oreste (II, 1-2), but the latter assures her of protection and offers her his throne despite her Trojan blood. She hesitates to accept his alliance (II, 3). Clitemnestre upbraids Oreste for his interest in Cassandre, but he defies his mother (II, 4). Enraged, Clitemnestre offers her hand and throne to Egiste if he will destroy Cassandre and Oreste. He agrees (II, 5-6). The people are celebrating the announcement of the Egiste-Clitemnestre marriage (II, 7) when Agamemnon's return becomes known. The couple is obliged to flee (II, 8).

Agamemnon's presence increases the pace of the action in the remainder of the tragedy. Clitemnestre decides to return to him (III, 1), but Oreste informs her that the king has discovered her perfidy and has slain Egiste. She runs from his vengeance (III, 2). Agamemnon declares that he will marry Cassandre and leave Clitemnestre to her ignominy (III, 3). Oreste and Cassandre decry the latter's marriage to Agamemnon (IV, 1), who suspects that he has a rival, although Cassandre assures him that she loves only the gods she serves (IV, 2). The king exiles his queen (IV, 3), and she calls upon Junon for vengeance (IV, 4). Egiste arises from the dead with a band of Greeks to oppose Trojan Cassandre as queen of the Greeks (IV, 5). Cassandre bids farewell to the Trojan captives of Agamemnon and reveals her plan to kill herself at her wedding (V, 1). She warns Agamemnon that he will be slain by Clitemnestre and Egiste, but he refuses to believe her. She agrees to marry him, although it means her death and other dire events: Oreste slaying his mother to avenge his father's death and Oreste's departure to find death among the Scythians (V, 2). Agamemnon is filled with anxiety (V, 3), and he is moved to return Cassandre to Oreste and to forgive Clitemnestre (V, 4). Oreste's happiness is shattered when Cassandre is stabbed by Clitemnestre, who has also murdered Agamemnon (V, 6). The tragedy ends with Oreste's sad vow for vengeance (V, 7).

BIBLIOGRAPHY: Lajarte I, 108; RGO IX, 115-68.

Cavalli, Pier Francesco (b. 14 February 1602, Crema; d. 17 January 1676, Venice), composer, studied music at Venice, where he also sang at the church of San Marco. Later in life, in 1640, he was appointed organist at this famous church, where he became choir master in 1668.

Cavalli was an incredibly prolific composer, and he wrote at least 40 operas in addition to discharging his ecclesiastical duties. His *Serse* (1654) was scheduled to be part of the festivities organized in 1660 for Louis XIV's marriage, and his *Ercole Amante* was composed for the inauguration of the great hall of the Tuileries, where it was executed on 1 February 1662. More recently, on 6 January 1916, his music was included in *Les Virtuosi de Mazarin,* a reconstruction of an Italian concert given in 1647 before young Louis XIV.

BIBLIOGRAPHY: AEM II, 926-32; BBD 296; EDS III, 268-71; ELM I, 500; NEO 129.

Céphale et Procris is a lyric tragedy in five acts and a prologue with a musical score by Mme Elizabeth Jacquet de La Guerre* and a libretto by Jean-François Duché de Vancy.* It was performed initially on 15 March 1694 at the Palais-Royal,* and its first run terminated before 1 October 1694. It was never revived, and the labored quality of the libretto and its diffuse intrigue doubtlessly contributed to its lack of popularity.

The prologue of *Céphale et Procris* presents Flore, Pan, Nerée, and their assembled retinues singing the praises of "the most powerful of kings." This introductory portion of the text is in the tradition of all the prologues presented during the war of the League of Augsburg: it develops the double theme of patriotism and love in its laudium of Louis XIV while alluding to the subject of the forthcoming composition.

The opera itself opens in a public square in Athens where Borée is complaining of Procris's indifference toward him and is accusing her of preferring Céphale to him. After the establishment of this simple triangle,

Procris admits her love for Céphale while explaining that she will abide by her father's choice of a husband for her. The situation here, then, recalls the opening of Pierre Corneille's *Le Cid*, where Chimène hopes that her father will select Don Rodrigue as her husband. The parallelism is maintained when Procris voices her misgivings about future events while insisting upon obeying her parent, but Duché's work also veers toward the Lullian pattern of lyric tragedy by adding the subplot of Arcas's love for Dorine. The serious weakness in the intrigue is its almost superfluous complexity, and spectators must have wondered why a third rival was added to the primary love affair and why the secondary situation had to be introduced at all. Procris's death by a stray arrow from Céphale's bow during his quarrel with Borée at the end of the opera does little to help the cause of work.
BIBLIOGRAPHY: Lajarte I, 63; RGO IV, 421-86.

Cesti, Marc' Antonio (b. 5 August 1623, Arezzo; d. 14 October 1669, Florence) was choir master for Ferdinand II de' Medici, and, at the end of his life, he held the same position with Leopold I of Vienna. He composed eight operas, of which the first and best known was *L'Orontea* (1649). An air by Corinda in this work was included in Léo Staats's *Mademoiselle de Nantes* (For *Mademoiselle de Nantes*, see twentieth-century volume), a reconstruction of a party given at Versailles during the time of Louis XIV. This predominantly choreographic work, also containing selections from the work of Lully* and Charpentier,* was staged at the Opéra on 9 December 1915.
BIBLIOGRAPHY: AEM II, 992-96; BBD 300; EDS III, 462-68; ELM I, 506; NEO 131.

Chappuzeau de Baugé, Daniel Paul (b. ?, Lyon; d. 1738, Paris?), librettist, was preparing for an ecclesiastical career after the completion of his formal studies, but he changed his mind suddenly to devote his energy to the composition of two fables that appeared in the *Mercure galant* for December 1680 and May 1681. Encouraged by this maiden effort, he created a heroic pastoral entitled *Coronis** for performance at the Royal Academy of Music in 1691.

This undertaking brought little fame and no fortune to the hopeful poet, and he obtained a position helping to gather taxes for the government of Louis XIV. He managed to amass an impressive fortune in his new position, and he never returned to writing as a career.
BIBLIOGRAPHY: CDDS I, 547; Lajarte I, 59; Parfaict brothers, *Dictionnaire des théâtres de Paris*, 7 vols. (Paris: Rozet, 1767) I, 391; L. Travenol and Jacques Durey de Noinville, *Histoire du théâtre de l'Opéra en France*, 2 vols. (Paris: Joseph Barbou, 1753) I, 195.

Charpentier, Marc-Antoine (b. 1634, Paris; d. 24 February 1704, Paris), composer, left his native city at the age of 15 to study music in Rome under Carissimi. He spent three years in Italy and returned to France to become acquainted with Luigi Rossi and other Italian musicians staying in Paris during the first decade of Louis XIV's reign. This group of foreign artistes was interested in religious composition, and their preferences led Charpentier to devote his attention to church music rather than to theatrical representations. But in 1672 the rupture between Lully* and Molière* resulted in Charpentier doing the music for *Le Malade Imaginaire* and the 1672 stagings of *La Comtesse d'Escarbagnas* and *Le Mariage forcé*. He continued to provide scores for the Théâtre Français until 1685, and his work was incorporated in *Circé* (1675) and *L'Inconnu* (1675) by Thomas Corneille* and Donneau de Visé, *Les Fous divertissants* (1680) by Raymond Poisson, *La Pierre philosophale* (1681), and the new version of Molière's *Psyché* performed in 1684.

Charpentier directed the chorus and strings maintained by the princess de Guise after 1680. When his protectress died, he moved on to provide religious music for the dauphin until 1686. Meanwhile in 1683 he was named to the post of subdirector of music for the royal chapel while assuming the duties of music master at the Jesuit college of Louis-le-Grand in the rue Saint-Antoine. His compositions at this time were almost exclusively religious in nature and included motets, hymns, and oratorios. He had some contact with the Royal Academy of Music at this point in his life because the artistes of this company sang at religious services despite their belonging to a condemned profession that even Lully had to renounce to receive absolution at the moment of his death. Yet, paradoxically enough, Charpentier was drawn toward theatrical music by the fact that the Jesuits asked him to compose music for two Christian tragedies they produced at their school, *Celsus* (1687) and *Saül* (1688). This latter work was staged with *David et Jonathas,* a work in French presented as an opera on the program and scored by Charpentier.

The death of Lully in 1687 and the end of his monopolistic control over musical compositions produced at the Palais-Royal* found Charpentier most qualified to replace the author of *Armide*, therefore, but it was not until 4 December 1693 that his *Médée* had its premiere at this theatre reserved for opera. Thomas Corneille* did the libretto. The king, his brother, and his eldest son heard and approved this work, which was never revived, although it was well received by the public at this time and was reviewed favorably by the *Mercure* for December 1693. This publication praised the performance of Mlle Le Rochois* in the title-rôle and called attention to two Italian airs it presented. The other major parts were sung by Mlle Moreau (Créuse), Dun (Créon), Du Mesny* (Jason). Campra included portions of its score in *Télémaque** in 1704. Titon du Tillet designated it as "a great success"; the story was employed in four other works later, although Charpentier's composition was never returned to the stage.

Médée was Charpentier's only contribution to the Royal Academy of Music because he was named music master of Sainte-Chapelle in 1698, a position he obtained through the intercession of the duke de Chartres. The composer passed the last six years of his life in the quietude of this chapel only a mile removed from the Palais-Royal. He died on 24 February 1704 at the age of seventy. The archives of Sainte-Chapelle reveal that he passed away at 7:00 A.M. and was laid to rest the following day after vespers.

The author of *Médée* left more than four hundred compositions that include sacred works for the most part, but his knowledge of music and his preference for the Italian manner resulted in Lully considering him a threat and trying to keep him in the shadows. Lully's fears were well founded, if only because Charpentier understood so clearly the relationship between music and the moods that opera created so constantly in the time of Lully's domination of the Palais-Royal. In the rules for musical composition that he wrote for his pupil, the duke d'Orléans, Charpentier presented a catalogue of the different emotional tones created by the various musical keys, and this brief list alone bespeaks his readiness to score almost any scene that Lully's librettists had conceived from the martial and festive prologue (D-major) to the amorous complaints of rejected heroines (E-minor).

Charpentier's music has been heard at the Opéra during the twentieth century because various composers have attempted to recreate certain musical events taking place before 1700: *Carême prenant* represents a concert in the time of Louis XIV, for example, and *Mademoiselle de Nantes* depicts a party given at Versailles during the early history of this château. Also, a revival of *Le Malade imaginaire* music by Charpentier was part of the celebration of the tricentennial of Molière's birth in 1922.

BIBLIOGRAPHY: AEM II, 1107-14; BBD 306; Bio univ VII, 677; Germaine Louise Micheline Crussard, *Un musicien français oublié: Marc-Antoine Charpentier, 1634-1704* (Paris: Floury, 1945); DBF VIII, 641-42; EDS III, 548-50; ELM I, 524; Lajarte I, 71; Robert W. Lowe, *Marc-Antoine Charpentier et l'opéra de collège* (Paris: G. P. Maisonneuve et Larose, 1966); NEO 133; TdT 490-91.

Circé had its premiere performance at the Palais-Royal* in October or November 1694. It was the fourth consecutive lyric tragedy in five acts and a prologue that failed to inspire spectators. It was never returned to the stage. This apparently diminishing success of the lyric tragedy was probably the earliest indication of the fact that composers and management alike were deluded if they thought that the Royal Academy of Music could endure forever by imitating Lully* and adding a bit of Italianate virtuosity to the score from time to time to obtain variety. The music of *Circé* was by Henri Desmarets,* and its librettist was Mme Gillot de Sainctonge.*

The brief prologue to *Circé* is set upon the banks of the Seine in a peaceful field to which Les Jeux and Les Plaisirs have fled to escape "a bloody war" and "cruel battles." As in the prologue of *Céphale et Procris,** "the triumphant Hero" has allowed love and peace to prosper in these places protected by "the great king" and "his august son." The nymph of the Seine exhorts her newly arrived guests to remain with her "under the august laws of the conqueror of the earth" until the return of peace. No mention is made in the prologue of the forthcoming production although some sort of allusion to it is usually made in the prologues of works staged at the time of the war of the League of Augsburg; for example, *Didon*.*

The intrigue of *Circé* features this sorceress's suspicions that Eolie may be her rival for Ulisse's affections and her transforming the latter's soldiers into "several sorts of monsters" to detain their leader on her island. Ulisse denies to Circé that he loves another woman, but she sees through his deception and seeks vengeance. He manages to escape from her clutches with Eolie despite Circé's attempts to stop them, and frustrated Circé transforms her island into a flaming and "frightful chaos." A subplot featuring the Astérie-Polite love affair parallels the Eolie-Ulisse involvement. The third member of the subordinate triangle is Elphénor, who allies himself with Circé so that Astérie will be obliged to accept his suit.

BIBLIOGRAPHY: DDO I, 244; Lajarte I, 63; RGO V, 1-66.

Cochereau, Jacques (b. ?; d. 17 July 1734, Paris), vocalist, left the army in Lille to sing in the chorus of the opera in this city. He married here, but he set out for Paris with his wife shortly after their wedding. He and Mme Cochereau were received into the Royal Academy of Music shortly after their arrival in the French capital, and he became the voice teacher of the daughters of Philippe d'Orléans.

Cochereau was quite successful at the Opéra, and he became one of the leading tenors at the theatre from 1702 until 1718. He appears to have made his debut at the Palais-Royal* singing minor rôles in *Les Fragments de Lully** and to have gone on to execute small parts in Campra's *Trancrède** and *Les Muses** in 1702-3. In the latter year, he was also cast as Phronyme in Lully's *Persée,** as L'Amour in a revival of the Florentine's *Psyché,** and finally as Orphée in Rebel's *Ulysse.** He was billed as Plutus in *Le Carnaval de la Folie** in 1704, the same year that he was assigned to a major rôle, Enée in Desmaret's *Didon.** He now did Hercule in *Alcide** in its 1705 revival as well as the title-rôle of *Bellérophon,** when the latter work was returned to the stage on 10 December 1705.

The tenor appeared in an almost countless number of revivals at the Opéra between 1705 and 1718. He performed in such parts as Athamas in *Philomèle** (1705), Apollon in *Alcyone** (1706), and Iphis in *Manto la fée** (1711), but he was cast more constantly in rôles in the popular opera-ballets and cognate types of compositions that were so popular during 1705-18. He was a mask in *La Vénitienne,** given its premiere on 26 May 1705, and he did both Damiro and Eraste in the first and third entrées of *Les Festes vénitiennes,** produced initially on 17 June 1710. After a minor assignment in the premiere of *Les Amours déguisés** on 22 August 1713, he did Léandre at the first representation of *Les Fêtes de Thalie** on 19 August 1714, and he created the Léandre in the first entrée of *Les Ages (for Les Ages,* see eighteenth-century volume) on 9 October 1718.

Cochereau was also a member of the Music of the King's Chamber. He remarried in 1714, and he left a son and daughter as well as a widow at his death.

BIBLIOGRAPHY: André Campra, *Les Festes vénitiennes,* ed. Alexandre Guilmant (Paris: Théodore Michaëlis, n. d.), 9; DBF IX, 67-68; EC I, 131-35; Fétis II, 328; Lajarte I, 105, 111-12, 114, 118-19, 121-22, 129.

Colasse, Pascal (b. 22 January 1649, Reims; d. 17 July 1709, Versailles), composer, was a choir boy at Saint Paul's church in Paris before coming to the attention of Jean-Baptiste Lully,* who made him his secretary and charged him with the completion of his operatic scores. He also led the orchestra of the Royal Academy of Music whenever Lully was indisposed or occupied with other matters. He became assistant music master of the royal chapel in 1687, the year that he attracted the attention of the public with his music for the last four acts of *Achille et Polyxène.** His great success was *Thétis et Pélée,** one of the outstanding works of the Lully school. After the staging of this "tragedy in music" in 1689, Colasse continued in the vein of lyric tragedy and did the scores for *Enée et Lavinie** in 1690, *Astrée** in 1692, *Jason** in 1696, *Canente** in 1700, and *Polyxène et Pyrrhus** in 1706. He obtained the position of Music Master of the Chamber in 1696 after scoring *Le Ballet de Villeneuve-Saint-Georges** in 1692, the opera-ballet *Les Saisons** in 1695, and the opera *La Naissance de Vénus** in 1696.

Colasse's position at Court was secure, and his income was far above average, but he seems to have been dissatisfied with his lot toward the end of his life. He renounced his musical career to pursue the study of alchemy, and he was extremely disturbed by the disastrous fire at the Lille theatre that he undertook to construct. Louis XIV made good his losses to some extent, but he was nevertheless crushed by poverty and in a mental condition bordering on madness at the time of his death. If there is any single reason for the oblivion into which his works have fallen, it is because they borrow so heavily from Lully. His music was used in *Carême prenant* (for *Carême prenant,* see twentieth-century volume) of 1916 for purely historical reasons.

BIBLIOGRAPHY: Bio univ VIII, 550; DBF IX, 181; Fétis II, 332-33; Robert M. Isherwood, *Music in the Service of the King: France in the Seventeenth Century* (Ithaca: Cornell University Press, 1973), 332-39; Lajarte I, 71-72; TdT 518.

Corneille, Thomas (b. 20 August 1625, Rouen; d. 8 December 1709, Andelys), librettist, was the younger brother of the famous dramatist Pierre Corneille. He studied at the Jesuit college of Rouen and embarked upon a law career before writing a series of comedies between 1647 and 1655. He turned to tragedy at about the age of 30, and his greatest success in this genre was *Timocrate.* He did nearly a dozen other tragedies prior to his later custom of alternating between comedy and tragedy. The volume of his works for the stage, nearly 30 in number, attests to his ability to manage a wide variety of amusing or serious subjects, although his technique was not always above reproach. He was elected to fill his brother's chair at the French Academy in 1685; he spent the last years of his life compiling a *Dictionnaire des arts et des sciences* (1694) and editing Vaugelas's *Remarques sur la langue française* (1687). He has a rôle in the history of French opera because he collaborated with Lully* on the composition of *Psyché* and *Bellérophon* during the interval of Quinault's* disgrace.

BIBLIOGRAPHY: Bio univ IX 232-35; Jules Carlez, *Pierre et Thomas Corneille, librettistes* (Caen: Blanc-Hardel, 1881); CG 128-35; DBF IX, 681-82; Lajarte I, 72; H. C. Lancaster, *A History of French Dramatic Literature in the Seventeenth Century*, 9 vols. (Baltimore: The Johns Hopkins Press, 1936) III, 874; Gustave Reynier, *Thomas Corneille, sa vie et son théâtre* (Paris: Hachette, 1892); TdT 380-84.

Coronis was designated as a heroic pastoral because it related the adventures of Apollon disguised as a shepherd and because its settings and certain episodes in it were in the pastoral tradition. Its libretto was the work of Chappuzeau de Baugé,* and its score was written by Theobaldo di Gatti.* It had its premiere at Paris on 23 March 1691, but its first run was unimpressive, and it was never returned to repertory. Baugé's work is remembered principally as having been the first of the four heroic pastorals mounted at the Palais-Royal* between 1691 and 1731: *Coronis* (1691), *Issé* (1697), *La Pastorale héroïque* (1730), *Endymion* (1731) (for Baugé's later works, see eighteenth-century volume).

The brief prologue of *Coronis* in two scenes features the Muses gathering to celebrate the delights of peace that have disappeared in the face of a cruel war continuing to ravish the face of the earth. The celebrants decide to honor Admète in the course of their festivities because his exploits and virtues are beyond parallel. Allusions to Admète's ridding the high seas of pirates and references not only to the Oriental ambassadors at his Court but also to his generous policy of protecting other monarchs point directly to the identification of Admète as Louis XIV.

The first act of the pastoral presents Apollon disguised as Tircis, Admète's shepherd, and it introduces the love intrigue by showing Apollon's suit of Coronis being rejected by her in favor of Daphnis (I, 1-2). Reverting to a pastoral device, Coronis awards her staff and flowers to Tircis for his superior argument in support of the constant lover (I, 3-5). The love element is then complicated further by the introduction of Apidamie as a second suitor of Daphnis (I, 5). The love intrigue is not simple in *Coronis*, therefore, because its heroine is pursued by two lovers, and one of these lovers in his turn has attracted the affections of two women, one of whom is the heroine.

The second act stresses Daphnis's preference for Coronis and his rejection of Apidamie (II, 1-3). The latter vows to punish Coronis for turning Daphnis into an apparent misogynist (II, 4) and tells her that it is she, Apidamie, whom Daphnis loves (II, 5). Coronis falls victim to this heartless stratagem (II, 6), but she still refuses to accept Apollon's suit after the god reveals his true identity and real power to her (II, 7-8). When Apollon finds out that he has been rejected even after having won the approval of his suit from Coronis's mother (III, 1-2), he destroys Coronis and Daphnis in a heartless rage (III, 7).

The lack of success that greeted *Coronis* is not difficult to understand, therefore, because its libretto is needlessly complicated and yet almost devoid of the spectacular element demanded by the public except for the palace built by Apollon to demonstrate his power. As a document, however, it has an evident interest by virtue of furnishing a clear indication of a continuing popularity of the pastoral manner in some quarters despite the preponderance of the lyric tragedy in repertory.

BIBLIOGRAPHY: Lajarte I, 59; RGO IV, 113-54.

Couperin, François (b. 10 November 1668, Paris; d. 12 September 1733, Paris), DIT Couperin le Grand, became organist at the church of Saint Gervais in Paris at age eleven after the death of his father. He learned quickly and became famous early because his compositions were soon known wherever organ music was heard. He has left an enormous corpus of music including 233 pieces for the harpichord, but his work has been heard on only one occasion at the Opéra, when George Skibine's *Pastorale* was danced at the Garnier palace on 20 December 1961 by Marjorie Tallchief and Jean-Paul Andréani. Couperin's work serves as the score for this ballet (for Andréani, M. Tallchief, and *La Pastorale*, see twentieth-century volume).

BIBLIOGRAPHY: AEM II, 1711-29; BBD 355-57; CBCM 71-78; ELM I, 600-606; Wilfrid Mellers, *Couperin* (New York: Roy, 1951); Thompson 384-85; Julien Tiersot, *Les Couperin* (Paris: Alcan, 1926), 38-112.

Créuse, also called *Créuse l'Athénienne*, is a lyric tragedy in five acts and a prologue for which La Coste* wrote the music. Pierre-Charles Roy* created its libretto. It enjoyed little success and was dropped after its first run from 5 April to 12 May 1712. It was billed on 22 dates.

In an ingenious prologue, La Fable and L'Histoire argue over the question of who between them has produced the most admirable heroes. They cannot agree, and they are obliged to call upon Apollon for a proper verdict. The god evades the issue by ordering them to combine their resources to retell the story of Créuse. The prologue anticipates the subject of the opera, but it follows the recent trend visible in *Diomède** and *Idoménée** whereby no mention is made of aged Louis XIV or of the current international situation.

The action of the tragedy itself is as complex as *Idoménée*. It begins with Créuse reminding her father that his son has been lost at sea with his mother. The king recalls a dream instructing him to consult the Oracle (I, 1). Créuse is angered by the prospect of a stranger occupying the throne of Athens, and she calls upon Apollon to protect the son that she has had by him (I, 2). Isménide interprets the continuing silence of the Oracle as a sign that Apollon demands a new minister in his temple; she names Idas to this position (I, 3). Idas has misgivings about his ministry because he was an abandoned orphan brought to the temple by a shepherd (I, 4-5).

The intrigue, then, appears to be less concerned with love than with the question of whether Athens will be ruled by Erectée's son, Créuse's son, or a total stranger. At the start of the second act, however, Phorbas complains of Isménide's indifference and threatens his suspected but unidentified rival (II, 1). Yet the intrigue returns immediately to the realm of politics, when Créuse complains to Isménide that her father will select a foreigner as his successor to the throne of Athens (II, 2). Idas and Erectée ask the Oracle to disclose the fate of the latter's son (II, 3); Idas is informed that he is the son of Erectée (II, 4). Angered by the certainty that Athens is to be ruled by a stranger, Créuse implores the Fates to tell her whether or not her son is alive (II, 5). She learns that Idas is not her brother and that her son lives. She vows vengeance (II, 6) and claims the throne from Idas while accusing the Oracle of deception. She determines to have Phorbas slay Idas (II, 7).

The intrigue moves more easily after the first two acts because the confrontations between characters have been prepared in such detailed fashion. Isménide deliberates declaring her love to Idas (III, 1), who divulges his love to Isménide (III, 2). A chorus and a ballet celebrating Apollon fail to persuade the god to reassure Idas or to satisfy Créuse (III, 4). Phorbas accuses Idas of dictating the Oracle's words to assure himself of power and position; Isménide refutes him by declaring that his own sister spread this story abroad on account of her hatred for him. Phorbas asserts that her love for Idas has blinded her (III, 5), and he swears vengeance (III, 6). Créuse joins with him, and the two conspirators call upon the demons of Hades to punish Idas (IV, 1-2). The infernal spirits appear armed with a vase of the Gorgon's blood to poison Idas at his wedding (IV, 3-4). Créuse beseeches her son to return to her (IV, 5).

The concluding act begins in an atmosphere of uncertainty because Créuse has doubts about herself when Isménide and Idas appear before the altar (V, 1-2). But she prevents the groom from drinking the fatal potion (V, 3). Finally, Apollon appears to explain the situation: Créuse's son has perished at sea, but Idas is the grandson of Apollon and Créuse. Idas is to occupy the throne of Athens, and Isménide will be his queen. Phorbas cannot disturb their rule, since Apollon has arranged his death (V, 4).

Roy explains in his preface to *Créuse* that he based his tragedy upon Euripides' *Io*, but he adds that he substituted the rôle of Créuse's father for that of her husband because he did not wish his heroine to be embarrassed by Apollon's revelation in V, 4 that he has had children by her. The basic situation found in Euripides is retained intact, however, because the Greek version presents the king as father of two children: Creusa born of a first marriage; a son born of a second marriage and lost at sea.

BIBLIOGRAPHY: Lajarte I, 115; RGO X, 389-446.

D

Danchet, Antoine (b. 7 October 1671, Riom; d. 28 February 1748, Paris), dramatist, was born in a tailor shop. While still a youth, he interrupted his studies at the Oratorian school in his native city to go to Paris. He completed his formal education in the capital and had a Latin ode printed there in 1691. He dedicated this learned piece of poetry to Père La Chaize, and the confessor to the king was pleased enough to reward Danchet by making him a professor of rhetoric at Chartres in 1692. He remained in the shadow of the famous cathedral until 1696, when he returned to Paris to serve as a tutor in the household of Colbert-Turgis. Then, in 1698, he wrote the poetry for two *divertissements** given before the king. Mme de Turgis refused to entrust her children to a man of the theatre, and she dismissed Danchet.

Left to his own resources, Danchet had no choice but to give himself over entirely to his art, and he became the exclusive librettist for Campra.* He provided this famous composer with the words for five lyric tragedies, two ballets, and a separate entrée for a third ballet between 1700 and 1705: *Hésione** in 1700, *Aréthuse** in 1701, *La Sérénade vénitienne** and *Tancrède** in 1702, *Les Muses** in 1703, *Iphigénie en Tauride** and *Télémaque** in 1704, and *Alcine** in 1705. He was invited to join the Academy of Inscriptions during this period on account of his skill with Latin verse, and he was elected to the French Academy in 1709. He resumed his partnership with Campra for *Les Festes vénitiennes** in 1710, *Idoménée** in 1712, *Télèphe** in 1713, and *Camille, reine des Volsques* in 1717. He became managing editor of the *Mercure de France* in 1727, and this position kept him busy until his death, although he did find time to write the words for *Achille et Déidamie* (for Danchet's post-1715 works, see eighteenth-century volume) in 1735.

BIBLIOGRAPHY: Bio univ X, 87; CG 193-219; DBF X, 78-79; Lajarte I, 160; H. C. Lancaster, *Sunset: A History of Parisian Drama in the Last Years of Louis XIV, 1701-1715* (Baltimore: The Johns Hopkins Press, 1945), 130-34.

Desmarets, Henri (b. 1662, Paris; d. 7 September 1741, Lunéville), composer, started his career as one of the music pages of Louis XIV, who awarded him a pension in 1683 because he was still too young to become royal choir master. He turned from religious to profane music in 1693, when his *Didon** was produced at the Palais-Royal.* He became one of the outstanding members of the Lullist school with *Circé** in 1694, *Théagène et Chariclée** in 1695, *Les Amours de Momus** in 1695, *Vénus et Adonis** in 1697, and *Les Festes galantes** in 1698.

In 1700, Desmarets visited his friend Gervais, master at the cathedral of Senlis, where he entered into a secret marriage with the daughter of an important municipal official. The girl's father charged the musician with kidnaping and seduction, and he was condemned to death. He ran off to Spain before the sentence could be executed, and he became choir master for Felipe V.

He could not support the Iberian climate, however, and he returned to Lunéville. His *Iphigénie en Tauride** was produced at the Palais-Royal in 1704, and he was named superintendent of music for the duke of Lorraine in this later period of his life, but his legal case was not reviewed until the time of the regency in 1722. He won the action ultimately, and his marriage was declared valid and existent. The duke d'Orléans increased his pension, and he lived comfortably until his death in 1741. His last work for the Royal Academy of Music was *Renaud* in 1722 (for *Renaud,* see eighteenth-century volume).

BIBLIOGRAPHY: Michel Antoine, *Henry Desmarest [sic], 1661-1741: biographie critique* (Paris: A. and J. Picard, 1965); Bio univ X, 521-22; DBF X, 1443-44; Fétis III, 4-5; Lajarte I, 72.

Desmatins, Mlle (b. 1670, Paris; d. 1708, Paris), singer, was the daughter of one of the king's violinists and a niece of the ballet master of the Opéra. She made her first appearance on the stage of the Opéra at age 12 on 18 April 1682 as a dancer and singer in *Persée,** but it was decided subsequently that she should devote her time and energy to developing her voice.

Mlle Desmatins started her career by doing parts of lesser importance like Sidonie or Phénice in *Armide,** Palès in *Cadmus et Hermione,** or Corcine in *Ariadne et Bacchus** because the presence of Mlle Le Rochois* on the stage of the Palais-Royal* kept her from assignments to major rôles until the time of the star's retirement. After the withdrawal of Mlle Le Rochois from the stage, however, Mlle Desmatins's popularity and capability were recognized, and she was given the responsibility of creating such parts as Vénus in *Hésione** on 21 December 1700, Sapho and Niobe in *Le Triomphe des Arts** on 16 May 1700, the heroine of Campra's *Iphigénie en Tauride** on 6 May 1704, and the female leads of *Alcine** and *Alcyone** on 15 January 1705 and 18 February 1706 respectively.

Mlle Desmatins was a striking beauty endowed with a noble bearing and understanding of drama, and she would have gone on to an even more impressive career if her health had not begun to falter as early as 1702, when her billings as Médée in *Médus, roi des Mèdes** had to be canceled. She died eventually in 1708 of an ulcerated liver.

BIBLIOGRAPHY: André Campra, *Les Festes vénitiennes,* ed. Alexandre Guilmant (Paris: Théodore Michaëlis, n.d.) 8; DBF X, 1454-55; EFC 133; Fétis Suppl. I, 261-62; GE XIV, 257-58; Lajarte I, 24-26, 35, 47-48, 53, 55-56, 58-60, 64-67; TdT 795.

Destouches, André-Cardinal (b. 1672, Paris; d. 1749, Paris), composer, was an adventurer rather than a musician in his youth when he went to Siam with Father Tachard, S.J. Only 16 years old at the time of this excursion, Destouches forgot his promise to Father Tachard that he would become a Jesuit and joined the second company of royal musketeers on his return from Asia in 1692. He was present at the siege of Namur. Later he took music lessons from Campra,* with whose aid he wrote *Issé** for representation at the Trianon and Paris in 1697. Encouraged by the success of this heroic pastoral, he went on to compose additional scores for the Royal Academy of Music: *Amadis de Grèce** and *Marthésie, reine des Amazones** in 1699, *Omphale** in 1701, *Le Carnaval et la Folie** in 1704, and *Callirhoé** in 1712. Destouches became superintendent of the king's music and general inspector of the Opéra in 1712-13, and he held these positions until 1721. Ten years after the staging of *Télémaque** in 1714 and *Sémiramis* (for *Sémiramis* and Destouches's subsequent works, see eighteenth-century volume) in 1718, he was made director of the Royal Academy of Music (1728-30). His last two titles for the Opéra were *Les Eléments* mounted initially at the Tuileries in 1721 and *Les Stratagèmes de l'Amour* billed for the first time at the Palais-Royal* on 28 March 1726. The greatest compliment ever paid Destouches was doubtlessly Louis XIV's remark that Destouches was the only musician who did not make him miss Lully.*

BIBLIOGRAPHY: Bio univ X, 565; DBF XI, 102; Kurt Dulle, *André Cardinal Destouches, 1672-1749* (University of Leipzig: Diss., 1909); Fétis III, 8; Robert M. Isherwood, *Music in the Service of the King: France in the Seventeenth Century* (Ithaca: Cornell University Press, 1973), 340-44, 348-49.

Didon was produced for the first time on 11 September 1693 at the Palais-Royal.* A lyric tragedy in five acts and a prologue, its musical score was by Henri Desmarets,* and its libretto was the first poem written for the Royal Academy of Music by a woman, Mme Gillot de Sainctonge.* *Didon* was only partially successful and was never revived, although it was staged with all available talent during its first and only run in the autumn of 1693. Marthe Le Rochois* sang the title-rôle, and Mlle Moreau filled the part of Anne. The male voices included Du Mesny,* Dun, and Moreau. Mlle La Fontaine* danced in the ballet opposite Magny and Lestang.*

The prologue resembles all other prologues given at the Palais-Royal during the war of the League of Augsburg: mythological figures support the action, Louis XIV is compared to Mars in an excessive laudium, and there is a fleeting allusion to the subject of the forthcoming tragedy.

The basic situation developed in *Didon* is the triangle formed by the heroine's rejection of Iarbe and her willingness to accept Enée as her king after the death of Sichée. The opening scenes are devoted almost exclusively to exchanges of promises of fidelity between Enée and Didon, and the second act makes manifest Iarbe's displeasure over his rejection by Didon.

After the decision of the gods to forbid the Didon-Enée marriage, the Carthaginian queen is crushed with misgivings and sadness. The ultimate outcome of the Didon-Enée situation is the subplot of the fourth act, then, and the librettist employs peripeteia here twice as if to underscore the instability of human affairs. Didon learns eventually that Enée has set sail for Sicily, of course, and she remains obedient to Sichée's command by killing herself with the dagger that her lover has given to her.

The treatment of the Dido story here is faithful to the account found in Vergil. It is based upon the identical premise that Aeneas cannot wed Dido because his destiny has pledged him to marriage with Lavinia.

BIBLIOGRAPHY: Lajarte I, 61-62; RGO IV, 281-344.

Diomède was a lyric tragedy in five acts and a prologue with a libretto by Jean-Louis-Ignace de La Serre* and music by Bertin de La Doue.* It had its premiere at the Palais-Royal* on 28 April 1710, and it went on to enjoy 25 representations by 15 June 1710, when it was withdrawn to permit the premiere of *Les Fêtes vénitiennes.** It was never revived.

The prologue of *Diomède* develops two themes: love is the only true source of happiness; all nature responds to its power. The slight intrigue involves Diomède about to travel to Cythère and Vénus's hostile reaction to this voyage.

Diomède is seen initially at the moment when he is beseeching Vénus to forgive him for opposing her at Troy. He announces his determination to appease her or to find solace in suicide, and he refuses to take his sister, Iphise, with him on his trip to Cythère (I, 1-2). When Iphise invites him to share in the games celebrating the founding of his new empire, he refuses lest Vénus seek vengeance by making him fall in love (I, 3). Iphise asserts that her fears for her brother sadden her despite her love for Daunus (I, 4). A chorus hails La Victoire and praises L'Amour (I, 5).

This simple situation involving a brother, a sister, and her suitor continues with Neptune and his retinue emerging from the sea to bid the winds be gentle for Vénus's voyage to Italy (II, 1). The mood changes abruptly with the arrival of the goddess because she bids the god of the sea to sink Diomède's fleet. Neptune reminds her that she has already punished Diomède by making him fall in love with his sister, but Vénus points out that Diomède is not really the brother of Iphise (II, 2). A chorus and a ballet of sailors from Diomède's fleet celebrate L'Amour again (II, 3) before embarking for Cythère (II, 4). Vénus and Neptune let loose fierce winds, and Diomède's fleet founders (II, 5-6).

After Diomède is crushed by Vénus, the protagonist finds himself in disarray on account of his love for Iphise, whom he views as his sister (III, 1). He urges her to welcome Daunus (III, 2), and she questions her feelings for her alleged brother (III, 3). Daunus proclaims his love to Iphise (III, 4-5), and a troupe of shepherds and pastors celebrates her suitor's valor and his love for Iphise (III, 6), who asserts that she must turn her attention to her brother (III, 7). But Daunus eavesdrops while Iphise questions herself about her love for him (IV, 1-2). He asks whether he has a rival, and her reactions to his questions lead him to accuse her of "a perfidious love" with her brother (IV, 3). Daunus tells Diomède that he has a rival for Iphise's hand (IV, 4), but nothing comes of this revelation, although Vénus reaffirms to Daunus that Diomède is his rival. The goddess adds that their love is not illegitimate, because Diomède was born of Tidée, while Iphise is the daughter of Sténélus. Vénus goes on to encourage Daunus to kidnap Iphise because Danaus will know before long that she is not his sister. The goddess completes her mischief by calling up La Discorde, La Terreur, and La Fureur to spread terror in the land (IV, 5). Minerva reproaches Vénus for her actions (IV, 6).

The solution to the intrigue comes rapidily. Diomède is horrified that he loves Iphise (V, 1), and he is overwhelmed upon beholding her and his guilt (V, 2). Daunus attacks Argypire, Diomède's capital, and Iphise attempts to follow Diomède going to the defense of his kingdom (V, 3-4). Diomède returns victorious to announce Daunus's death and his love for Iphise. Iphise admits her love for him, and Diomède is on the verge of suicide, when Minerva explains that their love is licit (V, 5-7).

BIBLIOGRAPHY: Lajarte I, 111; RGO X, 63-128.

Directors: The directorship of the Opéra was granted through a legal instrument issued by the Crown or by whatever post-1789 governmental agency was endowed with the power to confer this office. In the following list of directors at the Opéra, the dates given before the names mark the start of a director's tenure that comes to its legal end on the day of his successor's entrance into office.

28 June 1669: Pierre Perrin
13 March 1672: Jean-Baptiste Lully
27 June 1687: Jean-Nicolas de Francine
30 December 1698: Jean-Nicolas de Francine, Hyacinthe-Goureault du Monty
7 October 1704: Pierre Guyenet
12 December 1712: Jean-Nicolas de Francine, Hyacinthe-Goureault du Monty
8 January 1713: Mathurin Besnier, Etienne-Lambert Chomat, Louis-Etienne-François Duchesne, Pierre de Laval de Saint-Pont
2 December 1715: Duke d'Antin, Jean-Nicolas de Francine
8 February 1728: André-Cardinal Destouches
1 June 1730: Le prince de Carignan, Gruer
18 August 1731: Lecomte, Leboeuf
30 May 1733: Louis-Armand-Eugène de Thuret

18 March 1744: François Berger

1 January 1747: Guenot de Tréfontaine, Douet de Saint-Germain

1 January 1749: François Rebel, Louis-Joseph Francoeur

9 April 1755: Bontemps, Levasseur

13 March 1757: François Rebel, Louis-Joseph Francoeur

6 February 1767: Pierre-Montan Berton, Jean-Claude Trial (d. 23 June 1771)

29 July 1771: Pierre-Montan Berton, Antoine Dauvergne, Joliveau

18 April 1776: Denis-Pierre-Jean Papillon de la Ferté, Maréchal, des Entelles, Hébert, de la Touche, Bourboulon, Bussault (all directors of the Menus-Plaisirs)

18 October 1777: Anne-Pierre-Jacques Devismes de Valgay

19 February 1779: The City of Paris and Devismes de Valgay

19 March 1780: Pierre-Montan Berton (d. 14 May 1780)

22 July 1780: Antoine Dauvergne, François-Joseph Gossec

1 April 1785: Antoine Dauvergne, Louis-Joseph Francoeur, Pierre-Gabriel Gardel, Maximilien Gardel, Louis-Charles-Joseph Rey, Bocquet de Liancourt, Menageot, Lainez, Jansen, de La Salle

18 April 1790: Louis-Joseph Francoeur

29 February 1792: Jacques Cellerier, Louis-Joseph Francoeur

23 April 1798: Louis-Joseph Francoeur, Denesle, Bacot

12 September 1799: Anne-Pierre-Jacques Devismes de Valgay, Antoine-Joseph Bonnet de Treyches

23 December 1800: Antoine-Joseph Bonnet de Treyches

15 December 1801: Jacques Cellerier

20 December 1801: Étienne Morel de Chédeville

16 August 1802: Fourcroy

10 January 1803: Antoine-Joseph Bonnet de Treyches

1 November 1807: Louis-François Picard

18 January 1816: Denis-Pierre-Jean Papillon de la Ferté

30 October 1819: Giovanni Viotti

1 November 1821: François Habeneck

1 December 1824: Duplantys

12 July 1827: Émile Thimothée Lubbert

2 March 1831: Louis Désiré Véron

15 August 1835: Edmond Duponchel

15 November 1839: Edouard Monnais, Edmond Duponchel

1 June 1841: Edmond Duponchel, Léon Pillet

31 July 1847: Edmond Duponchel, Nestor Roqueplan

21 November 1849: Nestor Roqueplan

14 February 1853: Minister of State

1 July 1854: Nestor Roqueplan

11 November 1854: François-Louis Crosnier

1 July 1856: Alphonse Royer

20 December 1862: Émile Perrin

April-May 1871: Charles Garnier

1 July 1871: Olivier Halanzier-Dufresnoy

16 July 1879: Auguste-Emmanuel Vaucorbeil

1 December 1884: Eugène Ritt, Pedro Gailhard

2 January 1892: Bertrand

1 April 1893: Bertrand, Pedro Gailhard

1 January 1901: Pedro Gailhard

24 May 1907: Pedro Gailhard, P.-B. Gheusi

1 January 1908: André Messager, Broussan

1 January 1915: Jacques Rouché

14 January 1939: Legislation creating the Réunion des Théâtres Lyriques Nationaux was enacted on this date, and the title of general administrator was assigned to the official selected to head this new organization composed of the Opéra and the Opéra-Comique. The title of director was given to the heads of these two theatres who were to report to the general administration. The individuals named below occupied the post of general administrator.

15 January 1939: Jacques Rouché

21 February 1945: René Gadave, *interim*

23 June 1945: Maurice Lehmann

13 May 1946: Georges Hirsch

17 November 1951: Maurice Lehmann

1 October 1955: Jacques Ibert

13 April 1956: Georges Hirsch

8 March 1959: A.-M. Julien

19 April 1962: Georges Auric

1 October 1969: René Nicoly

2 June 1971: Daniel Lesur, *interim*

4 February 1972: Opéra-Comique closed by the government, and the Réunion des Théâtres Lyriques Nationaux passes out of existence for all practical purposes with the installation of the Opéra-Studio in the Salle Favart.

1 January 1973: Rolf Liebermann

1 September 1977: Opéra-Comique reopened by government and placed under control of general administrator and committee

1 September 1980: Bernard Lefort

10 June 1982: Committee led by Paul Puaux

1 July 1983: Massimo Bogianckino

Divertissement was at first an ordinary word used to indicate "an entertainment," but royal custom during the reign of Louis XIV endowed this noun with the special meaning of a lavish spectacle highlighted by theatrical activities ranging from extraordinary tableaux to operatic performances. Louis XIV arranged these entertainments to glorify certain memorable accomplishments in which he had a part, to celebrate the pre-Lenten season and win the admiration of his courtiers, or simply to hail the arrival of the Court at the different royal residences of Versailles, Fontaine-bleau, Chantilly, Marly, and Saint-Germain en Laye. Lully,* Molière,* and their comrades often provided the music and dramatic works that accompanied these sensational spectacles featuring banquets, fireworks, and water shows; the king selected a skilled staff of architects, engineers, and musicians to stage the theatrical portion of these extravaganzas, which praised his might and compassion. These *divertissements* took the form of a sumptuous masked ball on occasion, or they leaned toward the ballet, but they were always intended to honor the members of the royal family, some important national event, or the arrival of distinguished guests, such as ambassadors whom Louis XIV wished to impress. Yet these programs came to be classified only as *petits divertissements* because three of these festive occasions sponsored by the Sun King in 1664, 1668, and 1674 were so elaborate that they were described as *grands divertissements* by contemporary writers reporting upon them. These latter *divertissements* were usually unified by being based upon a single theme, and they were given to honor individuals like Anne of Austria and Marie-Thérèse or events like the peace of Aix-la-Chapelle. The most incredible of these "great entertainments" was the show that Louis XIV had staged for his 30,000 soldiers on the fortifications at Dunkirk with 700 drums, 80 cannon, and an orchestra of fifes, oboes, and trumpets. Lully's *Psyché* was also performed, and the enemy were left wondering how the French forces could wage war and produce opera simultaneously. These spectacles could last for days, moreover, as in the case of the *grand divertissement* of 1674, which was spread over 4, 11, 19, 28 July and 18, 31 August at Versailles, when Louis XIV decided to call attention to the valor and victories of his soldiers. Of course, there was a more modest significance in the word *divertissement* when it was applied simply to an interlude of singing and dancing in an operatic composition. This sort of *divertissement* could be nonessential to the evolution of the drama and purely decorative in nature, or it could be both decorative and a functional part of the intrigue. Lully used the word to describe a whole work in a single act, *L'Eglogue de Versailles,** and his *Cariselli** was billed as a "divertissement comique." Thus, a *divertissement* could designate a program, a single work, or a part of a work, and, in 1872, Lalo used the word as the title for a ballet, a development repeated by Serge Lifar (for Lalo and Lifar, see nineteenth- and twentieth-century volumes) in 1932.

BIBLIOGRAPHY: James R. Anthony, *French Baroque Music from Beaujoyeulx to Rameau* (New York: W. W. Norton, 1974), 417; Donald Jay Grout, *A Short History of the Opera* (New York: Columbia University Press, 1965), 499; Robert M. Isherwood, *Music in the Service of the King: France in the Seventeenth Century* (Ithaca: Cornell University Press, 1973), 248-80.

Duché de Vancy, Joseph-François (b. 29 October 1668, Paris; d. 14 December 1704, Paris), librettist, received an excellent education and obtained a commission as royal valet, a position that allowed him to approach influential personalities at Court. Duché de Vancy began to write for the Opéra in 1694, when he did the libretto for *Céphale et Procris.** He provided the words for Desmarets's* *Théagène et Chariclée** and *Les Amours de Momus** in 1695. His fourth libretto for the Royal Academy of Music was for the same composer's *Les Fêtes galantes** in 1698. He furnished a number of tragedies for the Comédie-Française and for Mme de Maintenon's charges at Saint-Cyr between 1699 and 1702, and the king and Mme de Maintenon were so pleased that they rewarded him with a purse of money.

Duché became associated with the count de Noailles, and the latter took him on a trip to Spain at the time that the duke d'Anjou was about to enter this country to occupy its throne. The poet won favor by distracting the princes making this long journey, and he also managed to attract the attention of Mme de Maintenon's niece. Thus, he continued to write for Saint-Cyr as well as for the Opéra after his return to Court. He composed the following works for the Palais-Royal* between 1701 and 1704: *Scylla** with music by Théobalde (Gatti*) in 1701; and *Iphigénie en Tauride,** another lyric tragedy that Danchet* had to finish for Duché, who had promised to renounce the theatre in the months before his death.

BIBLIOGRAPHY: Bio univ XI, 388; CG 149-53; DBF XI, 1215; Lajarte I, 73; H. C. Lancaster, *Sunset: A History of Parisian Drama in the Last Years of Louis XIV, 1701-1715* (Baltimore: The Johns Hopkins Press, 1945), 82-87; TdT 502-3.

Dumenil, sometimes written Du Mesny or du Mesnil (b. ?; d. 1715, Paris ?), was a cook in the service of the intendant Foucault before he made his debut as a tenor in Lully's* *Isis** in 1677. He was not held in very high esteem by his colleagues because he was given to drinking too heavily and to borrowing from the women of the company to pay his debts. He was billed frequently at the Palais-Royal* despite protests against his conduct, and he was cast as Alphée in the Paris premiere of Lully's *Proserpine** on 15 November 1680. He also sang the title-rôle of *Persée* at its world premiere on 17 April 1682, but his greatest accomplishment was his creation of Renaud in Lully's *Armide** on 15 February 1686. His other creations included these rôles:

Rôle	*Opera*	*Date*
Acis	*Acis et Galathée**	6 September 1686
Achille	*Achille et Polyxène**	7 November 1687
Pélée	*Thétis et Pélée**	11 January 1689
Turnus (?)	*Enée et Lavinie**	November 1690

Myrtil	Le Ballet de Villeneuve Saint-Georges*	1 September 1692
Enée	Didon*	11 September 1693
Jason	Médée*	2 December 1693
Bacchus	Ariadne et Bacchus*	February 1696
Octavio	L'Europe galante*	24 October 1697
Apollon	Issé*	17 December 1697

BIBLIOGRAPHY: Fétis III, 77; Lajarte I, 36, 42-43, 52-59, 62, 66, 83-87; TdT 799.

Dumoulin, David, was the youngest of the four dancing brothers at the Opéra and, like them, he has provided no specific information about the circumstances of his birth. The date and place of his death are likewise unknown.

David Dumoulin made his debut at the Royal Academy of Music in 1705, and it was not long before he became the most popular member of his family. Also, he proved to be a most effective performer, and the more important rôles of the day were assigned to Dupré, Blondy,* and him. He was selected frequently to partner the great danseuses of the time, Prévost,* Camargo, and especially Sallé (for Sallé and Camargo, see eighteenth-century volume). He retired on a pension in 1751.

The premieres in which he danced included:

Ballet	Premiere
Diomède	28 April 1710
Médée et Jason	24 April 1713
Les Festes de l'été	12 June 1716
Les Eléments	29 December 1721
Les Sens	5 June 1732
L'Empire de l'Amour	14 April 1733
Achille et Déidamie	24 February 1735
Les Indes galantes	23 August 1735
Les Romans	23 August 1736
Zaïde, reine de Grenade	3 September 1739

David also participated in a number of revivals between 1705 and 1751, and it was most often in these representations that he starred with the great ballerinas of his time. He danced with Camargo and Blondy in a *pas de trois* first, and he was assigned to partner Camargo subsequently in *Alcyone** on 9 May 1730, *Les Sens* on 5 June 1732, *Les Eléments* on 27 March 1734, and *Achille et Déidamie* on 24 February 1735. He was selected to dance with the famous Mlle Sallé in *Les Romans* in 1736 and in revivals of *Cadmus et Hermione,** *Atys,** and *Tancrède** in 1737.

BIBLIOGRAPHY: ACD 161; CODB 167; EDS V, 1120-21; Lajarte I, 22-23, 29-31, 97-99, 111, 117, 125-26, 137-39, 152-55, 173-77, 180, 189-90; L. Travenol and Jacques Durey de Noinville, *Histoire du théâtre de l'Opéra en France,* 2 vols. (Paris: Joseph Barbou, 1753) II, 57-58; Marian Hannah Winter, *The Pre-Romantic Ballet* (New York: Dance Horizons, 1975), 45, 48, 68, 85, 108, 162.

Dumoulin, François, dancer, has left no indication of his provenance and fate, although it is well known that he was a stepbrother of Henri Dumoulin.* He made his debut at the Opéra in about 1695 but did not retire from the stage until 1748. It is impossible to determine beyond a doubt the works in which François Dumoulin apeared because he and Henri Dumoulin began their careers at the same time, and their colleagues called them by their last names. In all probability, however, François contributed to the creation of the following works:

Ballet	Premiere
Issé	17 December 1697
Hésione	21 December 1700
Les Eléments	29 May 1725
Baiocco et Serpilla	7 June 1729

He also appeared in the revivals of *Psyché** (1703), *Didon** (1704), *Roland** (1705), *Thésée** (1701, 1720), and *Proserpine** (1741).

BIBLIOGRAPHY: EDS V, 1120-21; Lajarte I, 25-28, 33-34, 36-38, 48-49, 61-62, 86-87, 90-91, 137-39, 146; Marian Hannah Winter, *The Pre-Romantic Ballet* (New York: Dance Horizons, 1975), 13, 68.

Dumoulin, Henri, dancer, has left no details pertaining to his birth or death. Called the elder Duport, or Duport l'aîné, he appeared for the first time at the Royal Academy of Music as a dancer in 1695. He remained at the Opéra for 35 years and served simultaneously as ballet master at the Opéra-Comique between 1714 and 1719.

It is difficult to know beyond a doubt in which works Henri Dumoulin danced because he and his three brothers are called Dumoulin indiscriminately and without their baptismal names in the records of the Opéra. Yet it is probable that it was Henri who danced in the following six premieres:

Ballet	Premiere
Les Saisons	18 October 1695
Issé	17 December 1697
Hésione	21 December 1700
Omphale	10 November 1701
Tancrède	7 November 1702
Les Eléments	29 December 1721 (Tuileries)

BIBLIOGRAPHY: EDS V, 1120; Lajarte I, 64-65, 86-87, 90-91, 93-94, 97-98, 137-39; Marian Hannah Winter, *The Pre-Romantic Ballet* (New York: Dance Horizons, 1975), 68.

Dumoulin, Pierre, dancer, was a younger brother of François Dumoulin,* but no specific information about the time and place of his birth is available. It is known that he was still alive in 1756. As for his career as a dancer, it is recorded that he made his debut at the Opéra in *La Mort d'Hercule** on 23 June 1705. He withdrew from the stage in about 1749, and, in his career of 45 years, he won a reputation as an exciting soloist. He performed in at least four premieres during the height of his success:

Ballet	Premiere
Diomède	28 April 1710
Médée et Jason	24 April 1713
Les Eléments	29 May 1725
Baiocco e Serpilla	7 June 1729

He assisted in the revivals of *Thésée** (1707, 1720, 1729), *Persée** (1710), *Phaéton** (1730), and *Proserpine** (1741).

BIBLIOGRAPHY: EDS V 1120; Lajarte I, 25-28, 36-38, 42-45, 111, 117, 137-39, 146; Marian Hannah Winter, *The Pre-Romantic Ballet* (New York: Dance Horizons, 1975), 68.

E

L'Eglogue de Versailles is a short *divertissement** in one act of about a hundred lines that was first performed before the king at Versailles in 1668. Its libretto was written by Philippe Quinault*; Jean-Baptiste Lully* did its score. The king danced in its ballet with the marquis de Villeroy and the marquis de Rassan when it was mounted at Versailles for the first time. It was returned to the Court in July 1685, when it served as a curtain raiser for *L'Idylle sur la paix**; it was billed at the Palais-Royal* in the fall of this same year and was represented again at this same theatre with *Les Fêtes de L'Amour et de Bacchus** on 7 July 1696. It was also produced in Paris on 11 July 1700 with *Le Carnaval** and among the "fragments" offered there in the first half of 1717. It came to be known as *La Grotte de Versailles* after its revival in 1685 because its stage set reproduced "the grotto of Versailles."

The purpose of this pastoral had been to celebrate the return of the king to Court after the peace of Aix-la-Chapelle, and it was probably Quinault's words for Lully's music in this instance that first aroused the latter's interest in his future librettist. As might be expected, this short composition is a continuous laudium of Louis XIV, his grandeur, and his glory. The opening section features flutes and oboes in concert with a chorus of shepherds and shepherdesses, while Ménalque and Coridon provide the love interest. A so-called augmentation of the piece is in reality an extract from the last *intermède* of Molière's *Monsieur de Pourceaugnac*.

BIBLIOGRAPHY: Lajarte I, 50-51; RGO III, 81-90.

Enée et Lavinie is a lyric tragedy in five acts and a prologue by Fontenelle* for which Colasse* did the score. It had its premiere at the Palais-Royal* on 7 November 1690, but it was not very successful at this time or on 14 February 1758, when Dauvergne wrote new music for Fontenelle's text.

The opera is based upon the legendary account of the marriage of Aeneas and Lavinia described in the seventh book of Vergil's epic, but certain changes are made in the original story so that the dramatic representation of this episode in Roman history might be made acceptable on the stage. The principal modifications in Vergil's text are the establishment of the fact that Enée and Lavinie are already in love at the start of the opera and the presentation of Lavinie as the Chimène-like daughter who hopes that her father will select the suitor whom she prefers in the first place. After this exposition in the first act, the focus of attention is centered upon the conflict between Vénus and Junon and the oracular pronouncement that Lavinie's choice of a husband will be her own decision. The third act relates Lavinie's selection of Turnus as her husband, and the fourth act leads up to the Turnus-Enée duel with Vénus providing her son with special weapons forged by Vulcain. The death of Turnus results in a general peace and festive celebration that constitutes an appropriate grand finale.

The opera is more psychological and dramatic than epic, since the characters react to their problems on a human level. Yet this very humanization of the intrigue has a weakening effect upon the work in this instance: it reduces the action to a demonstration in fatalism by calling attention constantly to oracles. Perhaps even more serious is the damage done to Enée's heroic stature when he is reprimanded by Didon returned from the realm of the dead. In retrospect, *Enée et Lavinie* is a sad reminder that Pascal Colasse created only one real success for the Royal Academy of Music, *Thétis et Pélée.**

BIBLIOGRAPHY: Pascal Colasse, *Enée et Lavinie,* ed. Graham Sadler (Boston: Gregg International Publishers, 1972); Lajarte I, 59; RGO IV, 51-112.

L'Europe galante is an *opéra-ballet* in four entrées and a prologue that is generally considered the first work in its genre despite its structural similarity to early seventeenth-century *ballets à entrées* and *Les Saisons** by Pascal Colasse.* The libretto was by Antoine Houdard de La Motte,* and it was announced at first that the music was the work of Joseph Campra, a member of the orchestra at the Palais-Royal* and a brother to André Campra.* Crediting the score to the former musician was a subterfuge, however, because André Campra could not sign an operatic score with immunity: he was music master at Notre-Dame, and his name had already been affixed to a large quantity of religious music he had created in the chapels and cathedral to which he had become attached.

André Campra's authorship of profane works for the Royal Academy of Music was not long in becoming known, however, and he went on to write *Hésione,** *Tancrède,** and other works establishing him as the leading operatic composer of his time. It was in fact *L'Europe galante* that was responsible for settling the question of authors' royalties because the management of the Opéra offered such a small remuneration to Campra and La Motte that they refused to accept the ridiculous sum tendered. A dispute erupted, but influential figures intervened, and it was agreed that henceforth each author would receive 100 *livres* a performance for the first ten billings and 50 *livres* for each of the next ten representations with the text of his composition passing to the Royal Academy of Music after the twentieth staging. As Louis XIV had indicated in the original charter granting the monopoly of musical performances to Jean-Baptiste Lully,* the rights to the publication of works produced by the Academy were the property of the Florentine's successors.

L'Europe galante was so popular that it was revived a half-dozen times by the middle of the eighteenth century. Its first run appears to have lasted from 24 October until the end of December 1697 according to the incomplete records in the unpublished Le Journal de l'Opéra. It had 15 consecutive billings during its first revival lasting from 18 May to 20 June 1706. Its third run starting on 20 August 1715 was interrupted by the 27 August 1715 closing of the Palais-Royal* on the occasion of Louis XIV's illness and imminent death. The records for 1724 are also incomplete in Le Journal de l'Opéra, but it appears that L'Europe galante was brought back to the stage for the summer of 1724 and for the carnival season of 1725. It was during this latter run that the second entrée was dropped to make room for La Provençale, which had already been added to Les Fêtes de Thalie by Mouret* on 17 September 1722. L'Europe galante enjoyed another ten billings in November and December 1747.

The innovative character of L'Europe galante is not evident in its prologue, but it becomes clear in the first entrée that ancient mythology with its angry or lovesick gods and goddesses has been forgotten for a time at least. A prefatory note to eighteenth-century editions of the composition points to this development by indicating that the characters in the text are Europeans: "We have selected from the nations of Europe those whose character promises more play for the theatre: France, Spain, Italy, and Turkey. We have followed the ordinary ideas that people have of the personality of these peoples: the Frenchman is depicted as flighty, indiscreet, and given to flirting; the Spaniard, faithful and romantic; the Italian, jealous, sly, and violent; finally we have expressed, as far as the theatre would permit, the haughtiness and the dominance of the sultans, and the impetuousness of the sultanas." It was not until the 25th year of its existence, therefore, that the Royal Academy of Music presented a contemporary European upon its stage, and L'Europe galante was the 43d composition that it had accepted into repertory.

The principal rôles of L'Europe galante were filled by most of the famous artistes of the first half of the eighteenth century. At its premiere, Mlle Clément sang Vénus while Mlle Desmatins* did Céphise in La France and Zayde in La Turquie. Two parts were also created by Thévenard,* who appeared until 1736 as Sylvandre in La France and Zuliman in La Turquie. Mlle Moreau sang Olimpia, a rôle that was filled later by Mlle Erremans, who also did Céphise and Zayde in 1724 as well as Vénus and Doris in 1736. Jélyotte appeared as Octavio in 1747, when Mlle Fel sang Céphise, and Mlle Camargo (for Camargo, Fel, and Jélyotte, see eighteenth-century volume) starred in the ballet.

Campra managed to achieve a diversity of music in L'Europe galante, and there are a symphony in the prologue, a serenade in L'Espagne, and a ball with an orchestra and an Italian song in L'Italie. These are not the only passages worthy of note, of course, and musicologists continue to point to

Céphise's "Paisibles lieux, agréables retraites" in *La France* (scene 2), Don Pedro's "Sommeil, qui chaque nuit jouissez de ma Belle" in *L'Espagne* (scene 1), and Zayde's "Mes yeux, ne pourrez-vous jamais" in *La Turquie* (scene 1).

BIBLIOGRAPHY: André Campra, *L'Europe galante* (Farnborough, Hants, England: Gregg Press, 1967); André Campra, *L'Europe galante . . . reconstitué et reduit pour piano et chant par Théodore de Lajarte* (Paris: T. Michaëlis, 188?); Lajarte I, 83-85; Antoine Houdard de La Motte, *Oeuvres complètes*, 11 vols. (Genève: Slatkine Reprints, 1970), II, 134-45; RGO VI, 122-70; SS 62-63.

F

Les Festes de Thalie is an *opéra-ballet** in three entrées and a prologue that stands as a milestone in the history of the evolution of French opera because it was the first lyric comedy produced by the Royal Academy of Music: its characters employed current French in their speech and appeared on the stage in contemporary dress. Jean-Joseph Mouret* composed its musical score, and Joseph de Lafont* created its libretto. When it was mounted initially on 19 August 1714, it was composed of a prologue and three acts entitled *La Fille, La Femme,* and *La Veuve.* A fourth entrée entitled *La Critique des Festes de Thalie* was added on 9 October 1714. The work proved to be a success, and its first run included 48 straight billings from its premiere on 19 August until 27 November 1714. After the latter date, it was mounted on alternate dates for the 18 remaining programs of the year. It was revived in 1722, when *La Provençale* was substituted for *La Critique des festes de Thalie* on 17 September. This new act by the same authors was introduced into *L'Europe galante** on 22 February 1725 as well as into *Le Ballet des ballets* on 2 April 1726. *Les Festes de Thalie* was revived for another 36 consecutive representations between 2 June and 21 August 1735, and it was mounted on another 6 dates in November and December of this same year. It was returned to the stage in 1735. *La Provençale* was revived separately in 1745, and Candeille did new music for it in 1778.

Fittingly enough, the prologue is set upon the stage of the Palais-Royal,* where Melpomène is boasting that this theatre belongs to her: the sighs of love and the sounds of grief are the only true accompaniment for the royal and divine actions that transpire on these boards. Thalie accuses her sister of jealousy and reminds her that people tire of weeping before they tire of laughing. Apollon intervenes to suggest that the sisters reconcile their differences by contributing to the same compositions.

In *La Fille,* Cléon has been able to return to Marseille and his wife after ten years of slavery in Algiers because his friend Acaste has purchased his freedom (I, 1). Acaste is distraught because his courtship of Léonore has come to a standstill (I, 2) despite her mother's urgings that she accept his proposal of marriage before time destroys her charms (I, 3). Bélise is so impatient with her daughter that she advises Acaste to make Léonore jealous, and she offers herself as a candidate for his revised affections (I, 4).

When Léonore exits in protest, Acaste starts to pursue her, but he remains on stage to hear Bélise repeat her suggestion that she become his wife (I, 5). Cléon recognizes Bélise as his wife; he reproaches her for her inconstancy; Léonore realizes that Cléon is her father and points out to Acaste that he cannot marry her mother. Acaste replies that his marriage to Bélise was only a ploy to arouse her jealousy; he insists that he loves her alone and frees his Algerian captives. The liberated prisoners form a chorus and ballet to celebrate their freedom and the wedding of Acaste and Léonore (I, 6). Mlle Poussin* sang Léonore in the first run of the work, and the rôles of Acaste and Cléon were filled by Thévenard* and Dun (for Dun, see eighteenth-century volume).

La Femme opens with Caliste rejoicing that she has no rivals for her husband's affections (II, 1), but she adds that her husband is in fact organizing the present ball for her without knowing it because he was attracted to her at an earlier masked ball where he could not ascertain her true identity (II, 2). Caliste dons her mask, and Dorante is deceived once more; his valet Zerbin is similarly tricked into denouncing his wife to his masked wife, Dorine. Dorante insists in vain that Caliste remove her mask, but she observes to his amazement that his wife, Caliste, might object. He recovers long enough to admit that he loved Caliste once. She and Dorine unmask themselves at this point, and they forgive their grateful husbands (II, 3-4).

Situated in a hamlet, *La Veuve* revolves about Isabelle enjoying "the sweet liberty of widowhood" (III, 1). Doris asks whether wealthy Chrisogon or handsome Léandre will win her hand (III, 2), and each suitor claims to have won Isabelle's favor (III, 3), but the merry widow feigns grief to escape choosing between them (III, 4). The financier Léandre orders a *divertissement** to distract her (III, 5), but Isabelle decides to choose freedom over a second marriage (III, 6).

La Critique des Festes de Thalie recalls Molière* in its title and in its setting at the Palais-Royal, where Polymnie asserts that the ballet was well received on account of its music (scene 1). Terpsicore claims the same distinction for its dances (scene 2). Annoyed by this bickering, Apollon dispatches Momus to settle the quarrel (scene 3). The truce is celebrated in a festival of dance and song (scene 4).

BIBLIOGRAPHY: Lajarte I, 121-22; RGO XI, 178-232.

Les Festes vénitiennes is an *opéra-ballet** in three entrées and a prologue with music by André Campra* and words by Antoine Danchet.* This work was a welcome relief for Parisians who were tiring of the same operatic fare consisting of lyric tragedies cast invariably in the mould created by Lully* and Quinault.* It proved incredibly popular, therefore, and it perpetuated itself to the point where new entrées were written to replace the acts that seemed to be losing their appeal. When it was given for the first time on 17

June 1710, its entrées were entitled: prologue, *Le Triomphe de la Folie sur la Raison*; first entrée, *La Feste des barquerolles*; second entrée, *Les Sérénades et les Joueurs*; and third entrée, *L'Amour saltimbanque*. The composition ran in this form for ten straight performances until 8 July 1710, when *La Feste marine* became the first entrée. No further changes were made in the work until its 23d billing on 8 August 1710, when the prologue was suppressed, and *Le Bal* was added to it between the first and second acts. At its 34th showing on 5 September 1710, *Les Devins de la place Saint Marc* replaced *Les Sérénades et les Joueurs,* and the entrées were arranged in the following order: *La Feste marine, Le Bal, Les Devins de la place Saint Marc,* and *L'Amour saltimbanque.* The 51st mounting of *Les Festes vénitiennes* on 14 October 1740 saw *La Feste marine* eliminated, but a new act entitled *L'Opéra* was added as the fourth and last entrée. The very last entrée added was incorporated into the work in December 1710; it was presented as a miniature comedy and was entitled *Le Triomphe de la folie.* After its unprecedented success in 1710, Campra's work was revived in one form or another in 1712, 1713, 1721, 1731, 1732, 1740, 1750, and 1759. Rousseau's *Le Devin du village* was added to it for ten programs in October 1759 (see eighteenth-century volume for *Le Devin du village*). Nearly every artiste active during the first half of the eighteenth century had a part in it, and it would be too lengthy a task to indicate them all here. Suffice it to say that Mlles Dun, Journet,* and Poussin* sang at least two rôles in it during its first run, which also enjoyed the versatile services of Dun, Hardouin,* and Thévenard.*

BIBLIOGRAPHY: Brenner 176; DDO I, 449; Lajarte I, 111-14; Paul-Marie Masson, "*Les Fêtes vénitiennes* de Campra," *RdM* XIII (1932) 127-46, 214-26; Sonn I, 497-98; SS 63.

Les Fêtes de l'Amour et de Bacchus is a pastoral in three acts and a prologue that had its premiere at the Bel-Air* tennis court on 15 March 1672. This work has the distinction of being the composition with which Lully* started his career with the Royal Academy of Music. It was a pastiche of different dancing airs that the composer had already done for Benserade,* Molière,* and Quinault,* but it proved popular enough to be revived in 1689, 1696, 1706, 1716, and 1738.

The prologue to *Les Fêtes de l'Amour et de Bacchus* is striking because it is based upon the device of a theatre within a theatre and presents spectators upon the stage. This stage audience is composed of men and women from Switzerland and the provinces, especially Gascony, who clamor in vain for copies of the libretto of the work to be presented on the coming program. This lampooning of the Gascon dialect was doubtlessly intended as a satire of the Languedocian singers who had sung in productions by Perrin* and Sourdéac, the producers of earlier operas at the *jeu de paume* de la Bouteille.* The other prominent features of the prologue include the inevitable praise of Louis XIV and an antiphonal argument recalling the medieval *tension*. The debate in the prologue of *Les Fêtes de l'Amour et de Bacchus* is set in the form of a musical contest between Euterpe's pianissimo and Melpomène's fortissimo eulogies of the king's accomplishments in war and peace.

The pastoral itself is based upon Caliste's refusal to admit her love for pining Tircis (I, 1-4). When Caliste decides finally to reveal her feelings for her suitor (I, 5), Forestan and Silvandre abandon her to pay homage to Bacchus (I, 6). Forestan renews his suit for Caliste's hand, however, and his magicians and sorcerers deck him out in ridiculous dress (II, 1-3). After he discovers that he is being mocked on account of his ludicrous appearance, he rejoins Silvandre and the other members of Bacchus's band (II, 4). A subplot presents the Climène-Damon affair concluding in a reconciliation (II, 5-6).The followers of L'Amour and Bacchus stage a contest of song and dance (III, 1), and the dispute terminates in a general agreement that both gods have charms and powers that must be acknowledged (III, 2-3).

Les Fêtes de l'Amour et de Bacchus is interesting historically if not esthetically since it marks Lully's last total effort in the pastoral vein. His new operatic productions between 1673-1687 were restricted almost exclusively to lyric tragedies. The one striking exception was the heroic pastoral, *Acis et Galathée** (1686), which belies Lully's alleged aversion for the bucolic mode. It is also to be noted that Lully did Euterpe's rôle in the ornate style of the Italian aria whereas Melpomène's assertions and rebuttals of Euterpe are in the plain style of the French air. And it is the latter who is triumphant in the prologue debate, a victory that implies that the French manner is to be the dominant fashion in opera henceforth.

The music that Lully reused includes the *divertissement** of the last act of *Le Bourgeois Gentilhomme,* the *divertissement* from *Les Amants magnifiques,* the ballet from the *Fête de Versailles,* and the *divertissement* from the third act of *Georges Dandin.*

BIBLIOGRAPHY: Lajarte I, 21-22; Lionel de la Laurencie, *Lully* (Paris: Alcan, 1919), 34-37; Henry Prunières, *Lully* (Paris: Renouard, n.d.), 31-37; RGO I, 101-42; Ch. Nuitter and E. Thoinan, *Les origines de l'opéra français* (Paris: Plon, 1886), 282-86; Théodore Valensi, *Louis XIV et Lully* (Nice: Les E.L.F., 1951), 153-54.

Les Fêtes galantes was posted as a ballet with a score by Henri Desmarets* and a libretto by Jean-François Duché de Vancy.* Desmarets observed in a prefatory note to his work, "I have deliberated for a long time whether I should leave on this ballet the title that it was known to have two years ago, before there was any idea of writing *L'Europe galante* . . . . Chance brought the same characters into the minds of two persons.'' But there is little or no real similarity between the two compositions, one of which was a failure and the other a success: *L'Europe galante* is based upon three simple and unrelated plots, while *Les Fêtes galantes* has one of the most complicated intrigues to reach the stage of the Palais-Royal* before the death of Louis XIV. It had its premiere on 10 May 1698.

Strangely enough, the prologue of *Les Fêtes galantes* is so brief that it might be described as one short burst of song: Thalie enters singing the delights and pleasures that the new peace will bring, while Comus, Bacchus, and Thalie's retinue concur in a chorus.

The work itself deals with three friendly princes in love with the queen of Naples, who loves one of this trio, although this prince is also loved by one of the queen's relatives. In the first act, Carlos, Idas, and Sostrate identify themselves as princes of Sicily, Tuscany, and Persia. They pledge their mutual friendship and complain of the heartless beauty with whom they are in love before discovering that they all love Célime, queen of Naples (I, 1). Sostrate reveals to Célime that she is loved by all three princes (I, 2). Célime then confides to Cléonice that she loves Idas, and Cléonice assures Célime that Idas is in love with another woman despite what he has said; Cléonice's falsehood is prompted by her own love for Idas, and it is effective since Célime believes her (I, 3). Carlos tells Célime that Idas has left Naples (I, 4), but this prince and his retinue dressed as gypsies and Americans enter to amuse Célime with a concert and ballet (I, 5).

The situation becomes more involved in the second act, when Cléonice discourages Idas by telling him that Carlos is his successful rival for Célime's hand (II, 1-2); she completes her treachery by persuading Célime that Idas is in love with her, Cléonice (II, 3). Idas then describes aloud his love for Célime, and the latter overhears him and believes that he is speaking of his passion for Cléonice (II, 4). Rebuked and rebuffed by an outraged Célime, Idas swears vengeance (II, 5), and Carlos arrives with his singers and dancers to entertain Célime (II, 6-7), although she has disappeared (II, 8).

This complex plot, made so involved by Cléonice's lies, prepares a difficult third act. It begins with Sostrate telling Cléonice that he is aware that Idas has shunned Célime for her. Cléonice then explains to him that he should not repeat this information lest vain Célime forget him and try to win Idas from her through egotism (III, 1). Idas appears to propose to Cléonice that they wed without delay, but his constant allusions to Célime move Cléonice to accuse him of still being in love with the queen (III, 2). Idas swears to Célime that he loves Cléonice, however, and Célime asserts that she plans to wed Carlos (III, 3), although she admits to Cléonice that she is still in love with Idas and asks Cléonice to relinquish him to her (III, 4). Cléonice is too deeply in love with Idas to heed her request (III, 5), and Célime is not impressed by Sostrate's celebration in her honor: she informs him that she loves Carlos. But Carlos assures her that Idas still loves her (III, 6). Idas reveals to Célime that Cléonice has plotted against their love by using all manner of deception (III, 7). Finally aware of the truth, Célime explains to Carlos that she is to marry Idas, an announcement that shocks Carlos and Cléonice, besides demonstrating once more that love overcomes all obstacles. The work closes with the queen's Court celebrating her marriage to the prince of Tuscany (III, 9).

BIBLIOGRAPHY: Lajarte I, 87; RGO VI, 229-90.

Fontenelle, Bernard Le Bovier de (b. 11 February 1657, Rouen; d. 9 January 1757, Paris), librettist, distinguished himself even as a student at the Jesuit school in his native city. His teachers tried to persuade him to enter the Society of Jesus, and his father urged him to become a lawyer, but his early success in poetry and a trip to Paris in 1674 induced him to embark upon a literary career.

Yet Fontenelle did not find himself involved in a major project until he was invited to help his uncle, Thomas Corneille,* in the reworking of the libretto of Molière's *Psyché** for the Royal Academy of Music. It is impossible to measure the extent of Fontenelle's contribution to this opera in its new form because Thomas Corneille alone put the finishing touches on the final version, and the young writer's initial effort for the Palais-Royal* lost its identity in the process of this editing. Since Quinault* was still in exile from Court after the premiere of the new *Psyché* in 1678, the uncle asked his nephew to help him a second time. No public allusion was made to Fontenelle's part in the creation of *Bellérophon** until 1741, when he published a letter in the *Journal des Savants* to refute an assertion that this lyric tragedy was largely the work of Boileau. In his letter Fontenelle revealed that he had done the greatest portion of *Bellérophon* from a synopsis that his uncle had sent him in Rouen.

After *Psyché* and *Bellérophon* Fontenelle turned to legitimate tragedy and comedy, and he published the philosophical treatises and scientific popularizations that would win him international renown. Yet he continued to submit scripts to the jury of the Palais-Royal, where he was a frequent spectator and where he lived during the regency in an apartment given to him by the duke d'Orléans. His *Thétis et Pélée** had been a success in 1689, but *Enée et Lavinie** failed to arouse very much enthusiasm in 1690. It was not until forty years later that he did a libretto for the Opéra again, *Endymion* (for *Endymion,* see eighteenth-century volume). The unpublished *Journal de l'Opéra* notes on the occasion of the 29 November 1750 revival of *Thétis et Pélée,* "Fontenelle, author of the words, 93 years old, is present at the performance." It had been 62 years since he had finished this work.

BIBLIOGRAPHY: Bio univ XIV, 358-63; Suzanne Delorme, "Tableau chronologique de la vie et des oeuvres de Fontenelle avec les principaux synchronismes littéraires, philosophiques et scientifiques" and "Contribution à la bibliographie de Fontenelle," *RHS* 10 (1957), 301-9; Amédée Fayol, *Fontenelle* (Paris: Debresse, 1961); GDHS I, 462-66; Auguste Laborde-Milaà, *Fontenelle* (Paris: Hachette, 1905).

Les Fragments de Lully is a collection of pieces for which Lully* had written the music and for which different authors had supplied the words. It was given in its first form on 10 September 1702, and this type of *spectacle coupé* (see eighteenth-century volume for *spectacle coupé*) proved so popular that it was kept in the repertory, although new pieces were substituted for the old ones from time to time.

In its first form, *Les Fragments de Lully* was introduced by a prologue taken from *Les Fêtes de l'Amour et de Bacchus*,* with Polymnie exhorting her retinue to present a concert worthy of "the greatest king of the universe." Then followed four entrées: *La Fête marine* taken from *Le Bourgeois Gentilhomme* and *Les Jeux pythiens; Les Guerriers* borrowed from *Les Amours déguisés; La Bergerie* derived from *Les Muses,* *La Naissance de Vénus, Le Bourgeois Gentilhomme, La Princesse d'Elide, La Fête de Versailles; Les Bohémiens* derived from *Les Muses,* *Les Amours déguisés,* the ballet entitled *Alcidiane.*

The entrées incorporated into *Les Fragments* later were not always by Lully but more often by Campra.* The earliest titles added after the premiere included *Cariselli*;* *Le Triomphe de Vénus,* taken from *La Fête de Madame la Duchesse de la Ferté*; *La Sérénade vénitienne*;* *Le Bal interrompu* by Campra and Danchet.*

A new cluster of *Fragments* was billed on 8 February 1717: *La Grotte de Versailles*;* *La Sérénade vénitienne*; *L'Amour Médecin,* taken from *Les Muses*;* and *Le Bal interrompu* by Campra and Danchet. This combination was staged only seven times at the Palais-Royal* before being dropped on 28 February 1717.

BIBLIOGRAPHY: Lajarte I, 96-97; RGO VII, 391-468.

Francoeur, François (b. 28 September 1698, Paris; d. 6 August 1787, Paris), composer, learned to play the violin as a youth and earned a chair in the Palais-Royal* orchestra in 1710. He met his lifetime friend, François Rebel,* at the Royal Academy of Music about this time, when he was admitted to the Music of the King's Chamber. After 20 years of service, he became one of the famous "twenty-four violins" and then received the title of Composer of the Chamber from Louis XV in 1733. Rebel and Francoeur were both named inspectors of the Royal Academy of Music in 1736, and the management of the Opéra was entrusted to them in 1751. They performed these duties until their retirement in 1767. After leaving the Palais-Royal, Francoeur sold all his charges and offices to withdraw to a quiet life marred only by the pain of kidney stones. He was 89 years old at the time of his death, and with Rebel he had made a considerable contribution to the repertory of the Royal Academy of Music: *Pyrame et Thisbé* in 1726, *Tarsis et Julie* in 1728, *Scanderberg* in 1735, *Le Ballet de la paix* in 1738, *Les Augustales* and *Zélindor, roi des Sylphes* in 1744, *Ismène* in 1750, and *Le Prince de Noisy* (for Francoeur's compositions, see eighteenth-century volume). He also did two collections of sonatas for the violin.

BIBLIOGRAPHY: Bio univ XIV, 638-39; Fétis III, 311.

Fuzelier, Louis (b. 1672, Paris; d. 19 September 1752, Paris), playwright, was a prodigious producer of scripts for all the theatres of Paris in addition to being managing editor of the *Mercure de France* with La Bruère from November 1744 until September 1752. His name is associated with more than two hundred titles, and his compositions were performed at private homes, the Saint Laurent and Saint Germain fairs, Versailles, and Fontainebleau in addition to being mounted at the Comédie-Française and the Théâtre-Italien. His collaborators included Le Sage, d'Orneval, and Pannard, and he was accordingly one of the foundation stones of the Opéra-Comique while enjoying the distinction of working with Rameau (for Rameau, see eighteenth-century volume). Many of his texts are extant only in manuscript form in the Bibliothèque Nationale. His librettos for the Royal Academy of Music include *Les Amours déguisés,* * *Arion,* * *Les Ages,* *Les Festes grecques et romaines, La Reine des Péris, Les Indes galantes, L'Ecole des amours, Le Carnaval du Parnasse, Les Amours de Tempé, Phaétuse* (for Fuzelier's works for the Opéra, see eighteenth-century volume). In all, therefore, Fuzelier had ten musical works billed at the Palais-Royal* in addition to the comedies he contributed to the legitimate stage and the eighteen scripts he had accepted by the Italians.

BIBLIOGRAPHY: Bio univ XV, 309-10; Brenner 70-72; CG 177-81; H. C. Lancaster, *Sunset: A History of Parisian Drama in the Last Years of Louis XIV, 1701-1715* (Baltimore: The Johns Hopkins Press, 1945), 312-13, 329-31; Lajarte I, 161.

G

Gatti, Théobalde (b. 1650, Florence; d. 1727, Paris), composer, was known as Théobalde in France. He had already distinguished himself on the bass viol by the time he left his native country. Because he was so impressed by the overtures of Lully's* first lyric tragedies, he wished to meet their author. When he explained to his compatriot why he had come to Paris, Lully rewarded him with a chair in the orchestra of the Opéra. He held this position for nearly fifty years and was finally laid to rest in the church of Saint-Eustache in Paris. He published a collection of a dozen Italian airs besides contributing *Coronis** and *Scylla** to the Royal Academy of Music in 1691 and 1701 respectively.

BIBLIOGRAPHY: Fétis III, 422-23; Lajarte I, 59, 79, 92-93; TdT 621.

Gervais, Charles-Hubert (b. 19 February 1671, Paris; d. 15 January 1744, Paris) was a musician of average ability whose friends at Court obtained for him the position of music master of the chamber in the household of the duke d'Orléans during the regency. He became choir master for Louis XV after the latter's succession to the throne. His *Méduse** failed in 1697, and he did not have another work produced at the Palais-Royal* until 1716, when his *Hypermnestre* (for *Hypermnestre,* see eighteenth-century volume) was staged there. Castil-Blaze has reported that Philippe d'Orléans collaborated with Gervais to some extent on this composition, but it is more likely that it was the lost work, *Panthée,* to which the regent contributed his royal talents. This forgotten tragedy was performed in the apartments of the Palais-Royal, where the regent lived, but it was never offered to the public. Gervais's last effort for the Royal Academy of Music was *Les Amours de Protée* (for *Les Amours de Protée,* see eighteenth-century volume) of 1720. In addition to his operas, Gervais left a large group of motets that are still extant in manuscript form in the Bibliothèque Nationale in Paris.

BIBLIOGRAPHY: Fétis III, 466; Lajarte I, 67, 73, 126, 131-32.

Gilbert, Gabriel (b. 1610, Paris; d. 1680?, Paris), librettist, was a Parisian Protestant known more for his tragedies than his operas: his collaborator on *Téléphonte* (1642) was Cardinal Richelieu; his *Rodogune* (1644) seemed suspiciously similar to Pierre Corneille's play by the same title; his tragedy based upon the story of Hippolytus and Theseus anticipates Racine's *Phèdre* in more than one way. He was rather a contemporary of Corneille than a colleague of Boileau, and one of his most ardent admirers was Christina of Sweden, who invited him to take up residence at her Court in Stockholm just as she had asked Descartes to join her learned circle of academicians in the north. After the death of his royal protectress, Gilbert found a generous friend in M. d'Hervart, who was always ready to shelter and to support a gifted but indigent Protestant, and it was only through the intervention of this second patron that the playwright was spared the pain of poverty. His single contribution to the development of opera in France was the libretto he wrote for *Les Peines et les plaisirs de l'Amour** by Cambert* in 1672. This was Gilbert's last effort before his death sometime between 1673 and 1680.

BIBLIOGRAPHY: Bio univ XVI, 444-46; Eugène Haag, *La France protestante* (Paris: Cherbuliez, 1846-59); Lajarte I, 20; Eleanor J. Pellet, *A Forgotten French Dramatist, Gabriel Gilbert* (Baltimore: The Johns Hopkins Press, 1931); TdT 386-87.

Grotte de Versailles is a pastoral composition usually called *l'Eglogue de Versailles** because it was set in Versailles and performed there during the seventeenth century.

Guichard, Henri (b. ?; d. ?), librettist, appeared on the scene for the first time about 1670, when he became active at Court as superintendent of buildings for the duke d'Orléans, and his *Les Amours de Diane et d'Endymion* (1671) was given at Versailles. He took a special interest in musical affairs during the reign of Louis XIV because he held the license to give operas for a short time and because he and Lully* were involved in the latter's effort to win the monopoly to establish a musical theatre in France. The two men quarreled before long, however, and Lully accused his former associate of having plotted to kill him by poisoning his snuff. The scandal reached such preposterous proportions that an editor found it profitable to publish a volume entitled *Mémoires de Guichard contre Lully et de Lully contre Guichard* (1675). Only the king's intervention suppressed this quarrel.

After Lully's death in 1687, Guichard had his only contribution to the repertory of the Royal Academy of Music billed in 1705, *Ulysse,** for which the elder Rebel* had done the score. The composer left France to follow Philippe IV to Spain a few years later, and he established an opera house in Madrid at this time. It is believed that Guichard might have died in the Spanish capital.

BIBLIOGRAPHY: Brenner 77; CG 163-65; CDSS II, 1010; Fétis IV, 144; Lajarte I, 99, 161.

H

Hardouin (b. ?, Tréguier; d. circa 1725, Paris?), vocalist, joined the Royal Academy of Music in 1694 after having sung in provincial cathedrals of France. He was commissioned to replace Moreau as first bass at the Opéra, a rank that he held in the hierarchy of the Royal Academy of Music until 1697, when Thévenard* was able to dislodge him from this favored position on account of his waning popularity.

Hardouin remained with the Opéra for 23 years, however, because he refused to be discouraged by the preference shown to Thévenard by the public. He created at least 26 rôles in 22 compositions during his association with the theatre between 1694 and 1717. He sang two parts in *Issé** of 30 December 1697, Jupiter and Hylas; in *Iphigénie en Tauride** of 6 May 1704, L'Ordonnateur des Jeux and L'Océan; in *Les Fêtes vénitiennes** of 17 June 1710, Héraclite and Filinde; and in *Idoménée** of 12 January 1712, Eole and Arbas. As a bass, however, most of his rôles were gods, and he was cast as one of the divinities in Greek mythology in seven compositions:

Rôle	*Opera*	*Performance Date*
Mars	*Vénus et Adonis**	17 March 1697
Jupiter	*Marthésie, reine des Amazones**	9 November 1699
Jupiter	*Le Carnaval et la Folie**	3 January 1704
Momus	*La Vénitienne**	26 May 1705
Apollon	*Médée et Jason**	24 April 1713
Bacchus	*Les Amours déguisés**	22 August 1713
Jupiter	*Télèphe**	28 November 1713

The other operas in which he created parts set in a mythological, historical, or literary tradition were *Ariadne et Bacchus** (1696), *Le Triomphe des Arts** (1700), *Canente** (1700), *Hésione** (1799), *Médus, roi des Mèdes** (1702), *Cariselli** (1702), *Tancrède** (1702), *Les Muses** (1703), *Polyxène et Pyrrhus** (1706), *Les Fêtes de l'été* (1716), and *Camille, reine* *des Volsques* (1717) (for the last two works, see eighteenth-century volume).

BIBLIOGRAPHY: André Campra, *Les Festes vénitiennes,* ed. Alexandre Guilmant (Paris: Théodore Michaëlis, n.d.), 9; Fétis Suppl. I, 449; Lajarte I, 66-67, 86-87, 89-91, 100-103, 105, 109, 113-15, 117-20, 125, 127.

Hésione with music by André Campra* and a libretto by Antoine Danchet* is a lyric tragedy in five acts and a prologue. It was performed initially at the Palais-Royal* on 21 December 1700 and was revived for the first time in 1709, when it enjoyed 19 billings between 19 July and 30 August. It was returned to the stage once more on 13 September 1729; Lajarte asserts that it was given this year until the end of the following October. *Le Journal de l'Opéra* notes only a 31 January performance of *Hésione* in 1730, when its prologue was suppressed in favor of La Serre's* *La Pastorale héroique.** It was revived for the third and last time on 1 March 1743 and 1 October 1743; Mlle Romainville made her debut with the company in the title-rôle on 6 October of this same year.

The brief prologue of *Hésione* is set in Rome during the centennial games held to honor the sun. The priestess of the ceremony sees favorable signs for the future, and Le Soleil assures the Romans of victory and glory for their king.

The opera is not as simple as its prologue. It begins with Télamon regretting the pending Hésione-Anchise marriage on account of his love for the prospective bride (I, 1), although Vénus enters to promise him aid (I, 2-3). The king announces that Neptune is appeased and that the temple is to be consecrated for the celebration of Hésione's marriage (I, 4). A violent storm and earthquake interrupt the course of events, and a voice declares that Anchise is to go to Mount Ida to learn his fate (I, 5). Alone in the desert against Hésione's will (II, 1-2), Anchise beholds the wasteland turned into a flowering garden with the appearance of Vénus and her retinue. The goddess reveals her love for him, but he refuses to abandon Hésione (II, 3-6). The latter believes that Anchise is interested in Vénus (III, 1), and Télamon renews his suit for her hand without success (III, 2-3), although Vénus does promise to help him (III, 4-5).

The pace of the action quickens in the last two acts: Anchise is angered by Hésione's sudden love for Télamon (IV, 1); the lovers accuse each other of inconstancy until they realize that they have been bewitched by Vénus (IV, 2). Furious at their reconciliation, Vénus calls upon Neptune to destroy Troy (IV, 3-4). She is satisfied with the havoc wrought by a marine monster (V, 1), and Anchise asks her why he has not been able to slay this creature from the deep. She explains her plan to have Télamon win Hésione by killing the creature (V, 2). A rejoicing throng enters to announce the destruction of the monster by Télamon (V, 3); the hero and Hésione sail away together. Anchise swears to have revenge when the Greeks burn Troy (V, 4). Mercure discloses that the gods wish Anchise to cherish Vénus (V, 5).

The success and revivals of *Hésione* resulted in a number of artistes appearing in it. The title-rôle was filled by Mlles Moreau and Pélissier,* while Vénus was sung by Mlles Desmatins* and Antier.* Thévenard* and de Chassé executed the part of Anchise. On 31 August 1730 Mlle Le Maure returned to the Palais-Royal* after an absence of three years and scored a success in Colasse's work. She also appeared in it with Mlle Fel and the fabulous Jélyotte in 1743. Some of the popular dancers who performed in its ballet included Mlles Dangeville (1700), Sallé (1729), and Camargo (1743) (for Camargo, Fel, Jélyotte and Sallé, see eighteenth-century volume).

BIBLIOGRAPHY: Lajarte I, 90-91; RGO VII, 109-66.

Hippodamie is a lyric tragedy in five acts and a prologue with music by André Campra* and words by Pierre-Charles Roy.* This opera was inspired by Lucian's *Dialogues* with borrowings from Hyginus and Pindar. Like Roy's initial contribution to the repertory of the Royal Academy of Music, *Bradamante*,* his second work for the artistes was not especially popular: *Hippodamie* was billed only 14 times after its premiere on 6 March 1708, and it was never revived.

The rather singular prologue of Campra's opera presents a chorus of savages preparing to hunt down the hosts of the forest, but Vénus orders Les Grâces and Les Plaisirs to teach them to moderate their ways. Vénus interrupts again to tell her son that they must leave to defend Pelops, who is about to risk his life for Hippodamie.

The opera opens with a ceremony in honor of the men who have died in the attempt to win Hippodamie's hand. The heroine expresses the hope that this bloodshed will stop (I, 1), and she explains to Cléone that her father is suspicious of all her suitors because he believes that they are about to depose or to slay him. Yet Hippodamie has still another suitor despite her father's slaughter of all previous pretenders to her hand: Pelops, son of the king of Phrygia (I, 2). Eriphile discloses her love for Pelops (I, 3), whom the king has invited to his ceremony for his victims (I, 4). Pelops laments his apparently unrequited love for Hippodamie (I, 5), and Eriphile divulges her love for Pelops (II, 1). Pelops is reluctant to tell Eriphile that he loves Hippodamie (II, 2), and the latter accuses him of courting Eriphile, although he protests that it is she whom he loves. He adds that he has no fear of facing the fate of her previous admirers (II, 3). Encouraged by Hippodamie, Pelops encounters Neptune, who presents him with a team of divinely gifted horses (II, 4-5).

The king reproaches Eriphile for falling in love with Pelops, and Pelops challenges him to a duel (III, 1-3). Pelops readies himself for the encounter (III, 4-5). Eriphile regrets that Pelops prefers death to her love (IV, 1), and she reproaches Hippodamie for her approval of the endless bloodshed (IV, 2). Hippodamie contemplates suicide because she loves both combatants

(IV, 3), She loses her senses momentarily (IV, 4), but Pelops enters victorious at the end of the act (IV, 5). The king is still alive (V, 1), however, and he blames his daughter for his defeat (V, 2). Eriphile reminds him that she can restore him to power (V, 3), but Pelops returns his crown to him. Raging Eriphile is born aloft by the north winds, and the king gives his assent to the union of Pelops and Hippodamie (V, 4).

BIBLIOGRAPHY: Lajarte I, 110; RGO IX, 279-332.

I

Idoménée is a lyric tragedy in five acts and a prologue. Its musical score was created by André Campra,* and Antoine Danchet* did its libretto. It was one of Campra's more impressive compositions, although it enjoyed only a dozen performances during its first run between its premiere on 12 January 1712 and 31 January 1712. It was revived on 5 April 1731 according to *Le Journal de L'Opéra,* and it was mounted again in May and June of this same year before being dropped. Mlle Poussin did Vénus in the prologue opposite Hardouin* as Eole in 1712. Mlles Journet* and Antier* filled the principal female parts of Ilione and Dircé with the assistance of Thévenard* (Idoménée), Hardouin* (Arbas), and Mantienne (La Jalousie, Némésis). Mlle Prévost starred in the ballet, in which Mlle Camargo (for Mlle Camargo, see eighteenth-century volume) appeared in 1731.

Vénus asks Eole to dispatch his winds to blow Idoménée off course in the prologue, and the goddess assigns her attendants to his Court in gratitude for his compliance with her request (scenes 1-2). The prologue then closes with a hymn of praise to L'Amour, and no allusions are made to aged Louis XIV or to events on the international scene (scene 3).

The tragedy opens with Dircé's report that a storm has sunk all Greek ships except the one on which she and her companions were captives. Idoménée is probably dead, therefore, and Ilione is free to admit her love for Idamante, his son. She thinks sadly of her slain brothers and her father but reveals that Electre loves Idamante (I, 1). The establishment of the Electre-Idamante-Ilione triangle endows the meeting of Idamante and Ilione with immediate interest besides providing significance for the announcement by Idamante that his father is alive. Idamante frees the Trojans and declares his love to Ilione (I, 2). A chorus praises Ilione for cementing peace between the Greeks and the Trojans as thoroughly as Helen had interrupted it (I, 3). Electre reproaches Idamante for favoring the Trojans (I, 4), and events take a new turn with Arbas's revelation that Idoménée has perished at sea (I, 5). Electre is troubled because Idamante can now tempt his "Trojan slave" with offers of the throne, while she, the daughter of a king, is rejected. Inevitably, she swears vengeance (I, 6).

Idoménée does not remain dead, however, since he and his warriors reconvene after the storm on a beach strewn with wreckage. The Greeks have been rescued by Neptune, and Idoménée divulges his vow to sacrifice the first human he sees (II, 1-3). Idamante offers Idoménée refuge without recognizing him as his father. He tells him of his father's death at sea, but Idoménée knows that he is speaking with his son. He discloses his identity and bids his son not to follow him, an order which upsets uninformed Idamante (II, 4). Electre calls upon Vénus to aid her in her plan for revenge (II, 5-6), and the goddess summons La Jalousie to turn Idoménée against his son (II, 7-8).

This complex intrigue is not simplified by Idoménée's suspicions that Idamante freed Ilione because he loves her (III, 1). Idoménée accuses Ilione of rejecting him, therefore, because she loves Idamante (III, 2), but the remembrance of his obligation to sacrifice his son restrains his jealousy (III, 3). Electre is happy to leave Crète in the company of Idamante (III, 4-6), but Proteus and a monster emerge from the sea to remind defiant Idoménée of his vow (III, 7-8). Idamante decides to challenge the monster, and Ilione attempts to dissuade him. They declare their mutual love finally, although Ilione feels obliged to explain to Idamante that his father is his rival (IV, 1-3). Idoménée beseeches Neptune to withdraw his demand for his son's life (IV, 4-5). The dilemma appears to dissolve into thin air when Idamante slays the monster (IV, 6-7).

This tragicomedy situation turns to tragedy in the last act when Electre asks Idamante whether his father has consented to his marriage with the Trojan princess, Ilione. He confirms Electre's suspicions, and she threatens vengeance and suicide in her despair (V, 1). Ilione and Idamante pledge their love to each other (IV, 2), and Idoménée arrives to unite them (IV, 3). Némésis then reminds them of Idoménée's pledge to Neptune. The throne is shattered (V, 4). Idoménée goes mad and kills his son but is kept from suicide by the onlookers (IV, 5) in a conclusion that offers neither a grand finale nor a final disposition of three of its four main characters.

BIBLIOGRAPHY: Lajarte I, 114-15; RGO X, 315-88.

L'Idylle sur la paix was first performed in the Orangerie of Sceaux in 1685 and in Paris later on during this same year. The poem was written by Jean Racine with a score by Jean-Baptiste Lully.* It was designed to celebrate the continuing peace established by the signing of the Treaty of Ratisbonne on 15 August 1684. When it was mounted at Sceaux, it was produced before the king and the members of the royal family, who were the guests of the marquis de Seignelay. This work has the distinction of being the first Palais-Royal* production not created by Lully* and Philippe Quinault.*

This idyll might be described as an anthem in 87 lines. It presented a chorus singing the praises of peace with a recitative sustaining the theme. While recounting the blessings of peace, the text develops a laudium of Louis XIV by attributing the happiness of his people to his might and sense of justice.

The *Mercure galant* for July 1685 gives a detailed account of the reception held by the marquis de Seignelay for Louis XIV in his sumptuous gardens laid out by Le Nôtre, and Louis Racine recalls in his *Mémoires sur la vie de Jean Racine* that the text for *L'Idylle sur la paix* was the first profane verse that his father had published since 1677. The unpublished records of the Opéra indicate that the work was revived in the summer and in November or December of 1689 at the Palais-Royal. It served as a companion piece to *Les Fêtes de l'Amour et de Bacchus** on these later dates.

BIBLIOGRAPHY: Xavier de Courville, *"L'Idylle sur la paix* chantée dans l'Orangerie de Sceaux," *Revue critique des idées et livres* XXVII (1920), 411-23; Lajarte I, 49-50; Jean Racine, *Oeuvres,* 10 vols., ed. Paul Mesnard (Paris: Hachette, 1886) V, 79-89; RGO III, 1-72; R.H.F. Scott, *Jean-Baptiste Lully* (London: Peter Owen, 1973), 108-9.

Iphigénie en Tauride is a lyric tragedy in five acts and a prologue for which Henri Desmarets* and André Campra* did the music, and Joseph-François Duchy de Vancy* and Antoine Danchet* wrote the libretto. Since Desmarets was in Spain at the time of the production of this work, Campra undertook certain revisions in the score and created the prologue. The first run of *Iphigénie en Tauride* lasted for 33 performances between 6 May and 15 July 1704. Its first revival extended for 48 billings from 12 March to 25 August 1711. After a short run from 15 January to 31 January 1719, it was brought back to the stage again on 16 December 1734 and on 15 February 1735, but it was dropped after 3 May 1735, apparently because it returned only 611 *livres* to the box office. Its last series of performances at the Palais-Royal* did not take place until 1762, when it was presented 19 times between 16 November and 31 December and carried over into 1763 with another 4 representations on 2, 4, 7, and 9 January. It brought in as much as 3,965 *livres* 10 *sous* during its final run on 26 November 1762. Since it was in the repertory for nearly 60 years, a number of celebrated artistes appeared in it. The title-rôle was created by Mlle Desmatins,* and her successors in this part included Mlles Journet* (1711), Le Maure (1734), and Chevalier (1762). Oreste was sung by Thévenard* (1704), de Chassé (1734), and L'Arrivée (1762). Mlle Erremans appeared as Diane in 1734, a rôle created by Mlle Maupin* at the premiere (for Mlle Maure and M. L'Arrivée, see eighteenth-century volume). The list of dancers that executed the ballet in it is almost endless and includes such famous artistes as Mlles Subligny,* Camargo, Allard, and Vestris as well as Balon,* Dumoulin,* Dupré, d'Auberval, Vestris, and Lany (for Allard, Camargo, and Vestris, see eighteenth-century volume). Contemporary notices applauded Mlle Journet's* rendering of the heroine in 1719.

The prologue of *Iphigénie en Tauride* opens with the leader of the games in Délos directing his compatriots in singing the praises of Apollon. His purpose in promoting these public festivities is to defeat La Haine and La Discorde, who have brought strife to the world once again.

The opera opens with Iphigénie bewailing Agamemnon's cruelty, and she is filled with terror on account of a dream wherein she saw her parents giving her a knife to slay Oreste. She is also alarmed over the company of Greeks to be sacrificed by Thoas, king of Tauride, although Ismène assures her that her countrymen will be saved because Thoas loves the Greek princess with them (I, 1). Yet since Iphigénie is known in Tauride as the high priestess of Diane, Thoas orders her to sacrifice the captive Greeks to foil the prophesy of his death (I, 2-3). Thoas agrees subsequently to spare his prisoners if Electre accepts his love (I, 4-6).

The attention shifts to Oreste in the second act, when he and Pilade decide to rescue themselves by stealing the image and altar of Diane (II, 1), but Electre says she is going to make their deaths inevitable (II, 2). Oreste loses his senses under the stress of his predicament (II, 3). A symphony announces the coming of Diane and her retinue (II, 3). Thoas threatens to slay Oreste and the other Greeks on account of Electre's obduracy (III, 1). He relents at the last moment and liberates Oreste, Pilade, and the other Greeks. Oreste and Pilade disdain his condescending pardon (III, 2), however, and they accuse Electre of accepting Thoas's love because he had freed them. Disheartened, Electre decides to tell Thoas of her love for Pilade so that all misunderstandings may be made superfluous through their deaths (III, 3). A troubled Thoas orders Oreste led away before the celebration by the Scythes (III, 4-5). L'Océan warns Thoas that he is living his last day, and the Scythian king decides in panic to slay his prisoners, especially Electre (III, 6).

The fourth act returns to grieving Iphigénie, who urges Oreste to flee before she is obliged to slay him; he refuses lest the other Greeks be punished for his flight (IV, 1-2). Thoas is still resolved to sacrifice Electre and the Greeks to Diane (IV, 3), but Iphigénie is resourceful enough to delay their deaths (IV, 4). She urges Oreste to flee and discloses her identity to him; he reveals that he is her brother. They resolve to flee Tauride after nightfall (V, 1). Iphigénie hears the sound of arms (V, 2), and Electre explains that one of the Greeks has betrayed Oreste to Thoas, who has assaulted the Greeks (V, 3). Diane proclaims the death of Thoas and the marriage of Pilade to Electre. Freed, Oreste suggests that the Greeks embark for home (V, 4).

BIBLIOGRAPHY: Lajarte I, 102-3; RGO VIII, 233-90.

Isis was the fifth work created by Jean-Baptiste Lully* and Philippe Quinault* in collaboration. It was presented as a lyric tragedy in five acts and a prologue and was mounted initially before the king at Saint-Germain en Laye on 5 January 1677 before being performed at the Palais-Royal* in August of the same year.

The prologue of *Isis* is more like a classic frieze than a production for the stage as far as the characters and their disposition upon the scene are concerned: the setting is laid in the palace of La Renommée with Rumeurs and Bruits dancing attendance upon the goddess. La Renommée is visited by Apollon with his retinue of Muses and Arts Libéraux and by Neptune with his suite of Tritons. The members of these companies from the sky and the sea are equipped with violins, lutes, and trumpets. All that can possibly remain is the inevitable laudium of Louis XIV. This paean is immediately forthcoming as early as the first couplet of the prologue, where La Renommée speaks of "the glory and triumphant valor of the greatest of heroes." When Neptune sings of the recent exploits of this conqueror on the high seas, he is alluding to the recent French victory at Messina over the Dutch and Spanish navies, and there can be no doubt that the allusion is to Louis XIV. Yet the powerful leader of Apollon and Neptune is Jupiter, and the association of Louis XIV and Jupiter is of the greatest significance here: it will lead to Quinault's disgrace and dismissal from Court.

The libretto of *Isis* was the most simple and yet the most spectacular text that Quinault had created until now: the action is limited to the explanation and description of Junon's wrathful persecution of the heroine. The Jupiter-Isis-Hierax triangle is established in the first act, and Junon descends to earth to investigate her husband's errant ways in the second act. The remainder of the representation is devoted principally to Isis's punishments and suffering. After her lonely imprisonment under the eyes of Argus, the tortures arranged for her by relentless Furies include freezing in the icy north, burning before the flaming forges of the Chalybes, and witnessing the fearsome plottings of the Parques. Strangely enough, then, Isis is a pathetic rather than a dramatic figure, since Junon's anger falls upon her as a sudden, unavoidable, and crushing blow. The drama is provided by the constant struggle between Junon and Jupiter, who are reconciled only at the conclusion of the work that terminates in the apotheosis of Isis.

The selection of the Junon-Jupiter-Isis involvement as the subject for an opera was an especially happy choice, since it involved a goddess, a god, and a nymph. Any spectacle, no matter how extravagant or how imaginative it might be, was justifiable on the grounds that the actions and the destinies of its characters were not restricted to the human sphere. Isis could be carried to the far corners of the earth, to the regions beneath the sea, and into the far reaches of the sky because the power to transport her was divine and without limits. The cast involved in the production of *Isis* was large, varied, and spread abroad; it included choirs and bands of nymphs, sprites, shepherds, satyrs, the peoples of the north, spirits and demons of the underworld, and Egyptians. The apocalyptic scene of the Parques alone presented La Guerre and her Furies, Famine, L'Incendie, L'Inondation, and Les Maladies of all descriptions. The trio of the Parques in III, 7 was one of the highlights of Lully's music for *Isis,* and it was also another subordinate character, Pan, who executed the other memorable passage in this composition, "Ah! Quel dommage," in III, 6.

The striking feature of *Isis* is the frequency and diversity of its spectacles, which are so logically a part of its intrigue. Jupiter's relatively numerous entrances and exits are as natural as they are divine, and Junon's intrusions are as easily understood as her displeasure with her husband. In a word, the stage machinery is kept subservient to the action instead of being subordinated to the needs of the poet seeking a sensational event to enliven his action or a convenient device to resolve his too complicated situation. And this coordinated coming and going of gods and goddesses results in extra opportunities for the choreographer. There are *divertissements**in *Isis* at the close of the first and second acts, within the third and fourth acts, and at the conclusion of the work, which ends in the usual grand ballet. The scope and the variety of the settings, ballets, and *divertissements* entailed a large and skilled orchestra, and it is not surprising that *Isis* came to be known as "the musicians' opera."

Yet *Isis* was not a popular composition in the usual sense of the word. After its premiere at Court and its first run at the Palais-Royal, it was performed only once during the remaining 38 years of Louis XIV's reign, on 14 February 1704, according to the unpublished records of the Opéra. It was revived in 1717-18 and in 1732-33, but there is still a question regarding its lack of performances between 1677 and 1715. The answer is to be found in the wrath of Mme de Montespan. When *Isis* was being mounted in 1677, the king was shifting his favor from his mistress of the previous ten years to the attractive Mme de Ludres. He lavished presents upon his new favorite, and the affair became common knowledge at Court. Mme de Montespan was furious and did everything in her power to humiliate her. She managed finally to have her rival banished from Court. Enemies of Quinault as well as the usual gossipers pointed to allusions to the situation in his opera. The text abounded in passages that might apply to the king and his two mistresses, of course, and the Junoesque wrath of Mme de Montespan was directed finally at Quinault. Lully was obliged to dismiss his librettist, and Quinault followed Mme de Ludres into exile. And *Isis* was never returned to the stage during Louis XIV's lifetime except for the representation of 14 February 1704.

The principal rôles in *Isis* were created by Mlle Aubry* (*Io, Isis*), Mlle Saint-Christophe (*Junon*), Beaumavielle* (*Jupiter*). Godonesche sang *Pan,* and Beauchamp,* Pécourt,* Magny, and Boutteville danced in the ballet.

BIBLIOGRAPHY: DDO I, 588-89; Etienne Gros, *Philippe Quinault* (Paris: Champion, 1926), 534-35, 607-14; Lajarte I, 31-32; Lionel de La Laurencie, *Lully* (Paris: Alcan, 1919), 50-52, 154; Jean-Baptiste Lully, *Isis . . . reconstituée et réduite pour piano et chant par Théodore de Lajarte* (Paris: T. Michaëlis, 188?); Sonn I, 646-47.

Issé is a heroic pastoral in three acts and a prologue for which André-Cardinal Destouches* composed the musical score and Houdard de La Motte* wrote the libretto. It is considered to be Destouches's best score, although he was only 25 years old at the time of its premiere on 17 December 1697. *Issé* made such an impression on Louis XIV that he gave

Destouches a purse of 200 *louis* after its first staging at the Trianon. The work was taken to Court for the festivities honoring the marriage of the duke de Bourgogne, to whom *Issé* was dedicated. The artistes staged it initially at the Palais-Royal* on 30 December 1697, and it remained in the repertory for nearly 60 years. It was revived in five acts on 14 October 1708 and ran until the end of the year. A dozen years later, on 7 September 1719, *Issé* was heard again at the Palais-Royal, and on this occasion it inspired a parody entitled *Les Amours de Vincennes* performed by the Italians on 19 September 1719. It was billed at the Palais-Royal for runs beginning on 19 November 1733 and 14 November 1741; it was mounted for a single time in 1756 on 23 December. These many revivals resulted in nearly every prominent performer appearing in *Issé*. The title-rôle alone was sung by Mlles Le Rochois,* Desmatins,* Antier,* Le Maure, and Chevalier. Apollon was created by Du Mesny,* and Jélyotte started his career in it as a shepherd and Le Sommeil. Mlles Subligny,* Camargo, Dallemand, and Carville danced in it with Dun, Lany, and Dupré (for Le Maure, Dupré, Dun, Camargo, and Lany, see eighteenth-century volume).

The prologue is allegorical: the Garden of the Hesperides represents Abundance; the dragon who blocks its entrance stands for War, which suspends Commerce and closes the way to Abundance for the peoples that it divides. Finally, Hercules, who renders the Garden accessible to everybody by the defeat of the dragon, is the exact image of the king. The prologue begins with one of the Hesperides rejoicing that the dragon is preventing people from entering the garden, but Hercules enters to slay the dragon and make the fruits of the garden available to all the world. As the librettist explains, the prologue is essentially a laudium of Louis XIV.

The exposition of *Issé* establishes a triangle composed of Apollon-Issé-Hylas and offers Pan's fruitless suit for Doris's hand as a subplot. The intrigue starts with Apollon disguised as a simple shepherd and complaining of Issé's indifference toward him (I, 1-2). The heroine also refuses to lose her heart and liberty to Hylas (I, 3-4), who arranges a symphony and festival to accompany his declaration of love to Issé (I, 5). Still disguised as humble Philémon, Apollon reveals his love to Issé in vain (I, 6-7), and Doris rejects Pan (I, 8) before the act closes with a pastoral chorus singing the praises of youth and love (I, 9).

The last two acts of the work are concerned with the questions of whether Apollon will win the hand of Issé and whether Doris will yield to Pan's passionate entreaties. The resolution of the former problem begins with an optimistic Apollon waiting for Issé to consult the oracle of the oaks (II, 1) and Hylas regretting the apparent success of his rival (II, 2). Issé confirms her love for another man, and Hylas falls into deep despair (II, 3). Issé becomes alarmed at the oracle's pronouncement that Apollon loves her (II, 5). The Doris-Pan situation is settled when the former accepts her suitor's proposal (II, 4). A chorus sings the praises of Issé's beauty (II, 6).

Issé vows to remain faithful to Philémon (III, 1), and Le Sommeil enters to ease her fears of Apollon (III, 2). Issé awakens her to inform Hylas that she prefers Philémon to Apollon, and he despairs once more (III, 3). The Doris-Pan involvement is restored suddenly with Doris reproaching Pan for courting Temire and Pan accusing Doris of a flirtation with Iphis. They then decide that they are too fickle to remain constant to each other (III, 4-6). Issé protests to Philémon that she will never abandon him for Apollon, who proves his true identity to her by raising a magnificent palace before her eyes (III, 7). The peoples of the earth convene to sing the praises of the happy couple (III, 8).

BIBLIOGRAPHY: André-Cardinal Destouches, *Issé, pastorale héroique . . . reconstituée et réduite pour piano et chant par Hector Salomon* (Paris: T. Michaëlis, 188?); Lajarte I, 86-87; Antoine Houdard de La Motte, *Oeuvres complètes*, 11 vols. (Genève: Slatkin Reprints, 1970) II, 255-68; RGO VI, 172-228; IX, 333-86.

J

Le Jaloux trompé was a new title for Campra's* short score played in 1703 and 1717 under the title of *La Sérénade vénitienne.** This work was billed under its second title for the first time on 18 January 1731.

Jason is a lyric tragedy in five acts and a prologue for which Colasse* composed the score, and for which Jean-Baptiste Rousseau* wrote the libretto. It had its premiere at the Palais-Royal* on 6 January 1696. Its first and only run lasted until 5 February 1696 according to the unpublished *Le Journal de l'Opéra,* and its lack of success matched the more or less unenthusiastic receptions accorded to the other new lyric tragedies of this time such as *Céphale et Procris** and *Circé.**

The continuing war of the League of Augsburg had a certain influence upon the prologue of *Jason,* which presents La Paix asserting that peace is to be found only within Louis XIV's fortunate kingdom. The French monarch's enemies insist upon continuing the struggle because their obdurate fury will not permit them to understand that generous Louis is offering them calm and quietude in place of hideous war. As in *Théagène et Chariclée* and other compositions of this decade, then, *Jason* opens with a prologue that presents the contrast between the peace prevailing within France and the war that rages outside her borders despite the wisdom and magnanimity of Louis XIV. The opera itself is based upon the legend of the Golden Fleece and includes such well-known episodes as Jason breaking the wild bulls to the plow and subduing the warriors sprung from the earth. The love interest is furnished by the triangle formed of Médée's fierce passion for Jason and the latter's love for unfortunate Hipsipile.

BIBLIOGRAPHY: Lajarte I, 65; RGO V, 233-90; Sonn I, 661.

Jeu de paume is the French word used to designate an indoor tennis court. This game was so popular at one time that facilities were built in nearly every quarter of Paris to facilitate playing it in all weather and seasons, and a separate guild was formed to make balls and other equipment. The sport lost much of its popularity in the early years of the seventeenth century because the activities of the upper strata of society tended to center more and more around the king as time progressed, and it was not a pastime available to the less privileged members of the lower classes. These spacious structures fell idle, therefore, and theatrical groups saw in them ideal accommodations for their productions. The tennis court in the rue Mazarine became the home of Molière's* troupe after the death of this comedian, for example, and the court in the rue des Fossés-Saint-Germain-des-Prés was occupied by the newly founded Comédie-Française in 1689.

The Opéra occupied two of these structures in the early years of its history before transferring to the Palais-Royal* under Lully's* license. Their first theatre was located on the present site of numbers 42 and 44 rue Mazarine. It dated back to the reign of Henri IV and had been one of the more popular locations for playing tennis at this time. The letters patent assigning this facility to Perrin* and the members of his syndicate are dated 28 June 1669, and 1669 is inscribed on the curtain of the present Opéra to commemorate this grant. Perrin took possession of the building on 8 October 1670 after restoring it to suit his purposes. The first work mounted here was *Pomone.**

The structure in the rue Mazarine was abandoned temporarily, and its theatrical fixtures were ordered to be sold at auction when Lully obtained from Perrin the monopoly for giving operatic performances. Lully moved into the Bel-Air* tennis court at 13 rue de Vaugirard located near the Luxembourg palace. The new Royal Academy of Music that replaced Perrin's Academy of Opera performed its first work in these new quarters on 15 November 1672. It was entitled *Les Fêtes de l'Amour et de Bacchus.** After Lully left this theatre to stage *Alceste** at the Palais-Royal,* it was put to various uses, and, among other things, it became a fashionable riding academy between 1715 and 1730.

Four compositions in all had been produced at these first two homes of official French opera: *Pomone* and *Les Peines et les plaisirs de l'amour** in the *jeu de paume de la Bouteille** in the rue Mazarine; *Les Fêtes de l'Amour et de Bacchus** and *Cadmus et Hermione** in the *jeu de paume du Bel-Air* in the rue de Vaugirard.

Jolly, Antoine-François (b. 25 December 1672, Paris; d. 30 July 1753, Paris), librettist and playwright, made a late appearance on the theatrical scene in Paris: he was 36 years old when his first dramatic effort entitled *Méléagre** was produced at the Palais-Royal* in 1709; he was age 46 when his comedy *L'Ecole des amants* had its premiere at the Comédie-Française. Jolly also contributed a pair of comedies to the Théâtre-Italien, but his lack of success in the theatre led him to more scholarly endeavors, and he edited the works of Pierre and Thomas Corneille,* Molière,* and Racine. He then turned away from the stage completely to undertake paleological works at the urging of chancellor Séguier, and he brought to light a large quantity of manuscripts pertaining to the births, marriages, and deaths in noble families of France. Cardinal de Fleury named Jolly royal censor in 1737. *Méléagre* was his only libretto for the Royal Academy of Music.

BIBLIOGRAPHY: Bio univ XXI, 115-16; Brenner 80; GDHS I, 590; Lajarte I, 110-11.

Journet, Françoise (b. 16?, Lyon; d. 1722, Paris), singer, supported herself as a maid in the household of a wealthy merchant in Lyons until he went bankrupt. After she lost her position as a domestic, she married but learned almost immediately that her groom already had a wife, and she left him in 1687 for a career at the opera house in Lyons. She did so well in this theatre that she was invited to Paris. At first she met with a cool reception at the Opéra in the capital, and she was tempted to give up the stage, but her friends urged her not to be discouraged. She heeded their advice, and, with the support of Mlles Desmatins* and Le Rochois,* she went on to become one of the most applauded stars at the Opéra during the eighteenth century.

Mlle Journet made her debut at the Palais-Royal* on 26 December 1703 in Lully's *Armide,* * and she remained with the Royal Academy of Music until her deteriorating health obliged her to retire from the theatre in 1720. She appeared in eleven revivals during this 1703-20 interval, but none of these performances equalled her interpretation of the heroine's part in *Iphigénie en Tauride* * by Desmarets* and Campra* on 12 March 1711, when she may be said to have put this composition back into the repertory because it had aroused so little enthusiasm initially on 6 May 1704. The other ten revivals in which she performed were almost exclusively by Lully* and Campra: *Alcide* * and *Bellérophon* * in 1705, *Roland* * in 1706, *Tancrède* * and *Thésée* * in 1707, *Proserpine* * in 1715, *Alceste* * in 1716, *Vénus et Adonis* in 1717, and Lully's *Amadis* * and *Acis et Galathée* * in 1718.

Mlle Journet created rôles in 18 operas, opera ballets, and other assorted works during her association with the Royal Academy of Music. The first three new parts that she presented to the public were Progne in *Philomèle* * on 20 October 1705, Alcyone in *Alcyone* * on 18 February 1706, and Clytemnestre in *Cassandre* * on 22 June 1706. Then, after doing secondary characters in *Polyxène et Pyrrhus* * and *Bradamante* * on 21 October 1706 and 2 May 1707, respectively, she did another 14 rôles in 13 premieres on the following dates:

Rôle	Opera	Premiere
Iphise	*Les Festes vénitiennes* *	17 June 1710
Ziriane	*Manto la fée* *	29 January 1711
Ilione	*Idoménée*	12 January 1712
Callirhoë	*Callirhoë* *	27 December 1712

Médée	*Médée et Jason*	24 April 1713
La Haine and L'Estime	*Les Amours déguisés**	22 August 1713
Isménie	*Télèphe**	28 November 1713
Caliste	*Les Fêtes de Thalie**	19 August 1714
Calypso	*Télémaque**	29 November 1714
Bélise	*Les Fêtes de l'été*	12 June 1716
Camille	*Camille, reine des Volsques*	9 November 1717
Oenone	*Le Jugement de Paris*	14 June 1718
Artémise	*Les Plaisirs de la campagne*	10 August 1719

The singer is reputed to have acquired a fortune of nearly 900,000 *livres* during the speculation of the Regency period, but she is also said to have lost her fortune after the Law bubble burst as a result of monetary inflation in France.

BIBLIOGRAPHY: André Campra, *Les Fêtes vénitiennes,* ed. Alexandre Guilmant (Paris: Théodore Michaëlis, n.d.), 8; DDO 204; EFC 133-34; Fétis Suppl. II, 132-33; Arsène Houssaye, *Princesses de comédie et déesses d'opéra* (Paris: Henri Plon, 1860), 432-33; Lajarte I, 24-28, 34-38, 46-49, 52-55, 60-61, 106-9, 111-12, 114-15, 116-23, 125-28, 130; TdT 795; L. Travenol and Jacques Durey de Noinville, *Histoire du théâtre de l'Opéra en France,* 2 vols. (Paris: Joseph Barbou, 1753) II, 66.

L

La Barre, Michel de (b. 1675, Paris; d. 1743, Paris), composer, was a well-known flutist in his day, but his two compositions for the Royal Academy of Music did not meet with much success. His *Le Triomphe des Arts** was never revived after its first run in 1700, and *La Vénitienne** did not fare too well after its premiere on 26 May 1705. Not much else is known about him except that he wrote several duets and trios for his instrument.

BIBLIOGRAPHY: Fétis V, 146; GDHS II, 1; Lajarte I, 162.

La Coste, composer, whose first name and vital statistics are unknown, appeared upon the musical scene in Paris in 1693, when he started his career as a member of the chorus at the Palais-Royal.* He wrote an impressive number of scores for the Royal Academy of Music at the Opéra, and Francine selected him to be director of his orchestra. The works that he did for representation at Versailles and in Paris include *Aricie** in 1697, *Philomèle** in 1705, *Bradamante** in 1707, *Créuse** in 1712, *Télégone* in 1725, *Orion* in 1728, and *Biblis* in 1732 (for La Coste's post-1715 works, see eighteenth-century volume).

BIBLIOGRAPHY: Fétis V, 157; Lajarte I, 74.

Lafont, Joseph de (b. 1686, Paris; d. 1725, Passy), librettist, seemed destined for the practice of law until he became acquainted with La Thorillère and turned his attention to the theatre to write scripts for his new actor friend. His comedy *Danaé ou Jupiter Crispin* (1707) was staged when he was only 21 years old, and his initial contribution to the Palais-Royal* entitled *Les Festes de Thalie** was a sensation in 1714 by reason of being the first lyric comedy mounted by the Royal Academy of Music since its creation. He wrote two new entrées for this work to support its popularity: *La Critique des Festes de Thalie* (1714) and *La Provençale* (1722). His other three compositions performed by the Opéra were *Hypermnestre* in 1716, *Les Amours de Protée* in 1720, and the posthumously staged *Orion* in 1728 (for Lafont's post-1715 works, see eighteenth-century volume).

Lafont also worked on texts with Lesage and d'Orneval for the Opéra-Comique that was developing from the Saint-Germain and Saint-Laurent fairs at this time. The poet was a willing and constant worker, but his career was cut short at age 39 by his excessive dissipation, which undermined his health and reduced him to poverty despite his success as a writer.

BIBLIOGRAPHY: Bio univ XXII, 491; Brenner 83; CG 182-85; GDHS II, 17-18; Lajarte I, 162; H. C. Lancaster, *Sunset: A History of Parisian Drama in the Last Years of Louis XIV, 1701-1715* (Baltimore: The Johns Hopkins Press, 1945), 274-83; TdT 599.

La Fontaine, Jean de (b. July 1621, Château-Thierry; d. 13 April 1695, Paris), famous poet, studied at Reims and Paris before returning home and eventually marrying in 1647. Later he decided to leave his native town and wife to enter the household of the king's minister, Fouquet, and to make his way in more aristocratic circles, but his patron's disgrace induced him to quit Vaux for Limousin. Yet it was not long before he journeyed back to Paris to become an almost permanent house guest of the duchess de Bouillon before publishing *Psyché* in 1669; he lived subsequently with Mme de Sablière and M. d'Hervart while continuing to write. He created pieces for the legitimate theatre, but it was his *Contes* and especially his *Fables* that won him enduring and widespread fame. His lyric tragedy *Astrée** of 1692 was his only contribution to the Royal Academy of Music; Colasse* did its music. The libretto of this work has been published on many occasions, but its score remains in manuscript form among the holdings of the Bibliothèque Nationale in Paris.

BIBLIOGRAPHY: Ferdinand Gohin, *La Fontaine, études et recherches* (Paris: Garnier, 1937); André Hallays, *Jean de La Fontaine* (Paris: Perrin, 1922); J. de La Fontaine, *Oeuvres,* ed. Henri Régnier, 12 vols. (Paris: Hachette, 1883-92) VII, 507-53; Lajarte I, 59; Gustave Michaut, *La Fontaine*, 2 vols. (Paris: Hachette, 1913-14); idem, "Travaux récents sur La Fontaine," *RHL* XXIII (1916), 63-106; Louis Roche, *La Vie de Jean de La Fontaine* (Paris: Plon-Nourrit, 1913); Philip A. Wadsworth, *Young La Fontaine* (New York: AMS Press, 1952).

Lafontaine, Mlle de (b. 1655 ?; d. 1738?), ballerina, made her theatrical debut at the Opéra in Lully's* *Le Triomphe de l'Amour** in 1681, and this fact won for her the distinction of being the first professional danseuse of modern times. Her appearance in Lully's eleventh composition for the Royal Academy of Music was by no means the only aspect of her activity on the stage because she went on to lead the corps de ballet in other works by Lully and his contemporaries:

Ballet	Premiere
Persée*	17 April 1682
Phaéton	6 January 1683
Amadis	18 January 1684
Le Temple de la Paix*	October 1685
Armide*	15 February 1686
Didon*	11 September 1693

After her retirement, Mlle de Lafontaine regretted her profane career in the theatre and entered a convent to do penance for her past.

BIBLIOGRAPHY: ACD 281; ACPM 548; CODB 310; EDB 202; Lajarte I, 39-44, 46-47, 51-52, 61-62; TdT 799; Walter Terry, *Star Performance* (New York: Doubleday, 1954), 17-20; L. Travenol and Jacques Durey de Noinville, *Histoire du théâtre de l'Opéra en France*, 2 vols. (Paris: Joseph Barbou, 1753) II, 70.

La Grange, Joseph de Chancel de (b. 1 January 1676, Périgueux; d. 27 December 1758, Périgueux), dramatist and librettist, was known among his contemporaries as La Grange-Chancel. He, his two younger brothers, and a sister were taken to Bordeaux by their mother after the death of their father, and the three boys went to the Jesuit school in this city. Joseph proved to have an amazing memory, and he learned Latin quickly, besides devouring Corneille's tragedies and La Calprenède's romances. It is reported that he wrote poetry at the age of eight and then went on to compose a comedy the following year.

La Grange-Chancel was a child prodigy, therefore, and news of his precocity traveled from Bordeaux to Versailles. He was invited to Court, and he impressed the princess de Conti so favorably that she made him a page in her household. When he was sixteen, he dedicated his first tragedy to her, and the princess was so astonished at this accomplishment that she asked Racine to appraise it. The author of *Phèdre* was amazed in his turn after he had read this maiden effort, *Adherbal*. It was given later with great success under the title of *Jugurtha* at Paris on 8 January 1694, when its author was still in his teens. His protectress obtained a position for him with the duchess d'Orléans, mother of the future regent, and the youth continued to dedicate his talents to the service of the theatre. He contributed three librettos to the Royal Academy of Music in addition to his legitimate tragedies for the Comédie-Française: *Médus, roi des Mèdes** in 1702, *Cassandre** in 1706, and *Ariane* in 1717 (for *Ariane,* see eighteenth-century volume).

He could have passed the remainder of his life in writing plays and enjoying the security of his position, but he had the unfortunate idea of publishing his *Philippiques.* In this collection of libelous odes, he made all sorts of charges against the regent, the son of his former protectress. This tasteless attack upon the royal family did him no good, and he fled to Avignon. He did not escape his pursuers, however, and he was banished to the Sainte Marguerite islands. He was able to bribe his guards ultimately, and he made his way to Spain and Holland. He was about to take refuge in Poland when he received word that the regent was dead. He returned to France, therefore, and he settled down eventually in his paternal castle at Antoniat to work on the history of his native Périgord.

BIBLIOGRAPHY: Bio univ XXII, 521-23; Brenner 83; CG 158-64; GDHS II, 20-23; Lajarte I, 94-95, 108, 127, 162; H. C. Lancaster, *A History of French Dramatic Literature in the*

Seventeenth Century, 9 vols. (Baltimore: The Johns Hopkins Press, 1940) IV, 367-84; idem, *Sunset: A History of Parisian Drama in the Last Years of Louis XIV, 1701-1715* (Baltimore: The Johns Hopkins Press, 1945), 37-51.

Laguerre, Elisabeth-Claude Jacquet de (b. 1669, Paris; d. 27 June 1729, Paris), composer, became interested in music early in life and charmed Louis XIV at Court with a performance at the harpsichord when she was only fifteen. Mme de Montespan retained her in her entourage for three or four years after her first sensational programs for royalty. She married Marin de Laguerre, who was organist at the churches of Saint-Séverin and Saint-Gervais. They had a son who astonished his audiences by his ability at the harpsichord when he was only ten.

Mme de Laguerre was known for her capacity to improvise on the organ as well as on the harpsichord at a time when this gift was rare. In addition to *Cèphale et Procris,** produced at the Palais-Royal* in 1694, she wrote three books of cantatas for a single voice, some sonatas, and a collection of other pieces for the harpsichord. She executed a Te Deum at the Louvre in 1721 for the recovery of the young king. She was buried in Saint-Eustache in Paris.

BIBLIOGRAPHY: Fétis, V, 166-67; Lajarte I, 62, 74.

Lalande, Michel-Richard de (b. 15 December 1657, Paris; d. 18 June 1726, Versailles), composer, was the 15th child of an impoverished tailor, but he rose to become superintendent of music for Louis XIV and Louis XV. He started his long career as a choirboy in the church of Saint-Germain-l'Auxerrois, where he learned music under Chaperon. He proved to be an energetic and able student; he taught himself the violin, bass viol, and harpsichord. He lost his voice eventually at the age of 15, but one of his brothers-in-law provided him with food and shelter during this crucial period of his life. He applied in vain for a position as violinist with Lully,* and it is reported that this rejection prompted him to smash his violin in anger. He turned to the organ and managed to earn some money playing this instrument at four Parisian churches. When Louis XIV heard him at the organ of Saint-Germain, the king was impressed by his skill, but it was decided that Lalande was too young to take on the vacant position of royal organist, although Lully now seemed to smile upon him. The count de Noailles selected him to teach music to his daughters at this time, however, and Louis XIV suggested that he give lessons to the duchess d'Orléans as well. Lalande spent three years at Versailles, and the king was quick to reward him for his dedication and his talents. He made him master of the music of his chamber, and he named him to be one of the four superintendents of the royal chapel. In 1684 Lalande married Anne Rebel, one of the most accomplished vocalists at Versailles, and the king gave the bride a dowry and paid for the wedding. The couple had two daughters, and they inherited their mother's fine voice. Louis XIV was charmed by them and was sincerely saddened by their deaths in 1711, a year when personal tragedy also struck the monarch. He was most generous with Lalande after this blow, and he gave him a pension of 6,000 *livres* for his work with the Opéra as well as making him the only master of music for the royal chapel, a post held previously by four musicians. After the death of Louis XIV, Lalande lost his wife in 1722, and he asked Louis XV to replace him with Campra,* Bernier, or Gervais.* The Crown honored his request and awarded him an additional pension of 3,000 *livres* just before he wed his second wife, Mlle de Cury, in 1723. Three years later Lalande was dead. He had composed 60 motets for the Versailles chapel, and these pieces were published in 20 sumptuous volumes at royal expense. He did the music for Molière's *Mélicerte* and for the ballet *Les Eléments* (for *Les Eléments,* see eighteenth-century volume). Titon du Tillet reports that he had worked on several operas but had refused to publish them.

BIBLIOGRAPHY: Bio univ XXII, 603; Fétis V, 170-71; Lajarte I, 162-63; TdT 612-16.

La Motte, Antoine Houdard de (b. 17 January 1672, Paris; d. 26 December 1731, Paris), librettist, began his formal education with the Jesuits and went on to study law before renouncing the bar in favor of the theatre. His first work was a dismal failure at the Théâtre-Italien, and the mortified playwright decided to enter the Trappist order. After he had recovered from the blow to his pride, the refreshed author left the monastery to turn to the Royal Academy of Music with his successful *L'Europe galante** of 1697 for which Campra* had written a score between motets and Te Deums at Notre-Dame in Paris. La Motte tried his hand at odes, fables, and other sorts of nontheatrical poetry after his success at the Palais-Royal,* and he composed essays inspired by the famous dispute over the relative merits of ancient and modern authors, but he never lost interest in the theatre after the triumph of *L'Europe galante.* He contributed scripts to the Comédie-Française and to the duchess du Maine's private theatre at Sceaux; he favored the Royal Academy of Music with nearly a dozen librettos between 1699 and 1709. His first two lyric tragedies billed at the Palais-Royal were mounted in 1699: *Amadis de Grèce** and *Marthésie, reine des Amazones.** His other titles in this same genre included *Canente** in 1700, *Omphale** in 1701, *Alcyone** in 1706, and *Sémélé** in 1709. *Scanderberg* (for *Scanderberg,* see eighteenth-century volume) was staged posthumously in 1735. His ballets were entitled *Le Triomphe de Arts** in 1700, *Le Carnaval et la Folie** in 1704, and *La Vénitienne** in 1705. La Motte was elected to Thomas Corneille's* chair in the French Academy on 8 February 1710.

BIBLIOGRAPHY: Bio univ XX, 46-47; CG 158-64; Lajarte I, 161-62; H. C. Lancaster, *Sunset: A History of Parisian Drama in the Last Years of Louis XIV, 1701-1715* (Baltimore: The Johns Hopkins Press, 1945), 273-74; idem, *French Tragedy in the Time of Louis XV and Voltaire, 1715-1774* (Baltimore: The Johns Hopkins Press, 1950), 70-75, 78-94; TdT 655-57.

La Roque, Antoine de (b. 1672, Marseille; d. 3 October 1744, Paris) traveled to the Orient before joining the royal guard and losing a leg in the battle of Malplaquet in 1709. He returned to civilian life with a pension shortly after this misfortune. He became interested almost immediately in the Royal Academy of Music and joined forces with Pellegrin* to do librettos for *Médée et Jason** in 1713 and *Théonoé* (see eighteenth-century volume for *Théonoé*) in 1715. La Roque never wrote anything else for the Palais-Royal,* because he assumed the direction of the *Mercure de France* in 1721 and continued to guide the fortunes of this monthly periodical for three hundred twenty-one issues. He was buried in the church of Saint-Sulpice.

BIBLIOGRAPHY: Bio univ XXVI, 441-42; Brenner, 86; GDHS II, 45; Lajarte I, 117, 124, 163.

La Serre, Jean-Louis-Ignace de, sieur de l'Anglade (b. 1662, Cahors; d. 30 September 1756, Paris), librettist, was born of a noble family in Normandy, but he came to Paris early in life to enjoy himself among the gayer social circles of the time. An inveterate gambler, he is said to have lost 25,000 *livres* at the gaming tables of the capital. He turned to literature to recoup his fortune, and he wrote poetry and fiction as well as plays for the Comédie-Française and librettos for the Opéra. The latter theatre billed his *Polyxène et Pyrrhus** in 1706, but its lack of success did not deter him from submitting *Diomède** and *Polydore* to the same company in 1710 and 1720, respectively. His *Pirithous,* staged in 1723, is sometimes attributed to Seguineau, son of the secretary of a counselor of the Grand' Chambre, but no one disputes his authorship of the poem for *Pyrame et Thisbé* of 1726. He was encouraged by the applause inspired by his adaptation of Ovid's story of this pair of well-known lovers, and he went on to collaborate on another four titles posted at the Opéra during the next dozen years: *Tarsis et Julie* of 1728, *Pastorale héroïque* of 1730, *Scanderberg* of 1735, and *Nitétis* of 1741 (for La Serre's post-1715 works, see eighteenth-century volume). He was a close friend of Mlle de Lussan, who describes him under the name of Calemane in her novel, *La Comtesse de Gondez.*

BIBLIOGRAPHY: *Catalogue général des livres imprimés de la Bibliothèque Nationale*, 228 vols. (Paris: Imprimerie Nationale, 1926) LXXXIX, 600; CDHS II, 1039; GE XXIX, 1076-77; GDHS II, 46; Lajarte I, 109, 111, 130-31, 133-34, 141-42, 145, 148, 163, 177-78, 193.

Le Rochois, Marthe (b. 1658, Caen; d. 20 October 1728, Paris), singer, was left an orphan as a small child, but her uncle provided for her and arranged for her to receive a solid education. She was accepted into the Royal Academy of Music at age 19 in 1677, and she impressed Lully* so favorably that he did not hesitate to offer her a contract as a vocalist in his company.

Mlle Le Rochois made her debut in 1680 as Aréthuse in *Proserpine** by Lully. Her voice and stage presence won her stardom immediately, and she went on to play the female leads in Lully's *Persée** (1682), *Amadis** (1684), *Roland** (1685), *Armide** (1686), and *Acis et Galathée** (1686). She also appeared in his *Thésée* in 1688, *Atys** in 1689, and *Cadmus et Hermione** in 1690. After Lully's death she sang Polyxène in Colasse's* *Achille et Polyxène** (1687) and Thétis in the same composer's *Thétis et Pélée** (1689). Her other important parts included the female leads in Gillot de Sainctonge's* *Didon** (1693), Charpentier's* *Médée** (1693), Marais's* *Ariadne et Bacchus** (1696), and Desmarets's* *Vénus et Adonis** (1697). Success did not alter Mlle Le Rochois's personality, and her relationships with the members of the troupe and the successive directors of the Academy improved with the passage of time despite quarrels of various sorts that disturbed the regular conduct of affairs at the Palais-Royal.* In fact, it was as early as the production of *Armide** in 1686 that Le Rochois reached the peak of her career, although this work did not exert its maximum influence on theatregoers until Louis XIV approved it in a burst of regal enthusiasm.

The singer had been active for nearly two decades at the Royal Academy of Music by the time that *Vénus et Adonis** was produced in 1697, and she retired after appearing in *L'Europe galante,** staged initially on 24 October 1697, and after singing the title-rôle of *Issé,** given for the first time on 17 December 1697. When she withdrew from the theatre, she divided her time between her Paris residence and her summer cottage in Sartrouville-sur-Seine. She suffered greatly from her physical condition in her last years and was buried in the church of Saint-Eustache in Paris.

BIBLIOGRAPHY: AEM VIII, 658; Ellen Creathorne Clayton, *Queens of Song* (1865; reprint ed., Freeport, N.Y.: Books for Libraries Press, 1972), 43-46; EC II, 120-24; EFC 131-32; Fétis VII, 282; GE XXII, 74-75; Arsène Houssaye, *Princesses de Comédie et déesses d'opéra* (Paris: Henri Plon, 1860), 439-41; Lajarte I, 36-37, 42-43, 46-49, 53-54, 56, 61-62, 66-67, 85-86; TdT 790-95; Thurner 9-10; L. Travenol and Jacques Durey de Noinville, *Histoire de Théâtre de l'Opéra en France*, 2 vols. (Paris: Joseph Barbou, 1753) II, 58-65.

Lestang, sometimes written L'Estang, was the family name of a trio of dancers who distinguished themselves by their performances for the Royal Academy of Music during the reign of Louis XIV. Louis, the eldest of the group, seems to have made his debut on the stage of the Palais-Royal* with Beauchamp* in Lully's* *Cadmus et Hermione** during April 1673. He and Pécourt* danced together and came to enjoy the reputation of being among the most gifted artistes of their time. The elder Lestang is remembered as having appeared in:

Ballet	Date
Alceste*	19 January 1674
Thésée*	11 January 1675
Atys*	10 January 1676
Bellérophon*	31 January 1679
Proserpine*	3 February 1680

Le Triomphe de l'Amour *   21 January 1681

Amadis *   18 January 1684

Later, in 1685, Lestang danced in *Le Temple de la Paix* * at Fontainebleau, and, on 23 August 1688 he was cast in *Orontée* with his sister Geneviève for the production of this same work before the Court at Chantilly. He did very little composing, but it is asserted that he choreographed the first and fourth acts of *Achille et Polyxène* (1687). As an administrator he directed the dancing school incorporated into the Royal Academy of Music and Dance. He retired on a generous pension of 300 *livres*.

BIBLIOGRAPHY: EDS VI, 1430-41; Lajarte I, 22-26, 29, 34-39, 46; Marian Hannah Winter, *The Pre-Romantic Ballet* (New York: Dance Horizons, 1975), 69, 108; WT 13.

Lestang cadet, dancer, or the younger Estang, danced with his brother Louis in *Proserpine* * at Saint-Germain en Laye and Paris in 1680. Also, he represented Apollon in *Le Triomphe de l'Amour,* * and in 1681 he was cast in Molière's *Le Bourgeois Gentilhomme.* He appeared subsequently in *Didon* * in 1693, *Les Saisons* * in 1695, and in *Marthésie* * in 1699 at Fontainebleau and Paris.

BIBLIOGRAPHY: EDS VI, 1431; Lajarte I, 36-39, 61-62, 64-65. 89.

Lestang, Geneviève, ballerina, entered the Royal Academy of Music in 1683 and retired from it on a pension in 1689. She is remembered only for her interpretation of two minor rôles in *Orontée* produced in honor of the prince de Condé at Chantilly on 23 August 1688. Her brother, Louis, also appeared on this program.

BIBLIOGRAPHY: EDS VI, 1431.

Lully, Jean-Baptiste (b. 29 November 1632, Florence; d. 22 March 1687, Paris), composer, was baptized Giovanni Battista Lulli. He left his native city to come to Paris at the age of 12, and he passed the remainder of his life in France while adopting the French form of his name for reasons of convenience. He became a citizen of France in 1661.

Lully was brought to Paris because Mlle de Montpensier was looking for someone with whom she might practice her conversational Italian. Lully was already interested in music, and he played the violin in the orchestra maintained by his protectress, but his ambition to rise in social circles induced him to join the royal household during the time of the Fronde. The budding musician was not long in attracting the attention of the young monarch, and he was cast in no fewer than five parts in *Le Ballet de la nuit* as early as 23 February 1653. He was named "composer of instrumental music" for Louis XIV at this time on account of his skill with the violin, and his growing friendship with the king was strengthened by his organization at Court of a new group of musicians designated as the "Petits Violons."

But Lully was only too aware that he was amusing rather than impressing the king, and he set about to master the intricacies of composition. He then wrote a long underworld score for *Psyché** and did the music for *La Galanterie du temps* (1656). His name began to appear in contemporary gazettes, and he became the leading musical figure at Court with the music he created for three ballets by Benserade*: *L'Amour malade* (1657), *Alcidiane* (1658), and *La Raillerie* (1659). In 1660 he wrote a motet for the marriage of the king, and the following year he was appointed superintendent of music for the nation. His only rival now was Francesco Cavalli, whom Mazarin had invited to Paris, but Lully was equal to the challenge offered by his compatriot. He decided to become the champion of French music and to deprecate the ornate Italian style upon which he had been raised.

Lully's popularity was at its peak at this time, and he set about to fortify his position by becoming a French subject and by marrying Lambert's daughter. These maneuvers proved effective, and the delighted king rewarded him with a handsome income besides naming him music master for the royal family. Three daughters and three sons were born of the union between Jean-Baptiste Lully and Madeleine Lambert.

After his marriage, Lully wrote the music for nearly a dozen compositions by Molière* including such masterpieces as *Le Bourgeois Gentilhomme* (1670) and *La Comtesse d'Escarbagnas* (1671). In this 1664-71 interval, he also found time to do scores for five ballets by Benserade. His most immediately rewarding composition at this time was the motet *Plaude, laetare, Gallia,* which he did to honor the dauphin's baptism on 7 April 1668. Two weeks later the king issued a decree empowering Lully to indicate his sons as heirs to his royal positions.

Lully was wealthy, respected and powerful at Court, popular, and applauded by the public at this point in his life. His music for *Monsieur de Pourceaugnac* was better known than Molière's text; the symphonies and the pastoral music he had done for the *intermèdes* of *Amants magnifiques* were hailed as the great achievements of the decade. His airs for *Psyché* were hummed or even sung throughout the capital, and it seemed as though Lully and his music had reached into every corner of the kingdom. His career seemed complete, but events were conspiring to bring him new and even greater opportunites for power, wealth, and applause.

The monopoly for offering operatic productions to the public had been given to Perrin,* but this musical project favored by the government had foundered despite its popularity and financial success. Perrin had sold portions of his license to promoters who were less than honest, and he was thrown into jail. Upset by the chaos surrounding the plan to foster a national musical theatre, Colbert urged Lully to intervene. He moved quickly and bought Perrin's rights. Louis XIV approved the purchase. Letters patent were issued in Lully's favor on 13 March 1672, and the Royal

Academy of Music was created. Lully signed a lease for a theatre and coordinated passages from his previous works to prepare for his first bill in November 1672. He was offered the Palais-Royal* for his productions after the death of Molière, and the king gave him the sole right to use more than two voices and six violins. Lully's enemies were increasing in numbers, but the jealousy of his disgruntled competitors did not prevent him from posting at least one new title at the Palais-Royal nearly every year between 1672 and 1686.

These last years in Lully's career were a time of even greater glory for the Florentine, although a few unpleasant episodes took place in this interval. He had been distracted by a bitter quarrel that he had with Henri Guichard,* who had tried in vain to obtain a license to perform opera. Accusations and counteraccusations were made, and Guichard was charged finally with attempted murder. Lully's collaboration with Quinault* had also been disrupted when Mme de Montespan sought his librettist's disgrace with persistent vindictiveness because she found unpleasant allusions to herself in *Isis.** A third aggravation arose when his secretary started to claim credit for the more effective musical passages in *Isis,* and the composer had to discharge him from his service. These unwelcome incidents, coupled with the strain of maintaining the prestige of the Royal Academy of Music and his lax manner of living, undermined Lully's health, and he fell ill for the second time in his public career.

While theatregoers and his enemies were speculating about Lully's future, the king maintained his firm support of his superintendent of music in every way. The monarch's position became quite evident when he agreed to become the godfather of Lully's oldest son. He went so far as to direct that the ceremony be held at Fontainebleau in 1677, the year of the premiere of *Isis.** The composer had his own Te Deum sung on this occasion, and this work was repeated the following year for the marriage of Mlle d'Orléans. His *De Profundis* (1683) and his publication of a series of motets in 1684 also helped Lully from losing his favored position with Louis XIV, despite the king's increasing piety and Mme de Maintenon's growing influence upon royal attitudes. In any event, Lully never lost his powerful position as the king's foremost musician, and his last works were successful enough to silence any opposition to his rôle at Court or in Paris.

But fate was about to stop smiling upon the composer in a most unpredictable way and at a most unexpected moment. It began with an illness of the king, who recovered his health to the manifest joy of his subjects. Lully decided to share in the public rejoicing by having his Te Deum sung. He organized more than 150 singers and instrumentalists for the ceremony in the church of the Feuillants in the rue Saint-Honoré on 8 January 1687. It was a magnificent gesture of gratitude, but it cost Lully his life. In the process of conducting the performance, he struck his foot with the cane that he was using as a baton. The shock of the blow caused an abcess to form. His physicians recommended amputation. Lully hesitated. Gangrene set in and spread. The composer died on 22 March 1687 at the age of 55. His body was laid to rest in the Petits-Pères church.

Lully had started his musical career in France as a violinist in the household of Mlle de Montpensier, and at his death he was literally the master of French music. He had brooked no rivalry, but he did not avoid any of the numerous duties of his office. No form of musical entertainment could be offered in any theatre of the realm without his approval, and these powers, along with his constant activity and obvious talents as an administrator and artist, led Mme de Sévigné to exclaim one day in all sincerity, "I do not believe that there is any other music this side of heaven except Lully's."

He wrote the scores for the following dramatic works performed at the Royal Academy of Music: *Les Fêtes de l'Amour et de Bacchus** (Paris, 1672), *Cadmus et Hermione** (Paris, 1673), *Alceste** (Paris, 1674), *Thésée** (Saint-Germain en Laye and Paris, 1675), *Le Carnaval** (the Tuileries, 1668; Palais-Royal, 1675), *Atys** (Saint-Germain en Laye, 1675; Paris, 1677), *Isis** (Saint-Germain en Laye and Paris, 1677), *Psyché** (Paris, 1678), *Bellérophon** (Paris, 1679), *Proserpine** (Saint-Germain en Laye and Paris, 1680), *Le Triomphe de l'Amour** (Saint-Germain en Laye and Paris, 1681), *Persée** (Paris, 1682), *Phaéton** (Versailles and Paris, 1683), *Amadis** (Paris, 1684), *Roland** (Versailles and Paris, 1685), *L'Eglogue de Versailles** (Versailles and Paris, 1685), *Le Temple de la paix** (Fontainebleau and Paris, 1685), *Armide** (Paris, 1686), *Acis et Galathée** (château d'Anet and Paris, 1686), and *Achille et Polyxéne** (Paris, 1687).

Recently, Lully's music has found its way back to the stage of the Opéra because revivals of Molière's plays at the Garnier palace have entailed the concomitant use of his scores: *Le Sicilien* (1892), *Monsieur de Pourceaugnac* (1892, 1900), and *Le Bourgeois Gentilhomme* (1899, 1900, 1903, 1905). The production of Lully's *Le Triomphe de l'Amour** on 6 January 1925 resulted in this work enjoying a run of a dozen performances at the Garnier palace. Finally, compositions inspired by pre-1789 topics invariably used Lully's music in their scores. These included *Mademoiselle de Nantes* (1915), *Carême prenant* (1916), *L'Impromptu de Neuilly* (1929) (see twentieth-century volume for these works).

BIBLIOGRAPHY:David C. Cabeen and Jules Brody, *A Critical Bibliography of French Literature*, vol. 3, *The Seventeenth Century*, ed. Nathan Edelman (Syracuse, New York: Syracuse University Press, 1961), nos. 1608-1634; B. Champigneulle, "L'influence de Lully hors de la France," *Revue musicale* XXII (1946), 26-35; Jürgen Eppelsheim, *Das Orchester in den Werken Jean-Baptiste Lullys* (Tutzing: H. Schneider, 1961); Lionel de La Laurencie, *Lully* (Paris: F. Alcan, 1919); Jean L. Le Cerf de La Viéville, *Comparison de la musique italienne et de la musique française*, 3 vols. (Brussels: Foppens, 1704-1706); Jean-Baptiste Lully, *Oeuvres complètes*, ed. Henry Prunières, 10 vols. (Paris: Editions de la Revue musicale, 1931-38); L. Maurice-Amour, "Benserade, Michel Lambert et Lulli," *Cahiers de l'association internationale des études françaises* IX (1957), 53-76; Arthur Pougin, "L'orchestre de Lully," *Le Ménestrel* LXII (1896), 44-45, 59-60, 67-68, 76, 83-84, 91-92, 99-100; idem, "Les origines de l'opéra français: Cambert et Lully," *Revue d'art dramatique* XXI (1891), 129-55; Henry Prunières, *Lully: biographie critique* (Paris: Laurnes, n.d.); Ralph Henry Forster Scott, *Jean-Baptiste Lully* (London: Owen, 1973); Walter Storz, *Der Aufbau der Tänze in den Opern und Balletts Lully's, vom musikalischen Standpunkte aus betrachtet* (Göttingen: Inaug. Diss., 1928); Théodore Valensi, *Louis XIV et Lully* (Nice: Les E.L.F., 1951).

Lully, Jean-Louis (b. 24 September 1667, Paris; d. 28 December 1688, Paris), composer, was baptized in the church of Saint-Roch near the Palais-Royal* and his father's home. The third son of Jean-Baptiste Lully,* he was destined to inherit his famous father's positions at Court and in the Royal Academy of Music, but he died prematurely at age 21. He was buried in the church of the Petits-Pères. *Zéphire et Flore** was his only contribution to French operatic music; his brother, Louis Lully,* helped him with its score.

BIBLIOGRAPHY: Fétis V, 373; Lajarte I, 56-57.

Lully, Louis (b. 4 August 1664, Paris; d. 1 April 1734, Paris), composer, was the eldest son of Jean-Baptiste Lully,* whose genius he was not fortunate enough to inherit. He became superintendent and composer of the royal chamber after the death of his brother Jean-Louis Lully* in 1688, however, and he collaborated with him on the score of *Zéphire et Flore.** In 1690 his *Orphée** was mounted with little success at the Palais-Royal.* Three years later, on 3 February 1693, the Royal Academy of Music staged *Alcide,** which he had done with Marais.* His last work for the Opéra was *Le Ballet des saisons** of 1695. Louis Lully was still alive in 1703 because it was in the fall of this year that he executed a cantata entitled *Le Triomphe de la Raison* before the king at Fontainebleau. But the circumstances of his death are unknown. In 1916 Louis Lully's music was used in *Carême prenant* (for *Carême prenant*, see twentieth-century volume).

BIBLIOGRAPHY: Fétis V, 373; Lajarte I, 56-58, 60, 64-65, 76.

M

Manto la fée was billed as an opera, but its five acts and prologue recall the style of the lyric tragedy. Its score was written by Batistin* and its libretto was by Menesson. It had its premiere at the Palais-Royal* on 29 January 1711, but it had no billings after 5 February 1711. It was never revived. Mlle Desjardins sang Manto opposite Thévenard* as Licarcis. Mlle Journet* and Dun appeared as Ziriane and Merlin.

The prologue presents Merlin locked up to please his mistress but sallying forth to aid a friend who has fallen victim to love. The device of using the same character in the prologue and in the tragedy itself was not new, but the importance of Merlin in both parts of the production is striking.

Manto and Ismène emerge from a cloud at the opening of the opera to explain their special mission in Syria: Licarcis was dispatched to Syria by Manto to defend this country, but he has forgotten Manto and fallen in love with princess Ziriane (I, 1). This simple triangle is complicated by Ziriane's admission that she is in love with the stranger called Iphis (I, 2), who reveals to her that her father is preparing her marriage to Licarcis now that peace has been restored (I, 3). A chorus and a ballet celebrate the impending union of the hero and the princess (I, 4), but these festivities are interrupted by a storm, and Manto discloses that she has taken Ziriane prisoner (I, 5). Licarcis realizes that his failure to win Ziriane's hand will prevent his enjoying the prestigious rank to which he aspires (I, 6).

After this exposition establishing the quadrilateral love situation involving Manto, Licarcis, Ziriane, and Iphis, Merlin tells the story of how Manto lost her son at birth to kidnapers. The magician then gives to Iphis a ring that renders its wearer invisible (II, 1-2). Iphis meets Manto in his search for his beloved Ziriane, and she admits her love for him (II, 3-5). Licarcis tries to speak with Manto, but she flees, and Ismène informs him that Manto is no longer interested in him (II, 6). But Ziriane tells Licarcis to return to his first love, Manto (III, 1). Angered, Ziriane accuses Iphis of not loving her, but they are reconciled immediately (III, 2-3). Manto now laments her love for Iphis (III, 4), whom Licarcis tries to slay (III, 5). Manto evokes her spirits to protect Iphis, but they are buffeted about by winds that Merlin summons to protect Ziriane and to carry off vengeful Licarcis (III, 6). Ziriane declares her love for Iphis again (IV, 1), and

L'Amour rewards her constancy with a ballet, symphony, and chorus (IV, 2). Yet the princess is still alarmed for Iphis's life, although he is determined to protect her by giving Merlin's ring to her (IV, 3). Suddenly, Manto appears. She tries to stab Ziriane. Iphis prevents her, but Manto is able to snatch the ring from him. She recognizes it as the ring taken from her when her son was kidnaped. She resolves to throw Ziriane into prison and to save Iphis's life (IV, 5).

The last act is set before an arch laden with the trophies and statues of the warriors who have attempted to slay the dragon guarding the enchanted castle. The action here begins with Manto trying to find Iphis, who has just slain Licarcis (V, 1). She begins to question her feelings for him (V, 2) and tries to prevent him from attacking the dragon. He refuses to heed her warning and slays the dragon. Manto recognizes her son at last (V, 3). Merlin divulges that he kidnaped Iphis to train him as a hero. Ziriane and Iphis declare their love to each other (V, 4), and the grand finale celebrates love and glory (V, 5).

BIBLIOGRAPHY: Lajarte I, 114; RGO X, 253-314.

Marais, Marin (b. 31 March 1656, Paris; d. 15 August 1728, Paris), composer, was a celebrated violist remembered for having added a seventh string to the viol besides having developed a system that made possible the placing of greater tension on the three larger strings of this instrument. He began his musical career as a child in the choir of Sainte-Chapelle in Paris and became a pupil of Hotteman and Sainte-Colombe. Lully* also gave him some lessons in the art of dramatic composition. He entered the company of the Music of the King's Chamber in 1685 as a viol soloist and retained this position until 1725. He contributed four titles to the repertory of the Royal Academy of Music: *Alcide** in 1693; *Ariadne et Bacchus** in 1696; *Alcyone** in 1706; and *Sémélé** in 1709. He also published five volumes of pieces for the viol, the last of which appeared in 1725. Marais retired to a house in the rue Oursine a few years before his death to cultivate flowers in his private garden and to give private lessons during the week.

BIBLIOGRAPHY: James R. Anthony, *French Baroque Music from Beaujoyeulx to Rameau* (New York: W. W. Norton, 1974), 119-20, 329-33, 408 note 13; M. Barthélemy, "Les opéras de Marin Marais," *Revue belge de musicologie* VII (1953), 136-46; Fétis V, 438; Lajarte I, 60-61, 66, 76-77, 106-7, 110; TdT 624-27.

Marthésie, reine des Amazones is a lyric tragedy in five acts and a prologue. André-Cardinal Destouches* did the musical score, and Houdard de La Motte* wrote the libretto. The prologue and all five acts were performed initially on 11 October 1699 at Fontainebleau; the prologue and first act were presented at the royal suppers of 17 October 1699 and 25 October 1699. Selections from Destouches's work were sung the same month during the royal sojourn at Fontainebleau, and the entire work was mounted there once more on 11 November 1699. It had its Paris premiere on 9 November

1699 according to Lajarte and La Vallière, but the unpublished log of the Opéra dates its first representation at the Palais-Royal as 29 November. The tragedy was never revived. Mlles Maupin* (Cybèle), Desmatins* (Marthésie), and Moreau (Talestris) appeared in it with Hardouin* (Jupiter), Dun (Mars), and Thévenard* (Argapise). The ballet included Mlles Subligny,* Du Fort, Desplaces, and Dangeville opposite Pécourt,* Balon,* Lestang,* and Du Fort.

Cibèle dominates the prologue of *Marthésie* with her command to all divinities to celebrate Louis XIV's victories on land and on sea. Her exhortation is heeded, and Jupiter, Neptune, and Junon as well as a host of lesser gods join in the festivities.

The intrigue is built upon the fact that Marthésie and Talestris are captives of Argapise, who is determined to continue his war against the Amazons although he has already taken their queen and a member of her family prisoner. The two Amazons confess their love for their captor (I, 1), and Argapise prepares for battle with a sacrifice to the sun (I, 2), despite Talestris's warning that Mars is on the side of the Amazons and although she reveals her love to him (I, 3). Clouds cover the sacrifice to the sun, but Argapise rejects this omen (I, 4).

The second act opens with the surprising revelation that Marthésie is free after her forces have defeated Argapise and his Scythian army. Yet she is still the prisoner of her love for her foe, who is now her captive (II, 1) and in love with her (II, 2). She liberates her beloved and his warriors, but the Scythians flee before the approach of Mars (II, 3), who declares his love to an indifferent Marthésie (II, 4). Talestris laments her love for unresponsive Argapise, who still pursues the hand of uninterested Marthésie (III, 1-3). After Talestris and Argapise conclude their complaints about their unrequited loves (III, 4-5), Mars prevents the former from committing suicide and swears to slay both Marthésie and Argapise if the queen rejects his love (III, 6-8).

Marthésie dismisses Argapise once more but prevents him from killing himself while persuading Mars to spare him (IV, 1-2), and her triumphs are celebrated by the Greeks, Persians, Indians, and Egyptians at her Court (IV, 4). But Mars threatens again to slay Argapise (IV, 5), and she declares her love to the latter king (IV, 6). She entreats the darkness to protect her lover and herself (V, 1), and L'Hymen enters to celebrate her impending marriage (V, 2). Mars slays Argapise (V, 3-4), however, and Marthésie kills herself in grief to leave Mars alone and in despair (V, 5-6).

BIBLIOGRAPHY: Lajarte I, 89; Antoine Houdard de La Motte, *Oeuvres complètes*, 11 vols. (Genève: Slatkine Reprints, 1970) II, 156-70; RGO VI, 413-68.

Matho, Jean-Baptiste (b. 1660, Brittany; d. 1746, Versailles), composer, came from a Breton village to Versailles to enter the service of the royal chapel as a tenor in 1684. He became tutor in music to the children in the

royal family during his stay at Court. His sole contribution to the Royal Academy of Music was the score for *Arion** in 1714. He was 54 years old when this lyric tragedy was mounted at the Palais-Royal.*
BIBLIOGRAPHY: Fétis VI, 23; Lajarte I, 164.

Maupin, Mlle (b. 1673, Paris; d. 1707, Paris), singer, is remembered as the heroine of Théophile Gautier's novel by the same name, and any account of her life reads more like a romance than a biography.

Soon after Mlle Maupin's marriage, her husband left her in Paris to shift for herself while he went off to the provinces to tend to his new position with the government. Interested in athletics, the young bride took fencing lessons with a certain M. Seranne, and it was not long before she was using the foils with greater skill than her teacher, with whom she eloped. The couple assumed the name of d'Aubigny and earned some money by singing in the opera house at Bordeaux, where Mlle Maupin's lesbian tendencies overcame her, and she developed a passion for a young girl in the audience. The girl's friends placed her in a convent for her own protection, but Mlle Maupin was not to be outwitted. She applied for entrance into the same convent as a novice and was accepted. When one of the members of the community died, Mlle Maupin dug her up and put the corpse into the girl's bed. The singer then set fire to the latter's bedroom and abducted her while the flames burned the remains of the dead nun beyond recognition. Mlle Maupin, alias Mme d'Aubigny, was apprehended and condemned to death by fire, but she managed to escape justice by fleeing to the north.

The fugitive financed her trip to Paris by singing in cabarets, and, once she was back in the capital, she applied for admission to the singing school affiliated with the Royal Academy of Music. A short time later, on 4 December 1690, she made her debut as Pallas in a revival of Lully's *Cadmus et Hermione** (1673). The public was pleased with her performance in this rôle, and spectators applauded her enthusiastically on subsequent programs until her name became familiar to French theatregoers everywhere. She appeared in revivals of other works by Lully throughout the course of her career, and she created more than a score of rôles at the 16 premieres in which she had a part:

Rôle	*Opera*	*Premiere*
Une Magicienne	*Didon**	11 September 1693
Cérès	*Les Saisons**	18 October 1695
Cybèle	*Marthésie, reine des Amazones**	9 November 1699
Nénus, Campaspe	*Le Triomphe des arts**	16 May 1700
L'Aurore, Nérine	*Canente**	4 November 1700

Vénus, Une Prêtresse de Flore	Hésione*	21 December 1700
La Nymphe de la Seine, Thétis	Aréthuse*	14 July 1701
Une Grâce, Céphise	Omphale*	10 November 1701
Médée	Médus, roi des Mèdes*	23 July 1702
Clorinde	Tancrède*	7 November 1702
Pénélope	Ulysse*	21 January 1703
L'Amour médecin	Les Muses*	28 October 1703
La Folie	Le Carnaval et la Folie*	3 January 1704
Diane	Iphigénie en Tauride*	6 May 1704
La Félicité, Thétys	Télémaque*	11 November 1704
Isabelle	La Vénitienne*	26 May 1705

While she was at the Opéra, her ability to fence along with her preferences for masculine rôles and dress inspired tales about her prowess, and it was repeated everywhere how she had outfought Dumenil* and had taken his snuffbox only to prove her identity as his assailant by returning it to him the next day. The bully baron de Servan is reported to have been another of her victims after this overbearing braggart had cast aspersions on the character of the danseuse Pérignon.

At the height of her prowess and popularity, Maupin left France to accept a profitable contract in Brussels, where her success continued unabated until the Elector of Bavaria persuaded her to leave Belgium by offering her a handsome pension of 40,000 *francs*. The singer resolved to go to Spain, however, because she felt that she would be accepted with greater enthusiasm in Madrid. She was disappointed and had to accept employment as the private maid to the countess Marino. Disillusioned, she controlled her feelings until she was overcome by the temptation to play a practical joke on her mistress and had to flee to Paris.

But Mlle Maupin found the situation changed in the French capital, where competition for the principal rôles at the Opéra had become keen. The public was more demanding, and her irregular conduct had taken its toll on her beauty and voice. She decided to retire, if her course of action might be termed a retirement at this point in her life, and she returned all the presents that she had received from her admirers. Her thoughts turned toward a more pious way of life, and she wrote to her husband about her new resolves. He returned to her as quickly as he had left her a score of years before.

BIBLIOGRAPHY: André Campra, *Tancrède*, ed. Arthur Pougin (Paris: Théodore Michaëlis, n.d.), 4-7; EC II, 177-80; Ellen Clayton, *Queens of Song* (1865; reprint ed., Freeport, N.Y.: Books for Libraries Press, 1972), 47-51; EFC 35-39; Marie Pierre Yves et Léon Escudier, *Vie et aventures des cantatrices célèbres* (Paris: E. Dentu, 1856), 95-104; Fétis VI, 36-37; GE XXIII, 422; Arsène Houssaye, *Princesses de comédie et déesses d'opéra* (Paris: Henri Plon, 1860), 175-82; P. Lacome, "Les Etoiles du passé: Mlle Maupin," *AM* 14 (11 November 1875) 357-58, 14 (2 December 1875), 381-82; Lajarte I, 61-62, 64-65, 89-95, 97-98, 100-104; TdT 795.

Médée is a lyric tragedy in five acts and a prologue with a musical score by Marc-Antoine Charpentier* and a libretto by Thomas Corneille.* It has been described as the most significant work produced at the Palais-Royal* in the years immediately after the death of Jean-Baptiste Lully.* Titon du Tillet designated it as a great success, but *Le Journal de l'Opéra* lists no revivals for this work which seems to have had its only run from its premiere on 4 December 1693 until *Céphale et Procris** was given its initial representation at the Palais-Royal on 15 March 1694. Since Charpentier wrote the score, the music was Italianate to some degree whereas Corneille's libretto was exactly what Lully-oriented audiences expected. Even its ballets and choruses of demons and furies recalled the supernatural elements of *Amadis** and *Armide.*

The prologue describes the power of triumphant Louis XIV, and it voices the usual sentiments found in the prologues to such works as *Didon,** produced in Paris during the war of the League of Augsburg.

Corneille starts his tragedy at the moment in the legend when Médée suspects for the first time that Jason might be in love with Créuse despite the latter's alleged love for Oronte and Jason's marital tie to her. Jason assures Médée that he loves only her, however, although he admits immediately to Arcas that it is Créuse whom he loves. The exposition of *Médée* is quite laden, therefore, since it must present the love interest provided by the complicated Médée-Jason-Créuse-Oronte involvement without diminishing the importance of the public issue lodged in the struggle between Corinthe and Thessalie. Unfortunately, the tempo of the second act does not increase appreciably over the pace of the action in the first act, and this indecision surrounding the drama continues into the third act, where Médée tells Oronte that Créuse prefers Jason but then allows herself to accept Jason's word that he loves her. The last two acts move rapidly after Médée's plan for total vengeance is reached. As might be expected in any work featuring Medea, the conclusion to *Médée* is drenched in blood: Créon slays Oronte and commits suicide; Médée activates the poison in Créuse's dress and kills her children by Jason. The curtain descends upon a holocaust because the violent heroine summons her demons to burn her palace before flying off on the back of a fiery dragon.

BIBLIOGRAPHY: Marc-Antoine Charpentier, *Médée* (Farnborough, England: Gregg Press, 1968); Lajarte I, 62; RGO IV, 345-420.

Médée et Jason is a lyric tragedy in five acts and a prologue with a musical score by Salomon* and a libretto by abbé Simon-Joseph de Pellegrin* and Antoine de La Roque. It was popular and its prologue appealed strongly to patriotic audiences already aroused by the victory of Denain in the war of the Spanish succession. It was mounted 30 times between its premiere on 24 April and 20 June 1713. It was then withdrawn for revisions and returned to the stage of the Palais-Royal* for another 17 showings between 17 October and 21 November 1713. It was subsequently revived in 1727 for a third run lasting from 29 April to 13 July. The unpublished log of the Opéra lists its final performance on 18 March 1749. Mlle Journet* created the rôle of Médée.

At the start of the prologue, L'Europe is decrying the havoc wrought by war when Apollon declares that La Victoire is once again with the French and their model king. The ills of the world have ended, therefore, and it is time for Les Plaisirs, Les Amours, and Les Jeux to hold the center of the stage. Melpomène can find no one equal to the hero "who reigns over us." This prologue, then, is in the pattern of Lully*-Quinault* prologues with its laudium of Louis XIV, its allusions to contemporary international affairs, and its reference to the forthcoming opera.

The opera itself opens with Jason regretting having left Médée and his children to marry Créuse, who reveals that she is not eager to marry Jason (I, 1-2). Créon thanks Jason for having defeated the Athenians (I, 3), and the citizens and soldiers of Corinth honor him in song and dance (I, 4). Créuse reveals the frightening dream she has had of a chariot descending from the clouds with Médée in it: Créon's palace burst into flames; she and Jason tried to escape in vain, and he was slain (II, 1). Médée appears suddenly with her retinue of demons and magicians in a spectacle matching Créuse's dream. Médée threatens to slay Jason (II, 2) if he resists her will (II, 3-4).

Jason laments having exposed Créuse to Médée's jealous wrath, but he is distracted by the appearance of a magnificent palace graced with Démons disguised as Amours, Nymphes, and Plaisirs. They form a chorus and ballet to celebrate the pleasures of love (III, 1-2). Médée rages at Jason's independent attitude and swears vengeance (III, 5). Créuse believes that she has lost Jason to Médée, and she accuses him of infidelity; he protests in vain against her injustice (IV, 2). Créon mourns the desolation of his land, and Jason blames himself for attracting Médée to Corinth. They resolve to take a stand against the sorceress (IV, 3). Médée is captured, but Jason asks Créon to pardon her (IV, 4). He exiles her, and asks the gods to reduce him and his throne to dust if Médée is in Corinth at sunrise (IV, 5). Médée threatens Créon with his own words (IV, 6-7). The sailors enter to celebrate their departure from Greece, but a storm arises, and Médée cannot leave (IV, 8).

The last act is devoted to the sorceress' fury. She tells Jason that she is leaving Corinth and asks for custody of their children. He refuses, and she demands to see them. He agrees (V, 1-5). When Jason confronts Créuse, he argues that Médée's departure is proof of his fidelity (V, 6). A chorus and a ballet celebrate this return to harmony, but the rejoicing is interrupted by Créon's appearance: he is torn by torment and goes mad. He mistakes Créuse for Médée and tries to kill her. Jason tries to help him, but Médée's evil demons intercede, and Créon's palace is consumed in flames (V, 7-9). Médée enters in her chariot to announce Créuse's death. She kills Jason's children before disappearing into the sky. Jason tries to kill himself, but the Athenians restrain him (V, 10).

BIBLIOGRAPHY: Lajarte I, 117; RGO X, 545-608.

Médus, roi des Mèdes is a lyric tragedy in five acts and a prologue with a libretto by La Grange-Chancel* and a musical score by François Bouvard.* Its first and only run at the Palais-Royal* lasted from its premiere on Sunday, 23 July to Friday, 8 September 1702. It was billed on 21 consecutive programs.

The prologue of *Médus* presents La Fortune refusing to abandon Louis XIV. La Fortune adds that the protagonist of the forthcoming production provides only "a slight idea of the French empire."

The exposition of the opera presents a situation wherein Thoas loves Thomiris, who loves Médus loved by Médée. This Racinian intrigue of unrequited love is based upon the fact that Médée has come to Anticyre disguised as Mérope to restore her son to his proper rank, but she has also fallen in love (I, 1-2). Thomiris asks Médée-Mérope to halt the fighting in the city and reveals that it is not Thoas whom she loves (I, 3). Thoas enters to announce that the enemy has triumphed (I, 4), but Médus snatches victory from the jaws of defeat (I, 5). The king gives him Thomiris's hand in marriage amidst a general celebration that moves Médée to anger (I, 6-7). Happy to wed Médus, Thomiris defends him against jealous Thoas's accusation that this unknown warrior is not worthy of her (II, 1-2). After the engaged couple declare their love for each other (II, 3), the king suggests that Médus disclose his origins and rank to silence Thoas (II, 4). Médus calls upon Minerve to help him because the revelation that Médée is his mother will prevent his marriage to Thomiris (II, 5). Minerve gives him a golden sceptre and tells him to identify himself as the son of Créon (II, 6).

The lines of the conflict are now clearly drawn, therefore, and the stage is set for the first act of overt violence. Médée entertains the idea of killing Médus when she hears that Créon is his father, but an instinct tells her to spare him (III, 1). Thoas seeks Médée's aid in stopping the Médus-Thomiris marriage, and she agrees. Their first plan is to kill the king. A troupe of conspirators attempts this assassination, but Médus throws Minerve's golden sceptre among them, and they turn upon themselves in frenzy. Médus then steps in to slay Thoas, who beseeches Diane to avenge his murder. The "dark daughters of the Styx" appear and burn the city (III, 2-4).

Thomiris surveys the desolation wrought in the rather long third act (IV, 1), and Médée evokes the shade of Thoas (IV, 2), who declares that only the sacrifice of the foreigners in Anticyre can appease Diane (IV, 3). Médée decides to reveal her love for Médus to him (V, 1). Since Médus must die by Diane's decree, the king and Thomiris offer themselves as victims in his stead, and Médée reveals her true identity. Médus discloses that he is her son. Realizing that her love is maternal, Médée gives her permission for the Médus-Thomiris wedding (V, 2-3). Le Soleil descends to form the empire of the Mèdes for Médus (V, 4).

Mlle Desmatins* was replaced in the rôle of Médée by Mlle Maupin* because the former artiste was ill at the time of the production of *Médus*. Curiously enough, Mlle Le Rochois* refused this part according to unpublished documents in the Opéra library because she did not wish to play a sorceress who lacked a wand, a handkerchief and even a fan. The male singers included Boutelou, Dun, Hardouin,* and Thévenard.* The ballet was headed by Mlles Dangeville and Subligny* accompanied by Balon,* Bouteville, and du Mirail.

BIBLIOGRAPHY: Lajarte I, 94-95; RGO VII, 345-90.

Méduse is a lyric tragedy in five acts and a prologue. Its musical score was the work of Charles-Hubert Gervais,* and its libretto was by the abbé Claude Boyer.* It had its premiere at the Palais-Royal* on 13 January 1697, and its first run may have extended into the middle of March of the same year. It was dropped permanently before 17 March 1697. *Le Journal de l'Opéra* does not mention a revival of *Méduse* after the premiere of *Vénus et Adonis** on this date.

The prologue of *Méduse* provides a measure of relief from other prologues composed during the last decade of the seventeenth century: it is brief and is made up of only 44 verses sung by four characters and a chorus. Yet it manages nevertheless to cling to the regular formula in other respects. It sings the praises of love and of peace; it alludes to the subject of the forthcoming tragedy. It offers a laudium of Louis XIV, who is depicted as a great warrior fighting only because his enemies insist upon attacking him.

The opening scenes of *Méduse* establish an unusual situation by presenting Persée in love with Pallas and Neptune in love with Méduse, who alternates between pursuing Persée and accepting Neptune. The addition of Isménie to the intrigue complicates matters further because she is loved by Persée. The constant jealousy and rivalry among all these divinities palls after two or three acts, and Méduse's recurrent fits of rage lose their impact through repetition by the time that she has managed to capture Persée and

Isménie (IV, 1). The last act was designed to be an exercise in horror, and it is set ominously before the cave of the Gorgonnes, but the tragedy ends with Isménie being returned from stone to her original human form and with Persée free to seek glory in other lands.

Specifically, the last act opens with Méduse's decision to eliminate her rival for Persée's love, while Persée and Isménie resolve to die to circumvent Méduse's cruel plans (V, 1-2). Jupiter intervenes to assure the lovers that Minerve will thwart Méduse's intentions (V, 3). The Gorgonnes announce that Minerve has destroyed Méduse's charm and beauty, and Persée reveals that Méduse has transformed Isménie into a rock (V, 4-5). Persée resolves to kill himself, but compassionate Minerve restores Isménie to her original living form (V, 6-7). The goddess then whisks the lovers away to safety and eternal happiness (V, 8-9).

BIBLIOGRAPHY: Lajarte I, 67; RGO V, 415-68.

Méléagre is a lyric tragedy in five acts and a prologue for which François-Antoine Jolly* wrote the libretto and Baptistin* created the score. It had its premiere at the Palais-Royal* on 24 May 1709, but it had to be dropped after 24 performances on 16 July 1709. Although it was never revived, its prologue was used in the production of the pastiche entitled *Le Ballet sans titre* on 28 May 1726.

The prologue presents L'Italie regretting that she is no longer the glory of the universe, a distinction now enjoyed by La France, whose king has transported the greatness of the Caesars to the banks of the Seine. The two nations defend the virtues of their native music, but Apollon suspends their debate and rules that it is up to La France to guarantee the triumph of harmony.

The opera itself begins with Atalante expressing her discouragement because she has fallen in love with Méléagre and is obliged at the same time to protect Althée's lands against a savage monster and furious Diane (I, 1-2). Méléagre is Althée's son, and he thanks Atalante for her aid to his mother, but he shocks her into silence by declaring his love to her (I, 3). Méléagre and Plexippe urge their warriors to sing the glory of the "charming queen" who is about to slay the monster (I, 4). Plexippe is Althée's brother, and he complains of his secret and unrequited love for Atalante. He refuses to ask Althée to intercede with Atalante for him because her son is his rival (I, 5).

After the exposition establishes the triangle of Plexippe in love with Atalante who loves and is loved by Méléagre, the intrigue continues with Althée beseeching implacable Diane to cease her persecution of her people. She trembles at the recollection of a dream in which a flame representing her son's life was extinguished (II, 1), and the priestess with a chorus of citizens offers prayers to Diane (II, 2). While Althée and her subjects seek peace (II, 3), Méléagre slays the monster (II, 4).

Méléagre now reveals to Plexippe that he loves Atalante, and he decides to win an admission of love from her or perish because he has already divulged his love to her (III, 1). Plexippe regrets that he has concealed his love from Atalante (III, 2), and she protests that she does not love Méléagre (III, 3). Atalante continues to suppress her love for Méléagre (III, 4), but she admits finally that she loves him and warns him that Plexippe is his ruthless rival (III, 5). The people gather to celebrate the return of peace to their land (III, 6-7), but Plexippe vows to slay Méléagre (III, 8).

The Plexippe-Méléagre rivalry does not last long enough to provide any meaningful suspense for the final acts of the opera. The fourth act begins with the distracting spectacle of outraged Diane calling up the flames of Hades and making the earth tremble on account of the death of the monster (IV, 1). It is then learned that Plexippe is dead because his ghost asks Althée to punish his murderer, Méléagre (IV, 2-3). Althée swoons upon learning that she must take revenge upon her own son (IV, 4), and energetic Diane orders the Fates to instill in her heart an overwhelming hatred of her beloved Méléagre for killing Plexippe (IV, 5-6). Atalante and Méléagre declare their mutual love, and a chorus sings the praise of victory and peace (V, 1-2). Even Diane is thwarted when Althée confesses and condemns the crime she was meant to commit. She approves the marriage of her son and Atalante when Méléagre is attacked suddenly by poison (V, 3). The Fates enter to prevent Althée from saving her son (V, 4). He dies (V, 5). Atalante resolves to kill herself as the curtain falls (V, 6), and Diane's revenge is complete.

BIBLIOGRAPHY: Lajarte I, 110-11; RGO X, 2-62.

Molière (b. January 1622, Paris; d. 10 February 1673, Paris), playwright, was baptized Jean-Baptiste Poquelin. He assumed the stage name of Molière after joining the *Illustre Théâtre* group in 1642 because he wished to spare his family the embarrassment of having a son in the theatre. This first venture on the boards was a financial failure, and Molière was thrown into debtors' prison after the troupe could not pay their bill for candles. Restored to liberty eventually, Molière toured the provinces as an actor-author before returning to Paris. His initial efforts in the capital won him the favor of royalty, and he became the object of Louis XIV's special interest. He was able to establish his own theatre, therefore, and the story of the rest of his life is largely the history of the works he created and produced.

Molière's activity at Court brought him into close contact with Lully, of course, and he wrote ballets that the Florentine used to good advantage. Just before his death, Molière contributed to Lully's *Les Fêtes de l'Amour et de Bacchus** of 1672. The composer's *Le Carnaval** of 1675 borrowed from the third act of *Le Bourgeois Gentilhomme* for its first and fifth entrées; it derived its third entrée from *Monsieur de Pourceaugnac*. A *divertissement** in Italian supposedly excerpted from *Le Carnaval*,* and with words by Molière, was mounted at the Opéra in 1722 with music by Lully. Also inspired in the eighteenth century by Molière was Sedaine's *Amphitryon* of 1788.

Closer to our time, *Le Bourgeois Gentilhomme* in unabridged form with all five acts was staged at the Opéra in collaboration with the Comédie-Française on 30 December 1816, 13 March 1817, 11 December 1826, 30 January 1840, 15 January 1845, and 9 January 1852. The first representation of this comedy-ballet at Garnier's theatre with the Comédie-Française took place on 18 March 1899. *Le Dépit amoureux* as well as *Le Bourgeois Gentilhomme* were billed at the Opéra in 1900; they were offered in connection with the troupe of the Comédie-Française after the latter company's theatre burned earlier this same year. *Les Femmes savantes, Tartuffe,* and *Le Malade imaginaire* were posted under similar conditions in 1900, but *Le Mariage forcé* was not done at the Opéra until 28 April 1917 and 10 November 1927. Only the first act of *Le Misanthrope* was scheduled on 17 January 1922, although *Monsieur de Pourceaugnac* and *Le Sicilien* had been produced as early as 19 May 1892 in their entirety and *Les Précieuses ridicules* had been on a program at the Opéra even earlier, on 27 December 1881. *La Jalousie du Barbouillé* was staged in 1886.

BIBLIOGRAPHY: Antoine Adam, *Histoire de la littérature française au XVIIᵉ siecle*, 5 vols. (Paris: Domat, 1948-56) III, 181-418; René Bray, *Molière, homme de théâtre* (Paris, 1954); Pierre Brisson, *Molière, sa vie dans ses oeuvres* (Paris: Gallimard, 1943); Lajarte I, 21, 28, 132, 361; H. C. Lancaster, *A History of French Dramatic Literature in the XVIIth Century*, 9 vols. (Baltimore: The Johns Hopkins Press, 1929-42); Molière, *Oeuvres complètes*, ed. Despois and Mesnard, 14 vols. (Paris: Hachette, 1873-1900); Georges Mongrédien, *La vie privée de Molière* (Paris: Hachette, 1950); Richard Oliver, "Molière's Contribution to the Lyric Stage," *MQ* XXXIII (1947), 350-64; Alfred Simon, *Molière par lui-même* (Paris: Editions du Seuil, 1957); SW 345-47, 349, 351-54, 356-57.

Montéclair, Michel Pignolet de (b. 1666, Chaumont en Bassigny; d. September 1737, Paris), composer, came from a noble but poor family. He started his career as a choirboy in the cathedral of Langres, where he studied under Jean-Baptiste Moreau. He was attached to several other churches later, but he gave up this sort of work to enter the service of the prince de Vaudémont. He journeyed to Italy as music master to the prince and had an opportunity to study at Rome.

Montéclair was back in Paris by 1700 but did not join the orchestra of the Royal Academy of Music until 1707. He is credited with being the first musician to play the counterbass at the Palais-Royal,* an instrument that replaced the seven-stringed grand viol. Montéclair retired on a pension on 1 July 1737, only two months before his death. He composed the scores for the opera-ballet *Les Festes de l'été* in 1716 and for the lyric tragedy *Jephté* in 1732 (for *Les Festes de l'été* and *Jephté*, see eighteenth-century volume). He left some music for the flute and bass as well as motets and sonatas for the violin. His works also include essays on various aspects of harmony that put him into conflict with Rameau (for Rameau, see eighteenth-century volume).

BIBLIOGRAPHY: CG 259-60; Fétis VI, 179-80; Lajarte I, 125-26, 150-52, 164; Paul-Marie Masson, *L'Opéra de Rameau* (Paris: Laurens, 1930), 37; TdT 696-97.

Monteverdi, Claudio (b. May 1567, Cremona; d. 29 November 1643, Venice), composer, studied under the famous musician Ingegneri and published a collection of motets at age 15 in 1582. He entered the service of Vincenzo Gonzaga, duke of Mantua, as a singer and viola player in 1590, and he accompanied the duke on his expedition against the Turks in Hungary (1595-96) and on his trip to Flanders (1599). When his patron asked him to produce a musical composition for the stage in the style of the works that were being presented in Florence, Monteverdi responded with *La Favola d'Orfeo,* produced on 22 February 1607. He followed this initial effort with his lost *Arianna* and *Il Ballo delle Ingrate* of 1608.

The production of these works along with the publication of his madrigals in 1603-5 and of his *Scherzi musicali* in 1607 won for Monteverdi the reputation of being the leading composer of modern music in his time. His enemies were numerous and eloquent, however, and the death of his patron in 1612 resulted in his losing his post. He returned to his native Cremona for a while, but he was soon appointed choir master at the church of San Marco in Venice. Here, on the Adriatic, he spent much of his time during the last 30 years of his life writing religious compositions. However, he also turned again to composing for the theatre, and his works in this genre helped Venice to become the center of operatic activity in Italy. His last and most celebrated opera was *L'Incoronazione di Poppea* of 1642.

The repertory of the Opéra has not been affected deeply by Monteverdi despite the importance of his works in the history of the lyric theatre. His music was used in *Les Virtuosi de Mazarin* of 6 January 1916, but the score of this representation of a seventeenth-century concert also used music by Luigi Rossi* and Francesco Cavalli.* The music of all three Italian composers was used here for predominantly historical reasons rather than for any special esthetic effect. The sole instance where Monteverdi may be said to have had a genuine impact is the occasion of the revival of his *L'Incoronazione di Poppea* (for *L'Incoronazione di Poppea*, see twentieth-century volume) at the Opéra on 30 June 1979.

BIBLIOGRAPHY: AEM IX, 511-31; BBD 1179-80; EDS VII, 779-85; ELM III, 229-33; NEO 456-57; Henri Prunières, *Claudio Monteverdi* (London: Oxford, 1952); Hans Redlich, *Claude Monteverdi* (London: Oxford University Press, 1952); Thompson 1164-71.

Mouret, Jean-Joseph (b. 1682, Avignon; d. 22 December 1738, Charenton), composer, was the son of a silk merchant wealthy enough to provide his children with good educations. Mouret composed a few pieces of music that called attention to his talents before he was 20, and it was decided in 1707 that he should go to Paris. It was not long before he became superintendent of music for the duchess du Maine and composed several *divertissements** for this famous insomniac's nights at Sceaux. One of these pieces was entitled *Ragonde, ou la soirée du village* (1742). Mouret had six other operas and ballets produced by the Royal Academy of Music between 1714 and 1735: *Les Fêtes de Thalie** in 1714, *Ariane* in 1717, *Pirithoüs* in 1723, *Les Amours des dieux* in 1727, *Les Sens* in 1727, and *Les Grâces* in 1735 (for Mouret's post-1715 operas, see eighteenth-century volume).

Mouret distinguished himself at Court by winning the appointments of royal musician and director of the spiritual concerts. He lost both these posts in 1736, and he suffered an additional blow with the death of his protector, the duke du Maine. Threatened suddenly with poverty and this loss of prestige, he went mad. Finally, when he heard the chorus "Brisons nos fers" by Rameau, he kept on repeating this song until he was taken to the madhouse in Charenton.

BIBLIOGRAPHY: Fétis VI, 219; Lajarte I, 121-22, 127, 133-34, 152-53, 164-65, 174; TdT 703-6; Renée Viollier, "Les Divertissements de J.-J. Mouret pour la 'Comédie italienne' à Paris," *RdM* XXIII (1939), 65-71; idem, *Jean-Joseph Mouret, le musicien des grâces, 1682-1738* (Paris: Floury, 1952).

Les Muses is an opera-ballet in four entrées and a prologue for which André Campra* composed the music, and Antoine Danchet* wrote the libretto. It had its premiere at the Palais-Royal* on 28 October 1703, and its first run lasted until 25 November 1703. After these 15 representations, the work was never revived in its entirety, although portions of it were employed for the *Fragments* of 3 December 1711 and 8 February 1717. Mlles Desmatins,* Maupin,* and Sallé* filled featured rôles in *Les Muses,* and Dun, Hardouin,* and Thévenard* played opposite them.

The prologue features Momus, who regrets the departure of the muses from Parnasse. Yet they do return to their abode to celebrate the memory of great heroes and gods. Bacchus and Cérès offer an abundance of their gifts to sustain them, and Apollon declares that pastoral, satiric, tragic, and comic poetry are to compete in a contest judged by Momus.

The first entrée, *La Pastorale,* takes place in a rural setting. Palémon initiates the intrigue by speculating about whether Silvie's indifference toward him is caused by her interest in Arcas. The latter reveals to Palémon that he loves Sylvie, but he wonders if his royal status might not hinder his suit for this beautiful shepherdess. After a pastoral celebration, Arcas declares his love to her, but she rejects him. Furious, Arcas swears to identify his rival, but he abandons his plans for vengeance, when Palémon reveals himself to be his rival.

Although satire was a Roman creation, *La Satire* is set in a Greek temple adorned with the portraits of the cynic philosophers, and Diogène is presented as refusing to abandon his mocking manner because he finds some truth in all his comments. Aristippe suggests that flattery might be a more welcome manner of speech in this world, but Diogène dismisses the suggestion because he wishes to find out whether Laïs loves him. His satiric approach is effective, and he learns from Alcippe and Laïs that the latter prefers his rival.

In *La Tragédie,* Althée complains that her son wishes to depose her to place his beloved upon the throne. Her troubles are compounded when he murders her brother, and she finds herself sworn to kill her own child. These horrors are presented in about 30 lines, and one wonders how much more terror can be added to the parody without destroying its effectiveness. Yet after the traditional love scene with Atalante, Méléagre falls ill, and his mother reveals that she has poisoned him. Inevitably, she kills herself at the end of this brief carnival of perverse ambition and foul murder.

Also entitled *L'Amour médecin, La Comédie* features Ericine disguised as a physician. She has resorted to this ruse because her father wishes her to marry aged Géronte, although she prefers his lovesick son, Eraste. She heals her lover of his illness by impressing Géronte with her skill and persuading him that Eraste will die if he does not marry Ericine. The grand finale celebrates the lovers' wedding and the concomitant cure of the groom's ailment.

BIBLIOGRAPHY: Lajarte I, 100; RGO VIII, 111-80.

N

La Naissance de Vénus was produced as an opera with music by Pascal Colasse* and a libretto by the abbé Jean Pic. As with *Les Saisons,* * Colasse borrowed music for some portions of *La Naissance de Vénus* from manuscripts by Lully,* to which he had access. The description of the work as an opera had no special significance at this time, since this word was used to designate any composition sung throughout its representation. It had its premiere at the Palais-Royal* on 1 May 1696, but *Le Journal de L'Opéra* does not provide any other information about the dates and frequency of its billings. It was never revived, however, and it does not seem to have been produced after 6 July 1696.

As with *Didon,* * the prologue offers the usual tedious laudium of Louis XIV and observes that "the greatest king of the universe" protects France from invasion every March when war resumes. It is also revealed that the king suggested that the story of the birth of Vénus be adapted to operatic form.

The exposition of *La Naissance de Vénus* established a triangle by presenting Neptune's declaration of love for Amphitrite and then showing Nerée resentful that Amphitrite has turned her attention to Neptune. The librettist complicates matters further by introducing Vénus and providing her with two suitors, Neptune and Jupiter, before Vulcain has the opportunity to declare his love to the same goddess. After the creation of these rivalries, the intrigue hesitates briefly in the third act to accentuate and to exploit the perpetual drama of lyric tragedy: love versus hate and jealousy. Here irate Junon descends from the sky to chastise her errant husband, Jupiter, and to decree that Vénus will wed whom she despises most. Yet it is Jupiter who brings matters to a peaceful conclusion by ordering L'Amour to arrange the weddings of Doris and Nerée, Amphitrite and Neptune, and Vénus and Vulcain. He imposes his authority with a display of power featuring a shower of thunderbolts.

BIBLIOGRAPHY: Lajarte I, 66-67; RGO V, 353-414.

O

Olivet, Louis-Hilaire d', dancer, has left no indication of the dates or places of his birth and death, but he is remembered as one of the 13 original members of the Royal Academy of the Dance, and he was secretary of this official organization for a time. He danced as a follower of Bacchus in *Thésée* in 1675, and he represented an old fountain in *Atys** in 1676. He appeared as a dancing sailor in the 1678 revival of *Alceste** and helped to produce the choreography of the ballet *Divinité des richesses* incorporated into the 1704 version of *Isis.**

BIBLIOGRAPHY: EC II, 217; Lajarte I, 32; André Levinson, "Notes sur le ballet au XVIIᵉ siecle: Les danseurs de Lully," *RM* VI (January 1925), 54.

Omphale is a lyric tragedy in five acts and a prologue with music by André-Cardinal Destouches* and a libretto by Houdard de La Motte.* It was mounted for the king at Versailles on 27 February 1702 nearly four months after its premiere at the Palais-Royal* on 10 November 1701. Its first run of 29 representations ended on 8 January 1702. It was revived in 1721 and 1733, and Mlle Pélissier (for Mlle Pélissier, see eighteenth-century volume) succeeded Mlle Moreau in the title-rôle on this latter occasion. It was also revived in 1735 and 1752, and the *Journal de l'Opéra* notes that it was produced with a *pas de six* on 22 February 1735 and with an "air italien" and *pas de trois* on 21 and 26 March 1735.

In the prologue to *Omphale,* L'Amour and his lively retinue have La Jalousie in chains, and Les Grâces are singing the praises of love, when Junon enters to ask the son of Vénus to humble Alcide. L'Amour complies by freeing La Jalousie to attack Alcide.

The first act of the tragedy takes place before a series of triumphal arches raised to the glory of Alcide, and the action starts with the announcement of a new victory by this hero, who reveals to Iphis his tormented love for Omphale and his fears of what Argine may do (I, 1-3). Omphale organizes a triumph in behalf of Alcide for freeing her people from the tyranny of a monster, and he admits his love to her (I, 4), although she loves Iphis (II, 1). Iphis divulges that he loves Omphale (II, 2).

The intrigue moves to greater complexity when Hercule lays the spoils of his victory at Omphale's feet, and he orders his prisoners to sing of his love for her. Junon's demons interrupt the festivities (II, 3), and Argine arrives on a dragon to upraid Alcide for his fickle heart.

After Argine is certain of Alcide's love for Omphale, she swears vengeance (III, 1-3) and casts a spell over him (III, 4). She is about to slay her rival when Alcide wrests the dagger from her hand. Enraged, Argine orders her demons to kidnap Omphale (III, 5-6). The latter manages to convince Argine that she is not in love with Alcide, who reports this revelation to Iphis. Despairing, Alcide vows to kill her unknown lover (IV, 1-2), and he asks jealous Argine for aid (IV, 3). The sorceress summons her demons and prepares a sacrifice to Proserpine and Pluton. Tirésie appears before her with the decree that Alcide will never love her (IV, 4). Alcide is overcome by the sudden announcement that Omphale and Iphis are to wed (IV, 5), and the prospective bride prays that Alcide and Argine will leave Sardis (V, 1-2). She admits her love for Iphis (V, 3). Torn between love and hatred, Alcide declares that he will smile upon the marriage (V, 4).

BIBLIOGRAPHY: Antoine Houdard de La Motte, *Oeuvres complètes*, 11 vols. (Genève: Slatkine Reprints, 1970) II, 204-19; Lajarte I, 93-94; RGO VII, 277-344.

Opéra, names of. The word "Opéra" has always designated the Paris opera company affiliated with the French Government since its foundation by Louis XIV in the seventeenth century, although this institution has always had a second name that reflected its official relationship with the government. Thus, changes in government on account of revolutions have resulted in this theatrical entity being renamed on 24 occasions over the past 300 years. Here are the two dozen titles and the dates of their adoption.

Adoption Date	*Title*
28 June 1669	Académie d'opéra
13 March 1672	Académie royale de musique
24 June 1791	Opéra
29 June 1791	Académie de musique
17 September 1791	Académie royale de musique
15 August 1792	Académie de musique
12 August 1793	Opéra
18 October 1793	Opéra national
7 August 1794	Théâtre des Arts
2 February 1797	Théâtre de la République et des Arts
24 August 1802	Théâtre de l'Opéra
29 June 1804	Académie impériale de musique

3 April 1814	Académie de musique
5 April 1814	Académie royale de musique
21 March 1815	Académie impériale de musique
9 July 1815	Académie royale de musique
4 August 1830	Théâtre de l'Opéra
10 August 1830	Académie royale de musique
26 February 1848	Théâtre de la Nation
29 March 1848	Opéra
2 September 1850	Académie nationale de musique
2 December 1852	Académie impériale de musique
1 July 1854	Théâtre impériale de l'Opéra
12 July 1871	Théâtre national de l'Opéra

Opéra-ballet was a musical form of theatrical entertainment that grew out of the *ballets à entrées* of the early seventeenth century; it enjoyed its greatest growth and popularity in the first half of the eighteenth century. *L'Europe galante** of 1697 is considered to be the first fully developed *opéra-ballet,* but *Les Saisons** of 1695 is so typical of the genre that it is mentioned as the most distinct prototype of this sort of composition. The importance of the dance in these works led many authors and other individuals concerned with their production to accept them merely as ballets, but it was quite clear to certain writers of the eighteenth century that they were dealing with a totally new form of entertainment. Cahusac (for Cahusac, see eighteenth-century volume), for example, was obliged to observe flatly in 1754 that "*L'Europe galante* is the earliest of our works which was not like an opera by Quinault."

Specifically, the *opéra-ballet* had to have as many separate plots as it had entrées, and the entrées were connected only by some overall concept or theme that was usually announced in the title, for example, *Les Sens* (for *Les Eléments* and *Les Sens,* see eighteenth-century volume). Marmontel saw this quite clearly when he wrote for Diderot's *Encyclopédie* that the *opéra-ballet* is made up of independent acts united under a collective idea like the elements, the muses, or the senses, but with the intrigue and characters of these acts being unrelated to each other. A second distinct property of the *opéra-ballet* was its rejection of ancient mythology in favor of more contemporary scenes and people, for example, *L'Europe galante** of 1697, which is the first of the regular *opéra-ballets,* presents Italian and Spanish lovers in Italian and Spanish settings. This tendency to lean toward less heroic subjects and more varied content suggests that this genre grew so rapidly in the first decades of the eighteenth century because Lully* was dead, Louis XIV had adopted a more secluded style of living, and the Court was becoming less concentrated at Versailles. As in the regency of Philippe d'Orléans (1715-1723), moreover, there was a growing taste for more diverse and less monumental art. The musical theatre reflected this popular disposition and presented in the *opéra-ballet* three or four short units of entertaining and even comic action to meet the demands of spectators no longer inclined to sit through five acts of a single and elaborate involvement such as the lyric tragedy offered.

The principal composers of *opéra-ballets* in the eighteenth century included Campra,* Mouret,* Destouches,* and especially Rameau (for Rameau, see eighteenth-century volume), whose scores in a single act were more often than not exactly in the manner of an entrée from an *opéra-ballet*. The term *opéra-ballet* was used later in the nineteenth and twentieth centuries, but, strangely enough, this phrase came to assume a vague and indistinct meaning after 1789, when the ballet was a regular and intrinsic part of the opera itself. It has also been suggested that the *opéra-ballet* was the precursory form of the modern spectacular ballet.

BIBLIOGRAPHY: J. R. Anthony, "The French *Opéra-ballet* in the Early 18th Century: Problems of Definition and Classification," *Journal of the American Musicological Society,* XVIII (1965), 197-206.

Opera buffa, comic intermezzos initially inserted between the acts of *opera seria.** Comic scenes were included in Italian opera in the seventeenth century, but they were soon dropped from serious works, probably on account of contemporary obedience to the classical injunction against including comic and tragic elements in the same work. The comic aspect of operatic productions was not banished from the theatre, however, because it constituted an essential part of theatrical entertainment as Italian actors and audiences expected it to be. The outcome was that the comic material was relegated to a position between the acts of the *opera seria** to provide comic relief for the program. It became an *intermezzo*. Thus isolated, the *opera buffa* attained its own identity in the eighteenth century, and the Italians became its masters as well as its founders. A separate theatre was established in Naples for the production of works in this genre as early as 1709. Vinci's *Zite'n galera* (1722) is generally considered to be the prototype of the *opera buffa,* and Pergolesi's *Lo frate 'nnammorato* (1732) and *La Serva padrona* (for *La Serva padrona,* see eighteenth-century volume) are acknowledged as the first accomplished examples of this type of production.

The *opera buffa* was by no means heroic, but it was rather in the tradition of the *commedia dell'arte* with its standard gestures, ready improvisations, and everyday situations based on the domestic trials and triumphs of such stock characters as the domineering master of the household, his shrewish wife, and the crafty servants usually associated with legitimate farce. The plot was often hinged to a falsehood, a disguise, or some other deception designed to work to the advantage of the underdog in a contrived and deliberately complicated plot. The score developed to match this sort of libretto was perforce alternately gay, mocking, cajoling, threatening, or wistful in mood. The music was homophonic, and it found variety in abrupt changes in register. The motifs were of short duration, and staccato passages abounded. The recitative was relieved from time to time by arias and duets that exploited key moments in the intrigue.

The *opera buffa* made its first great assault upon the French musical theatre during the *guerre des bouffons,* when no fewer than thirteen of these *intermezzi* or burlesque operas were staged at the Palais-Royal* between 1 August 1752 and 7 March 1754. Another 14 of these Italian compositions were produced at the same theatre from 11 June 1778 until 8 March 1786, during the second phase of the *guerre des bouffons* in the time of Gluck and Piccinni (for Gluck and Piccinni, see eighteenth-century volume). The enduring contribution made to the theatre by the *opera buffa* and the quarrels it provoked was the impetus that they provided in the development of *opéra-comique* in France.

BIBLIOGRAPHY: Werner Bollert, *Die Buffoopern Baldassare Galuppis* (Bottrop: Buch-und Kunstdruckerei W. Postberg, 1935); Noël Boyer, *La Guerre des bouffons et la musique française (1752-1754)* (Paris: Les Editions de la Nouvelle France, 1945); André Guillaume Contant d'Orville, *Histoire de l'opéra bouffon* (Paris: chez Grangé, 1768); Andrea della Corte, *Figuras y motivas de lo opera bufa italiano* (Buenos Aires: La Revista de Musica, 1928); Lionel de La Laurencie, *Les Bouffons (1752-1754)* (Paris: Publications de la Revue S.I.M., 1912); idem, "Deux Imitateurs français des bouffons: Blavet et Dauvergne," *Année musicale* 2 (1912), 65-125; Louisette Reichenburg, *Contributions à l'histoire de la "Querelle des Bouffons"* (Paris: Nizet et Bastard, 1937); Ruggero Vené, "The Origin of *Opera Buffa,*" MQ XXI (1935), 33-38.

Opera Houses: Fire and politics caused the Opéra to move from time to time, and the following list of theatres presents in chronological order the facilities used by the troupe during the past 300 years.

Legal Possession or First Program	*Opera House*
19 March 1671	La Bouteille* tennis court
15 November 1672	Le Bel-Air* tennis court
16 June 1673	Palais-Royal* theatre, burned 6 April 1763
24 January 1764	Hall of Machines, Tuileries, burned May 1871
26 January 1770	Palais-Royal theatre, burned 8 June 1781
14 August 1781	Menus-Plaisirs theatre, demolished 1910
7 August 1794	Montansier theatre, demolished 1820-21
19 April 1820	Favart theatre, burned 13-14 January 1838

15 May 1821	Louvois theatre
16 August 1821	rue Le Peletier theatre, burned 29 October 1873
19 January 1874	Ventadour theatre
5 January 1875	Garnier theatre
1 August 1936	Sarah Bernhardt theatre
30 November 1936	Champs-Elysées theatre
21 February 1937	Garnier theatre
14 October 1939	Favart theatre
16 November 1939	Garnier theatre

Opera seria was a term coined to designate an Italian form of musico-theatrical entertainment from which comic scenes had been dropped. The expression means literally "serious opera"; it came into being as a result of reforms proposed by such Italian dramatists as Apostolo Zeno (1668-1750), who felt that greater importance should be attached to the Aristotelian precept against commingling the two genres of comedy and tragedy in a single work. Pietro Metastasio (1698-1782) subsequently added more stringent controls upon the literary tenets to be obeyed in the writing of librettos. In general, for example, the composition of the poem was to be unified by expunging characters or scenes that were clever and striking but patently superfluous. The drama was to be reduced to its simplest components and left unimpeded by ornate excursions into virtuosity or the addition of such failure-proof theatrical devices as the introduction of animals and children for their own sake. The recitativo was to be accompanied by a disciplined score that was to be followed. Chorus and ballet had to contribute directly and energetically to the development of the work rather than being allowed to stand apart as separate units of entertainment. The principle of validity should obtain especially in the presentation of historical subjects, and no effort was to be spared in documenting the adventures and destiny of protagonists known for their social, political, or even personal significance. The closest French counterpart to the Italian *opera seria* was the lyric tragedy developed by Lully* as a French national form. It reached its height in France, as in other countries, at the flood stage of the baroque tide and when the glory of the Bourbons was at its apogee.

Orphée, with a score by Louis Lully* and a libretto by Du Boullay,* was the first lyric tragedy in three acts billed at the Palais-Royal.* This distinction was not enough to guarantee the success of *Orphée* because the unpublished log of the Opéra indicates that its first and only run extended from 21

February to 8 April 1690. Its singular intrigue presented married protagonists defending their marital love against the adulterous intentions of a spurned but persistent rival.

Lullist prologues were normally set in the spring or in the summer with sunny skies prevailing, but this prologue by the younger Lully is laid in a frozen clime featuring snow, ice, and shivering people. A troupe of potential spectators enters in search of a theatrical program and encounters Winter complaining that no one is grateful to him for suspending war and restoring entertainment. The assemblage rejects him, and Vénus descends from the heavens in her chariot and accompanied by Amour and the Grâces. Winter flees to yield the place to Printemps; Jeux and Plaisirs engage in a ballet. Vénus announces the return of Orphée and sings the praises of this hero against whom the entire universe conspires in vain. Louis Lully follows the pattern set by his father for the composition of prologues by including a laudium of the king and a fleeting reference to the current war of the League of Augsburg as well as an allusion to the subject of the forthcoming entertainment. His use of machines to enhance the spectacle, his employment of a chorus and ballet to achieve variety of tone, and his transformation of the setting within the prologue to supply added relief from monotony are standard devices of the period.

The material of the Orphée-Euridice myth is distributed over three acts that transpire before, during, and after the protagonist's descent into the netherworld to return his beloved to her rightful place among the living. The action is instituted by Orasie's complaint that Orphée has rejected her and by her concomitant decision to destroy Euridice by arranging for a poisonous viper to bite her (I, 1-3). After unsuspecting Euridice is bitten by the venomous serpent, she obliges Orphée to remain alive so that he can rescue her from Hades through the power of his music (I, 8).

The second act takes place on the banks of the Styx with Euridice as a subject of Pluton and with Orphée as a minstrel invading his realm (II, 1-3). Orphée is allowed to escort Euridice back to earth on condition that he refrain from gazing upon her beauty (II, 9). He defeats his own cause at the last moment by looking at her inadvertently. Returned to earth, Orphée continues to shun Orasie (III, 1), and he devotes his time to playing his lyre for groups of charmed animals (III, 2). Ultimately, however, Orphée and his magical instrument are destroyed by the Bacchantes sent to do away with him (III, 6).

The libretto of *Orphée* is devoid of innovations and modifications, therefore, and it depends exclusively for its visual effects upon the scenes inherent in the original legend. The first act relies for its effects and motivation almost exclusively upon Orasie's jealousy and passion, but some originality was apparently achieved in the fifth and sixth scenes devoted to the chorus and ballet depicting Euridice's death among the flowers. The second act has a certain unavoidable interest by being set in Hades, and its underworld characters afford a resultant picturesque appeal, but the central device of the entire act is the music of Orphée, heard in the distance (II, 2-4) and then on the stage (II, 5-10). The last act presents the disheartening spectacle of the protagonist stripped of his powers, love, and life; the successive blows that contribute to his destruction are so thorough and effective that the spectators could do little else besides take refuge in a sort of numb indifference to his undeserved fate. It was probably the complete annihilation of Orphée that led spectators to reject this work, which violated the first canon of contemporary opera that true love triumphs over all.

BIBLIOGRAPHY: Lajarte I, 58; RGO IV, 1-50.

P

Palais-Royal was the residence of Cardinal Richelieu, whose interest in the stage induced him to build a private theatre in his own home. It was constructed in 1639 and could accommodate 1,200 spectators, but it was not used as a theatre until the cardinal's play *Mirame* was produced there on 14 January 1641. After the death of Richelieu in 1642, the facility passed to the Crown and fell into neglect until it was used by Molière between 1661 and 1673. When the comedian died, Louis XIV assigned the Palais-Royal to Lully,* who profited by his good fortune to present his operas on its stage. Philippe d'Orléans resided in the palace after the death of Louis XIV, and he had machinery installed in the theatre to raise the floor of the pit to the level of the stage so that a larger dance floor would be available for his fabulous soirées. Yet the Opéra continued to present programs here without interruption until it caught fire early on the morning of 6 April 1763. The theatre was completely gutted in this conflagration, and the company was obliged to look elsewhere for facilities. The Crown gave the artistes permission to move into the *salle des machines* at the Tuileries until Moreau could complete a second Palais-Royal (for the second Palais-Royal, see eighteenth-century volume) across the way from the site of the old theatre in the rue Saint-Honoré. The company had performed previously in the Salle de La Bouteille* in the rue Mazarine and in the Salle du Bel-Air* between 1671 and 1673.

BIBLIOGRAPHY: Max Aghion, *Le théâtre à Paris au XVIIIe siècle* (Paris: Librairie de France, n.d.), 191-94, 203-4; Pierre D'Espezel, *Le Palais-Royal* (Paris: Calmann-Lévy, 1936), 87-88, 117-18, 124-25, 128; Emile Dupezard, *Le Palais-royal de Paris* (Paris: Ch. Eggimann, 1911); idem, *Le Palais-Royal de Paris; architecture et décoration de Louis XV à nos jours* (Paris: Librairie centrale d'art et d'architecture, 1911); Jacques Hillairet, *Dictionnaire historique des rues de Paris,* 2 vols. (Paris: Les Editions de minuit, 1963) II, 431-32; Eugène Hugot, *Histoire littéraire, critique et anecdotique du théâtre du Palais-royal* (Paris: P. Ollendorff, 1886); L. Augé de Lassus, *La vie au Palais-Royal* (Paris: H. Daragon, 1904), 40-44, 60-63; André Lejeune et Stéphane Wolff, *Les quinze salles de l'Opéra de Paris* (Paris: Librairie théâtrale, 1955), 17-21; François Lesure, *L'Opéra classique français* (Genève: Editions Minkoff, 1972), 5 and plate 10; Jean Marot, *Le magnifique chasteau de Richelieu, en général et en particulier* (Paris: 16?); Charles Nuitter, *Le Nouvel Opéra* (Paris: Hachette, 1875), 5-6; Spire Pitou, "The *Comédie française* and the *Palais royal* Interlude of 1716-1723," SVEC LXIV (1968), 225-31.

Pécourt, Guillaume-Louis (b. 1653, Paris; d. 1729, Paris), dancer, was the son of a royal courier and had the opportunity to study dancing at Court under the direction of Beauchamp.* When it became obvious that he was endowed with unusual talent, he was admitted to the Royal Academy of Music, and Lully* gave him the chance to perform in the ballet of *Cadmus et Hermione** for his 1674 debut at the Palais-Royal.* He would appear again in this lyric tragedy during its 1690-91 revival.

Lully was assured immediately that Pécourt had the noble bearing and dignified manner essential to the execution of the ballets in his works, and he assigned the young dancer to the corps de ballet for *Thésée** and *Atys** in 1675; *Isis** in 1677; *Bellérophon** in 1679; the seventh, fourteenth, and eighteenth entrées of *Le Triomphe de l'Amour** in 1681; the rôle of *premier danseur* opposite Mlle Lafontaine in *Persée** in 1682; and *Amadis** in 1684. He was one of six members of the Academy selected for the staging of *Le Temple de la Paix** in 1685.

After an interval of more than a decade, Pécourt resumed his activities at the theatre in 1697 by taking part in the premiere of *Vénus et Adonis.** He was likewise a member of the ballet for the initial representations of *Marthésie, reine des Amazones** in 1699, *Hésione** in 1700, and *Cariselli** in 1702. Yet except for appearing in the premiere of *Camille, reine des Volsques* (for *Camille, reine des Volsques,* see eighteenth-century volume) on 9 November 1717, Pécourt did little on the stage beyond appearing in revivals of Lully's works later in his career. Indeed, if it is agreed that he retired from the stage to devote all his energy to choreographing certain texts for the Court and for the Academy, it would have to be supposed concomitantly that there was a Pécourt *père* and a Pécourt *fils*, with the latter having been trained by his father to master Lully's ballets for their revivals.

Aside from his dancing, Pécourt is remembered for having been one of the first choreographers to try to establish a code to permit written descriptions of the moves in ballets. La Bruyère has left a portrait of the composer-dancer in his *Les Caractères* under the name of Bathylle.

BIBLIOGAPHY: ACD 358-59; ACPM 717; CODB 408; EDB 273; GE XXVI, 208; Lajarte I, 22-23, 25-26, 29-32, 34-35, 38-40, 42-43, 46, 51-52, 67, 89-90, 93-97, 127; André Levinson, "Notes sur le ballet au XVIIe siècle: Les danseurs de Lully," *RM* VI (January 1925), 52; Louis Pécour, *Recueil de danses & La Nouvelle Gaillarde* (New York: Dance Horizons, n.d.); TdT 800; Marian Hannah Winter, *The Pre-Romantic Ballet* (New York: Dance Horizons, 1975), 4, 46, 48, 108, 109, 149, 162, 260; WT 13.

Les Peines et les plaisirs de l'amour is the second operatic work staged in Paris under the egis of the Academy of Opera at the *Jeu de paume de la Bouteille.** Cambert* was the author of the musical score for this composition in five acts, and Gilbert* was its librettist. The precise date of the premiere of this pastoral is uncertain, but accounts agree generally that it was performed initially in February or March 1672.

Pomone* had been based upon the love of two gods for a goddess, but Gabriel Gilbert's libretto presents two nymphs in love with Apollon. The later intrigue is complicated by the death of one rival at the hands of the other nymph, although this act of violence occurs before the curtain goes up. The action that follows the murder is quite simple: Apollon mourns Climène's death (I), and Vénus orders Mercure to return her to the living (II); Apollon is attracted to Climène, now alive and disguised as a shepherdess (III); Astérie bemoans her unrequited love (IV), and Apollon is reunited with Climène (V).

This Ovidian story is prefaced with the requisite laudium of Louis XIV. The scenery changes with each act and even within the act itself. Machinery is used to lower and raise the characters between heaven and earth, and the grand finale offers the spectacle of Apollon returning to the skies with Climène to pursue his daily course from east to west. The verse forms extend from the baroque alexandrine of twelve syllables to only four syllables. The shorter verses are assigned most often to choristers and are arranged to create an antiphonal effect. The ballet is developed to the point where it appears to separate itself almost from the main course of the action, for example, the dance of spectres before Climène's tomb (II, 4). The *chanson* is used almost constantly to develop a melody in two or four voices executing refrains or merely repeating previous motifs.

It is not known what artistes appeared in *Les Peines et les plaisirs de l'amour,* but Chouquet suggests that the leads were filled by Mlles Aubry* and Brigogne as Philis and Climène, respectively, opposite Beaumavielle,* Clédière, and Tholet singing Faune, Apollon, and Pan.

BIBLIOGRAPHY: Robert Cambert, *Les Peines et les plaisirs de l'amour,* ed. J. B. Wekerlin (Paris: Théodore Michaëlis, 1881); Lajarte I, 20; RGO I, 49-100.

Pellegrin, Simon-Joseph (b. 1663, Marseille; d. 5 September 1745, Paris), librettist, entered a religious community in Moutiers at an early age, but he became bored with this sequestered life before long and signed up as a chaplain on a vessel plying between France and North America. He returned to his native land permanently in 1703, and he decided to enter the poetry contest sponsored by the French Academy in 1704. His *Epître sur le glorieux succès des armes de Sa Majesté* carried off the laurels, although another poem he had composed and sent to Paris was also considered for the award. It became known eventually that a poet-cleric from the Midi had almost won the contest twice, and Mme de Maintenon expressed a desire to meet him. Pellegrin came to Paris and Versailles, therefore, and he received the necessary dispensation allowing him to remain in the capital. Yet he found it difficult to live on the small sums he received for the performance of his ecclesiastical duties, and he embarked upon a unique venture to provide himself with the bare necessities of life: he opened a poetry shop to sell love poems, satirical pieces, flattering compliments, and rhymed expressions of gratitude.

He began to work for the theatres and had two tragedies accepted by the Comédie-Française in 1706 and 1707. Cardinal de Noailles was archbishop of Paris at this time, and he did not fail to notice the abbé Pellegrin's curious ways and unbecoming interest in the theatre, and he condemned his conduct. Fortunately for the abbé, he managed to obtain a position as drama critic for the *Mercure*. The poet-reporter-playwright spent the rest of his life composing works of piety, translations of the classics, plays, and a limited number of scripts for the Royal Academy of Music. His first libretto here was *Médée et Jason** in 1713 followed by *Télémaque** in 1714. Later on he did the words for *Renaud ou la suite d'Armide* in 1722, and it was not until 1733 that he contributed the poem for *Hippolyte et Aricie* (for *Renaud* and *Hippolyte et Aricie,* see eighteenth-century volume). His greatest distinction was probably having done the libretto for Rameau's first work at the Opéra. It should be noted finally that neither literary historians nor musicologists have ever settled the question of the extent of Mlle Barbier's collaboration with the abbé (for Mlle Barbier, see eighteenth-century volume).

BIBLIOGRAPHY: Bio univ XXXII, 393-94; Brenner 109-10; CG 245-69; GDHS II, 360; Lajarte I, 165-66; H. C. Lancaster, *Sunset: A History of Parisian Drama in the Last Years of Louis XIV, 1701-1715* (Baltimore: The Johns Hopkins Press, 1945), 124-30; idem, *French Tragedy in the Time of Louis XV and Voltaire, 1715-1774* (Baltimore: The Johns Hopkins Press, 1950), 112-16.

Perrin, Pierre (b. 1620, Lyon; d. 1676, Paris), impresario, was known as the abbé Perrin; he adopted his ecclesiastical title only to guarantee himself a certain social standing, and it was not long before he managed to obtain the position of presenting ambassadors to Gaston, duke of Orléans, an honor he shared with the famous poet and friend of Mme de Rambouillet, Vincent Voiture. The year of his arrival at Gaston's Court, he embarked upon a musical career by presenting at Issy in the home of M. de LaHaye *Le Pastorale d'Issy* for which Robert Cambert* had done the music. The success of this venture encouraged him to compose *Ariane ou le mariage de Bacchus,* which Cambert also set.

It was at about this time that the marquis de Sourdéac was in the process of perfecting mechanical devices for the staging of spectacular machine plays, and Perrin made his acquaintance on the occasion of the mounting of Pierre Corneille's *La Toison d'or* at the marquis's country residence in Normandy. The death of Mazarin interrupted Perrin's plans momentarily, but he did not forget his success with musical representations, and he obtained permission on 28 June 1669 to give performances of this sort before the public. His initial program under his royal license was *Pomone** in March 1671. Greed and jealousy within his theatrical company disrupted his organization, and Lully* managed to obtain the rights to his monopoly in 1672. Perrin renounced any active connection with the Royal Academy of Music founded by Lully, and he left France for England, but he had won the unquestioned distinction of having founded the first officially recognized opera company in his native land.

BIBLIOGRAPHY: Bio univ XXXII, 536-37; Norman Demuth, *French Opera: Its Development to the Revolution* (Sussex: Dufour, 1964), 102-3, 106-13, 117, App. 13, 14; Arthur Pougin, *Les Vrais créateurs de l'opéra français: Perrin et Cambert* (Paris: Charavay, 1881); TdT 385-86.

Persée is the sixth work that Jean-Baptiste Lully* and Philippe Quinault* wrote in collaboration for the Royal Academy of Music and the second composition upon which they worked together after the librettist had incurred royal disfavor on account of alleged allusions to Mme de Montespan in *Isis.* * *Le Journal de l'Opéra* asserts that it was performed for the first time on 17 April 1682 at the Palais-Royal* with the king, the queen, and the dauphin present. Mlle Desmatins* appeared in it on this occasion as a singer and a dancer, although she was only 12 years old.

The prologue of *Persée* presents La Fortune and La Vertu forgetting their differences to sing the praises of Louis, and the sole spectacle consists of the sudden adornment of the stage with flowers and statues to hail La Fortune. It is announced that Persée will be brought back to life on this occasion because he resembles the Sun King. Quinault had always stressed L'Amour and La Gloire in his previous prologues, and it is interesting to find here that he speaks of La Vertu. One can attribute this change to Mme de Maintenon's increasing influence at Court. It was she who was promoting a more austere and devout atmosphere at Versailles.

The intrigue of *Persée* is based upon the situation of two lovers pursued by two thwarted suitors, and the supernatural element is provided by the recurrent operatic theme of the hero slaying the monster only to encounter a second peril before winning the heroine's hand. The central love affair is between Persée and Andromède. Phinée, the uncle of Andromède, offers the initial complication because his brother had promised his daughter to him in marriage. The queen's sister, Mérope, creates the second problem by falling in love with Persée and by encouraging the Andromède-Phinée marriage so that the hero will be free to marry her. Thus, Mérope is in love with Persée, who loves and is loved by Andromède, who has been promised by her father to Phinée. A sufficient number of wondrous and captivating spectacles are interspersed among the ensuing complications. Cassiope orders games to be held to appease Junon, and the principal feature of the program is a dance contest (I). A troupe of dancing Cyclopes brings to Persée a sword forged by Vulcain (II, 8); a band of militant nymphs presents him with Pallas's buckler of diamonds (II, 9); a company of divinities from Hades offers him Pluton's helmet (II, 10). The most elaborately produced tableau is the struggle between Persée and Méduse. Contrary to the Aristotelian precept forbidding bloodshed on the stage, he slays her in full view of the spectators, and monsters "of a terrible and bizarre appearance" are born of her blood to fly, to crawl, or to run about the stage.

The representation of the Andromède-Persée story was not a complete innovation. An *intermède* entitled Andromède had been produced in 1624, and Corneille had dramatized the legend in 1650. The ultimate source of the story was Ovid's *Metamorphoses,* and it seems that Quinault used Corneille's play as well as Ovid's poem in the preparation of his own version.

The entire score of *Persée* is not extant because it was not yet customary to print the music as well as the libretto of compositions mounted by the Royal Academy of Music. But enough of Lully's work is available, and it is known that certain passages of *Persée* were especially favored by the public. The first act was applauded for the Mérope-Andromède-Phinée trio, "Ah! Que l'amour cause d'alarmes" (I, 4), and for Mérope's air, "Ah! Je garderai bien mon coeur" (I, 3). The scene of the Gorgons in the third act, Phinée's air "L'Amour meurt dans mon coeur" (IV, 3), and the chorus of Tritons and Néréides singing "Descendons dans l'eau" (IV, 6) also brought applause, as did the high priest and the chorus singing "Hymen! O doux Hymen" (V, 3).

Persée was sung at Versailles before the king in July and August 1682, although Louis XIV had not yet made this palace his permanent residence. It was the composition offered on the free program of 6 August 1682 at the Palais-Royal*; this bill was gratis to celebrate the birth of the duke de Bourgogne. The first run of *Persée* in Paris lasted from April to August 1682, when it was replaced by *Alceste.** It continued to be well liked by audiences, however, and it was returned to the stage on 10 April 1687. It was revived subsequently in 1703, 1710, 1722-23, 1737, and 1748.

BIBLIOGRAPHY: DDO II, 861-62; Etienne Gros, *Philippe Quinault* (Paris: Champion, 1926), 535-36, 578-84, 619-22, 672; Lajarte I, 42-44; Lionel de La Laurencie, *Lully* (Paris: Alcan, 1919), 61-62, 157-58; Sonn I, 864.

Phaéton is the first lyric tragedy by Jean-Baptiste Lully* and Philippe Quinault* to have its world premiere at Versailles, where it was mounted initially and without machinery on 6 January 1683. It was produced for the first time at the Palais-Royal* on 27 April 1683, and its first run was interrupted only by the death of the queen on 30 July 1683. It was brought back to the stage at the end of the period of mourning thirty days later and continued its run until 12 or 13 January 1684. Fanchon Moreau, mistress of Monseigneur, made her debut in the premiere of *Phaéton* at the age of 15. The work was well received and went on to enjoy revivals in 1682, 1702, 1710, 1721, 1730, and 1742.

As in *Isis** and *Persée,** the characters in *Phaéton* are of divine and human status, but the hero furnishes the physical means of communication between the heavens and Egypt. The love interest is based upon the mutual attraction between Phaéton and Théone, and the obstacle is provided by the former's quest for power and glory: he rejects Théone to seek the hand of Libie because she is the daughter of the king and despite her love for Epaphus (I). Phaéton's ambitions are realized when Mérope gives Libie to him as a bride (II). The action hesitates momentarily at this point because Epaphus vows vengeance, and the conflict resolves itself into the question of whether the Epaphus-Jupiter combination or the Phaéton-Soleil faction will triumph (III). Le Soleil acknowledges that Phaéton is his son, and he allows his offspring to ride off into the morning sky (IV). Phaéton loses control of his horses, and Jupiter is obliged to strike him down to save the earth from incineration (V).

There are really only two episodes in the entire presentation: the hero's wild ride through the sky and his death. This lack of opportunity to produce spectacular events on the stage with machines was remedied by having recourse to a generous supply of *divertissements**: Protée and Triton emerging from the sea (I, 5 and 7); the ceremony of the king offering his daughter to Phaéton (II, 5); the temple of Isis filled with dancing furies, phantoms, and flames (III, 5); the singing and dancing in the palace of Le Soleil throughout act IV; the honoring of Phaéton and his prowess (V, 4).

Phaéton was quite popular with the general public, and it became known as "the people's opera" just as *Atys** earned the title of "the king's opera" and *Isis** came to be called "the musician's opera" on account of its score. Some of the music spread throughout Paris and was heard everywhere; for example, "Hélas! Une chaîne belle" in the last act, which also included Lully's favorite air entitled "Que mon sort serait doux." Libie opened the first act with the very popular "Heureuse une âme indifférente." Another striking passage was the chorus of Heures singing "Dans ce palais" in IV, 2 before Phaéton confronts Le Soleil.

Phaéton enjoyed the added distinction of having been the first work mounted by the Academy of Music at Lyons when this institution was founded there in 1687. Contemporary accounts assert that people came from 30 miles around to hear it.

BIBLIOGRAPHY: DDO II, 871-72; Etienne Gros, *Philippe Quinault* (Paris: Champion, 1926), 141-44, 531-32, 622-24, 677-78; Lajarte I, 44-45; Lionel de La Laurencie, *Lully* (Paris: Alcan, 1919), 63-64, 158; Jean-Baptiste Lully, *Phaéton . . . reconstituée et reduite pour piano et chant par Théodore de Lajarte* (Paris: T. Michaëlis, 1883); RGO II, 369-430; R.H.F. Scott, *Jean-Baptiste Lully* (London: Peter Owen, 1973), 96-97; Sonn I, 869.

Philomèle is a lyric tragedy in five acts and a prologue with a score by La Coste* and a libretto by Roy*. It was the librettist's first contribution to the Royal Academy of Music and had its premiere on 20 October 1705. Its first run lasted until *Le Triomphe de l'Amour* was returned to the Palais-Royal* on 26 November 1705. It was revived on 8 October 1709 and 27 April 1723.

The principal rôles were created by Mlle Desmatins* (Philomèle), Mlle Journet (Progné), and Thévenard* (Terée). In 1723 these parts were filled by Mlle Le Maure, Mlle Antier,* and de Chassé.

The prologue presents Vénus lamenting the terrors of war and Mars's subsequent announcement of another victory by Louis XIV and the return of peace. Vénus and Mars are reconciled, and the assembled shepherds sing the praises of L'Amour while listening to a song by Philomèle.

Based upon the sixth book of Ovid's *Metamorphoses,* the intrigue develops from Progné's love for her husband, Terée, who is in love with his sister-in-law, Philomèle, who loves and is loved by Athamas. This situation, recalling the plots of *Alcine** and *Tancrède,** is established by Progné's brief explanation that her husband's adulterous love could imperil all four individuals concerned (I, 1). The danger becomes more acute when Terée reveals to his wife and to the assembled Athenians that he has postponed Philomèle's trip from Thrace to Athens (I, 2-5). He declares his love to Philomèle ultimately, but she reminds him that he is married to her sister (I, 6-7).

Philomèle laments her predicament but opposes Athamas's plan to seek vengeance against Terée (II, 1-2). Minerve consoles the distressed couple (II, 3). Terée accepts Arcas's suggestion that he repudiate Progné to wed Philomèle, and Progné accuses him of betraying her (II, 5). Ignoring Philomèle's feelings and Athamas's anger, Terée threatens to slay Philomèle if she rejects his suit (III, 1). Athamas renounces his love for Philomèle to protect her, and guards lead him away to certain death if Philomèle rejects Terée. Philomèle weakens under duress, however, although she assures Terée that she will kill herself after the ceremony making her his wife (III, 2-5). The temple and the statue of Hymen disappear to signal the displeasure of the gods with Terée's tyranny.

Progné has recovered from her despair and shock, and her companions urge her to pursue vengeance (IV, 1). She and her sister decide to seek justice for the death of Athamas, who has been slain by raging Terée between the third and fourth acts (IV, 2). Philomèle exhorts a company of infernal demons to kill his son (IV, 3), but Progné protests against this bloody plan (IV, 4). Yet she accepts a dagger to murder Terée and joins in the chorus of Bacchantes to burn his palace to the ground in a scene (IV, 5) which the *Mercure* (1734) will call "one of the most frightening and beautiful" spectacles ever presented at the Palais-Royal.

Philomèle watches the flames devour the palace (V, 1-3), and a troop of Minerve's servants dressed as sailors arrive to accompany her to Greece (V, 4). Progné kills her son by Terée (V, 5) and leaves for Athens with her sister. Terée is burned to death in the opera, although he is transformed into a sea gull in the *Metamorphoses*; Roy provides only the slightest hint that Philomèle and her sister will become a nightingale and a swallow.

BIBLIOGRAPHY: Lajarte I, 106; RGO IX, 1-64.

Les Plaisirs de la paix is a ballet in three acts and a prologue joined by four *intermèdes*. Louis-Thomas Bourgeois* composed its score, and Menesson created its libretto. It was billed on 26 dates between its premiere on 29 April 1715 and 21 June 1715, but it was never returned to the stage of the Palais-Royal.*

The preface to the printed version of the ballet explains that the work is an allegory: L'Hyver represents the calm that prevails in Europe at the moment; the action taking place in the palace of L'Hyver signifies the quiet accomplishments achieved in Europe during the summer of 1715 before Louis XIV's death.

The prologue presents Vénus descending from the brilliant skies with her company of Amours and Grâces. She praises the virtues of the season and leads her retinue in songs and dances honoring L'Amour and the continuing peace.

The intrigue of the first entrée could scarcely be more simple. Licidas complains of Céphise's indifference to him (I, 1), and Céphise laments Licidas's failure to pay attention to her (I, 2). When Licidas protests his love to her, she admits her love for him (I, 3). A ball is then held in the palace built by the Cyclopes, and two Italian singers praise the charms of love in their own language (I, 4-5).

An *intermède* featuring Bacchus leads into the second act wherein Licas sings the praises of this god (II, 1). Timante extols the charms of love, but Licas pays homage to Bacchus again before leaving Timante with Iris. The latter couple declare their mutual love, and Iris decides to upset Licas by pretending to be infatuated with him (II, 2-3). Cliton addresses a drinking song to his empty bottle, and his master, Licas, scolds him for his bibulousness. Iris pretends not to see Licas as she describes her disenchantment with Timante and her sudden affection for Licas. The latter breaks his bottle and glass in his pledge of love to Iris, but she rejects him for his inconstancy (II, 5). Timante invites Iris to their wedding feast, and the theatre opens to disclose a group of drinkers in the midst of a celebration (II, 6-8).

The third entrée, *Le Jaloux puni ou la sérénade,* was presented as a comedy and centers upon Alcantor, who is jealous of Clarice and furious with his rival (III, 1). When he meets Clarice in the street at night, she explains that she is on her way to a concert. She rebukes him for his jealousy, and he proposes marriage in vain. He swears to slay his rivals wherever he finds them (III, 2). Licis and Clarice plan to announce their betrothal at a ball, but Gusman enters to play a serenade before entering the ballroom where his friend Licis is to meet him and his fellow artists (III, 3-6). Alcantor wishes to know why Licis is at the ball with Gusman, and the latter's answer reveals that Licis and Clarice have wed (III, 7). The curtain falls after a ballet and chorus in honor of love.

BIBLIOGRAPHY: Lajarte I, 123-24; RGO XI, 233-300.

Polyxène et Pyrrhus, sometimes called *Polyxène*, is a lyric tragedy in five acts and a prologue with music by Colasse* and a libretto by La Serre.* This composition was seen only 17 times during its first run from 21 October to 23 November 1706 at the Palais-Royal.*

Obviously imitating the prologue of *Cassandre,** the prologue of *Polyxène et Pyrrhus* presents Mercure ordering the inhabitants of a newly built city to watch the gods bringing them a glorious destiny. Neptune, Jupiter, and Minerve arrive simultaneously. Neptune claims the responsibility of protecting the city and presents its citizens with a river. Minerve guarantees them peace to pursue the arts even in time of war. She offers them an olive tree. Jupiter suggests that the city be called Athens.

The opera opens with Polyxène rejecting Pyrrhus despite her love for him because he has killed Priam (I, 1-2). When he insists upon his love for her, she reminds him of his past deeds and suggests that he court Erixène, sister of the king of Thrace (I, 3). Erixène arranges a celebration in the absence of Polymnestor (I, 4), but the festivities are interrupted by an untimely darkness and the emergence of Achille's shade to order the sacrifice of Polyxène (I, 5). Pyrrhus refuses to kill his beloved Polyxène (II, 1), and Ulysse supports Achille's command, but Pyrrhus insists that he will prevent Polyxène's sacrifice to Calchas despite the Greek's wish that this be done (II, 2-3). He assures Polyxène of his protection (II, 4-5), and Vénus urges her to accept his aid (II, 6-7).

The question of whether or not Polyxène will be sacrificed remains the central issue at the start of the third act, where Erixène warns Pyrrhus of the Greeks's anger if he helps her rival (III, 1-2). Polyxène and her Trojan retinue lament their destiny, but Pyrrhus reassures them once again (III, 3-4). Grateful, Polyxène admits her love to Pyrrhus, even though he is a Greek (III, 5), and she offers her life to her enemy (III, 6). Ulysse declares that the Greeks are now armed (III, 7). Junon and Minerve urge Pyrrhus to accept either the Greek or Trojan faction, and he opts for the Trojans (III, 8). Polyxène decides to flee, and Pyrrhus follows her (IV, 1). Erixène faints from jealousy at this development (IV, 2), and Iris orders her transported to the cavern of La Jalousie (IV, 3). La Jalousie takes possession of Erixène, who reports the flight of Pyrrhus and Polyxène to Ulysse (IV, 4-6).

Matters draw closer to a conclusion when Erixène wonders why she wishes Polyxène's death (V, 1), and, when the Greeks and Thracians enter on their way back to Greece (V, 2), Ulysse tells Erixène that he found but could not slay Polyxène (V, 3). Calchas announces that the Greeks must sacrifice Polyxène before they set sail for home (V, 4), and Pyrrhus enters with his troops to rescue her (V, 5). The confrontation is finally defined, therefore, but Polyxène sacrifices herself, and Pyrrhus's followers have to restrain him from following her in death (V, 6).

BIBLIOGRAPHY: Lajarte I, 109; RGO IX, 169-226.

Pomone was the first opera produced in France under the license given to Pierre Perrin* by letters patent establishing an Academy of Opera. A pastoral in five acts with a score by Cambert,* its libretto is based upon a simple plot. Pomone dismisses Vertumne and Faune, who are rivals for her hand (I). Vertumne rejects Beroë and laments his fruitless pursuit of Pomone (II). Vertumne resorts to disguising himself as Plutus and Bacchus to win Pomone's favor, but he meets with failure again (III). He then assumes the form of Beroë and is dismissed for the fourth time. He is accepted finally by offering Pomone his love without disguise or guile (IV), and their wedding is celebrated in a festival of song and dance (V).

This banal story of love triumphant provided the occasion for enough supernatural incidents, meteorological phenomena, and sudden metamorphoses to sustain the production to the satisfaction of audiences, and the spectacle offered enough ballet, burlesque, and song to please spectators accustomed to the *comédie-ballet* already developed by Molière* and Lully.* The effects achieved by   Sourdéac's mechanical devices were sensational enough to compare favorably with those of the machine plays mounted at the Marais theatre and the Tuileries.* The finale with a large cloud chasing ten small clouds from the sky must have been hailed as an accomplishment of the first order in scenic manipulation.

The real shortcomings in the composition are in the libretto, which becomes ludicrous at times; for example, the passage where Vertumne exhorts Pomone to join her fruit with his truffles and mushrooms (I, 3). The low comedy scene where Faune cannot grasp the elusive bottle of wine to assuage his thirst (III, 9) is clever enough, but his talk of a full belly and the gestures indicating cuckoldry (V, 9) seem better suited to gross farce.

The question of the identity of the artistes who performed in *Pomone* has been resolved by Nuitter (for Nuitter, see nineteenth-century volume) who uncovered a legal instrument bearing the signatures of these artistes. It is impossible to tell what rôles were assigned to them, but their names have been established as members of the first formally established operatic company in France: François Beaumavielle,* Pierre Rossignol, Bernard Clédière, Pierre Taulet, Jean Bourel-Miracle, Tranquille La Tellier, Antoine Lemercier, Marie-Madeleine Jossier, femme Cartillier DITE Cartilly, Marie Hardy, and Marie-Elisabeth Bouet. It is likely that Beaumavielle and Mlle Cartilly did Vertumne and Pomone.

BIBLIOGRAPHY: Robert Cambert, *Pomone, 1er acte avec accompagnement de piano,* ed. J. B. Wekerlin (Paris: Théodore Michaëlis, n.d.); Lajarte I, 19-20; RGO I, 1-48.

Poussin, Mme (b. ?; d. 1743?), vocalist, appeared on the operatic scene as early as 1699, when she was assigned to the chorus of the Royal Academy of Music. She was still performing this same service for the company in the revival of *Le Triomphe de l'Amour* during 1705, when she did Aglaure and Diane in the third and fourth entrées of this work. She was then assigned regularly to secondary rôles and to whatever comic parts were available, tasks she performed with distinction. She was given a part in *Cassandre** of 1706, and she was billed subsequently in the following works, in which she created the characters indicated:

Rôle	Opera	Premiere
La Folie	Les Festes vénitiennes*	17 June 1710
Vénus	Idoménée*	12 January 1712
L'Europe	Médée et Jason*	24 April 1713
Vénus	Les Amours déguisés*	22 August 1713
Junon	Télèphe*	28 November 1713
Thalie, Léonore, Dorise	Les Festes de Thalie*	19 August 1714
Climène	Les Fêtes de l'été	12 June 1716
Flore	Camille, reine des Volsques	9 November 1717
Hébé, Lucinde	Les Ages	9 October 1718

Mme Poussin was left a widow only a short time after she married the singer Poussin, but she was apparently still alive in 1741.

BIBLIOGRAPHY: André Campra, *Les Festes vénitiennes,* ed. Alexandre Guilmant (Paris: Théodore Michaëlis, n.d.), 8-9; EFC 134; Lajarte I, 111-12, 114-15, 117-22, 125, 127, 129.

Prévost, Françoise (b. 1680; d. 1741), dancer, was a pupil of Blondy,* but her performances in the extremely popular *Atys** created a first impression that she belonged to the generation after Lully.* She replaced Mlle de Subligny* as première danseuse in 1705, and she scored striking successes on the stage of the insomniac duchess du Maine's theatre at Sceaux. She reached the apex of her glory as a soloist in *Les Caractères de la danse* in 1720, but her physical endurance and agility did not keep pace with her interest in the ballet, and she spent the later years of her life teaching her art to younger performers.

Mlle Prévost appeared in the creations or revivals of more than 30 works during the course of her career:

Les Saisons* (1695)
Iphigénie en Tauride* (1704)
Télémaque* (1704)
Bellérophon* (1705)
Alcine* (1705)
La Vénitienne* (1705)

Philomèle* (1705)
Cassandre* (1706)
Polyxène et Pyrrhus* (1706)
Amadis* (1707)
Bradamante* (1707)
Les Festes vénitiennes* (1710)
Idoménée* (1712)
Callirhoë* (1712)
Thétis et Pélée* (1712)
Armide* (1713)
Médée et Jason* (1713)
Les Amours déguisés* (1713)
Télèphe* (1713)
Proserpine* (1715)
Zéphyre et Flore* (1715)
L'Europe galante* (1715)
Roland* (1716)
Vénus et Adonis* (1717)
Le Jugement de Paris (1718)
Polydore (1720)
Les Amours de Protée (1720)
Pirithoüs (1723)
Amadis de Grèce* (1724)
Télégone (1725)
Les Stratagèmes de l'Amour (1726)
Pyrame et Thisbé (1726)

(See eighteenth-century volume for post-1715 works in which Mlle Prévost appeared.)

Mlle Prévost's most celebrated pupils were Marie Sallé and Camargo (for Camargo, see eighteenth-century volume), who accepted their teacher's revolutionary conviction that the ballet has a mimetic function that should bring it closer to the drama being developed. Thus, she was in her fashion an immediate precursor of Noverre and his *ballets d'action*. Rameau himself recognized the importance of her ideas and the validity of her dancing. He wrote in his *Le Maître à danser* (1734), "all the rules are contained in a single one of her dances." Even the government recognized her worth as an artist by giving her a bonus of 800 *livres* in 1711 for having "extremely contributed to the success of the operas in which she had been employed."

BIBLIOGRAPHY: ACPM 387; CODB 425; EDS VIII, 459; Lajarte I, 29-30, 34-35, 46-49, 52-53, 56-59, 64-65, 85, 102-4, 106, 108-9, 112, 114-20, 128, 130-31, 133, 140-41; Parmenia Migel, *The Ballerinas from the Court of Louis XIV to Pavlova* (New York: Macmillan, 1972), 11-12; Mark Edward Perugini, *A pageant of the dance and ballet* (London: Jarrolds, 1946), 108, 114, 133.

Proserpine was the first composition produced by Jean-Baptiste Lully* and Philippe Quinault* after the latter had been banished from Court through the influence of Mme de Montespan. Quinault was back in favor by June 1679, and *Proserpine* had its first performance at Saint-Germain en Laye on 3 February 1680. It was billed at the Palais-Royal* for the first time on 15 November 1680, and its first run extended into March of the following year. It was revived twice during the reign of Louis XIV: 31 July to 27 November 1699 and for a single billing on 7 March 1715. It was mounted again in the eighteenth century in 1727, when it was enhanced by new scenery by Servandoni and Rousseau with Bertin in charge of the machinery. Its last two revivals were posted in 1741 and 1758. An interesting note describing Servandoni's 1727 set for the cavern of La Discorde is still extant: ". . . escaping light can be seen coming from the top of the cavern, through crevices, between rocks, to illuminate this dreadful place." The waterfall of the fifth act is made with "several sides of silver gauze that form the cascade; by means of two wheels, each twelve feet in diameter," the movement of the water is reproduced.

The tale of Proserpine and of her being carried off to Hades by Pluto was a story that had already furnished material for several ballets and plays in the seventeenth century, but Quinault went directly to Ovid's *Metamorphoses* for his documentation. Unfortunately, he tried to use nearly every detail in Ovid besides adding some developments of his own. The first act affords a most striking example of an overloaded exposition, and it presents Alphée-Aréthuse and Jupiter-Cérès in love, the departure of Cérès for Phyrigie, and another paean to Louis XIV, which is thinly disguised as a laudium of Jupiter. The second act is concerned with two nearly unrelated developments: the reconciliation between Alphée and Aréthuse; the kidnaping of Proserpine by Pluton. An attempt at unification is made in the third act when Alphée and Aréthuse depart for Hades in quest of Proserpine. The remainder of the action is devoted to depicting Cérès' wrath at the disappearance of her daughter. The last two acts alone are simple and direct by reason of dealing exclusively with Pluton's attempts to woo Proserpine (IV) and with the pacification of Cérès (V). Some spectators found this action too slow and even boring while complaining that the fourth act was nothing more than a long lament by the heroine. Other critics leveled the charge that the intrigue was too dispersed. Yet in fairness to Quinault, it must be said that these alleged weaknesses of structure and presentation were in fact the very moments that the librettist went out of his way to create so that Lully could diversify his music. Quinault's introduction of Ascalaphe might seem superfluous, for example, but his incorporation into the libretto allowed the composer to attempt the innovation of a duet for two bass voices when Ascalaphe and Pluton sing "L'Amour, comblé de gloire" (II, 7). Similarly, the duet of Proserpine and Pluton in IV, 4 and Jupiter's "Je suis roy des Enfers" in the same scene add nothing to the drama, but they are excellent opera.

Unlike the intrigue in *Atys** and *Isis,** the plot of *Proserpine* provides unparalleled opportunities for the use of machines because the characters and their retinues come from heaven (Jupiter), earth (Cérès), and Hades (Pluton). As always, Mercure constitutes the bridge among them. The first act uses machines in the flights of Mercure and Cérès, when the latter enters her chariot pulled by dragons. The demons of Hades emerge in the second act, and Mount Etna flames in the background at the start of the third act. The last act features a sumptuous entrance by Pluton and Proserpine. The divine stature of the personages involved here and the epic sweep of their actions make *Proserpine* a more truly heroic opera in the grand manner of the late seventeenth century than any composition yet mounted at the Palais-Royal. In retrospect, it is perhaps not as dramatic as one might desire, and it lacks compositional unity, but it is as typical of its era as a painting by Poussin or the façade of Versailles.

BIBLIOGRAPHY: DDO II, 913-14; Etienne Gros, *Philippe Quinault* (Paris: Champion, 1926), 130-33, 531, 544-52, 614-19; Lajarte I, 36-38; Lionel de La Laurencie, *Lully* (Paris: Alcan, 1919), 155-56; Jean-Baptiste Lully, *Proserpine . . . reconstituée et reduite pour piano et chant par Théodore de Lajarte* (Paris: T. Michaëlis, 18?); RGO II, 197-268; Sonn I, 900.

Psyché was the first work created by Jean-Baptiste Lully* and Thomas Corneille* after the banishment from Court of Lully's first librettist, Philippe Quinault.* It had its premiere at the Palais-Royal* on 18 April 1678.

Although *Psyché* is alleged to have been written in haste, it offered Lully a well-unified text based upon the legend of the love affair between Cupid and Psyché. The action moves clearly and simply from act to act. Psyché is informed by the oracle that she must sacrifice herself to protect her people, and she consents to die only to be carried off at the last moment by a group of Zéphires (I). She finds that she has been whisked away from earth because L'Amour loves her (II). Swearing vengeance, Vénus gives Psyché a magic lamp to enable her to see and to know her son, an act which she has been forbidden to perform. After Psyché has gazed upon L'Amour, she finds that she has lost her love. Vénus is implacable and refuses to help her unless she can obtain Proserpine's chest of cosmetics (III). Psyché is successful in her quest in the underworld (IV), but she is overcome by vapors after opening Proserphine's coffer. She is revived when Jupiter intervenes to restore peace and love throughout the universe (IV).

The libretto that Lully accepted from Thomas Corneille was a reworked version of the original *Psyché* first performed in the great hall of the Tuileries on 17 January 1671. This earlier work had likewise been the fruit of a collaboration with music by Lully and the poem divided among three writers. Molière* had done the prologue and the early scenes of the first three acts, and its two stagings at the Tuileries in 1671 had caused so much comment that Molière brought it back to his own theatre, where it proved to be one of his most successful productions before his death. When Thomas Corneille was asked to adapt this machine play to an operatic libretto, he made a considerable number of changes in the intrigue; for example, he deleted the start of Molière's third act and changed the motivation for L'Amour leaving Psychè. Most of his alterations were inspired by the desire to achieve a more visual presentation of the Psyché story.

The work did not prove very popular in its new form, although it was revised twice. It was brought back to the stage of the Palais-Royal for a run of 45 performances between 10 June and 18 September 1703, and it enjoyed 27 consecutive billings between 22 June and 20 August 1713. Thomas Corneille was so discouraged by the cool reception *Psyché* received in 1678 that he would have broken off with Lully if the king had not suggested that he continue to contribute to the Royal Academy of Music. His next work for Lully was *Bellérophon.* *

BIBLIOGRAPHY: DDO I, 915-16; Jacques Heuzey, "Notes sur un dessin représentant la Salle des Machines au XVIIe siècle," *RHT* 6 (1954), 60-67; Lajarte I, 33; H. C. Lancaster, *A History of French Dramatic Literature in the Seventeenth Century,* 9 vols. (Baltimore: The Johns Hopkins Press, 1936) III, 520-23; Jean-Baptiste Lully, *Psyché . . . reconstituée et réduite pour piano et chant par Théodore de Lajarte* (Paris: T. Michaëlis, 188?); Molière, *Oeuvres,* ed. Eugène Despois and Paul Mesnard, 14 vols. (Paris: Hachette, 1883) VIII, 245-384; RGO II, 69-134; Charles I. Silin, *Benserade and His Ballets de Cour* (Baltimore: The Johns Hopkins Press, 1940), 254-61; Sonn I, 904.

Q

Quinault, Jean-Baptiste Maurice (b.?, Paris; d. 1744, Gien), composer, was known as the elder Quinault, but only scant information about his birth and death has been recorded. He was involved principally with the Comédie-Française, where he made his debut as Hippolyte in Racine's *Phèdre* in 1712; so many members of his family belonged to this troupe that Voltaire referred to them as "the Quinault tribe."

Jean-Baptiste Maurice Quinault was a competent musician as well as an actor, and he sang in productions mounted by the company whenever his services as a vocalist were required for the performance of *divertissements.* * His only contribution to the Royal Academy of Music was the score he did for *Les Amours des déesses* (for *Les Amours des déesses*, see eighteenth-century volume) of 1729.

BIBLIOGRAPHY: Fétis VII, 153; Lajarte I, 146-47, 166; H. C. Lancaster, *Sunset: A History of Parisian Drama in the Last Years of Louis XIV, 1701-1715* (Baltimore: The Johns Hopkins Press, 1945), 21-22.

Quinault, Philippe (b. 3 June 1635, Paris; d. 26 November 1688, Paris), librettist, was born of humble origins but made an early start in the theatre when his mentor, Tristan l'Hermite, persuaded the royal troupe of actors to accept his first work. *Les Rivales* proved to be a successful comedy, and the 18-year-old dramatist was encouraged to continue to write for the theatre. He produced three comedies, six tragicomedies, and a tragedy by the time that he had reached his 25th birthday. His *Amalasonthe* had captured the king's fancy on 14 November 1657 and had won him a royal gift; his *Stratonice* (1660) had attracted the attention of all Paris.

A few months after the premiere of *Stratonice,* Quinault married a young and wealthy widow, Louise Goujon, who brought him an immense dowry. An eighteenth-century rumor reported that his new wife made him renounce the theatre, except for the composition of operas, but the dramatist did six more plays in the course of the decade following his marriage. His work at this time included *Lysis et Hespérie,* written to celebrate the wedding of Louis XIV and given before him at the Louvre on 9 December 1660. The manuscript of this allegorical pastoral is lost. Quinault was obviously trying to win royal favor at this moment in his life, however, and it is not difficult to imagine the sort of eulogy he wrote on this occasion. He dedicated his *Agrippa* (1661) to the young monarch the following year. The playwright was now haunting the halls of the Louvre; he had bought a position in the royal household; he was known personally to Louis XIV. The summit of success came with *Astrate,* which the king selected for a private performance in December 1664 or January 1665. After still another triumph with *La Mère coquette* (1665), Quinault retired from the theatre for three years, perhaps on account of the bitter quarrels in which his literary activity had involved him.

But Quinault returned to the theatre and an active rôle at Court in 1668 with *L'Eglogue de Versailles,* * produced as part of the great festival held at Versailles to celebrate the peace of Aix-la-Chapelle. The king danced in the ballet for which Lully* had written the music, and the dramatist was now officially recognized as one of the men of letters capable of being charged with the celebration of Louis XIV's deeds and glory, and he was elected to the French Academy soon after the premiere of *L'Eglogue de Versailles.* Quinault reached the age of 36 in 1671. He had created 17 compositions for the theatre in addition to being the author of *Lysis et Hespérie,* the *intermèdes* for *Psyche,* * and *L'Eglogue de Versailles.* He had already collaborated twice with Lully, and, when the Italian superintendent of the king's music obtained the monopoly to present opera in France, he invited Quinault to become his librettist.

The first fruit of the Lully-Quinault collaboration was *Les Fêtes de l'Amour et de Bacchus.* * The two authors produced five operas between 1673 and 1678, and their partnership was interrupted only because Mme de Montespan had Quinault dismissed from Court on account of certain allegedly humiliating references to her in his *Isis.* *

Lully continued to score operas for Louis XIV after Quinault's disgrace in 1677, but he was not overly impressed with the verse that he was receiving from Thomas Corneille* and Bernard de Fontenelle,* and he set about to have his former librettist restored to royal favor. Quinault worked toward his reinstatement by cultivating the good will of Colbert. The diminishing influence of Mme de Montespan at Court also helped Quinault's cause, and it was not long before he was able to leave his exile.

The second phase of the Quinault-Lully partnership began with *Proserpine* * in 1680 and lasted for another seven years until the premiere of *Armide* * in 1686. The two men contributed a ballet, a ballet-opera, and five operas to the repertory of the Royal Academy of Music during this second period of their cooperative authorship. Their association was brought to an end only by Quinault's growing religious scruples about his career in the profane theatre and by his letter to the king asking to be relieved of his duties as Lully's poet.

Their association lasted over a period of 14 years, however, and it was based upon a mutual agreement that was never broken. Lully was to pay

Quinault the sum of 4,000 *livres* a year in return for which Quinault was to supply the composer with a libretto every 12 months. The librettist lived up to his end of the contract by furnishing his composer with a pastoral, a ballet, an opera-ballet, and 13 operas. He had also done the poem for Lully's *L'Eglogue de Versailles* in 1668, the work which had aroused the musician's interest in him in the first place. Quinault had likewise contributed to the ballet-tragedy *Psyché* of 1671, for which Lully had written the score.

Quinault enjoys the distinction of having prepared the first work staged by Lully under the auspices of the Royal Academy of Music, *Les Fêtes de l'Amour et de Bacchus*. He supplied the words for 14 of the first 17 titles that this organization sponsored under the aegis of Lully. The inspiration for his texts ranges from the mythological subjects found in Ovid to the accounts of medieval heroes glorified in old French romances and Italian Renaissance epics. His poetry lacked the forcefulness of Pierre Corneille's tragedies, and he did not possess the poetic gift of Racine, but he did create the lyric tragedy to serve as a vehicle for contemporary vocal and instrumental music, and he perfected this form in the course of providing Lully with texts that demonstrated that the French language could be accommodated to dramatic song. He was able to blend the already existing ballet, the pastoral, and the machine play into a new and effective theatrical medium that was different from the Italian opera and that would allow these independent forms to contribute to a unified effect.

Quinault provided the poems for the following compositions mounted by the Royal Academy of Music: *Les Fêtes de l'Amour et de Bacchus** (1672), pastoral; *Cadmus et Hermione** (1673), "tragedy in music"; *Alceste** (1674), lyric tragedy; *Thésée** (1675), lyric tragedy; *Atys** (1676), lyric tragedy; *Isis** (1677), lyric tragedy; *Proserpine** (1680), lyric tragedy; *Le Triomphe de l'Amour** (1681), ballet; *Persée** (1682), lyric tragedy; *Phaéton** (1683), lyric tragedy; *L'Eglogue de Versailles** (1668, 1685), *divertissement*; Le Temple de la paix** (1685), opera-ballet; and *Armide** (1686), lyric tragedy.

BIBLIOGRAPHY: David C. Cabeen and Jules Brody, *A Critical Bibliography of French Literature: The Seventeenth Century*, ed. Nathan Edelman (Syracuse, N.Y.: Syracuse University Press, 1961), nos. 1779-1783; Etienne Gros, *Philippe Quinault* (Paris: Champion, 1926); H. C. Lancaster, *A History of French Dramatic Literature in the Seventeenth Century*, 9 vols. (Baltimore: The Johns Hopkins Press, 1929-1942).

R

Rebel, François (b. 19 June 1701, Paris; d. 7 November 1775, Paris), composer, was the son of Jean-Féry Rebel. Admitted to the orchestra of the Royal Academy of Music at age 13 in 1714, he was still a member of this musical organization in 1738. He was a close friend of Francoeur,* also a violinist at the Opéra, and the two men collaborated not only on the composition of operas but also as inspectors and then as directors of the company between 1751 and 1767. Louis XV rewarded François Rebel with the Order of Saint Michel and the position of superintendent of royal music. Finally, in 1772, he became general administrator of the Opéra, but his age obliged him to resign from this post on 1 April 1775.

These many administrative duties did not prevent him from writing a De Profundis, a Te Deum, and eight operas: *Pyrame et Thisbé* of 1726, *Tarsis et Julie* of 1728, *La Paix* of 1738, *Les Augustales* of 1744, *Zélindor* of 1745, *Ismène* of 1750, and *Le Prince de Noisy* of 1760 (for the post-1715 Rebel-Francoeur works, see eighteenth-century volume). These theatrical works were done with Francoeur, as was his cantata entitled *Le Trophée* and executed in 1745 to celebrate the battle of Fontenoy.

BIBLIOGRAPHY: AEM XI, 86-87; Bio univ XIV, 638-39 under Francoeur; Brenner 116; Fétis VII, 193-94; Lajarte I, 141-42, 145, 166-67, 185-86, 200-202, 215-16, 241-42, and II, 249; LXIX XIII, 761.

Rebel, Jean-Féry (b. April 1661, Paris; d. January 1747), composer, was the son of Jean Rebel* and a pupil of his father and Lully* at the Court of Louis XIV. He became a member and then the conductor of the orchestra at the Opéra, and, from 1705 to 1746, he served in the *violons du roi*.

Rebel contributed a single opera to the repertory of the Royal Academy of Music. It was entitled *Ulysse,* * and it had its world premiere at the Opéra on 21 January 1703. His ballet entitled *Les Eléments* was danced intially at the Tuileries on 27 September 1737. This work later attracted the attention of Serge Lifar (for Serge Lifar, see twentieth-century volume) who rechoreographed it for presentation at the Petit Trianon in Versailles on 29 June 1950. Its scenario was edited for this occasion by Lucien Coutaud.

BIBLIOGRAPHY: AEM XI, 83-88; BBD 1401; EDS VIII, 761-62; ELM III, 552-53; Grove XII, 70.

Regnard, Jean-François (b. February 1655, Paris; d. 4 September 1709, Normandy), librettist, was born into a wealthy family of Parisian merchants. He lost his father when he was still an infant, but his mother undertook to provide him with an excellent education. After he had finished his schooling, he traveled to Italy and Constantinople. He was returning to France by ship after a second trip to Italy when he was captured by pirates and sold into slavery in Algiers. He was put to work making wicker cages for birds and was confined to quarters that he remembered later with horror. He and his companions were ransomed eventually, and their captivity ended in May 1679. The future playwright had passed eight months in the hold of the privateer's ship and in his "dark and stinking dwelling" ashore. After he was safe in Europe, he set out on still another voyage with his friend Fercourt, and they visited Sweden, Poland, and Austria. Once back in Paris, Regnard purchased a position in the government and started to write plays for the Comédie-Française and the Théâtre-Italien; his only contribution to the Royal Academy of Music was the libretto for Campra's* *Le Carnaval de Venise,* a ballet that attracted the attention of all Paris. Regnard purchased an estate in Normandy in 1699, and he moved there without delay to spend the remainder of his life in ease and comfort.

BIBLIOGRAPHY: Bio univ XXXV, 329-32; David C. Cabeen and Jules Brody, *A Critical Bibliography of French Literature: The Seventeenth Century*, ed. Nathan Edelman (Syracuse, N.Y.: Syracuse University Press, 1961), nos. 1787, 1820-48; GDSS II, 427-29; Joseph Guyot, *Le Poète J.-Fr. Regnard en son chasteau de Grillon* (Paris: A. Picard, 1907); André Hallays, *Regnard* (Paris: Berger-Levrault, 1929); H. C. Lancaster, *A History of French Dramatic Literature in Seventeenth Century,* 9 vols. (Baltimore: The Johns Hopkins Press, 1940) IV, 731-54; J.-F. Regnard, *La Provençale*, ed. Edmond Pilon (Paris: Bossard, 1920).

Roland is the tenth opera in five acts created by Jean-Baptiste Lully* and Philippe Quinault.* It had its world premiere in the Riding School at Versailles on 8 January 1685 before the king, and, like *Phaéton,* it was produced without machines on this occasion, not a difficult task for the stage production engineer Carlo Vigarani,* since only the fifth act required mechanical devices for its staging. In all, the work was performed eight times at Court by 3 March 1685. Two of these performances were attended by the archbishop of Paris and the Siamese ambassadors. It opened in Paris at the Palais-Royal* on 8 March 1685.

Roland is unique among the compositions that Lully and Quinault wrote before 1685 because the principal action is psychological with the drama taking place within the characters themselves. Their struggles arise from the passions that stir within their own beings rather than from their efforts to appease or thwart the gods. The only supernatural interference in the work occurs when recourse is had to magical rather than to divine powers to restore the hero's sanity. For *Roland* is based upon Ariosto's *Orlando furioso*, cantos XIX, XXIII, XXIV, XXX, XXXIX, wherein the circumstances related to the protagonist's loss of his reason are described. The material borrowed from the opera's source is rearranged, abridged, or expanded, however, and the later work moves in quite different directions, with even Roland's loss of his reason resulting in frustrated ravings rather than in psycopathic violence (IV, 6).

The intrigue itself is quite simple. The exposition presents Roland in love with Angélique, who loves and is loved by Médor. When Roland returns from the wars to rejoin Angélique, she and Médor proclaim their mutual love in a reconciliation (II), which leads to the coronation of Médor and to the lovers' decision to sail away from the scene of their cares (III). Rejected, Roland loses control of his senses (IV), and Logostille puts him to sleep to relieve him of his despair. Roland revives with his sanity intact and resolves to devote himself henceforth to the pursuit of glory (V). Thus, *Roland* was an opera in the honored pattern of legitimate classical drama wherein a main character was torn between love and duty in a moment of irresolution. It is not by chance that *Roland* neglected machines and spectacles to rely upon the dance and the chorus, which were the indigenous elements of true tragedy in the original tradition.

Roland came to be considered one of Lully's most effective works before long, and it enjoyed great success from the start with Mlle Le Rochois* as Angélique and Beaumavielle* in the title-rôle assisted by Du Mesny as Médor and Mlle Armand in the part of Thémire. It was revived on 12 February 1705 and 15 November 1709 according to the unpublished *Journal de l'Opéra,* which notes that a parody of it entitled *Pierrot Roland* was given at the Foire Saint-Germain on 3 February 1709. It was brought back to the stage of the Palais-Royal for its third revival on 11 November 1727, and it continued to be billed through September 1728. It was performed again between 19 December 1743 and 16 March 1744, although only three acts were mounted toward the end of this run. At this time de Chassé sang Roland, a rôle that had been filled by Thévenard* for 43 years. In his turn, de Chassé went on to sing this rôle for the next 42 years. Three passages from *Roland* never failed to evoke applause during these years: Médor's air, "Ah! Quel tourment" in I, 3; the chorus of "Quand on vient dans ce boccage" in IV, 3 and of "Roland, courez aux armes" in V, 3.

BIBLIOGRAPHY: DDO II, 972-75; Etienne Gros, *Philippe Quinault* (Paris: Champion, 1926), 536-37, 569-72, 629-32, 674-76; Lajarte, I, 48-49; Lionel de La Laurencie, *Lully* (Paris: Alcan, 1919), 67-68, 161-63; Henry Prunières, *Lully* (Paris: Henri Laurens, n.d.), 101; RGO III, 1-72; Sonn I, 947-48.

Rossi, Luigi (b. 1597 or 1598, Torremaggiore, Foggia; d. 19 February 1653, Rome), composer, studied in Naples and then moved to Rome to enter the service of Marc' Antonio Borghese. Subsequently he joined the staff of cardinal Barberini, and events took a sinister turn for Rossi when he was in the employ of the cardinal because Innocent X succeeded Urbain VIII in 1644, and the new pope was a declared enemy of Barberini. The Barberini family found it prudent to flee Rome, therefore, and Rossi fled with his employers to find refuge in France under Mazarin. Thus, it was proper and even inevitable that Rossi's music be included in the score of Henri Prunières's *Les Virtuosi de Mazarin* (for *Les Virtuosi de Mazarin*, see twentieth-century volume) of 6 January 1916, which reconstructed a concert allegedly given before young Louis XIV in 1647, when Mazarin was still prime minister of France.

BIBLIOGRAPHY: AEM XI, 938-42; BBD 1457; EDS VIII, 1231-32; ELM III, 593; Grove VII, 242-43.

Rousseau, Jean-Baptiste (b. 6 April 1670, Paris; d. 17 March 1741, Brussels), librettist, was the son of a shoemaker who gave each of his two sons an excellent education despite his modest station in life. Contemporary gossip asserted that Jean-Baptiste ignored his father as soon as fortune smiled upon him, and the poet's future enemies never lost an opportunity to recall his filial ingratitude.

Rousseau started his career in the theatre with a comedy entitled *Le Café* (1694), but the public did not take kindly to this work. Deciding to court success elsewhere, he wrote *Jason** for the Royal Academy of Music in 1696. His first contribution to the Opéra was no more successful than his previous effort at the Comédie-Française, but he persisted and prepared the libretto for *Vénus et Adonis** in 1697. This composition proved as unrewarding as *Jason*, and Rousseau decided to make still another effort at the Comédie-Française with *Le Flatteur* and *Le Capricieux*, but he was again dissatisfied with the results of his work. Disgruntled, he looked for enemies to blame for his misfortunes and found ready targets among the regular patrons of the café Laurent, especially Danchet,* whose *Hésione** was enjoying a sustained run at the Palais-Royal.* Like Roy, Rousseau turned to satire for revenge, and it was not long before he found that his parodic verse and epigrams had stirred up a storm beyond his control. Hostility toward him increased in nearly every quarter, and, when he sought election to the French Academy ten years later, a second rash of satiric verse recalled Rousseau's previous writings of a libelous nature. Rousseau decided to enter the courts to defend his reputation, but this maneuver ended in a disaster: he was found guilty of having circulated defamatory writings, and he was banished from the kingdom. It was inevitable that Rousseau's theatrical activity should come to an end with this decree of 7 April 1712, although he had 29 more years to live in exile in Switzerland, Austria, and Belgium.

BIBLIOGRAPHY: Bio univ XXXVI, 608-11; Brenner 121; CG 146-49; Lajarte I, 65, 67; H. C. Lancaster, *A History of French Dramatic Literature in the Seventeenth Century*, 9 vols. (Baltimore: The Johns Hopkins Press, 1940) IV, 847-55; TdT 732-52.

Roy, Pierre-Charles (b. 1683, Paris; d. 23 October 1764, Paris), librettist, was not interested as a youth in pursuing a legal career, although his father had purchased for him a position as a lawyer at the Châtelet. He turned to writing instead of law, and he submitted entries in the poetry contests held by the French Academy and the Jeux Floraux in addition to preparing librettos for the Royal Academy of Music. He was soon known as "a prodigy of wit" and was only 22 years old at the time of his first opera, *Philomèle,* * in 1705. Yet he did not rest upon these laurels, and his second composition, *Bradamante,* * was ready for presentation to the public by 2 May 1707. His third libretto for the Palais-Royal,* *Hippodamie,* * had its premiere on 6 March 1708. Roy had won five poetry contests between this latter date and 1712, the year of his *Créuse* * and *Callirhoé.* *

Roy was as ambitious as he was energetic, and he sought election to the French Academy after having contributed his *Les Captifs* to the Comédie-Française and certain texts to the duchess du Maine's famous nights at Sceaux. He was now only 32, but he had already acquired some influential enemies among the Forty Immortals, and his candidacy for a chair in the Academy was rejected. Roy was not inclined to accept defeat gracefully, and he began to write vicious satire. His epigrams became venomous, but his bitterness did not interfere with his activities as a librettist, and his contributions to the repertory of the Palais-Royal came to eclipse even those of Danchet,* Bernard,* and Cahusac (for Cahusac, see eighteenth-century volume). He did the words for *Sémiramis* in 1718 and for his acclaimed *Les Eléments* in 1721 (for Roy's post-1715 works see eighteenth-century volume). Roy had climbed about as high as he could go by the time he was 40, and his downfall was thereby the more dramatic. On 9 December 1724, Roy was arrested for certain slanderous writings and thrown into the Bastille. He was sentenced to banishment from Paris, a painful verdict that still left him free to collaborate with Destouches.*

The poet was allowed to return to Paris on 22 June 1725, and his new ballet, *Les Stratagèmes de l'Amour,* had its premiere in 1726. Roy tried to bury the past by composing flattering verse directed at the Crown, and he became an eighteenth-century Malherbe by writing, if not reforming, French poetry at Court. His enemies were still at work, however, and he was returned to prison in March 1728 and subsequently sent into his second exile. He married in July 1729 and returned to writing; his *Le Ballet des sens* was ready for representation on 6 June 1732. It was well received, but the quality of the librettist's work declined thereafter, and his *Les Grâces* of 1735 as well as his *Le Ballet de la Paix* of 1737 were not greeted with the usual enthusiasm. After election to the Order of Saint Michel in 1742, Roy produced a series of works honoring the king and other members of the royal family. He passed his last decade on earth suffering from the effects of a serious stroke.

BIBLIOGRAPHY: Bio univ XXXV, 666-67; Brenner 121; CG 218-37; GDHS II, 495; Elliot H. Polinger, *Pierre-Charles Roy* (New York: Publications of the Institute of French Studies, 1930).

S

Saint-Jean (?) is known exclusively as the author of the libretto for Marais's *Ariadne et Bacchus** of 1696, and his first name as well as the salient features of his life and interests remain a mystery.

BIBLIOGRAPHY: Brenner 123; CDSS III, 1802; GDSS 922; Lajarte I, 66.

Saintonge, Louise-Geneviève Gillot (b. 1650, Paris; d. 24 March 1718, Paris), librettist, was a daughter of Mme Gillot de Beaucour and the wife of a lawyer named Saintonge or Sainctonge. Nothing is known of her life except these sparse details and her bibliography that includes the librettos for two works staged at the Royal Academy of Music, *Didon** and *Circé.* Mme Saintonge created a ballet entitled *Le Charme des saisons,* but it could not be billed at the Palais-Royal* because the abbé Pic had already had his *Les Saisons** performed there in 1695.

BIBLIOGRAPHY: Bio univ XXXVII, 376-77; Brenner 12; Lajarte I, 61, 63; TdT 563.

Les Saisons was one of two *opéra-ballets* given in 1695 to relieve a run of six consecutive lyric tragedies. It fitted the definition of its genre by incorporating as many plots as it had acts and by having each of its four parts contribute to the theme announced in the title.

Le Printemps ou l'Amour coquet is laid in a verdant setting where Le Printemps recalls all the joy and beauty that come to the earth in his season. *L'Eté ou l'Amour constant et fidèle* presents L'Eté pointing to the precious gifts that his bounty secures for mankind. L'Automne notes in *L'Automne ou l'Amour possible dans l'état du mariage* that Bacchus is especially dependent upon him, although he is responsible for completing the many other tasks left unfinished by Le Printemps and L'Eté. L'Hiver boasts in *L'Hiver ou l'Amour brutal* that he restores peace and entertainment to the world when it becomes too cold to wage war. Apollon enters in the grand finale to review the claims and merits of the seasons and to establish harmony among them. As indicated in their subtitles, each of the entrées develops a love affair.

Although the music for *Les Saisons* was attributed to Louis Lully* and Colasse,* Lajarte noticed that Colasse and the late (that is, Jean-Baptiste) Lully were cited as the composers. This collaboration is quite plausible, because Colasse had been the elder Lully's secretary and had had access to his manuscripts before and after his death. The abbé Jean Pic did the libretto.

Les Saisons has weaknesses as far as its structure is concerned, but its historical importance is sufficient reason to recall it: it was this work that started the tradition of the *opéra-ballet** at the Palais-Royal* by furnishing the inspiration for Campra's* *L'Europe galante** of 1697. Its esthetic shortcomings are to be excused at least partially because even as early as 1695 the public was beginning to demand a lighter and more varied form of entertainment than the lyric tragedy, with its complicated plot extending over five acts.

The work was a success and was revived on three occasions after a first run extending from 18 October 1695 until 5 January 1696. It was returned to the stage of the Palais-Royal sometime during February-May 1700. It was mounted without its prologue on two dozen dates between 12 July and 4 September 1712 and finally with the masquerade from *Monsieur de Pourceaugnac* from 16 to 23 June 1722. The leading danseuses at its premiere were Mlles Dangeville and Prévost* opposite Boutteville, Du Mirail, and Lestang.* The vocalists included Mlles Desmatins,* Maupin,* and Moreau with Boutelou,* Dun, and Thévenard* singing the male rôles.

BIBLIOGRAPHY: Lajarte I, 64-65; Jean-Baptiste Lully and Pascal Colasse, *Les Saisons, reconstitué et reduit pour piano et chant par Louis Soumis et introduction par H. Lavoix fils* (Paris: Théodore Michaëlis, n.d.); RGO V, 185-232.

Salomon (b. 1661, Provence; d. 1731, Versailles), composer, came to Paris as a boy to study the bass viol under Sainte-Colombe. He obtained a position in the royal chapel when he was 51 years old according to Fétis, who contradicts the Parfaict brothers' statement that Salomon was much younger at the time of his entrance into royal service. His two contributions to the repertory of the Royal Academy of Music were lyric tragedies: *Médée et Jason** in 1713 and *Théonoé* (for *Théonoé,* see eighteenth-century volume) in 1715.

BIBLIOGRAPHY: Fétis VII, 386; Lajarte I, 168.

Scylla is a lyric tragedy in five acts and a prologue with a libretto by Jean-François Duché de Vancy* and music by the Florentine Teobaldo di Gatti,* known in France as Théobalde. The opera had its premiere at the Palais-Royal* on 16 September 1701, and its first run lasted through its 24th billing on 13 September 1701. It was withdrawn for revision and brought back to the stage with a new prologue and three reworked acts on 20 December 1701. It enjoyed seven representations before being dropped again on 12 January 1702; it was revived in October 1720 and September 1732.

The prologue of *Scylla* presents L'Envie assembling a troupe of warriors risen from Hades to attack La France, but they disperse at the sight of their intended victim. Apollon annnounces to La France that her greatest joy and prosperity are at hand. After the inevitable laudium of Louis XIV, it is revealed that the coming production will deal with Scylla and her unhappy love.

The tragedy begins with Scylla lamenting her inappropriate passion for the invader, Minos, and her regrettable indifference toward Dardanus, whom she used to love (I, 1-2). Dardanus declares that he and Scylla can now marry because her father and Minos have laid down their arms (I, 3). Capis decries the truce that Minos and Nisus have decreed because the cessation of hostilities permits the marriage of Scylla and Dardanus, whom she loves. Ismène promises to help her to break the armistice (I, 4). Nisus, Minos, and their followers enter singing the praises of peace, but thunder interrupts their rejoicing. As in *Tancrède,* therefore, the exposition in *Scylla* establishes a chain of unrequited loves reminiscent of Racinian plots: Capis loves Dardanus in love with Scylla, who loves Minos. This situation will kaleidoscope under the impact of events, and Scylla will find herself being courted by the man she loves.

The second act opens with Minos and Scylla confessing their love to each other; the latter promises to delay her marriage to Dardanus (II, 1-2). Capis thinks that Dardanus has rejected Scylla (II, 3-4), and Ismène summons up demons from Hades to help her win his love (II, 5). Ismène and her brother Artémidor, also a magician, reassure Capis (III, 1), but Dardanus complains of his unrequited love (III, 2-3). Artémidor conjures up the mausoleum of Tirésie, and the latter announces that Dardanus should reject Scylla in favor of Capis (III, 4). But Dardanus ignores her, and she swears vengeance (III, 5-6).

The situation becomes complicated in the fourth act, when Minos explains to Scylla that he must leave her because her father has declared war (IV, 1-2). Scylla laments (IV, 3), and her father complains of being obliged to break the truce (IV, 4). A chorus of shepherds sings the praises of La Paix (IV, 4-5), who descends from the clouds to warn Nisus of Ismène's trickery (IV, 6). La Discorde urges him to punish Minos (IV, 7-8). Scylla confesses that she has been treacherous enough to cut the protective lock of hair from her father's head (V, 1), but a chorus arrives announcing Minos's defeat (V, 2). This news proves false when Doris reveals the deaths of Nisus, Dardanus, and Capis along with the victory of Minos (V, 3-4). Scylla blames herself for her father's defeat and swallows poison to die at Minos's feet (V, 5).

BIBLIOGRAPHY: Lajarte I, 92-93; RGO VII, 215-76.

Sémélé is a lyric tragedy in five acts and a prologue with music by Marais* and a libretto by Houdard de La Motte.* Like *Bradamante** and *Hippodamie,** it was not a very popular composition and was never revived, although it was billed on 25 dates between its premiere on 9 April 1709 and its last performance on 21 May 1709.

The prologue of *Sémélé* centers on Bacchus's apotheosis with a chorus and Apollon singing the new god's praises. No effort is made to allude to the subject matter of the forthcoming opera, and Louis XIV is not extolled.

The tragedy begins with Cadmus informing Sémélé that Adraste has defeated the enemy and has won her hand as his reward (I, 1). Desperate, the heroine decides that she must obey her father and marry Adraste despite her love for Idas (I, 2), but an earthquake shakes the temple, and Furies fly off with the hero's trophies of victory (I, 3).

A minor plot is introduced at the start of the second act: Mercure enters disguised as Arbate and reveals his love for Dorine (II, 1). The action returns to the principal intrigue immediately, however, when Jupiter disguised as Idas rebukes Sémélé for rejecting him. She protests that she had to accept Adraste in spite of herself, and Jupiter responds by disclosing his true identity (II, 2). The god then orders a celebration in honor of Sémélé and himself (II, 3). Sémélé explains to Adraste that she cannot reject a god, and her former suitor attacks Jupiter (II, 4), only to be swallowed up in a dense cloud (II, 5). When he is liberated, Adraste calls upon Junon for aid (III, 1). The goddess promises him that Jupiter will be called to task shortly (III, 2), and she threatens Sémélé for her impertinent and too ambitious love (III, 3). Since Sémélé rejoices over Jupiter's love for her, Junon is obliged to disguise herself as Sémélé's nurse to gain her rival's confidence. She suggests to Sémélé that she loves an imposter and that it is not unusual for mortals to pretend to perform superhuman feats to impress other people. She supports her allegation by calling forth the Furies and Demons of Hades (III, 4-5). Junon argues further that Sémélé can remove her suspicions by daring her suitor to appear before her in all his divine glory (III, 5).

The secondary plot is revived at the start of the fourth act when Arbate reveals himself to be Mercure, but Dorine rejects him because he will be no more constant than Jupiter (IV, 1). The latter god orders a celebration for Sémélé (IV, 2). He is alarmed at her sadness, and she admits her doubts about his divine identity. He hesitates to display his glory, and she refuses to believe that he is Jupiter (IV, 3). Jupiter regrets that he must be the agent of her death if he is to convince her (IV, 4). Finally, Sémélé agrees that her suitor is the ruler of the gods, and she begs him to descend again to earth (V, 1). Adraste thinks that Junon has deceived him with false promises, and he rages against Jupiter too (V, 2). Jupiter comes down from the heavens amidst deafening thunder and scorching flame (V, 3). Adraste urges his beloved Sémélé to flee before he dies, and Sémélé is carried off into the empyrean (V, 4).

BIBLIOGRAPHY: Lajarte I, 110; Antoine Houdard de La Motte, *Oeuvres complètes,* 11 vols. (Genève: Slatkine Reprints, 1970) II, 268-81; RGO IX, 387-437.

La Sérénade vénitienne is a ballet entrée included in *Les Fragments de Lully** and staged in 1702. It was revived in 1703 and 1707; it was revised and billed under the title of *Le Jaloux trompé* in 1731.

The intrigue was designed to entertain rather than to edify, and it begins with Le Docteur complaining that he has fallen in love with youthful Léonore, despite his advanced age. Like Molière's cautious husband in *L'Ecole des maris,* he has locked his beloved in his house for safekeeping, and he depends upon his wealth to make him attractive. He frees her momentarily to suggest that she marry him in return for her liberty, but she protests that she prefers slavery to marriage with him. He confines her to his house again, but Eraste kidnaps her.

BIBLIOGRAPHY: Lajarte I, 97.

Subligny, Marie-Thérèse Perdou de (b. 1666; d. 1741, Paris?) danced with the corps de ballet of the royal Academy of Music between 1689 and 1707. She appeared in the ballets of eleven works by Lully* during their revivals in this period: *Atys,** *Cadmus et Hermione,** *Proserpine,** *Le Carnaval,** *Amadis de Gaule,** *Acis et Galathée,** *Armide,** *Persée,** *Psyché,** *Isis,** and *Roland.** She was also billed to dance in Campra's *L'Europe galante,** *Hésione,** *Alcine,** *Aréthuse,** *Les Muses,** *Télémaque,** and *Tancrède** between 1697 and 1707 as well as in Destouches's *Issé,** *Omphale,** *Amadis de Grèce,** *Marthésie,** and *Le Carnaval et la Folie,** and assorted pieces like Colasse's *Canente** (1700), Théobalde's *Scylla** (1701), and Bouvart's *Médus** (1702).

Mlle de Subligny has a certain historical importance because she was one of the first dancers of noble birth to perform professionally at the Palais-Royal.* She was also the first professional ballerina to appear on the stage in England (1700-2). Her career is also noteworthy for its length and for the number of rôles in which she was cast because dancers were limited in her day to presenting striking configurations rather than interpreting dramatic situations evolving from the matrix work. Her satisfactory service with the corps de ballet is verified by her attainment of the rank of première danseuse.

The ballerina appears to have been admired for her unprepossessing personality and beauty, although critics objected at times that her feet and knees were inclined to turn inward. Her father was a gentleman and interested in literary matters, and she carried letters of introduction to John Locke from the abbé Dubos and Fontenelle on her trip to England. Inelegantly enough, the last document pertaining to her activities is Paris is a complaint of 8 May 1735 by Louis Francoeur of the royal violins. The complainant asserts that Mlle Subligny ruined his black suit and wig by dumping the contents of a chamber pot upon him in the rue Saint-Honoré.

BIBLIOGRAPHY: ACPM 868; CODB 506-7; EC II, 295-99; EDS IX, 529; Lajarte I, 23, 30. 37, 53, 55, 60, 86, 90-95, 98, 101, 103-6; André Levinson, "Notes sur le ballet au XVIIe siècle: Les danseurs de Lully," *RM* VI (January 1925), 54-55; Parmenia Migel, *The Ballerinas from the Court of Louis XIV to Pavlova* (New York: Macmillan, 1972), 9-10; L. Travenol and Jacques Durey de Noinville, *Histoire du Théâtre de l'Opéra en France,* 2 vols. (Paris: Joseph Barbou, 1753) II, 70-71.

T

Tancrède is a lyric tragedy in five acts and a prologue for which André Campra* scored the music and Antoine Danchet* wrote the libretto. It had its premiere at the Palais-Royal* on 7 November 1702, and the unpublished *Journal de l'Opéra* records in November and December of this year that it was continued with *Les Fragments de Lully** until 23 January 1703. *Tancrède* was extremely popular, and it was revived successfully on numerous occasions between 1707 and 1764. When it was returned to the stage five years after its first run, it underwent certain modifications for its 13 billings between 20 October and 15 November 1707, when Mlles Armand and Journet* sang Clorinde. Then, on 8 June 1717, it was presented again with new corrections, and it was heard in this emended form for 30 programs until 15 August 1717. It was also during this series of bookings that *Tancrède* was followed by a symphonic composition by the elder Rebel* to which Blondy,* Laval, and Mlle Camargo (for Camargo, see eighteenth-century volume) danced a *pas de trois* with great success. This miniature ballet presented a dancing teacher and his two students in a series of dances. De Chassé filled the part of Tancrède in the revivals of 1738 and 1750, and Larrivée followed him in this rôle in 1764 (for de Chassé and Larrivée, see eighteenth-century volume). *Tancrède* was applauded at the start of its career at the Palais-Royal doubtlessly because Campra was so skilled in writing for the voice that he was able to compose the part of Clorinde especially for Mlle Maupin.* In fact, *Tancrède* is the first opera to have a rôle for a contralto. The selections that impressed audiences most favorably were the bass duet by Isménor et Argant, "Suivons la fureur et la rage" (I, 2), and the aria by Herminie, "Cessez, mes yeux, de contraindre vos larmes" (III, 2).

The prologue of *Tancrède* presents a benevolent sorcerer and his suite calling upon La Paix to assist them in a celebration, but the goddess explains that war has broken out again. This allusion to the war of the Spanish succession is followed by a propagandistic note reassuring spectators at the Palais-Royal that "the famous people from the banks of the Seine" are being led once more by a king gentle in peace and valiant in war. The tragedy itself recounts the love affair of Clorinde and Tancrède, with the protagonist slaying his beloved Clorinde because he mistakes her for Argant.

BIBLIOGRAPHY: André Campra, *Tancrède reconstituée et reduite pour piano et chant par Alexandre Guilmant* (Paris: T. Michaëlis, 188?); Lajarte I, 97-99; RGO VIII, 1-56.

Télémaque was billed as a tragedy in five acts and a prologue. It was designated frequently as "fragments from the moderns" and had its premiere at the Palais-Royal on 11 November 1704. Its first run lasted through 13 January 1705 for 37 representations. It was heard on 16 November 1704 by the dauphin in the company of the duchess de Bourgogne, the duke de Berry, and the princess de Conty, but it was never taken to Versailles or Fontainebleau.

Campra* and Danchet* were responsible for its production, and the latter explains in the preface to his libretto that the success of *Les Fragments de Lully** induced the decision to create an operatic work composed of the more striking extracts from certain "modern operas" that were not impressive enough in their totality to justify being revived in their complete form. This was difficult but possible, the poet continues, by selecting the story of Télémaque and coordinating certain admired pieces of music with it. Thus, Danchet wrote connecting words for certain already extant texts, and Campra set them to music. The adopted passages included extracts from *Énée et Lavinie** by Colasse* and *Aréthuse** by Campra for the prologue; from *Astrée** by Colasse, *Enée et Lavinie* again, and *Canente** by Colasse for the first act; *Aréthuse* again for the second act; *Médée** by Charpentier* and *Canente* again for the third act; *Le Carnaval de Venise** by Campra, *Ariane** by Marais,* and *Circé** by Desmarets* for the fourth act; *Le Carnaval de Venise* again, *Les Fêtes galantes** by Desmarets, *Canente* again, *Ulysse** by Rebel,* and *Circé* and *Aréthuse* again for the fifth act.

The prologue resulting from this interweaving of selections from previous compositions presents La Félicité descending to earth and Le Printemps encouraging the flowers to beautify the countryside.

The action of the opera itself is simple and begins with the presentation of Calipso troubled by her love for Télémaque and worried over his continued absence (I, 1-2). Vénus announces to Calipso that L'Amour has overcome Télémaque (I, 3), and she resolves to determine whom he loves (I, 4). Eucaris reveals that she and the son of Ulysse are in love (I, 5). The exposition also establishes that Neptune is a suitor for the hand of Calipso.

Calipso is interrogating evasive Télémaque (II, 1) when Neptune frightens her away (II, 2). The god enters singing the praise of Vénus, but he becomes suspicious and threatening because he cannot find Calipso (II, 3-5). Eucaris and Télémaque declare their love for each other (III, 1), and jealous Calipso summons up the Furies from Hades to frighten Eucaris, but Neptune dismisses these evil spirits to exact his own vengeance (III, 2-4). He is still pondering the proper punishment for his rival when Minerve restrains him (IV, 1-2). The goddess puts Télémaque to sleep (IV, 3-4), but she awakens him from this spell to order him to flee because Neptune loves Eucaris, and Calipso is planning to harm him (IV, 5). Angry Calipso plans a "celebration" for Eucaris and Télémaque so that she may slay them together (V, 1-3), but they escape in hasty flight (V, 4).

BIBLIOGRAPHY: Lajarte I, 104; RGO VIII, 291-332.

Télémaque is a lyric tragedy in five acts and a prologue with a score by André-Cardinal Destouches* and a libretto by the abbé Simon-Joseph de Pellegrin.* The story is inspired by the first book of Fénelon's *Télémaque*, in which Calypso falls in love with the shipwrecked protagonist, and by the sixth book, which recounts the love affair of Télémaque and Eucharis. Destouches's work had its premiere on 29 November 1714 and enjoyed ten performances during the rest of the year. A parody of it was offered at the Saint-Germain fair in 1715. It was revived on 23 February 1730, but it was billed only five times during its second and last run.

The prologue of the tragedy is an uninhibited laudium of Louis XIV, supposedly ordered by Minerva to celebrate the peace that the French king has brought to Europe. Apollon assists in this display of gratitude for the end of the war of the Spanish Succession, and L'Amour constructs a pyramid to the king's glory at the close of the celebration.

Télémaque is set on the island of Ogygie which is battered by floods. Here Eucharis has fallen in love with a shipwrecked stranger (I, 1-2). Calypso is angered by the devastation wrought by Neptune upon her kingdom and by the god's request that she sacrifice Ulysse's blood (I, 3). Adraste announces that the gods have united to bring new destruction to the land, and he rails against Neptune for having prevented his marriage to Calypso (I, 4). Calypso summons her demons from the underworld, and they direct her to erect an altar for the sacrifice, because Neptune will supply Ulysse's blood (I, 5-6). She agrees. The principal dramatic interest is provided by the conflict between Calypso and Neptune, with the love element supplied by Eucharis's apparently unrequited love for a handsome stranger, and by Adraste's frustrated love for Calypso.

Télémaque enters to share in the sacrifice. Idas warns him against Eucharis and reminds him that he is to wed Antiope (II, 1). Télémaque reveals to Eurcharis that he is the son of Ulysse, and she urges him to flee because Neptune is demanding Ulysse's blood (II, 2). The high priestess and her entourage pray to Neptune to deliver the sacrificial victim (II, 3). Télémaque offers himself, but Calypso orders him spared at the last moment (II, 4). Adraste swears to slay Télémaque (III, 1-2) and informs Calypso of his vow (III, 3). Calypso admits her love for Télémaque (III, 4-5), who tells her that he is embarking because Neptune has been appeased

(III, 6). Calypso conjures up an enchanted palace and orders her attendants to entertain Télémaque (III, 7), but he is determined to sail away in search of Ulysse (III, 8). Eucharis decides to renounce Télémaque to spare his life (IV, 1), but she cannot persuade him to reject her in favor of Calypso (IV, 2). The latter notices that he shuns her, and she suspects that she has a rival. Angry (IV, 3), she consults the high priestess of L'Amour, but the Oracle foretells that Télémaque and Antiope are to reign over Itaque (IV, 4). Calypso is furious to learn from Adraste, wounded mortally by Télémaque, that the latter is in love with Eucharis (IV, 5-6). Calypso resolves to slay them both (IV, 7).

The conclusion of the tragedy is reached rapidly when Calypso permits Télémaque to embark while she holds Eucharis for execution (V, 1-2). Télémaque determines to rescue his beloved, and she reveals that she is Antiope, his destined queen in Itaque (V, 4). Télémaque's forces arrive by ship to rescue Antiope, but Calypso's demons put the fleet to the torch (V, 5-6). The hero calls upon Minerva for help, and the goddess descends from the skies to arrange the lovers' rescue (V, 7-8).

BIBLIOGRAPHY: Brenner 220; DDO II, 1070; Lajarte I, 123; Sonn I, 1057.

Télèphe is a lyric tragedy in five acts and a prologue with music by André Campra* and words by Antoine Danchet.* It enjoyed 19 performances including its premiere on 23 November 1713; it was dropped after its 24 December 1713 billing. The title-rôle was sung by Thévenard,* with Mlles Journet* and Pestel as Isménie and Arsinoë, respectively. Hardouin* did the part of Eurite, the tyrant of Mysie. Mlles Guyot and Prévost* appeared in the ballet with Dumoulin.*

The gods and goddesses of the earth, sea, skies, and underworld are gathered in the prologue for the apotheosis of Hercule. Junon approves of the ceremony that Jupiter has prepared. The wedding of Hercule and La Jeunesse is announced, and Vénus and her retinue lead in the celebration.

In the tragedy Télèphe is separated from his beloved Isménie, and, in searching for her, he has entered and defended Eurite's kingdom. In gratitude, the king offers him his sister as his bride, but he rejects this arrangement, because Arsame is already in love with Arsinoë, and he wishes to continue to look for Isménie. Thus, the early exposition of *Télèphe* establishes two love affairs (Isménie-Télèphe, Arsame-Arsinoë) instead of a triangle. It is also made clear that the protagonist comes from unknown but apparently humble origins (I, 1-2). The action is complicated when Arsame discovers Arsinoë's love for Télèphe (I, 3). After a celebration inspired by the return of peace, Eurite reveals his fears that Télèphe's popularity might prompt him to usurp the throne. He suggests that Télèphe be asked to leave Mysie, and he describes the doubts that have haunted him since he killed Teutras and took possession of his kingdom. Arsinoë suggests that he marry Isménie after announcing that she is the sister of Teutras (I, 5).

The second act reunites Isménie and Télèphe with Eurite demanding the former's hand in marriage (II, 1-2). The rites for Apollon are performed in a *divertissement,* * and the Oracle foretells that Isménie will wed the king of Mysie before nightfall (II, 3). Télèphe resolves to tell Eurite of his great love for Isménie in the hope that the king will release her (II, 4). Isménie reveals her love for Télèphe to Arsinoë, and the latter vows to take vengeance against her (II, 5-6). Her first tactic is to explain to Eurite that Isménie and Télèphe are in love so that she may have her brother and his power on her side. Their alliance is weakened by the king's persistent desire to protect Isménie (III, 1). Eurite threatens Isménie (III, 2), but Télèphe swears to protect her (III, 3). When he offers to take Eurite's throne for her, she interprets his scheme as a plot for power and threatens to marry Eurite. Crushed, Télèphe threatens suicide, and the entire matter ends in the reconciliation of the two lovers (III, 4). Isménie learns finally that she is the daughter of Teutras, and the people of Pergame hail her as their ruler (III, 5-6).

Isménie now recalls the death of her father at the altar of Hercule and vows to avenge him. Télèphe suggests that he slay Eurite at the forthcoming celebration honoring Hercule (IV, 1-2). Eurite launches his counterplot by offering Arsinoë's hand to Arsame if the latter will kill Télèphe. Arsame refuses out of gratitude for Télèphe's past favors to him (IV, 3-5), and the rites for Hercule start (IV, 6). Yet all is not well in Pergame because Télèphe has been arrested on Eurite's orders, and the people have risen in revolt (IV, 7).

The conclusion of the tragedy is prepared by Arsame's instigating a move to free Télèphe (V, 1-2). Arsinoë threatens to punish the rioters and swears to Isménie that she will pay for her love for Télèphe (V, 3). Her menacings are in vain because Télèphe and Arsame announce the death of Eurite. Defiant Arsinoë responds by offering her life to Télèphe, but Arsame surrenders himself to her, and she stabs herself in despair. Arsame cannot bear the death of his beloved Arsinoë, and he commits suicide to leave Télèphe and Isménie as king and queen of Pergame. Hercule, La Gloire, and the people celebrate their succession, and Hercule announces that Télèphe is his son (V, 4-6).

BIBLIOGRAPHY: Lajarte I, 119-20; RGO XI, 111-76.

Le Temple de la paix is the only *opéra-ballet* * that Jean-Baptiste Lully* and Philippe Quinault* created for the Royal Academy of Music, although they had already contributed the straight ballet entitled *Le Triomphe de l'Amour* * to the repertory. *Le Temple de la paix* was mounted for the first time at Fontainebleau on 20 October 1685, and Louis XIV attended its premiere to watch the members of his Court perform in it. It was taken to Paris in November 1685, but it was never revived in the capital.

Like *L'Idylle sur la paix,* * this work was offered as a pastoral celebration hailing the peace that Europe seemed certain to enjoy after the signing of the Treaty of Ratisbonne on 15 August 1684. Since all France is depicted as being grateful to a heroic and magnanimous king, the shepherdesses and shepherds appearing in colonial and provincial dress are cast as Bretons, Basques, Africans, and American Indians. *Le Temple de la paix,* then, was intended to serve as a universal salute to Louis XIV.

This composition enjoyed only limited success, although it was designed to provide a gay, swift, and picturesque spectacle with its variegated costumes and exotic characters. Lully pointed out in its preface that it was meant to be "a mythological and allegorical allusion" to the marriage of the dauphin, but its representation created the impression of a kaleidoscopic parade rather than an allegorical communication.

The six entrées of *Le Temple de la paix* were prefaced by a chorus of nymphs, shepherds, and shepherdesses announcing the forthcoming festival in honor of "an always conquering king" who has assured a peaceful life for all his subjects. The chorus and certain characters continue their panegyric of this hero in the first two entrées, and Basques perform native dances while singing in French during the third entrée. The "daughters of Brittany" appear in the fourth tableau to announce their intention of enjoying the peace without losing their liberty to love. The American Indians proclaim their satisfaction with their status as subjects of France in the fifth segment before a second love affair between Licidas and Amarallis is introduced. The Africans perform in much the same manner in their concluding scene.

Le Temple de la paix was staged a dozen times at Fontainebleau and Versailles between 20 October 1685 and 21 January 1686. It was taken to the latter royal residence on 3 December 1685 because the Court had ended their autumn sojourn at Fontainebleau and had returned to Versailles for the winter. It was billed at the Palais-Royal* for three months beginning in November 1685. Strangely enough, Paris audiences did not seem to tire of it during this interval, and Lully did not have to resort to a revival of one of his previous successes to keep the public entertained while he was completing *Armide.* *

BIBLIOGRAPHY: Lajarte I, 51-52; RGO III, 92-120.

Théagène et Chariclée, sometimes spelled *Téagène et Cariclée*, is a lyric tragedy in five acts and a prologue with music by Desmarets* and a libretto by Duché de Vancy.* It was based upon Heliodorus's romance of the same title, but its librettist took liberties with the original tale to achieve spectacular effects for the stage. Alexandre Hardy had dramatized this ancient novel of adventure at the beginning of the seventeenth century, and Mlle de Scudéry had helped make it better known by acknowledging it to be one of the models of her own fiction. Yet the opera was not very successful, and it was never revived after its first run extending from 3 February 1695 until sometime in April or May of the same year.

After the usual laudium of Louis XIV in the prologue, the intrigue of the tragedy itself is set into motion without delay and in medias res by Chariclée's complaint that she has fallen in love with a man whom she will never see again and by Tisbé's announcement that Méroebe will defeat Egypt and ask for Chariclée's hand in marriage. Duché then manages to achieve a *coup de théâtre:* Méroebe enters with his first contingent of prisoners, and Chariclée discovers her beloved Théagène among them. The political aspect of the action is brought into focus by Hidaspe's victory over Egypt. The supernatural element is introduced by Arsace calling upon the demons of Hades to carry Tisbé, Méroebe, Chariclée, and herself to the banks of the Styx. Arsace remains in control of the situation until Hidaspe recognizes Chariclée as his daughter and prevents her execution. Arsace then kills herself in despair, and the king gives his blessing to the marriage of Théagène and Chariclée.

BIBLIOGRAPHY: Lajarte I, 63; RGO V, 67-134.

Thésée was the second work done by Jean-Baptiste Lully* and Philippe Quinault* for the Palais-Royal,* but it had its premiere at Saint-Germain en Laye on 11 January 1675 and was not mounted at the artistes' own theatre until 12 May 1675.

The success of *Alceste** probably induced Quinault to model the prologue of *Thésée* after the introductory portion of his previous work: the earlier prologue had been set in the Tuileries; the prefatory section of *Thésée* is laid in Versailles and its gardens, where Plaisirs and Jeux lament the absence of the king away at war. Bacchus, Cérès, and their sportive followers enliven the spectacle that ends in a festival of joyous song and dance for which Lully wrote his usual "glorious" music. Vénus's air, "Revenez, revenez," is the most arresting portion of the prologue music.

The main plot is reminiscent of a Racinian tragedy with its quadrilateral situation: Médée loves Thésée in love with Eglé, who loves Thésée while being loved by Egée. The subplot based upon the affections of Arcas and Cléone is never developed beyond the point of inspiring a few scenes of debate that furnish intervals of relief. The action is not initiated in the usual manner of expositions but to the accompaniment of a noisy battle raging in Athens between the enemies and supporters of Egée. The first act presents Egée suppressing the revolt with Thésée's help and proposing marriage to Eglé, although he is supposed to wed Médée. Thésée becomes Egée's rival for the throne of Athens as well as for the hand of Eglé, when the Athenians seek him as their king (II).

Rejected and raging like Racine's Hermione in *Andromaque,* Médée threatens Eglé on account of Thésée's indifference towards her (III). When Thésée and Eglé refuse to abandon each other even in the face of Médée's fury and sworn vengeance, peace and quiet are restored after Egée recognizes Thésée as his son, and Minerva descends from the sky to protect the lovers (IV, V).

The libretto for *Thésée* is not too well composed: the subplot is established only to be ignored; Médée changes her mind too drastically and too rapidly; the conflict never settles down into a simple direction. It should be acknowledged, however, that the spectacles are unified with the action, since the furies, monsters, and demons as well as the denizens of the underworld are all ancillary to the major events.

Thésée may not have been one of Lully's greatest works, but it was one of his most popular compositions. It was retained in the repertory for more than a century and was still attracting money to the box office after Gluck's works had had their premieres. It was mounted again at Saint-Germain en Laye on 16 February 1677. It was revived more than a dozen times between 1679 and 1782. Mondonville (for Mondonville, see eighteenth-century volume) did a new score for it in 1767.

The celebrated singers who performed in it include Mlles Le Maure, Fel, and Sophie Arnould among the women and Jélyotte, Legros, and de Chassé among the men. Mlles Camargo, Carville, and Allard danced in its ballets as did Dangeville, Dupré, Laval and d'Auberval (for Jélyotte, de Chassé, and Camargo, see eighteenth-century volume).

Lully created at least four noteworthy passages for *Thésée:* the chorus of the priestesses in I, 4; the duet by the two old men in II, 6; Médée's recitative in II, 9, "Dépit mortel"; and Médeé's invocation in III, 6, "Sortez, ombres, sortez."

BIBLIOGRAPHY: DDO II, 1083-84; Etienne Gros, *Philippe Quinault* (Paris: Champion, 1926), 111-12, 530-31, 599-603; Lajarte I, 25-28; Lionel de La Laurencie, *Lully* (Paris: Alcan, 1919), 43-45; Jean-Baptiste Lully, *Thésée . . . reconstituée et réduite pour piano et chant par Théodore de Lajarte* (Paris: T. Michaëlis, 1883); RGO I, 273-346; Sonn I, 1068-89.

Thétis et Pélée was the first work produced by the Royal Academy of Music under the direction of Lully's* son-in-law, Francine. It was a lyric tragedy in five acts and a prologue for which Colasse* composed the score and Fontenelle* did the libretto.

Staged initially in 1689, its prologue was almost exclusively an ornate laudium of the dauphin. La Victoire announces her intention of crowning the young hero with success, and Le Soleil reveals his plans to light up his triumphs. This brief introduction to *Thétis et Pélée* is in the nature of a patriotic rally.

The legend of Thétis and Pélée had already been used by Benserade* in a ballet in 1654, and there had been an allusion to it in *Le Triomphe de l'Amour et de Bacchus** in 1681. Pindar speaks of the love between this couple, and Ovid relates it at length in the *Metamorphoses* IX, 221-65. Fontenelle's version differs from these ancient sources because he depicts his hero and heroine in love before the work begins. Aware of the Horatian rule to start his intrigue in medias res, he initiates his action by presenting Neptune's passion for Thétis as the obstacle to the Pélée-Thétis love while complicating the situation further by producing Doris as Thétis's rival for Pélée's affections and offering Jupiter as a third suitor for Thétis's hand. Thus, Fontenelle depicts two gods and a mortal pursuing a goddess in love with an earthling loved by another goddess. The variety of scenes evolving among this quintet of lovers offers an almost unlimited range of dramatic confrontations, but a conclusion is reached after the lovers find themselves free to marry by virtue of Doris, Jupiter, and Neptune withdrawing from the scene.

A tableau was offered at the start of the third act of the opera where the "ministers" of Destin sing of the power and glory of their master. Collé notes in his *Journal historique* (I, 317-18) that the anticlerical tone of this passage moved the archbishop of Paris to attempt to suppress the scene. Fontenelle is reported to have observed in the face of this ecclesiastical objection to his work, "I don't interfere with his clergy, let him keep away from mine."

Thétis et Pélée was quite successful and was revived in 1699, 1708, 1712, 1723, 1736, and 1750. After its premiere at the Palais-Royal* on 11 January 1689, *Le Journal de l'Opéra* indicates that it was given the following month without machines at Court on two dates including 16 February. The dauphin attended both performances at Court as well as the Paris premiere, and he was doubtlessly pleased to hear the prologue, which flattered him so generously. The unpublished records of the Opéra point out that Fontenelle was present at the theatre on 29 November 1750; he was 93 years old at the time, and it had been 62 years to the day since the premiere of *Thétis et Pélée* had been given. The receipts on this occasion reached 4,256 *livres* 10 *sous*.

Many of the famous artistes of the first half of the eighteenth century appeared in Colasse's composition including Mlles Le Rochois,* Desmatins,* Antier,* and Chevalier as Thétis. Pélée was sung by Du Mesny* and Jélyotte (for Jélyotte, see eighteenth-century volume).

BIBLIOGRAPHY: Pascal Colasse, *Thétis et Pélée, reconstituée et reduite pour piano et chant par Louis Soumis* (Paris: T. Michaëlis, 1880); Lajarte I, 57-58; RGO III, 331-94.

Thévenard, Gabriel-Vincent (b. 10 August 1669, Orléans; d. 24 August 1741, Paris), vocalist, worked in his father's business establishment until his compatriots heard him sing and advised him to develop his voice and to earn his livelihood by singing. He went to Paris and took voice lessons. He distinguished himself as a student, and he went on to win an audition at the Opéra, where he became one of the leading basses of his day after making his debut at the Royal Academy of Music in 1695. Inevitably, he sang secondary rôles at first, but it was not long before he became the substitute for the elder Dun.* When the composer Destouches* was made director of the Opéra, he took the trouble to coach Thévenard, who was intelligent enough to profit by this expert instruction, and he rose to become a star. He was quite popular during his 30 years on the stage, and his appearances with Le Rochois* were especially applauded.

As a bass, Thévenard created a number of rôles in which he was a soothsayer, a god, a prophet, a sage, or some other type of character endowed with the power to understand the present and to anticipate the future. It was not usual to encounter a bass cast in the title-rôle of an opera because he was normally an interpreter of events, a prophet of tragedy, or an adviser of heroes. He was ancillary to the action rather than a leading force influencing the unfolding of events. Yet Thévenard was cast in the title-rôle or shared top billing in no fewer than thirteen compositions at the time of their premieres:

Rôle	Opera	Premiere
Amadis	Amadis de Grèce*	26 March 1699
Médus	Médus, roi des Mèdes*	23 July 1702
Tancrède	Tancrède*	7 November 1702
Le Carnaval	Le Carnaval et la Folie*	3 January 1704
Pyrrhus	Polyxène et Pyrrhus*	21 October 1706
Idoménée	Idoménée*	12 January 1712
Mars	Les Amours de Mars et de Vénus	6 September 1712
Télèphe	Télèphe*	28 November 1713
Pâris	Le Jugement de Pâris	14 June 1718
Polydore	Polydore	15 February 1720
Protée	Les Amours de Protée	16 May 1720
Télégone	Télégone	6 November 1725
Pyrame	Pyrame et Thisbé	17 October 1726

(See eighteenth-century volume for 1718-26 works.)

The 1697-1729 period was a time when mythological subjects were still popular at the Palais-Royal,* of course, and Thévenard's personal repertory could not avoid reflecting this predilection for classical mythology in art, in literature, and in music. He was cast as a Greek divinity in at least seven works in which he was not a major character. As indicated previously, he was billed in these parts simply because he was the best bass available. He represented the gods in the premieres of seven works:

God	Opera	Premiere
Mars	*Vénus et Adonis* *	17 March 1697
Jupiter	*Issé* *	30 December 1697
Bacchus	*Les Muses* *	28 October 1703
Apollon	*Les Festes de Thalie* *	19 August 1714
Apollon	*Les Festes grecques et romaines*	13 July 1723
Neptune, Bacchus	*Les Amours des dieux*	16 September 1727
Saturne	*Le Parnasse*	5 October 1729

(See eighteenth-century volume for 1723-29 works.)

More frequently, the bass was cast as a ruler or warrior found in Trojan, Greek, Arabic, or Medieval history or legend, or he was the product of the librettist's imagination:

Rôle	Opera	Premiere
Sylvandre, Zuliman	*L'Europe galante* *	24 October 1697
Argapise	*Marthésie, reine des Amazones* *	9 November 1699
Picus	*Canente* *	4 November 1700
Alphée	*Aréthuse* *	14 July 1701
Eraste	*La Sérénade vénitienne* *	10 September 1702
Athlante	*Alcine* *	15 January 1705
Le Carnaval, Léandre	*Les Festes vénitiennes* *	17 June 1710
Licarcis	*Manto la fée* *	29 January 1711
Corisus	*Callirhoë* *	27 December 1712
Diomède, Ovide	*Les Amours déguisés* *	23 August 1713
Adraste	*Télémaque* *	29 November 1714
Licas	*Les Plaisirs de la paix* *	29 April 1715
Thestor	*Théonoé*	3 December 1715
Almon	*Camille, roi des Volsques*	9 November 1717
Eraste	*Les Ages*	9 October 1718
Valère	*Les Plaisirs de la campagne*	10 August 1719
Ixion, Valère	*Les Eléments*	29 May 1725

(See eighteenth-century volume for *Théonoé* and 1716-25 works.)

The rôles created by Thévenard that were more obviously in debt to legend, saga, myth, or even a specific literary source included:

Rôle	Opera	Premiere
Pygmalion	*Le Triomphe des arts**	16 May 1700
Anchise	*Hésione**	21 December 1700
Alcide	*Omphale**	10 November 1701
Oreste	*Iphigénie en Tauride**	6 May 1704
Agamemnon	*Cassandre**	22 June 1706
Roger	*Bradamante**	2 May 1707
Créon	*Médée et Jason**	24 April 1713
Eurylas	*Arion**	10 April 1714
Danaüs	*Hypermnestre*	3 November 1716
Thésée	*Ariane*	6 April 1717
Nourredin	*La Reine des Péris*	10 April 1725

(See eighteenth-century volume for 1716-25 works.)

The most difficult of Thévenard's rôles to classify is probably one of the parts he sang for a revival of *Les Festes vénitiennes*, "un Français."

BIBLIOGRAPHY: AEM XIII, 330-31; André Campra, *Les Festes vénitiennes*, ed. Alexandre Guilmant (Paris: Théodore Michaëlis, n.d.), 9; EC II, 307-13; Fétis VIII, 212; Lajarte I, 67, 83-86, 88-95, 97-98, 100-105, 108-9, 111-12, 114-24, 126-31, 133-35, 137-38, 140-43, 147; TdT 797-99; L. Travenol and Jacques Durey de Noinville, *Histoire du théâtre de l'Opéra en France*, 2 vols. (Paris: Joseph Barbou, 1753) II, 54-57.

Le Triomphe de l'Amour is a ballet in twenty entrées with music by Jean-Baptiste Lully,* a libretto by Philippe Quinault,* and choreography by Isaac de Benserade.* It was danced for the first time on 21 January 1681 at Saint-Germain en Laye after two postponements caused by the illness of the dauphin. Louis XIV commissioned the work to please the dauphine, who was fond of music and dancing. The king himself had lost some of his active interest in the dance, and the return of the royal ballet to Court after an absence of ten years was a signal event. It aroused such enthusiasm that the lords and ladies of the Court joined in with the professional artistes for its gala premiere featuring magnificent costumes and dazzling jewels. The presence of ladies of noble and royal blood on the stage opened the way for women to dance regularly with the company. *Le Journal de l'Opéra* notes on 10 May 1681, "For the first time, introduction of danseuses into the ballets of the Opéra."

It has been remarked that *Le Triomphe de l'Amour* is best viewed as an opera because its libretto has a certain unity and its production depends in such large measure upon its music as well as upon the dance. Its libretto is in fact unified to a remarkable degree despite the large number of entrées it includes because each entrée leads up to and acknowledges the triumph of love. When Jupiter appears finally at the conclusion of the composition to announce that L'Amour is indeed omnipotent and irresistible, the gods, semigods, and mortals sing their agreement with his pronouncement before the grand ballet celebrates the titularly announced "triumph of Love." Thus, while the entrées differ in the pageantry, characters, and choreography developed, they are bound together by the single theme of love victorious. *Le Triomphe de l'Amour* is a seminal *opéra-ballet** and not an expanded *divertissement.**

Lully's work was revived on 6 May 1682 and 11 September 1705. It was billed for 25 representations during this last run that continued until 8 December with but a single interruption on 26 November 1705. The *Journal de l'Opéra* specifies that, for the 11 September 1705 performance, "Danchet and Campra changed this ballet almost entirely by putting it into a prologue and four entrées: I, *Mars et Vénus;* II, *Amphitrite et Neptune;* III, *Diane et Endymion;* IV, *Ariane et Bacchus.*"

BIBLIOGRAPHY: DDO II, 1099-1111; Etienne Gros, *Philippe Quinault* (Paris: Champion, 1926), 134-38, 638-43; Lajarte I, 38-41; Lionel de La Laurencie, *Lully* (Paris: Alcan, 1919), 56-58, 156-57; Jean-Baptiste Lully, *Le Triomphe de l'Amour*, ed. Paul Angerer (Wien: Doblinger, 1959); RGO II, 269-98; Charles Silin, *Benserade and His Ballets de Cour* (Baltimore: The Johns Hopkins Press, 1940), 392-400; Sonn I, 1093; SS 60-62.

Le Triomphe des arts is an *opéra-ballet** in five acts with music by Michel de La Barre* and a libretto by Houdard de La Motte.* It had its premiere at the Palais-Royal* on 16 May 1700, and its first and only run extended for 24 performances until 19 July 1700.

The first entrée, entitled *L'Architecture,* presented Apollon agreeing with Vénus that L'Amour be honored in a new temple built for him, but Apollon insists that Louis XIV have an even greater share in this homage. Sapho complains of her inconstant lover in *La Poésie,* and a chorus of lovers praises Vénus and L'Amour before the despairing poetess throws herself into the sea.

Amphion charms Niobé with his song in *La Musique,* and he offers her a crown while a throne is prepared for them. *La Peinture* transpires in Alexandre's palace, where Apelle has painted the story of the Macedonian hero. A slight intrigue is developed from the triangle of Alexandre loving Campaspe despite the mutual love between Campaspe and the artist, and the act ends with a chorus of the painter's disciples celebrating his glory and happiness upon winning Campaspe's hand.

La Sculpture presents Pigmalion urging La Propetide to forgive his senseless love for his statue, but she continues to upbraid him for his folly. Vénus produces a solution for this dilemma by turning La Propetide to stone and animating the statue.

Ballot de Sauvot revised the libretto of *Pigmalion,* and Rameau composed fresh music for this retouched poem (for Ballot de Sauvot and Rameau, see eighteenth-century volume).

The performers appearing in *Le Triomphe des arts* included Mlle Maupin* (Vénus, III; La Propetide, V) with Hardouin* as Amphion (III) and Thévenard* as Pygmalion.

BIBLIOGRAPHY: CL II, 1101; Lajarte I, 89-90; Antoine Houdard de La Motte, *Oeuvres complètes,* 11 vols. (Genève: Slatkine Reprints, 1970) II, 170-91; RGO VII, 1-48; Sonn I, 1094.

Tuileries, Salle des Machines. Louis XIV gave the order to complete the Tuileries, located opposite the Louvre, and the Salle des Machines was among the units of the palace finished in the seventeenth century by Le Vau and his son-in-law d'Orbay. The world premiere of *Psyché* by Corneille, Lully,* Molière,* and Quinault* was staged in this theatre in 1671, but it was not until 24 January 1764 that the Opéra moved into the Salle des Machines, situated between the pavillon de l'Horloge and the pavillon de Marsan. The Royal Academy of Music continued to use this facility until 23 January 1770, when the members of the company left it to occupy the new Palais-Royal,* which was constructed specifically for them. They had spent seven years in this temporary facility.

The Salle des Machines was destroyed during the Commune uprising and the burning of the Tuileries in May 1871.

BIBLIOGRAPHY: Max Aghion, *Le Théâtre à Paris au XVIIIe siècle* (Paris: Librairie de France, n.d.), 204-5; Jacques Heuzey, "Notes sur un dessin représentant la Salle des Machines au XVIIe siècle," *RHT* 6 (1954), 60-67; Jacques Hillairet, *Dictionnaire historique des rues de Paris,* 2 vols. (Paris: Les Editions de minuit, 1963) I, 574-75; André Lejeune and Stéphane Wolff, *Les quinze salles de l'Opéra de Paris* (Paris: Librairie théâtrale, 1955), 21-22; Charles Nuitter, *Le Nouvel Opéra* (Paris: Hachette, 1875), 7.

U

Ulysse was billed as a tragedy in five acts and a prologue. Its music was by the elder Rebel,* and its libretto was written by Guichard.* It was not a very successful work, and it was never revived after its first run. It had its premiere at the Palais-Royal* on 23 January 1703. A tale circulated in 1703 to the effect that Guichard had sold the royalties to his work before its production, and after its failure he said, "You cannot judge the worth of my opera without having seen the sixth act: that of the notary."

The prologue of *Ulysse* presents Orphée giving a concert for the creatures of the forest. The nymph of the Seine joins the audience with her retinue, and she explains that she and her companions are paying honor to "the hero of the Seine." The last three lines of the prologue announce hurriedly that Ulysse and his deeds have furnished the inspiration for the coming tragedy.

The opera opens with a suitor of Pénélope, Urilas, complaining that he cannot persuade her to show any interest in him (I, 1) and with Circé promising to help him win her affections (I, 2). But cunning Circé has also promised Pénélope that Ulysse will return home before long because she knows that he is already on his way back to Itaque, and she hopes to win his heart by promoting Pénélope's infidelity (I, 3). Ulysse's wife deplores his absence (I, 4-6), but Circé assures her that his return is at hand (I, 7) while tempting her to listen to Urilas's suit (I, 8-9). Pénélope reproaches herself for thinking of Urilas, who seeks help from Junon (II, 1). But the goddess keeps Pénélope faithful to Ulysse (II, 2), and Urilas regrets her interference (II, 3). Finally, Circé urges Urilas to kidnap Pénélope (II, 4). She then orders her Furies to ignore Junon and to raise a magnificent palace for Ulysse (II, 5-6).

It may be said that the second half of *Ulysse* begins with the entrance of the protagonist at the end of the second act, although he does not return to Pénélope even at this point in the action. He sends Euriloque into Itaque, however, while Circé's demons disguise themselves as Tritons and Néreides to entertain in his sumptuous palace (III, 1-3). Circé convinces Ulysse that she will help him against his enemies, and she gives him an enchanted sword (III, 4-5). Ulysse falls under her spell once again, and they make plans to leave Itaque (III, 6). But Euriloque sees through the enchantress's trickery, and he persuades Ulysse to discard the weapon. Ulysse agrees and returns to his senses. He will return to Itaque to defend his kingdom (IV, 1). Circé upbraids him for his change of heart and destroys the palace (IV, 2), but Ulysse remains firm despite Circé's fury and the sudden transformation of his soldiers into stone. Ulysse despairs finally, however, and he attempts suicide. Euriloque and Circé interfere with his attempt upon his own life (IV, 4), and his soldiers are returned to the living (IV, 5). Ulysse is unmoved by Circé's generosity, and she condemns his followers to blindness. Mercure descends from the heavens to break this last cruel enchantment and to urge Ulysse to return to Pénélope and to scatter his rivals (IV, 6-8).

Ulysse apparently has not yet suffered enough because tireless Circé swears to slay Télémaque before his eyes (IV, 9). Ulysse defeats his enemies (V, 1-2), however, although a storm interrupts his triumphant celebration (V, 3-4). Télémaque appears in chains within a cloud, and next to him is Circé holding a dagger (V, 5). She invites Ulysse to move closer so that the blood will drop on him, a touch only Circé could add, but Pallas intervenes quickly to thwart the enchantress and to bring peace to Ulysse and Pénélope (V, 6).

BIBLIOGRAPHY: Lajarte I, 99; VIII, 57-110.

V

Vaugirard, rue de, was the location of the Bel-Air* tennis court to which Lully* moved his opera company. The troupe had been performing until then in the tennis court called La Bouteille,* situated in the rue Mazarine. The Florentine inaugurated this structure near the Luxembourg palace on 15 November 1672, but he left it within a year to open with *Pomone** at the first Palais-Royal* theatre on 17 June 1673. After the departure of Lully's troupe from the Bel-Air tennis court, this structure was converted into a riding academy.

BIBLIOGRAPHY: André Lejeune et Stéphane Wolff, *Les quinze salles de l'Opéra de Paris* (Paris: Librairie Théâtrale, 1955), 16-17; Charles Nuitter, *Le Nouvel Opéra* (Paris: Hachette, 1875), 4.

La Vénitienne is a comedy-ballet in three acts and a prologue with music by La Barre* and a libretto by Houdard de La Motte.* It had its premiere at the Palais-Royal* on 26 May 1705, and its first run of 12 performances ended on 21 June 1705. Only its third act was revived to form a portion of *Les Nouveaux Fragments* of 3 December 1711. The pastiche of 28 May 1726 entitled *Le Ballet sans titre* also incorporated the third act of *La Vénitienne* for its third *divertissement.** Dauvergne (for Dauvergne, see eighteenth-century volume), who was inclined to provide older works with new scores, created new music for La Barre's work on 6 May 1768, but he met with as little success as his predecessors.

The prologue to this comedy-ballet is a brief presentation of Momus asking the Italian comedians and Euterpe to help him to amuse the dauphin.

Isabelle reproaches Léonore for stealing the affections of Octave. Léonore asserts that she is interested not in Octave but in a masked stranger whom she has just met (I, 1-2). Isabelle then reveals privately that she was the stranger with whom misled Léonore fell in love (I, 3). Octave declares his love to an unsympathetic Léonore (I, 4-5) before the act ends in an entertainment (I, 6-8). Octave disguises himself as his valet; Zerbin dons the dress of his master; Zerbin falls asleep from too much wine (II, 1-2). Isabelle comes upon his sleeping form and mistakes him for Octave. Angry, she tries to stab him, but his voice reveals that he is Zerbin. He explains that his errant master has gone to consult Isménide about the future of his love for Léonore (II, 3). When Octave returns, Isabelle takes advantage of the darkness in the cave to imitate an oracle and to order Octave to abandon Léonore for her (II, 4). Léonore is rebuking Octave once again for his inconstancy, when her "beloved" enters in "his" mask, and Léonore requests "him" to reveal "his" identity. Octave reproaches Léonore for her new love (III, 1-2). When angry Octave threatens to stab her, Isabelle tears off her mask, and Léonore leaves in disarray (III, 3). Octave and Isabelle are reconciled, Spinette and Zerbin announce their troth, and the comedy ends amidst general rejoicing (III, 4-5).

Mlles Maupin* and Desmatins* starred in the leading female parts opposite Hardouin,* Chopelet, Dun, and Boutelou *fils*. Mlles Prévost,* Dangeville, and Saligny executed the ballet with Balon,* Blondy,* and Dumoulin.*

BIBLIOGRAPHY: Lajarte I, 105; Antoine Houdard de La Motte, *Oeuvres complètes*, 11 vols. (Genève: Slatkine Reprints, 1970) II, 233-43; RGO VIII, 393-436.

Vénus et Adonis was billed as a lyric tragedy in five acts and a prologue. Henri Desmarets* wrote its musical score, and Jean-Baptiste Rousseau* was the author of its libretto. *Le Journal de l'Opéra* is unsure about the exact date of its premiere and notes that it was offered for the first time at the Palais-Royal* on 17 March 1697 according to the eighteenth-century bibliographers Léris and La Vallière, while the Parfaict brothers and Duchesne believe it had its initial representation sometime in April 1697. *Vénus et Adonis* was dropped to make room for the premiere of *Aricie** on 9 June 1697 but returned to the stage almost immediately on 17 August 1697. Curiously enough, it was revived for the last time on 17 August 1717, exactly 20 years to the day after its first revival; it was billed until 12 September 1717. This work was the only composition by Desmarets to enjoy even a modest measure of success.

The prologue of *Vénus et Adonis* reverts to the recurrent theme developed in prologues composed at the end of the seventeenth century: "the torch of war" burns everywhere in the world except in France, protected by "the ever victorious king" whose glory has spread "even to the wild climes where the gods are almost unknown."

The intrigue of the tragedy is based upon a Vénus-Adonis-Cydipe triangle that occupies the first three acts with three basic developments: Cydipe mourns because her love for Adonis is unrequited; Vénus and Adonis declare their mutual love; Cydipe calls upon Mars for assistance. The action assumes a more tragic tone in the last two acts, although it must be acknowledged that the effect produced by Mars's change in attitude diminishes the impact of the drama: he threatens to slay Adonis only to transfer his wrath to the unsuspecting Cypriots. Also, Adonis's rôle becomes stereotyped, when he is summoned to slay the monster and to save the people only to meet death himself.

The principal rôles were created by Mlles Le Rochois* and Desmatins* as Vénus and Cydipe, respectively, with Dun as Adonis and Harouin* in the rôle of Mars. In 1717, Mlle Journet* did Vénus with Mlle Antier* as Cydipe; Cochereau* and Thévenard* sang Adonis and Mars. The members of the ballet included Mlles Dupré, Guyot, La Ferrière, and Prévost* opposite Dangeville, Dumoulin,* Javillier, Maltayre, and Pécourt.*

BIBLIOGRAPHY: Lajarte I, 67; RGO VI, 1-62.

Vigarani, Carlo (b. 1623, Reggio, Emilia; d. 1752, Paris ?), architect and scenery designer, came to Paris in 1659 with his father, an engineer also interested in the theatre. It was not long before young Vigarani came to the attention of Louis XIV, and he was accordingly commissioned to prepare the settings for the sumptuous programs that the king was in the habit of ordering for celebrations at Court.

Vigarani's work for certain plays created by Molière* for staging at Versailles won him the title of "inventor of machines" for the ballets and *fêtes* sponsored by royalty, and he remained an associate of Jean-Baptiste Lully* until 1675. His most important project for the Opéra was the renovation of the Palais-Royal,* the opera house of the Royal Academy of Music.

Z

Zéphire et Flore has a certain historical interest if only because it was the first composition given at the Palais-Royal* to which Jean-Baptiste Lully* did not make a direct contribution. An *opéra-ballet* in three acts and a prologue, its score was written by Louis and Jean-Louis de Lully,* and its libretto was by Michel du Boullay.* It was given initially on 22 March 1688, the first anniversary of the death of the composers' father. The unpublished *Journal de l'Opéra* does not specify how many performances it enjoyed during its first run, but it was not a popular work and was replaced in April by a revival of *Armide.** *Zéphire et Flore* was returned to the stage on 23 June 1715, however, and it was billed for 25 consecutive programs at this time before being dropped from the repertory on 18 August 1715. Louis de Lully* never lived to see his work revived because he had died at the age of 21 on 28 December 1688 after succeeding his father as superintendent of the king's music. It is a curious irony that this ineffectual work came to be associated with the deaths of Louis XIV, Jean-Baptiste Lully, and its own composer.

The prologues of *Pomone,** *Alceste,** and *Thésée** had been set near the Louvre or at Versailles, and Lully's sons followed this procedure by choosing the new Trianon palace as the locale for the prologue of *Zéphire et Flore.* If previous laudia of Louis XIV seem tedious in retrospect, the opening lines of this work surpass them easily in banality. Most annoying is the repeated use of "Héros" and "Gloire"; the adjective *grand* is applied to the king three times in thirteen short stanzas. The employment of such rimes as *gloire:victoire* and *chants:champs* does little to enhance the verse.

Zéphire et Flore offers an almost unique example of a composition so baroque that it runs the constant risk of degenerating into a parody of its own style. The first act is set in Flore's empire, and flowers fill the stage. The set for the second act is equally cluttered with its "thick forest and raised rocks." The grotto of Borée in the mountains of Thrace is more chaste (III), but this vista is transformed into a magnificent palace without delay. The overstatements in the sets are matched by the extravagance of the theme, which can only be described as meteorological: gentle Zéphire must struggle against harsh Borée for the hand of beautiful Flore, who prefers tender treatment and the friendly sun to protect her from the icy embrace of the northern winds. Such precious concepts as Le Soleil reassuring Flore (III, 9) or Borée frightening her retinue (II, 5) might have been tolerated in a ballet, but even the age of Louis XIV could not endure an entire program based upon this commonplace conceit.

BIBLIOGRAPHY: Lajarte I, 56-57; RGO III, 281-330.

THE REPERTORY, 1671-1715

The following three bibliographical lists of works billed at the Opéra and at Court are arranged chronologically from the time of the founding of the royal opera company by Louis XIV in 1671 until the death of this monarch in 1715. The first list presents the entire repertory between 19 March 1671 and 1 September 1715, regardless of genre, while the second catalogue contains only lyric works, and the third bibliography provides the titles of the ballets involved. In the separate entries, the title of the work is followed by notations indicating the genre to which the composition in question belongs and the number of acts, parts, or tableaux into which it is divided. The names of the composer and the librettist are then provided, and the choreographer's identity is established for ballets. The date furnished at the end of each entry indicates the date of the world premiere of the work at the Opéra if only a single date is given. If a composition was mounted first at Court, that is, at Versailles or Fontainebleau, both the date of this private representation and of its subsequent premiere in Paris are recorded. The double dates are furnished so that it will be easy to obtain a measure of the time interval between the world premiere of a given opera and its critical staging at the public theatre in the capital. Lastly, it must be noted that the dates for the creations of some works at the Opéra during the first two decades of the history of this theatre are moot or vague. In such cases, the unpublished *Journal de l'Opera* has been followed.

Abbreviations

a.	act, acts
alleg. ball.	allegorical ballet
anac.	Anacreontic
ball.-com.	ballet comedy, comedy ballet
ball. lyr.	lyric ballet
ball.-op	ballet-opera
bros.	brothers
chor.	choreographer, choreography
com.	comedy, comic

com.-ball.	comedy-ballet
com.-op.	comedy-opera
div.	*divertissement* or entertainment
dr.	drama, dramatic
fai.	fairy
fant.	fantastic
her.	heroic
hist.	historical
inter.	intermède, intermezzo
ital.	Italian
lyr.	lyric
masc.	masquerade
nos.	numbers
op.	opera
op.-ball.	opera-ballet
pant.-ball.	pantomime ballet
past.	pastoral
pro.	prologue
rom.	romantic, Romantic
trag.	tragedy, tragic
trag.-op.	tragedy-opera
trans.	translation, translated, translator

Entire Repertory

Pomone, past., pro. and 5a.; music, Cambert; words, abbé Perrin; 19 March 1671.

Les Peines et les plaisirs de l'amour, past., pro. and 5a.; music, Cambert; words, Gilbert; 8 April 1672.

Les Fêtes de l'Amour et de Bacchus, past., pro. and 3a.; music, Desbrosses and Lully; words, Benserade, Périgny, Molière, Quinault; 15 November 1672.

Cadmus et Hermione, lyr. trag., pro. and 5a.; music, Lully; words, Quinault; 1 February 1673.

Alceste, lyr. trag., pro. and 5a.; music, Lully; words, Quinault; 19 January 1674.

Thésée, lyr. trag., pro. and 5a.; music, Lully; words, Quinault; Saint-Germain en Laye on 11 January 1675 and at the Opéra April 1675.

Le Carnaval, masc., pro. and 9 entrées; music, Lully; words, Benserade, Lully, Molière, Quinault; 18 January 1668 at the Tuileries; at the Opéra on 17 October 1675.

Atys, lyr. trag., pro. and 5a.; music, Lully; words, Quinault; Saint-Germain en Laye on 10 January 1676 and at the Opéra in August 1675.

Isis, lyr. trag., pro. and 5a.; music, Lully; words, Quinault; Saint-Germain en Laye on 5 January 1677 and at the Opéra in August 1677.

Psyché, lyr. trag., pro. and 5a.; music, Lully; words, Thomas Corneille; 18 April 1678.

Bellérophon, lyr. trag., pro. and 5a.; music, Lully; words, Thomas Corneille and Fontenelle; 31 January 1679.

Proserpine, lyr. trag., pro. and 5a.; music, Lully; words, Quinault; Saint-Germain en Laye on 3 February 1680 and at the Opéra on 15 November 1680.

Le Triomphe de l'Amour, ball., 20 entrées; music, Lully; words, Benserade, Quinault; Saint-Germain en Laye on 21 January 1681 and at the Opéra on 6 May 1681.

Persée, lyr. trag., pro. and 5a.; music, Lully; words, Quinault; 17 April 1682.

Phaéton, lyr. trag., pro. and 5a.; music, Lully; words, Quinault; Versailles on 6 January 1683 and at the Opéra on 27 April 1683.

Amadis de Gaule, lyr. trag., pro. and 5a.; music, Lully; words, Quinault; 16 January 1684.

Roland, lyr. trag., pro. and 5a.; music, Lully; words, Quinault; at Versailles on 18 January 1685 and at the Opéra on 8 March 1685.

L'Idylle sur la paix, past., 1a.; music, Lully; words, Jean Racine; Sceaux on 16 July 1685 and at the Opéra in November 1685.

L'Eglogue de Versailles, div., 1a.; music, Lully; words, Quinault; Versailles and then at the Opéra, 1685.

Le Temple de la paix, op.-ball., pro. and 6a.; music, Lully; words, Quinault; Fontainebleau on 20 October 1685 and the Opéra in November 1685.

Armide, trag., pro. and 5a.; music, Lully; words, Quinault; 15 February 1686.

Acis et Galathée, her. past., pro. and 3a.; music, Lully; words, Campistron; at duke de Vendôme's château d'Anet on 6 September 1686 and at the Opéra on 17 September 1686.

Achille et Polyxène, lyr. trag., pro. and 5a.; music, Lully, Colasse; words, Campistron; 7 November 1687.

Zéphire et Flore, op.-ball., pro. and 3a.; music, Louis and Jean-Louis de Lully; words, du Boullay; 22 March 1688.

Thétis et Pélée, lyr. trag., pro. and 5a.; music, Colasse; words, Fontenelle; 11 January 1689.

Orphée, lyr. trag., pro. and 3a.; music, Louis Lully; words, du Boullay; 21 February 1690 or 8 April 1690.

Enée et Lavinie, lyr. trag., pro. and 5a.; music, Colasse; words, Fontenelle; 7 November 1690.

Coronis, her. past., pro. and 3a.; music, Teobaldo di Gatti DIT Théobalde; words, Chappuzeau de Beaugé; 23 March 1691.

Astrée, lyr. trag., pro. and 5a.; music, Colasse; words, La Fontaine; 11 November 1691.

Le Ballet de Villeneuve-Saint-Georges, ball., 3 entrées; music, Colasse; words, Banzi; 1 September 1692 at Villeneuve-Saint-Georges, and at Opéra in October 1692.

Alcide, lyr. trag., pro. and 5a.; music, Louis Lully and Marais; words, Campistron; 3 February 1693.

Didon, lyr. trag., pro. and 5a.; music, Desmarets; words, Mme Gillot de Sainctonge; 5 June 1693 or 11 September 1693.

Médée, lyr. trag., pro. and 5a.; music, Charpentier; words, Thomas Corneille; 4 December 1693.

Céphale et Procris, lyr. trag., pro. and 5a.; music, Mme Jacquet de Laguerre; words, Duché; 15 March 1694.

Circé, lyr. trag., pro. and 5a.; music, Desmarets; words, Mme Gillot de Sainctonge; 1 October 1694.

Théagène et Chariclée, lyr. trag., pro. and 5a.; music, Desmarets; words, Duché; 3 February 1695.

Les Amours de Momus, op.-ball., pro. and 3a.; music, Desmarets; words, Duché; 25 May 1695.

Les Saisons, op.-ball., pro. and 4a.; music, Louis de Lully, Colasse; words, abbé Pic; 18 October 1695.

Jason, ou la toison d'or, lyr. trag., pro. and 5a.; music, Colasse; words, J.-B. Rousseau; 6 January 1696.

Ariadne et Bacchus, lyr. trag., pro. and 5a.; music, Marais; words, Saint-Jean; 23 February 1696 or 8 March 1696.

La Naissance de Vénus, opera, pro. and 5a.; music, Colasse; words, abbé Pic; 1 May 1696.

Méduse, lyr. trag., pro. and 5a.; music, C.-H. Gervais; words, abbé Boyer; 13 January 1697.

Vénus et Adonis, lyr. trag., pro. and 5a.; music, Desmarets; words, J.-B. Rousseau; 17 March 1697 or April 1697.

Aricie, op.-ball., pro. and 5a.; music, La Coste; words, abbé Pic; 9 June 1697.

L'Europe galante, op.-ball., pro. and 4 entrées; music, Campra; words, La Motte; 24 October 1697.

Issé, her. past., pro. and 3a.; music, Destouches; words, Houdard de La Motte; 17 December 1697 at Trianon and at the Opéra on 30 December 1697.

Les Fêtes galantes, ballet, pro. and 3a.; music, Destouches; words, La Motte; 10 May 1698.

Le Carnaval de Venise, ball.-op., pro. and 3a.; music, Campra; words, Regnard; 20 January 1699 or 28 February 1699.

Amadis de Grèce, lyr. trag., pro. and 5a.; music, Destouches; words, La Motte; 26 March 1699.

Marthésie, reine des Amazones, lyr. trag., pro. and 5a.; music, Destouches; words, Houdard de La Motte; Fontainebleau on 11 October 1699 and at the Opéra on 29 October 1699.

Le Triomphe des arts, op.-ball., 5 entrées; music, Michel de La Barre; words, Antoine Houdard de La Motte; 16 May 1700.

Canente, lyr. trag., pro. and 5a.; music, Colasse; words, La Motte; 4 November 1700.

Hésione, lyr. trag., pro. and 5a.; music, Campra; words, Danchet; 21 December 1700.

Aréthuse, op.-ball., pro. and 3a.; music, Campra; words, Danchet; 14 July 1701.

Scylla, lyr. trag., pro. and 5a.; music, Teobaldo di Gatti; words, Duché; 16 September 1701.

Omphale, lyr. trag., pro. and 5a.; music, Destouches; words, La Motte; 10 November 1701.

Médus, roi des Mèdes, lyr. trag., pro. and 5a.; music, Bouvard; words, La Grange-Chancel; 23 July 1702.

Les Fragments de Lully, ballet, pro. and 4 entrées; music, Campra; words, Danchet; 10 September 1702.

Tancrède, lyr. trag., pro. and 5a.; music, Campra; words, Danchet; 7 November 1702.

Ulysse, lyr. trag., pro. and 5a.; music, J.-François Rebel; words, Henri Guichard; 21 January 1703.

Le Carnaval et la folie, com.-ball., pro. and 4a.; music, Destouches; words, Antoine Houdard de La Motte; Fontainebleau on 3 January 1703, at the Opéra on 14 October 1703.

Les Muses, op.-ball., pro. and 4 entrées; music, Campra; words, Danchet; 28 October 1703.

Iphigénie en Tauride, lyr. trag., pro. and 5a.; music, Campra, Desmarets; words, Danchet, Duché; 6 May 1704.

Télémaque, trag., pro. and 5a. of fragments; edited and arranged by Campra (music) and Danchet (words); 11 November 1704.

Alcine, lyr. trag., pro. and 5a.; music, Campra; words, Danchet; 15 January 1705.

La Vénitienne, com.-ball., pro. and 3a.; music, La Barre; words, La Motte; 26 May 1705.

Philomèle, lyr. trag., pro. and 5a.; music, La Coste; words, Roy; 20 October 1705.

Alcyone, lyr. trag., pro. and 5a.; music, Marais; words, La Motte; 18 February 1706.

Cassandre, lyr. trag., pro. and 5a.; music, Bouvard, Bertin; words, La Grange-Chancel; 22 June 1706.

Polyxène et Pyrrhus, lyr. trag., pro. and 5a.; music, Colasse; words, La Serre; 21 October 1706.

Bradamante, lyr. trag., pro. and 5a.; music, La Coste; words, Roy; 2 May 1707.

Hippodamie, lyr. trag., pro. and 5a.; music, Campra; words, Roy; 6 March 1708.

Sémélé, lyr. trag., pro. and 5a.; music, Marais; words, La Motte; 9 April 1709.

Méléagre, lyr. trag., pro. and 5a.; music, Batistin Stuck; words, Jolly; 24 May 1709.

Diomède, lyr. trag., pro. and 5a.; music, Bertin; words, La Serre; 28 April 1710.

Les Festes vénitiennes, com.-ball., pro. and 3a.; music, Campra; words, Danchet; 17 June 1710.

Manto la fée, lyr. trag., pro. and 5a.; music, Batistin Stuck; words, Menesson; 29 January 1711.

Idoménée, lyr. trag., pro. and 5a.; music, Campra; words, Danchet; 12 January 1712.

Créuse l'Athénienne, lyr. trag., pro. and 5a.; music, La Coste; words, Roy; 5 April 1712.

Les Amours de Mars et de Vénus, com.-ball., pro. and 3a.; music, Campra; words, Danchet; 6 September 1712.

Callirhoé, lyr. trag., pro. and 5a.; music, Destouches; words, Roy; 27 December 1712.

Médée et Jason, lyr. trag., pro. and 5a.; music, Salomon; words, abbé Pellegrin; 24 April 1713.

Les Amours déguisés, ball.-op., pro. and 3a.; music, Bourgeois; words, Fuzelier; 22 August 1713.

Télèphe, lyr. trag., pro. and 5a.; music, Campra; words, Danchet; 28 November 1713.

Arion, lyr. trag., pro. and 5a.; music, Matho; words, Fuzelier; 10 April 1714.

Les Festes de Thalie, ballet, pro. and 3a.; music, Mouret; words, Lafont; 14 August 1714.

Télémaque, lyr. trag., pro. and 5a.; music, Destouches; words, abbé Pellegrin; 29 November 1714.

Les Plaisirs de la paix, ballet, pro. and 3a. with 4 inter.; music, Bourgeois; words, Menesson; 29 April 1715.

Lyric Repertory

Cadmus et Hermione, lyr. trag., pro. and 5a.; music, Lully; words, Quinault; 1 February 1673.

Alceste, lyr. trag., pro. and 5a.; music, Lully; words, Quinault; 19 January 1674.

Thésée, lyr. trag., pro. and 5a.; music, Lully; words, Quinault; Saint-Germain en Laye on 11 January 1675 and at the Opéra April 1675.

Atys, lyr. trag., pro. and 5a.; music, Lully; words, Quinault; Saint-Germain en Laye on 10 January 1676 and at the Opéra in August 1675.

Le Carnaval, masc., pro. and 9 entrées; music, Lully; words, Benserade, Lully, Molière, Quinault; 18 January 1668 at the Tuileries; at the Opéra on 17 October 1675.

Isis, lyr. trag., pro. and 5a.; music, Lully; words, Quinault; Saint-Germain en Laye on 5 January 1677 and at the Opéra in August 1677.

Psyché, lyr. trag., pro. and 5a.; music, Lully; words, Thomas Corneille; 18 April 1678.

Bellérophon, lyr. trag., pro. and 5a.; music, Lully; words, Thomas Corneille and Fontenelle; 31 January 1679.

Proserpine, lyr. trag., pro. and 5a.; music, Lully; words, Quinault; Saint-Germain en Laye on 3 February 1680 and at the Opéra on 15 November 1680.

Persée, lyr. trag., pro. and 5a.; music, Lully; words, Quinault; 17 April 1682.

Phaéton, lyr. trag., pro. and 5a.; music, Lully; words, Quinault; Versailles on 6 January 1683 and at the Opéra on 27 April 1683.

Amadis de Gaule, lyr. trag., pro. and 5a.; music, Lully; words, Quinault; 16 January 1684.

L'Eglogue de Versailles, div., 1a.; music, Lully; words, Quinault; Versailles and then at the Opéra, 1685.

Roland, lyr. trag., pro. and 5a.; music, Lully; words, Quinault; at Versailles on 18 January 1685 and at the Opéra on 8 March 1685.

Armide, trag., pro. and 5a.; music, Lully; words, Quinault; 15 February 1686.

Achille et Polyxène, lyr. trag., pro. and 5a.; music, Lully, Colasse; words, Campistron; 7 November 1687.

Thétis et Pélée, lyr. trag., pro. and 5a.; music, Colasse; words, Fontenelle; 11 January 1689.

Orphée, lyr. trag., pro. and 3a.; music, Louis de Lully; words, du Boullay; 21 February 1690 or 8 April 1690.

Enée et Lavinie, lyr. trag., pro. and 5a.; music, Colasse; words, Fontenelle; 7 November 1690.

Astrée, lyr. trag., pro. and 5a.; music, Colasse; words, La Fontaine; 11 November 1691.

Alcide, lyr. trag., pro. and 5a.; music, Louis Lully and Marais; words, Campistron; 3 February 1693.

Didon, lyr. trag., pro. and 5a.; music, Desmarets; words, Mme Gillot de Sainctonge; 5 June 1693 or 11 September 1693.

Médée, lyr. trag., pro. and 5a.; music, Charpentier; words, Thomas Corneille; 4 December 1693.

Céphale et Procris, lyr. trag., pro. and 5a.; music, Mme Jacquet de Laguerre; words, Duché; 15 March 1694.

Circé, lyr. trag., pro. and 5a.; music, Desmarets; words, Mme Gillot de Sainctonge; 1 October 1694.

Théagène et Chariclée, lyr. trag., pro. and 5a.; music, Desmarets; words, Duché; 3 February 1695.

Jason, ou la toison d'or, lyr. trag., pro. and 5a.; music, Colasse; words, J.-B. Rousseau; 6 January 1696.

Ariadne et Bacchus, lyr. trag., pro. and 5a.; music, Marais; words, Saint-Jean; 23 February 1696 or 8 March 1696.

La Naissance de Vénus, opera, pro. and 5a.; music, Colasse; words, abbé Pic; 1 May 1696.

Méduse, lyr. trag., pro. and 5a.; music, C.-H. Gervais; words, abbé Boyer; 13 January 1696.

Vénus et Adonis, lyr. trag., pro. and 5a.; music, Desmarets; words, J.-B. Rousseau; 17 March 1697 or April 1697.

Amadis de Grèce, lyr. trag., pro. and 5a.; music, Destouches; words, La Motte; 26 March 1699.

Marthésie, reine des Amazones, lyr. trag., pro. and 5a.; music, Destouches; words, Houdard de La Motte; Fontainebleau on 11 October 1699 and at the Opéra on 29 October 1699.

Canente, lyr. trag., pro. and 5a.; music, Colasse; words, La Motte; 4 November 1700.

Hésione, lyr. trag., pro. and 5a.; music, Campra; words, Danchet; 21 December 1700.

Scylla, lyr. trag., pro. and 5a.; music, Teobaldo di Gatti; words, Duché; 16 September 1701.

Omphale, lyr. trag., pro. and 5a.; music, Destouches; words, La Motte; 10 November 1701.

Médus, roi des Mèdes, lyr. trag., pro. and 5a.; music, Bouvard; words, La Grange-Chancel; 23 July 1702.

Tancrède, lyr. trag., pro. and 5a.; music, Campra; words, Danchet; 7 November 1702.

Ulysse, lyr. trag., pro. and 5a.; music, J.-François Rebel; words, Henri Guichard; 21 January 1703.

Iphigénie en Tauride, lyr. trag., pro. and 5a.; music, Campra, Desmarets; words, Danchet, Duché; 6 May 1704.

Télémaque, trag., pro. and 5a. of fragments; edited and arranged by Campra (music) and Danchet (words); 11 November 1704.

Alcine, lyr. trag., pro. and 5a.; music, Campra; words, Danchet; 15 January 1705.

Philomèle, lyr. trag., pro. and 5a.; music, La Coste; words, Roy; 20 October 1705.

Alcyone, lyr. trag., pro. and 5a.; music, Marais; words, La Motte; 18 February 1706.

Cassandre, lyr. trag., pro. and 5a.; music, Bouvard, Bertin; words, La Grange-Chancel; 22 June 1706.

Polyxène et Pyrrhus, lyr. trag., pro. and 5a.; music, Colasse; words, La Serre; 21 October 1706.

Bradamante, lyr. trag., pro. and 5a.; music, La Coste; words, Roy; 2 May 1707.

Hippodamie, lyr. trag., pro. and 5a.; music, Campra; words, Roy; 6 March 1708.

Sémélé, lyr. trag., pro. and 5a.; music, Marais; words, La Motte; 9 April 1709.

Méléagre, lyr. trag., pro. and 5a.; music, Batistin Stuck; words, Jolly; 24 May 1709.

Diomède, lyr. trag., pro. and 5a.; music, Bertin; words, La Serre; 28 April 1710.

Manto la fée, lyr. trag., pro. and 5a.; music, Batistin Stuck; words, Menesson; 29 January 1711.

Idoménée, lyr. trag., pro. and 5a.; music, Campra; words, Danchet; 12 January 1712.

Créuse l'Athénienne, lyr. trag., pro. and 5a.; music, La Coste; words, Roy; 5 April 1712.

Callirhoé, lyr. trag., pro. and 5a.; music, Destouches; words, Roy; 27 December 1712.

Médée et Jason, lyr. trag., pro. and 5a.; music, Salomon; words, abbé Pellegrin; 24 April 1713.

Télèphe, lyr. trag., pro. and 5a.; music, Campra; words, Danchet; 28 November 1713.

Arion, lyr. trag., pro. and 5a.; music, Matho; words, Fuzelier; 10 April 1714.

Télémaque, lyr. trag., pro. and 5a.; music, Destouches; words, abbé Pellegrin; 29 November 1714.

Choreographic Repertory

Pomone, past., pro. and 5a.; music, Cambert; words, abbé Perrin; 19 March 1671.

Les Peines et les plaisirs de l'amour, past., pro. and 5a.; music, Cambert; words, Gilbert; 8 April 1672.

Les Fêtes de l'Amour et de Bacchus, past., pro., and 3a.; music, Desbrosses and Lully; words, Benserade, Périgny, Molière, Quinault; 15 November 1672.

Le Triomphe de l'Amour, ball., 20 entrées; music, Lully; words, Benserade, Quinault; Saint-Germain en Laye on 21 January 1681 and at the Opéra on 6 May 1681.

L'Idylle sur la paix, past., 1a.; music, Lully; words, Jean Racine; Sceaux on 16 July 1685 and at the Opéra in November 1685.

Le Temple de la paix, op.-ball., pro. and 6a.; music, Lully; words, Quinault; Fontainebleau on 20 October 1685 and the Opéra in November 1685.

Acis et Galathée, her. past., pro. and 3a.; music, Lully; words, Campistron; at duke de Vendôme's château d'Anet on 6 September 1686 and at the Opéra on 17 September 1686.

Zéphire et Flore, op.-ball., pro. and 3a.; music, Louis and Jean-Louis Lully; words, du Boullay; 22 March 1688.

Coronis, her. past., pro. and 3a.; music, Teobaldo di Gatti DIT Théobalde; words, Chappuzeau de Beaugé; 23 March 1691.

Le Ballet de Villeneuve-Saint-Georges, ball., 3 entrées; music, Colasse; words, Banzi; 1 September 1692 at Villeneuve-Saint-Georges, and at Opéra in October 1692.

Les Amours de Momus, op.-ball., pro. and 3a.; music, Desmarets; words, Duché; 25 May 1695.

Les Saisons, op.-ball., pro. and 4a.; music, Louis de Lully, Colasse; words, abbé Pic; 18 October 1695.

Aricie, op.-ball., pro. and 5a.; music, La Coste; words, abbé Pic; 9 June 1697.

L'Europe galante, op.-ball., pro. and 4 entrées; music, Campra; words, La Motte; 24 October 1697.

Issé, her. past., pro. and 3a.; music, Destouches; words, Houdard de La Motte; 17 December 1697 at Trianon and at the Opéra on 30 December 1697.

Les Fêtes galantes, ballet, pro., and 3a.; music, Destouches; words, La Motte; 10 May 1698.

Le Carnaval de Venise, ball.-op., pro. and 3a.; music, Campra; words, Regnard; 20 January 1699, or 28 February 1699.

Le Triomphe des arts, op.-ball., 5 entrées; music, Michel de La Barre; words, Antoine Houdard de La Motte; 16 May 1700.

Aréthuse, op.-ball., pro. and 3a.; music, Campra; words, Danchet; 14 July 1701.

Les Fragments de Lully, ballet, pro. and 4 entrées; music, Campra; words, Danchet; 10 September 1702.

Le Carnaval et la folie, com.-ball., pro. and 4a.; music, Destouches; words, Antoine Houdard de La Motte; Fontainebleau on 3 January 1703; at the Opéra on 14 October 1703.

Les Muses, op.-ball., pro. and 4 entrées; music, Campra; words, Danchet; 28 October 1703.

La Vénitienne, com.-ball., pro. and 3a.; music, La Barre; words, La Motte; 26 May 1705.

Les Festes vénitiennes, com.-ball., pro. and 3a.; music, Campra; words, Danchet; 17 June 1710.

Les Amours de Mars et de Vénus, com.-ball., pro. and 3a.; music, Campra; words, Danchet; 6 September 1712.

Les Amours déguisés, ball-op., pro. and 3a.; music, Bourgeois; words, Fuzelier; 22 August 1713.

Les Festes de Thalie, ballet, pro. and 3a.; music, Mouret; words, Lafont; 14 August 1714.

Les Plaisirs de la paix, ballet, pro. and 3a., with 4 inter.; music, Bourgeois; words, Menesson; 29 April 1715.

LEADING FEMALE SINGERS, 1671-1982

Leading female singers at the Opéra with dates of their debuts with the company:

Marie Jossier DITE Cartilly 1671
Marie-Madeleine Brigogne 1671
Marie Aubry 1671
Verdier 167-
Saint-Christophe 1676
Louison Moreau 1680
Fanchon Moreau 1683
Marthe Le Rochois 1678
Desmatins 1682
Maupin 1686
Souris *aînée* 17--
Souris *cadette* 17--
Marie Antier 1711
Journet 1716
Tulou 1718
Catherine Nicole Lemaure 1721
Erremans 1721
Pélissier 1726
Marie Fel 1726
Petitpas 1727
Bourbonnais 1735
Marie-Angélique Coupé 1738
Marie-Jeanne Fesch DITE
 Chevalier 1740
Cartou 1740
Rotisset de Romainville 1740
Léris de Latude DITE Clairon 1742
De Metz 1744
Marie-Jeanne Lemière, or Mme
 Larrivée 1750
Sophie Arnould 1758
Françoise Campagne DITE
 Duplant 1761

Durancy 1762
Henriette Adélaïde de Villars DITE
 Beaumesnil 1766
Rosalie Levasseur 1766
Anne-Victoire Dervieux 1767
Clavel DITE Saint-Huberty 1777
Gavaudan *aînée,* or Mme Lainez 1780
Domergue DITE Aurore 1782
Dupuis 1782
Maillard 1782
Gavaudan *cadette* 1783
Dozon, or Mme Chéron 1784
Mme Saint-Aubin 1786
Chevalier, or Mme Branchu 1800
Armand 1801
Mme Albert-Himm 1806
Armand *nièce* 1808
Mme Grassari 1816
Mme Dabadie nee Louise Zulmé
 Leroux 1821
Mme Jawurek 1821
Lebrun 1825
Cinthie-Montalant, or Mme Damoreau-
 Cinti 1826
Mme Dorus-Gras nee Julie van
 Steenkiste 1830
Cornélie Falcon 1831
Flécheux 1835
Marietta Brambilla 1835
Nau 1835
Mme Duprez 1837
Rosine Stoltz 1837
Nathan-Treillet 1839

Pauline Garcia, or Mme Viardot 1849
Castellan 1849
Mme Marietta Alboni 1850
Rosine Laborde 1850
Mme Tedesco 1851
Angiolina Bosio or Mme Xinda
    Velonis 1852
Sophie Cruwel DITE Cruvelli 1854
Mme Adélaïde Borghi-Mamo 1856
Mme Gueymard-Lauters 1857
Marie Sax or Sasse 1860
Mme Vandenheuvel-Duprez 1860
Marie Battu 1864
Mauduit 1865
Rosine Bloch 1867
Hisson 1867
Christine Nilsson 1868
Fursch-Madier 1868
Mme Miolan-Carvalho 1868
Fidès Devriès 1871
Marie Belval 1874
Adelina Patti 1874
Daram 1874
Gabrielle Krauss 1875
Alphonsine Richard 1877
Heilbron 1879
Eva Dufranne 1880
Norton-Lilian Nordica 1882
Mme Marie Lureau-Escalaïs 1882
Emma Eames 1883
Adèle Isaac 1883
D'Ervilly 1884
Mme Rose Caron 1885
Rosa Bosman 1885
Charlotte-Marie Agussol 1888
Félia Litvinne 1889
Mme Nellie Melba 1889
Mme C. Fierens 1890
Mme Meyriane Héglon-Leroux 1890
Mme Blanche Deschamps-Jehin 1891
Lucienne Bréval 1892
Mme Marguerite Carrère-Xanrof 1892
Mme Alba Chrétien-Vaguet 1893
Sybil Sanderson 1893
Louise Grandjean 1895
Marie Lafargue 1895
Aïno Ackté 1897

Marie Delna 1898
Marianne Flahaut 1898
Jeanne Hatto 1899
Goulancourt 1901
Rose Féart 1902
Marcelle Demougeot 1902
Lucy Arbell 1903
Antoinette Laute-Brun 1903
Jeanne Lindsay 1903
Agnès Borgo 1904
Géraldine Farrar 1905
Marthe Chenal 1905
Gabrielle Notick 1906
Louise Mancini 1906
Henriette Doyen 1906
Ketty Lapeyrette 1908
Jeanne Campredon 1908
Lucy Isnardon 1908
Léonie Courbières 1908
Jeanne Cosset 1908
Mary Garden 1908
Maria Kousnietzoff 1908
Yvonne Gall 1908
Marie Charbonnel 1908
Jeanne Bourdon 1909
Dubois-Lauger 1910
Lyse Charny 1910
Alice Daumas 1910
Lucile Panis 1911
Gauley-Texier 1911
Madeleine Bugg 1913
Rose Montazel 1914
Marie-Thérèse Haramboure 1915
Germaine Lubin 1916
Mireille Berthon 1917
Jane Cros 1917
Marguerite Choquet 1918
Jeanne Laval 1918
Yvonne Courso 1918
Françoise Rosay 1919
Ninon Vallin 1920
Fanny Heldy 1920
Gabrielle Ritter-Ciampi 1921
Marguerite Monsy 1921
Cécile Rex 1921
Jeanne Montfort 1921
Madeleine Lalande 1921

Maryse Beaujon 1921
Georgette Caro 1922
Andrée Marilliet 1922
Marcelle Denya 1923
Marthe Nespoulos 1923
Marisa Ferrer 1924
Louise Barthe 1925
Eidé Noréna 1925
Marguerite Lloberès 1925
Marcelle Mahieu 1926
Laure Tessandra 1926
Yvonne Gervais 1927
Marcelle Bunlet 1928
Lotte Lehmann 1928
Jeanne Manceau 1928
Suzanne Lumière 1929
Germaine Hoerner 1929
Milly Morère 1930
Jemmy Bachillat 1931
Renée Mahe 1931
Odette Ricquier 1932
Marie-Antoinette Almona 1933
Marjorie Lawrence 1933
Eliette Schenneberg 1934
Solange Delmas 1934
Lily Pons 1935
Antoinette Couvidoux 1936
Renée Gilly 1936
Anita Volfer 1936
Solange Bonni-Pellieux 1938
Eliane Carrier 1938
Hélène Bouvier 1939
Huguette Saint-Arnaud 1939
Jeanne Segala 1940
Janine Micheau 1940
Elisabeth Schwarzkopf 1941
Geori Boué 1942
Suzanne Juyol 1942
Solange Michel 1942
Jacqueline Lucazeau 1944
Mado Robin 1945
Gisèle Desmoutiers 1946
Inès Chabal 1946
Jacqueline Brumaire 1946
Suzanne Chauvelot 1946
Denise Duval 1947
Renée Doria 1947

Georgette Camart 1948
Jacqueline Cauchard 1948
Marcelle Croisier 1948
Agnès Disney 1948
Denise Boursin 1949
Margaret Mas 1949
Geneviève Serres 1951
Berthe Montmart 1951
Régine Crespin 1951
Jeannine Collard 1951
Denise Scharley 1951
Rita Gorr 1952
Paulette Chalanda 1952
Christiane Castelli 1952
Liliane Berton 1952
Monique de Pondeau 1952
Martha Angelici 1953
Agnès Léger 1953
Isabelle Andréani 1954
Lyne Cumia 1955
Elise Kahn 1956
Georgette Spanellys 1956
Léna Pastor 1957
Andréa Guiot 1957
Jacqueline Broudeur 1958
Denise Monteil 1958
Mady Mesplé 1958
Maria Callas 1958
Jane Rhodes 1958
Jane Berbié 1959
Irène Jaumillot 1959
Andrée Esposito 1959
Jacqueline Silvy 1960
Nadine Sautereau 1960
Térésa Stich-Randall 1960
Rosanna Carteri 1961
Michèle Le Bris 1961
Christiane Eda-Pierre 1962
Francine Arrazau 1962
Regina Resnik 1964
Hélia T'Hézan 1964
Birgit Nilsson 1966
Nadine Denize 1967
Françoise Garner 1967
Leontyne Price 1968
Hélène Garett 1969
Patricia Dupont 1969

Christa Ludwig 1971
Renée Auphan 1971
Danièle Perriers 1972
Eliane Lublin 1972
Teresa Berganza 1972
Montserrat Caballé 1972
Gwyneth Jones 1973
Jocelyn Taillon 1973
Anna Ringart 1973
Mireilla Freni 1973

Jeannette Pilou 1973
Margaret Price 1973
Frederica von Stade 1973
Martina Arroyo 1973
Katia Ricciarelli 1974
Arline Saunders 1974
Kiri Te Kanawa 1975
Annick Dutertre 1976
Danièle Chlostawa 1977
Valérie Masterson 1977

LEADING MALE SINGERS, 1671-1982

Leading male singers at the Opéra with dates of their debuts with the troupe:

Clédière 1671
Beaumavielle 1671
Bourel-Miracle 1671
Taulet 1671
Rossignol 1671
Lemercier 1671
Thévenard 1675
Dumenil 1676
Gaye 1676
Dun *père* 1686
Mantienne 1695
Hardouin 1697
Boutelou 1697
Cochereau 1702
Muraire 1715
Dun *fils* 1716
Dubourg 1718
De Chassé de Chinais 1720
Tribou 1721
Cuvillier 1724
Jélyotte 1733
Person 1735
Le Page 1735
Bérard 1736
Le Page *cadet* c. 1737
Cuvillier *fils* 1738
Chapotin 1741
Latour 1742
Poirier 1745
Gélin 1750
Larrivée 1755
Pillot 1755
Le Gros 1764
Lainez or Lainé 1773

Moreau 1776
Chéron 1778
Lays 1779
Rousseau 1780
Chénard 1782
Chardini 1786
Andrieu 1786
Chollet 1787
Villoteau 1792
H. Dérivis 1803
Nourrit *père* 1803
Levasseur 1813
Prévost *fils* 1814
Lecomte 1817
A. Dupont 1818
Damoreau 1819
Ad. Nourrit 1821
Lafont 1823
F. Prévost 1824
Massol 1825
Dabadie *jeune* 1828
Prosper Dérivis 1831
Wartel 1831
Duprez 1837
Marié 1840
Obin 1844
Roger 1848
Gueymard 1848
Chapuis 1851
Bonnehée 1853
Coulon 1853
Belval 1855
Sapin 1856
Faure 1861

Niemann 1861
Caron 1862
Grisy 1862
Villaret 1863
David 1865
Ponsard 1867
Gaspard 1867
V. Maurel 1868
Bosquin 1869
Bouhy 1871
Gailhard 1871
Bataille 1871
J. Lassalle 1872
Achard 1873
Auguez 1873
Vergnet 1874
Manoury 1874
L. Gresse 1875
Boudouresque 1875
Berardi 1876
H. Sellier 1878
H. Devriès 1878
Lorrain 1879
Dubulle 1879
Dereims 1879
Melchissédic 1879
Escalaïs 1883
Plançon 1883
Ed. de Reszké 1885
J. de Reszké 1885
Duc 1885
Martapoura 1886
Muratet 1886
F. Delmas 1886
Ballard 1887
Affre 1890
Vaguet 1890
Douaillier 1890
Van Dyck 1891
Renaud 1891
Fournets 1892
Saleza 1892
Alvarez 1892
Noté 1893
Narçon 1893
Bartet 1893
Cancelier 1894

Delpouget 1894
Paty 1896
Tamango 1897
L. Laffitte 1898
Gonguet 1900
Nivette 1900
Rousselière 1900
Riddez 1900
A. Gresse 1901
Gilly 1902
G. Dubois 1902
Triadou 1903
Scaremberg 1903
Muratore 1905
Plamondon 1906
Nansen 1907
Cerdan 1907
Duclos 1907
Dangès 1908
Lequien 1908
Caruso 1908
Vanni-Marcoux 1908
Journet 1908
Revol 1908
Teissie 1908
Franz 1909
Fabert 1909
Campagnola 1910
R. Lassalle 1911
E. Rouard 1912
Couzinou 1913
John Sullivan 1914
L. Ernst 1915
Huberty 1916
Rambaud 1917
G. Mahieux 1919
Soria 1919
Dalerant 1921
Bordon 1922
Peyre 1922
F. Ansseau 1922
C. Cambon 1924
Thill 1924
R. Gilles 1926
Verdière 1926
André Pernet 1928
J. Claverie 1928

J. Deleu 1928
Endrèze 1929
José de Trevi 1930
P. Froumenty 1930
M. Singher 1930
J. Forest 1931
José Luccioni 1931
H. Etcheverry 1932
E. Chastenet 1932
H. Médus 1933
P. Cabanel 1933
R. Gourgues 1934
José Beckmans 1935
Charles-Paul 1935
L. Noguera 1935
G. Nore 1935
C. Rouquetty 1935
M. Clavère 1936
A. Delorme 1939
J. Petitpas 1939
A. Richard 1939
A. Philippe 1942
M. Dens 1947
J. Giovanetti 1947
J. Giraudeau 1947
P. Savignol 1948
R. Bianco 1948
Libéro de Luca 1948
M. Roux 1950
J. Borthayre 1951
A. Laroze 1952
H. Legay 1952
R. Massard 1952
X. Depraz 1952
G. Vaillant 1952
G. Serkoyan 1952
W. Windgassen 1954
E. Blanc 1954
A. Vanzo 1954
Nicolai Gedda 1954

C. Hector 1954
M. Huylbrock 1954
P. Finel 1954
A. Lance 1956
G. Chapuis 1956
G. Botiaux 1956
T. Poncet 1957
J.-P. Laffage 1958
G. Bacquier 1958
J.-P. Hurteau 1958
G. Chauvet 1959
M. Cadiou 1959
R. Gouttebroze 1959
J. Haas 1960
L. Quilico 1962
R. Soyer 1963
H. Beirer 1964
J. Vickers 1973
M. Agnetti 1973
C. Cossutta 1973
J. van Dam 1973
P. Domingo 1973
R. Dumé 1973
F. Dumont 1973
J. Dupouy 1973
T. Krause 1973
J. Mars 1973
C. Méloni 1973
K. Moll 1973
M. Sénéchal 1973
R. Soyer 1973
N. Ghiaurov 1974
R. Massard 1974
R. Raimond 1974
J.-L. Soumagnas 1974
J. Bastin 1975
M. Vento 1975
J. Macurdy 1977
K. Riegel 1978

LEADING FEMALE DANCERS, 1671-1982

Leading danseuses at the Opéra with the dates of their debuts with the Ballet de l'Opéra:

Lafontaine 1681
Desmatins 1682
Marie-Thérèse de Subligny 1688
Marie-Cathérine Guyot 1689
Babet Dufort 1690
Françoise Prévost 1699
Michelle de Dangeville 1699
Jeanne-Eléanore Thibert 1722
Marie-Antoinette Petit 1722
Richelet 1723
Marie-Anne de Camargo 1726
Marie Sallé 1727
Barbarina Campanini 1739
Louise-Madeleine Lany 1743
Marie-Françoise Lyonnois 1744
La Batte 1750
Louise Rey (Mme Pitrot) 1751
Teresa Vestris 1751
Asselin 1758
Marie Allard 1761
Marguerite-Angélique Peslin 1761
Marie-Madeleine Guimard 1762
Dervieux 1765
Heinel 1767
Anne-Marguerite Dorival 1773
Théodore, nee M.-M. Crépé 1777
Cécilé Dumesnil 1777
Rose, nee Marie-Rose Pole 1782
Victoire Saulnier 1784
Louise Langlois 1784
Marie-Anne Miller (Mme Gardel) 1786
Laure 1786
Geneviève-Sophie Chevigny 1789

Emilie Collomb 1790
Mafleuret Clotilde 1793
Aimée 1793
Louise Chameroy 1796
Marie-Jeanne Saulnier 1796
Emilie Bigottini 1801
Fanny Bias 1807
Geneviève Gosselin 1809
Lise Noblet 1818
Pauline Montessu, nee Paul 1820
Amélie Legallois 1822
Julia de Varennes 1823
Pauline Leroux 1826
Marie Taglioni 1827
Pauline Duvernay 1831
Fanny Elssler 1834
Adèle Dumilâtre 1840
Marie Guy-Stéphan 1840
Carlotta Grisi 1841
Adeline Plunkett 1845
Flora Fabbri 1845
Sofia Fuoco 1846
Célestine Emarot 1847
Fanny Cerrito 1847
Louise Taglioni 1848
Louise Marquet 1851
Nadejda Bogdanova 1851
Carolina Rosati 1853
Claudina Couqui (Cucchi) 1855
Caterina Beretta 1855
Amalia Ferraris 1856
Zina Mérante 1857
Emma Livry 1858

Zina Richard 1860
Léontine Beaugrand 1861
Marie Petipa 1861
Angelina Fioretti 1863
Laure Fonta 1863
Martha Mouravieva 1863
Eugénie Fiocre 1864
Marie Sanlaville 1864
Amina Boschetti 1864
Guglielmina Salvioni 1864
Adèle Grantzow 1866
Annette Mérante 1866
Giuseppina Bozzachi 1870
Rita Sangalli 1875
Rosita Mauri 1879
Julia Subra 1879
Emma Sandrini 1888
Carlotta Zambelli 1894
Marthe Urban 1903
Anna Johnsson 1906
Aïda Boni 1907
Jeanne Schwarz 1910
Camille Bos 1911
Suzanne Lorcia 1917
Yvonne Daunt 1918
Olga Spessivtseva 1924
Tamara Toumanova 1929

Yvette Chauviré 1934
Madeleine Lafon 1935
Lycette Darsonval 1935
Micheline Bardin 1936
Christiane Vaussard 1936
Solange Schwarz 1937
Claude Bessy 1945
Maria Tallchief 1947
Jacqueline Rayet 1948
Liane Daydé 1948
Nina Vyroubova 1950
Claire Motte 1951
Christiane Vlassi 1952
Josette Amiel 1952
Marjorie Tallchief 1957
Nanon Thibon 1958
Wilfride Piollet 1960
Noëlla Pontis 1960
Francesca Zumbo 1963
Claudette Scouarnec 1972
Ghislaine Thesmar 1972
Patrice Bart 1972
Carolyn Carlson 1973
Elisabeth Platel 1975
Dominique Khalfouni 1978
Florence Clerc 1978
Claude Vulpian 1978

LEADING MALE DANCERS, 1671-1982

Outstanding danseurs of the Opéra with dates of their debuts with the Ballet de l'Opéra.

P. Beauchamp 1673
L. Lestang 1673
L. Pécour 1674
Bouteville 1675
Noblet 1675
M. Blondy 1691
J. Balon 1691
F. Dumoulin 1695
A.-F. Dangeville 1699
D. Dumoulin 1705
A. de Laval 1706
L. Dupré 1714
Dumay 1736
J.-B. Lany 1741
P. Sodi DIT Pietro 1744
Lyonnois 1746
Gaétan Vestris 1748
Maximilien Gardel 1759
J. Dauberval 1761
Pierre Gardel 1772
August Vestris 1772
Louis Nivelon 1777
Louis Milon 1783
Ch. Beaupré 1789
Ch. Didelot 1791
A.-J.-J. Deshayes 1798
J. Aumer 1798
Armand Vestris 1800
L. Duport 1800
F. Taglioni 1800
L. Henry 1803
Decombe DIT Albert 1803
S. Taglioni 1806

Montjoie 1808
Antoine Paul 1813
Antoine Coulon 1816
Carlo Blasis 1817
Ferdinand 1818
L. Gosselin 1820
A. Bournonville 1826
Paul Taglioni 1827
Jules Perrot 1830
J. Mazilier 1830
E. Coralli 1834
A. Mabille 1835
A. Guerra 1836
Lucien Petipa 1839
A. Saint-Léon 1847
F. Berthier 1847
L. Mérante 1848
M. Beauchet 1851
A. Chapuy 1855
D. Segarelli 1856
Miguel Vasquez 1874
Léo Staats 1898
Gustave Ricaux 1901
Albert Aveline 1905
Serge Peretti 1922
Serge Lifar 1922
Roger Ritz 1930
Max Bozzoni 1936
Michel Renault 1940
Jean-Paul Andréani 1945
Alexandre Kalioujny 1947
Jean Babilée 1949
Youly Algaroff 1952

Jean-Pierre Franchetti 1953
Attilio Labis 1954
Peter van Dijk 1955
George Skibine 1957
Cyril Atanassoff 1957
Jean-Pierre Bonnefous 1959
Patrice Bart 1959

Flemming Flindt 1961
Georges Piletta 1961
Jean Guizérix 1964
Michael Denard 1965
J.-Y. Lormeau 1971
Charles Jude 1973
Patrick Dupond 1976

INDEX

Italic page numbers indicate the location of the entries in the encyclopedia.

About the Author

Spire Pitou is Professor Emeritus of French Language and Literature at the University of Delaware. He has written *La Calprenède's "Faramond": A Study of the Sources, Structure, and Reputation of the Novel* and *The Text and Sources of Chateaubrun's Lost "Ajax."* He has collaborated on *A Critical Bibliography of French Literature: The Seventeenth Century, A Critical Bibliography of French Literature: The Eighteenth Century, Supplement,* and *Encyclopedia of World Literature* and has published articles in French and English in international scholarly journals such as the *Australian Journal of French Studies, Modern Language Review, XVIIᵉ, Romanische Forschungen, Studi Francesi, Annales Jean-Jacques Rousseau, Modern Language Notes,* and *Publications of the Modern Language Association of America.*